THE FLUORESCENT LIGHT GLISTENS OFF YOUR HEAD

Other DILBERT books from Andrews McMeel Publishing

It's Not Funny If I Have to Explain It
ISBN: 0-7407-4658-8

Don't Stand Where the Comet Is Assumed to Strike Oil
ISBN: 0-7407-4539-5

Words You Don't Want to Hear During Your Annual Performance Review
ISBN: 0-7407-3805-4

When Body Language Goes Bad
ISBN: 0-7407-3298-6

What Do You Call a Sociopath in a Cubicle? Answer: A Coworker
ISBN: 0-7407-2663-3

Another Day in Cubicle Paradise
ISBN: 0-7407-2194-1

When Did Ignorance Become a Point of View?
ISBN: 0-7407-1839-8

Excuse Me While I Wag
ISBN: 0-7407-1390-6

Dilbert—A Treasury of Sunday Strips: Version 00
ISBN: 0-7407-0531-8

Random Acts of Management
ISBN: 0-7407-0453-2

Dilbert Gives You the Business
ISBN: 0-7407-0338-2 hardcover
ISBN: 0-7407-0003-0 paperback

Don't Step in the Leadership
ISBN: 0-8362-7844-5

Journey to Cubeville
ISBN: 0-8362-7175-0 hardcover
ISBN: 0-8362-6745-1 paperback

I'm Not Anti-Business, I'm Anti-Idiot
ISBN: 0-8362-5182-2

Seven Years of Highly Defective People
ISBN: 0-8362-5129-6 hardcover
ISBN: 0-8362-3668-8 paperback

Casual Day Has Gone Too Far
ISBN: 0-8362-2899-5

Fugitive from the Cubicle Police
ISBN: 0-8362-2119-2

Still Pumped from Using the Mouse
ISBN: 0-8362-1026-3

It's Obvious You Won't Survive by Your Wits Alone
ISBN: 0-8362-0415-8

Bring Me the Head of Willy the Mailboy!
ISBN: 0-8362-1779-9

Shave the Whales
ISBN: 0-8362-1740-3

Dogbert's Clues for the Clueless
ISBN: 0-8362-1737-3

Build a Better Life by Stealing Office Supplies
ISBN: 0-8362-1757-8

Always Postpone Meetings with Time-Wasting Morons
ISBN: 0-8362-1758-6

For ordering information, call 1-800-223-2336.

THE FLUORESCENT LIGHT GLISTENS OFF YOUR HEAD

A DILBERT™ BOOK
BY SCOTT ADAMS

**Andrews McMeel
Publishing**

Kansas City

05 06 07 08 09 BBG 10 9 8 7 6 5 4 3 2 1

ISBN: 0-7407-5113-1

Library of Congress Control Number: 2004115387

www.dilbert.com

For my friends.
Thank you for putting up with me.

Introduction

Whenever I see anyone wearing stylish clothes that fit, I'm envious and amazed. I have been chasing that dream for years. Maybe it's time to let it go.

Part of the problem is that my clothing sizes are all imaginary numbers. For example, my pants size is the square root of negative five, and my shirts are "Extra Smedium." My strategy is to buy a much larger size than I can possibly wear, and let the washing machine and dryer do their thing. Over time, a shirt will shrink to the point where only a Ken doll can wear it, and even he complains that it makes him look gay. There will be a one-week period where the shirt is precisely the right size. That period falls one year after the shirt has gone horribly out of style. So I wash it a few more times, staple shut the sleeve and neck holes, and use it as a cleaning mitten. I have over four hundred of them.

Recently I learned that pleated pants are an embarrassing fashion blunder. This knowledge sent me into a pant-buying frenzy. I rushed to the mall and bought five pairs of pleat-free pants—my most prolific pant-shopping trip ever. I felt the shopper's high that I'd always heard about, intoxicated by my bounteous fortune of pants. That's enough pants to wear a different one every day of the week, not counting weekends when I wear culottes.

I took my pants treasure to a professional alterations place to get them shortened to a fashionable bunching atop my shoes. They were splendid, stylish, perfectly fitted. One week later, after the first laundry cycle, I donated all five pairs to Goodwill, where they will be used to clothe disadvantaged puppets. While it lasted, it was divine. I have no regrets.

Compounding my challenge, I've reached an age where, by universal agreement, I'm not allowed to dress fashionably anyway. I've considered taking up golf just so I can have a reason to look "like that." Or maybe, since I'm arguably an artist, I'll just come up with a look that's all my own. I'm thinking along the lines of a beret, but instead of wearing it on my head, I'll cut two holes in it and wear it like a Speedo. Then all I need is a cape and a monocle. That's the sort of look that never goes out of fashion.

Speaking of fashion, one thing that never goes out of style is membership to Dogbert's New Ruling Class (DNRC). Join now and be by his side when he conquers the world and makes everyone else our domestic servants. To be a member all you need to do is sign up for the free *Dilbert* newsletter that is published approximately whenever I feel like it—about five times a year if you're lucky.

To subscribe or unsubscribe, go to www.dilbert.com. If you have problems with the automated subscription method, write to newsletter@unitedmedia.com.

S. Adams

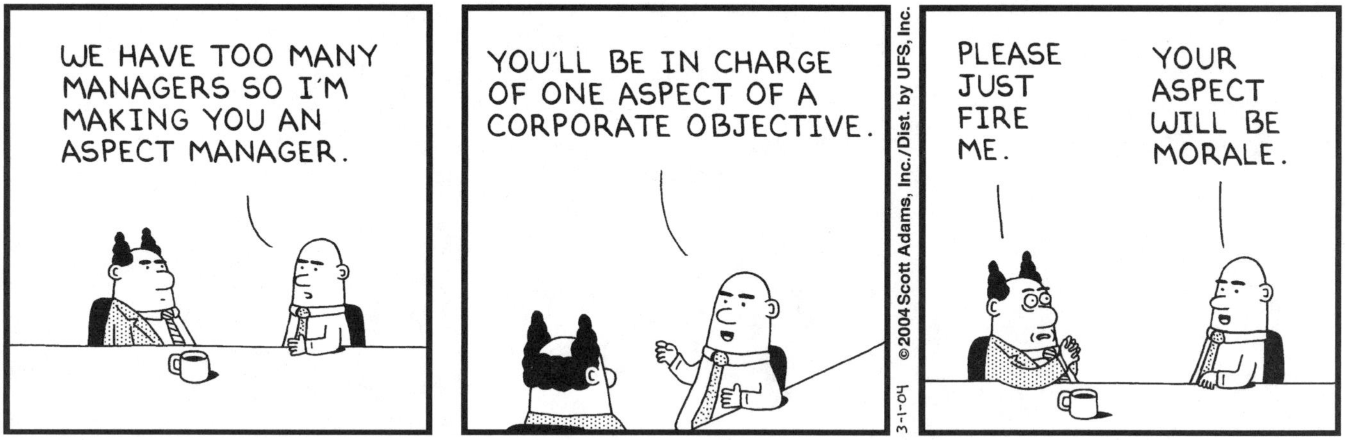
WE HAVE TOO MANY MANAGERS SO I'M MAKING YOU AN ASPECT MANAGER.
YOU'LL BE IN CHARGE OF ONE ASPECT OF A CORPORATE OBJECTIVE.
©2004 Scott Adams, Inc./Dist. by UFS, Inc.
3-1-04
PLEASE JUST FIRE ME.
YOUR ASPECT WILL BE MORALE.

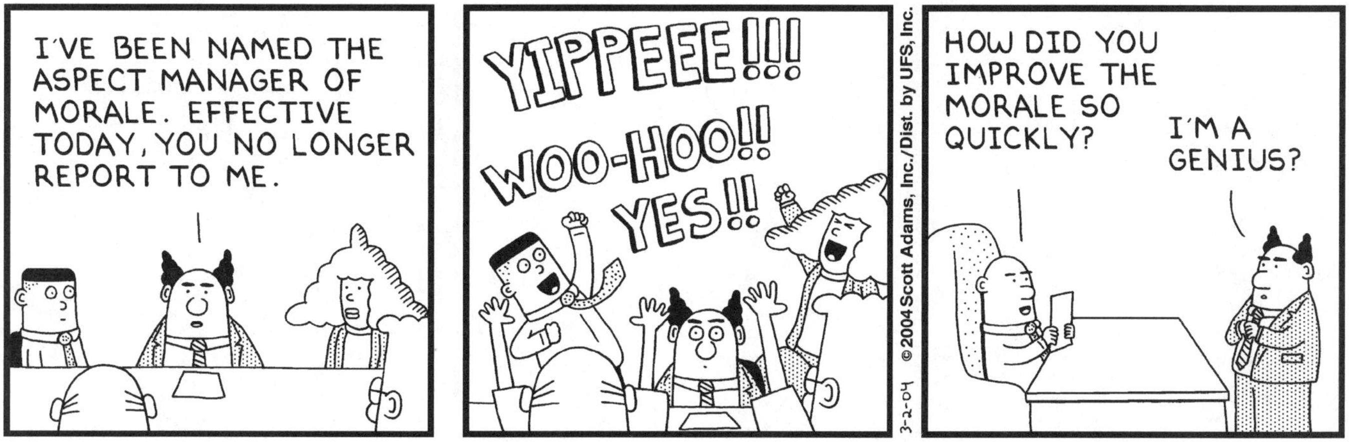
I'VE BEEN NAMED THE ASPECT MANAGER OF MORALE. EFFECTIVE TODAY, YOU NO LONGER REPORT TO ME.
YIPPEEE!!!
WOO-HOO!!
YES!!
©2004 Scott Adams, Inc./Dist. by UFS, Inc.
3-2-04
HOW DID YOU IMPROVE THE MORALE SO QUICKLY?
I'M A GENIUS?

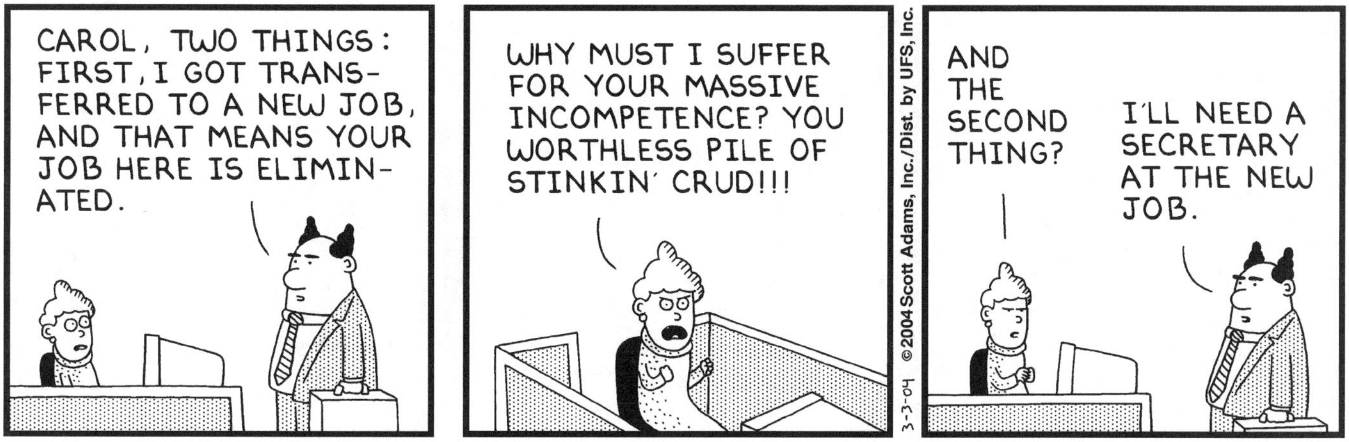
CAROL, TWO THINGS: FIRST, I GOT TRANS-FERRED TO A NEW JOB, AND THAT MEANS YOUR JOB HERE IS ELIMIN-ATED.
WHY MUST I SUFFER FOR YOUR MASSIVE INCOMPETENCE? YOU WORTHLESS PILE OF STINKIN' CRUD!!!
©2004 Scott Adams, Inc./Dist. by UFS, Inc.
3-3-04
AND THE SECOND THING?
I'LL NEED A SECRETARY AT THE NEW JOB.

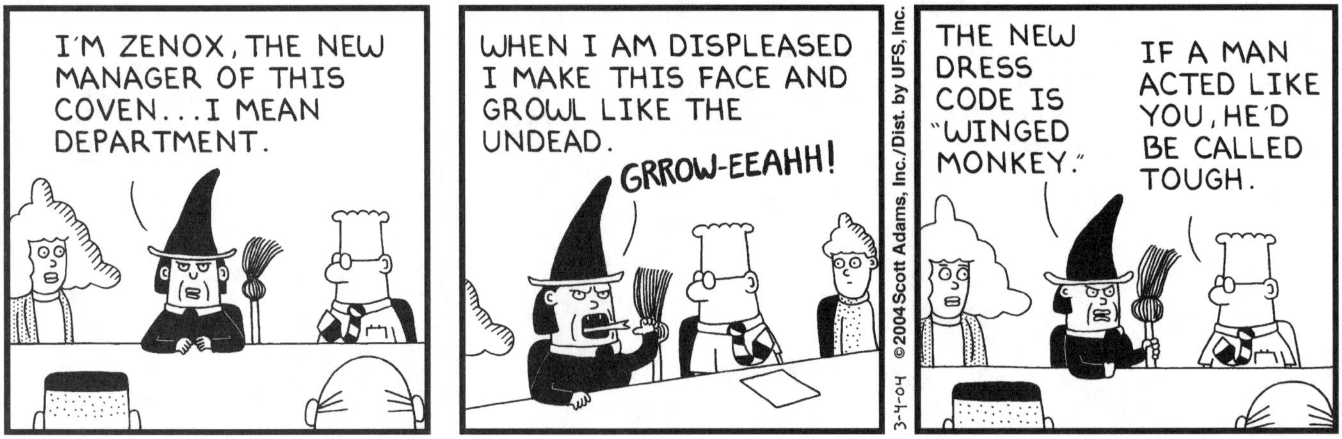
I'M ZENOX, THE NEW MANAGER OF THIS COVEN...I MEAN DEPARTMENT.
WHEN I AM DISPLEASED I MAKE THIS FACE AND GROWL LIKE THE UNDEAD.
GRROW-EEAHH!
3-4-04 ©2004 Scott Adams, Inc./Dist. by UFS, Inc.
THE NEW DRESS CODE IS "WINGED MONKEY."
IF A MAN ACTED LIKE YOU, HE'D BE CALLED TOUGH.

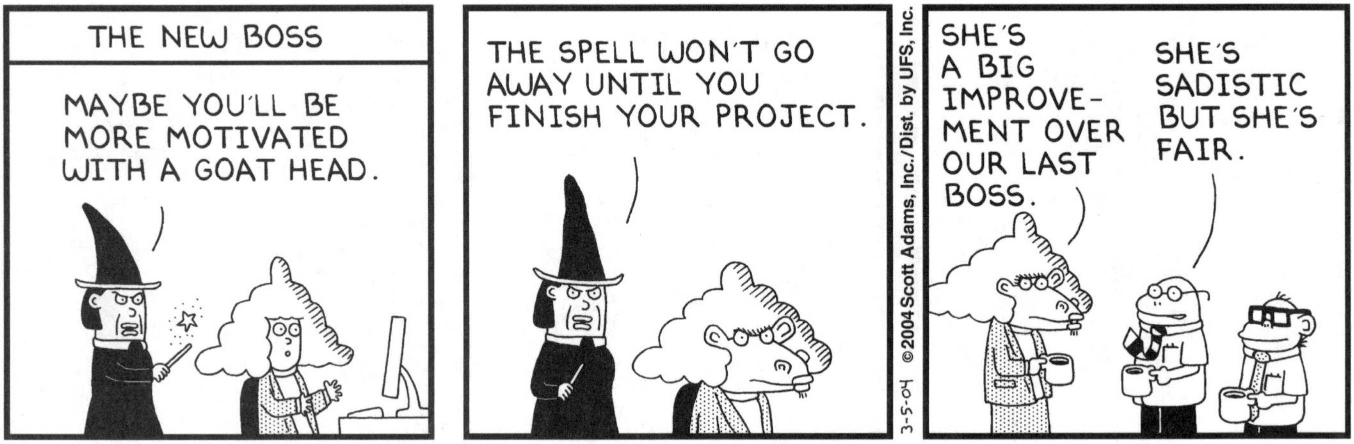
THE NEW BOSS
MAYBE YOU'LL BE MORE MOTIVATED WITH A GOAT HEAD.
THE SPELL WON'T GO AWAY UNTIL YOU FINISH YOUR PROJECT.
3-5-04 ©2004 Scott Adams, Inc./Dist. by UFS, Inc.
SHE'S A BIG IMPROVE-MENT OVER OUR LAST BOSS.
SHE'S SADISTIC BUT SHE'S FAIR.

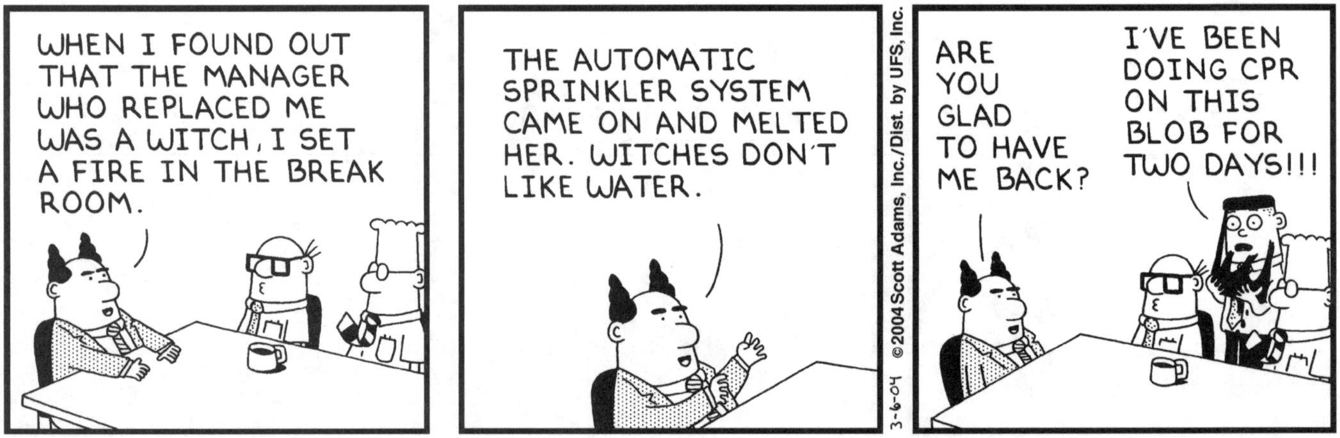
WHEN I FOUND OUT THAT THE MANAGER WHO REPLACED ME WAS A WITCH, I SET A FIRE IN THE BREAK ROOM.
THE AUTOMATIC SPRINKLER SYSTEM CAME ON AND MELTED HER. WITCHES DON'T LIKE WATER.
3-6-04 ©2004 Scott Adams, Inc./Dist. by UFS, Inc.
ARE YOU GLAD TO HAVE ME BACK?
I'VE BEEN DOING CPR ON THIS BLOB FOR TWO DAYS!!!

I WORKED NIGHTS AND WEEKENDS TO FINISH MY PROJECT AHEAD OF SCHEDULE.
GOOD. HERE'S MORE WORK.
I DON'T UNDERSTAND.
AM I BEING PUNISHED FOR WORKING HARD?
©2004 Scott Adams, Inc./Dist. by UFS, Inc.
NO, YOU'RE BEING REWARDED WITH EXCITING NEW CHALLENGES.
SPROING!
WHY DOES THE PLANT GROW FASTER WHEN YOU SAY THINGS LIKE THAT?
NO REASON.
3-7-04
STOP THAT!
ANYWAY, YOUR ANNUAL PERFORMANCE REVIEW WILL REWARD YOUR HARD WORK.
THAT IS ONE WELL-FERTILIZED PLANT.

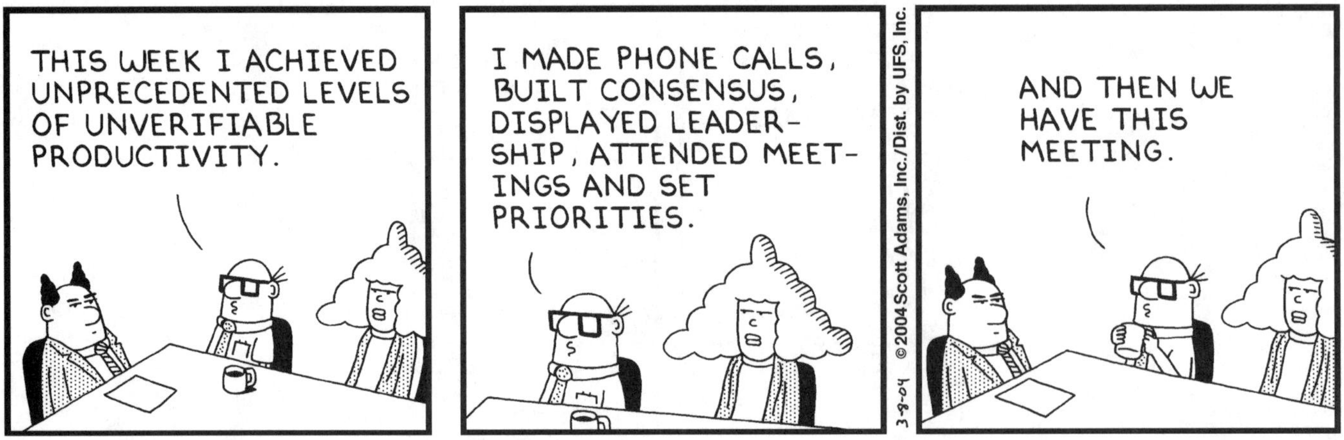
THIS WEEK I ACHIEVED UNPRECEDENTED LEVELS OF UNVERIFIABLE PRODUCTIVITY.
I MADE PHONE CALLS, BUILT CONSENSUS, DISPLAYED LEADER-SHIP, ATTENDED MEET-INGS AND SET PRIORITIES.
AND THEN WE HAVE THIS MEETING.
3-8-04 © 2004 Scott Adams, Inc./Dist. by UFS, Inc.

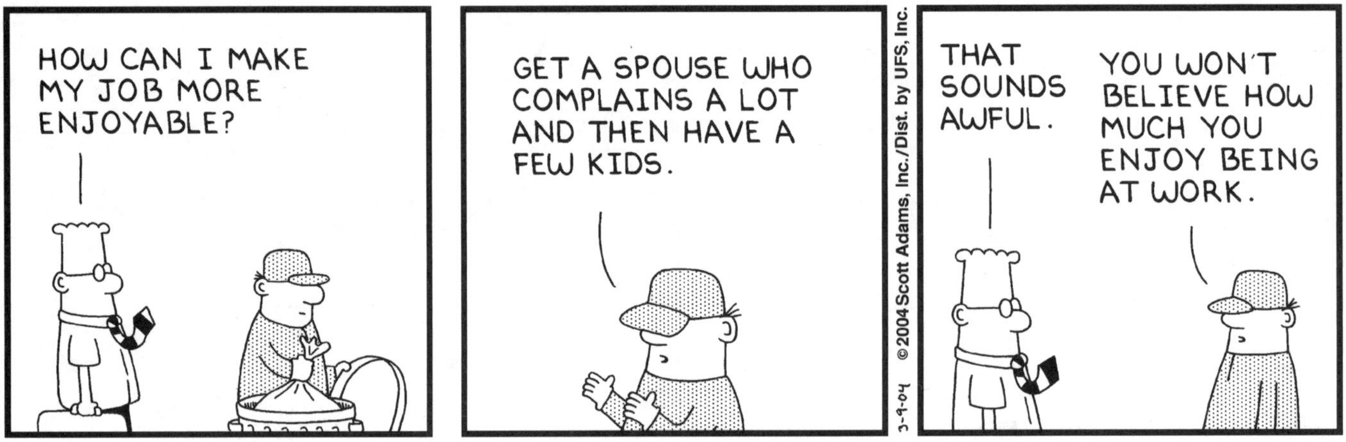
HOW CAN I MAKE MY JOB MORE ENJOYABLE?
GET A SPOUSE WHO COMPLAINS A LOT AND THEN HAVE A FEW KIDS.
THAT SOUNDS AWFUL.
YOU WON'T BELIEVE HOW MUCH YOU ENJOY BEING AT WORK.
3-9-04 © 2004 Scott Adams, Inc./Dist. by UFS, Inc.

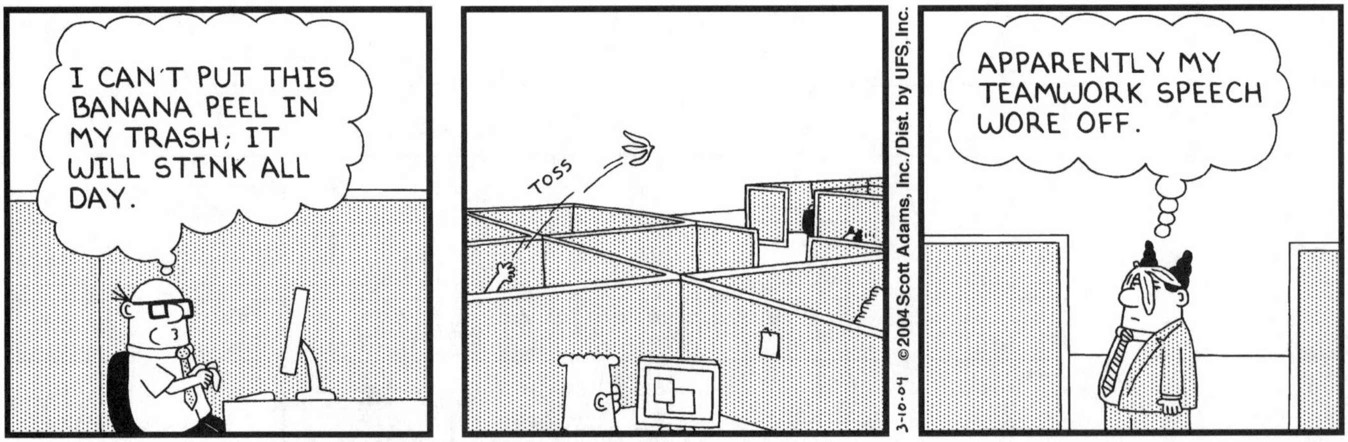
I CAN'T PUT THIS BANANA PEEL IN MY TRASH; IT WILL STINK ALL DAY.
TOSS
APPARENTLY MY TEAMWORK SPEECH WORE OFF.
3-10-04 © 2004 Scott Adams, Inc./Dist. by UFS, Inc.

WE ONLY HAVE A 10% REPEAT CUSTOMER RATE WHEREAS PRISONS HAVE A 70% RATE OF RECIDIVISM.

WE NEED TO FOCUS OUR MARKETING ON CRIMINALS BECAUSE THEY DON'T LEARN FROM EXPERIENCE.

ORDER NOW AND GET A FREE KNUCKLE TATTOO PLUS OUR FREE BOOK "1,001 NICKNAMES FOR WOMEN."

IT'S CALLED A 360-DEGREE REVIEW. YOU GET TO EVALUATE ME AT NO RISK OF RETRIBUTION.

NO MATTER WHAT YOU SAY ABOUT ME, YOU WILL ONLY BE JUDGED ON THE QUALITY OF YOUR WORK.

SOMETIMES YOU ARE LAZY, EVIL AND MANIPULATIVE.

THE QUALITY OF YOUR WORK JUST WENT WAY DOWN.

YOU CAN MANIPULATE PEOPLE BY LYING ABOUT WHAT OTHER PEOPLE SAID.

IF YOUR VICTIM GOES TO THE SOURCE AND DISCOVERS YOUR TREACHERY, SAY, "OF COURSE HE TELLS **YOU** THAT."

YOUR ADVICE DOESN'T SOUND HEALTHY.

THAT'S NOT WHAT THE MAYO CLINIC SAID.

I NEED A DAY OFF TO ATTEND MY TWIN SISTER'S FUNERAL.
A WHOLE DAY?? HOW WELL DID YOU KNOW HER?
SHE... WAS... MY... TWIN.
BUT NOT IDENTICAL!
©2004 Scott Adams, Inc. /Dist. by UFS, Inc.
HOW DOES THAT MATTER?
WELL...SHE DIDN'T EVEN LOOK LIKE YOU.
AND YET YOU WANT A WHOLE DAY OFF FOR A SERVICE THAT TAKES FIFTEEN MINUTES.
3-14-03
GAAA!!! IT WOULD BE IMPOSSIBLE TO BE MORE INSENSI-TIVE!!!!
I'LL COMPROMISE. MY PET GERBIL IS ON HIS LAST LEGS. I'LL GIVE YOU THE DAY OFF IF YOU TOSS HIM IN THE CASKET SO I DON'T HAVE TO BURY HIM MYSELF.
WHEN DO YOU THINK IT WILL DIE?
DEPENDS. HOW MUCH DOES YOUR SISTER WEIGH?

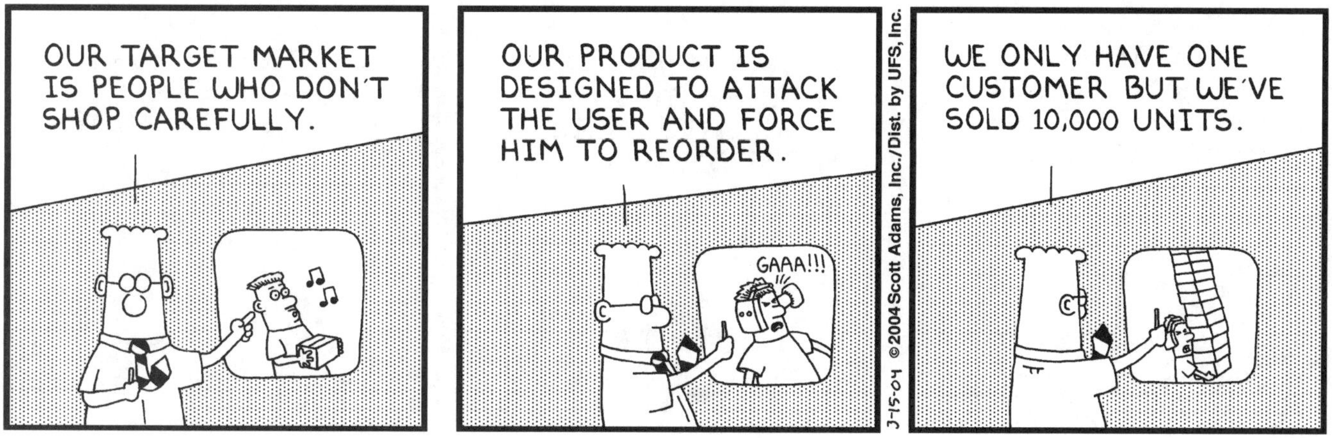
OUR TARGET MARKET IS PEOPLE WHO DON'T SHOP CAREFULLY.
OUR PRODUCT IS DESIGNED TO ATTACK THE USER AND FORCE HIM TO REORDER.
GAAA!!!
3-15-04 ©2004 Scott Adams, Inc./Dist. by UFS, Inc.
WE ONLY HAVE ONE CUSTOMER BUT WE'VE SOLD 10,000 UNITS.

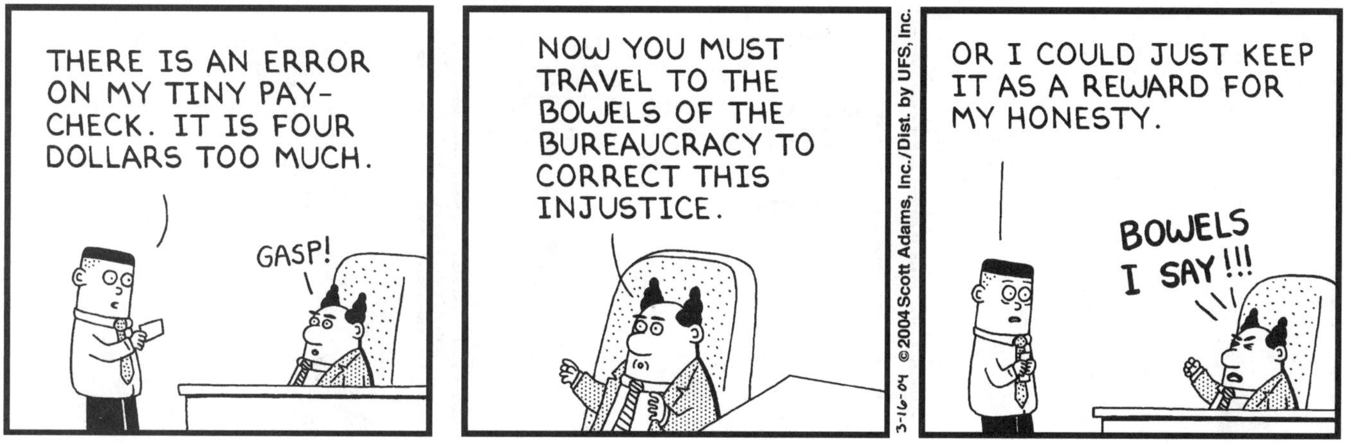
THERE IS AN ERROR ON MY TINY PAY-CHECK. IT IS FOUR DOLLARS TOO MUCH.
GASP!
NOW YOU MUST TRAVEL TO THE BOWELS OF THE BUREAUCRACY TO CORRECT THIS INJUSTICE.
3-16-04 ©2004 Scott Adams, Inc./Dist. by UFS, Inc.
OR I COULD JUST KEEP IT AS A REWARD FOR MY HONESTY.
BOWELS I SAY!!!

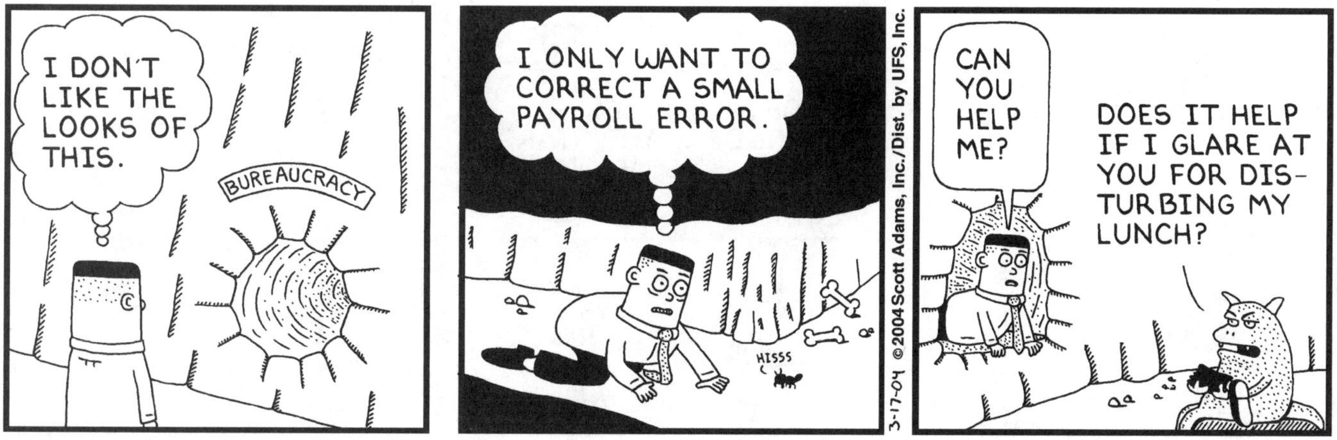
I DON'T LIKE THE LOOKS OF THIS.
BUREAUCRACY
I ONLY WANT TO CORRECT A SMALL PAYROLL ERROR.
HISSS
3-17-04 ©2004 Scott Adams, Inc./Dist. by UFS, Inc.
CAN YOU HELP ME?
DOES IT HELP IF I GLARE AT YOU FOR DIS-TURBING MY LUNCH?

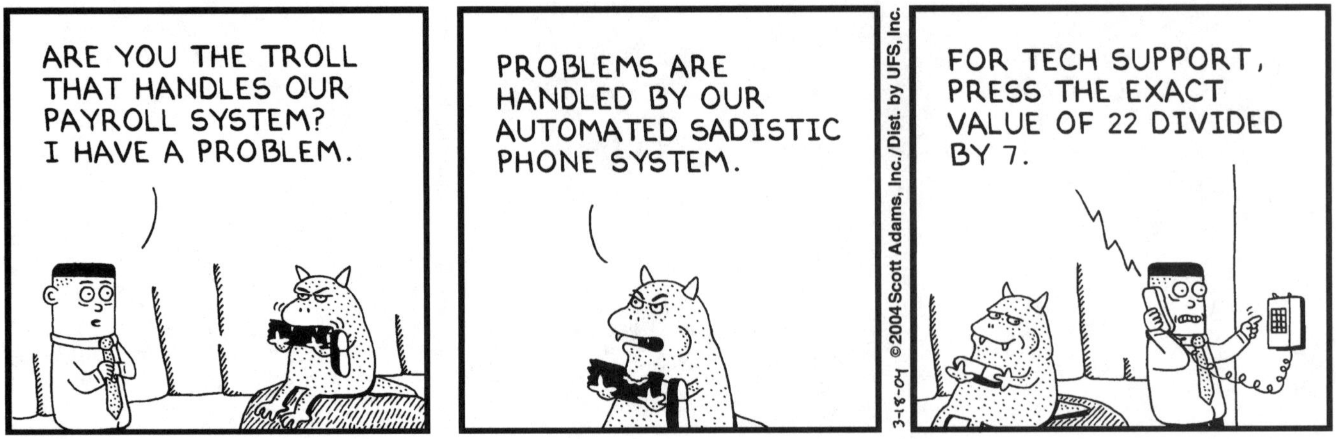
ARE YOU THE TROLL THAT HANDLES OUR PAYROLL SYSTEM? I HAVE A PROBLEM.
PROBLEMS ARE HANDLED BY OUR AUTOMATED SADISTIC PHONE SYSTEM.
3-18-04 ©2004 Scott Adams, Inc./Dist. by UFS, Inc.
FOR TECH SUPPORT, PRESS THE EXACT VALUE OF 22 DIVIDED BY 7.

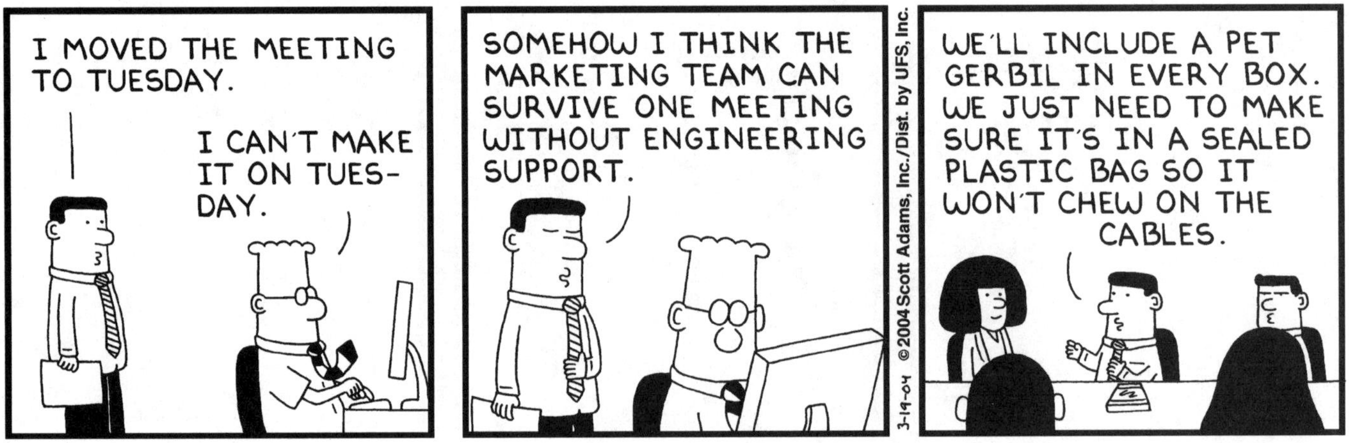
I MOVED THE MEETING TO TUESDAY.
I CAN'T MAKE IT ON TUES-DAY.
SOMEHOW I THINK THE MARKETING TEAM CAN SURVIVE ONE MEETING WITHOUT ENGINEERING SUPPORT.
3-19-04 ©2004 Scott Adams, Inc./Dist. by UFS, Inc.
WE'LL INCLUDE A PET GERBIL IN EVERY BOX. WE JUST NEED TO MAKE SURE IT'S IN A SEALED PLASTIC BAG SO IT WON'T CHEW ON THE CABLES.

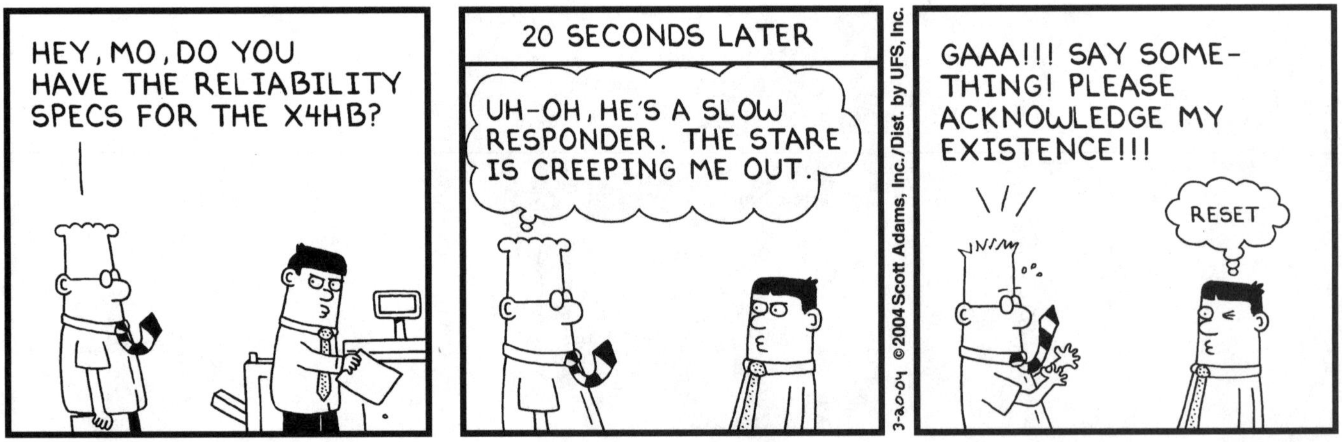
HEY, MO, DO YOU HAVE THE RELIABILITY SPECS FOR THE X4HB?
20 SECONDS LATER
UH-OH, HE'S A SLOW RESPONDER. THE STARE IS CREEPING ME OUT.
3-20-04 ©2004 Scott Adams, Inc./Dist. by UFS, Inc.
GAAA!!! SAY SOME-THING! PLEASE ACKNOWLEDGE MY EXISTENCE!!!
RESET

OUR DIRECTOR OF MARKETING WILL GIVE US AN UPDATE.
WE SPENT OUR ENTIRE MARKETING BUDGET BUYING A RACEHORSE.
WE NAMED THE HORSE AFTER OUR FLAGSHIP PRODUCT BECAUSE THEY'RE BOTH FAST.
GET IT?
©2004 Scott Adams, Inc./Dist. by UFS, Inc.
UNFORTUNATELY WE DIDN'T HAVE ENOUGH BUDGET FOR A TOP THOROUGHBRED.
OUR HORSE BROKE ITS LEG WALKING TO THE STARTING GATE, SO WE SHOT IT.
3-21-04
NEXT YEAR WE PLAN TO SPONSOR A SAIL-BOAT.
ANYWAY... YOUR LUNCH TODAY IS BROUGHT TO YOU BY THE MARKETING DEPART-MENT.
ENJOY!
HEY, MY ROAST BEEF SANDWICH HAS A PIECE OF LEAD IN IT.

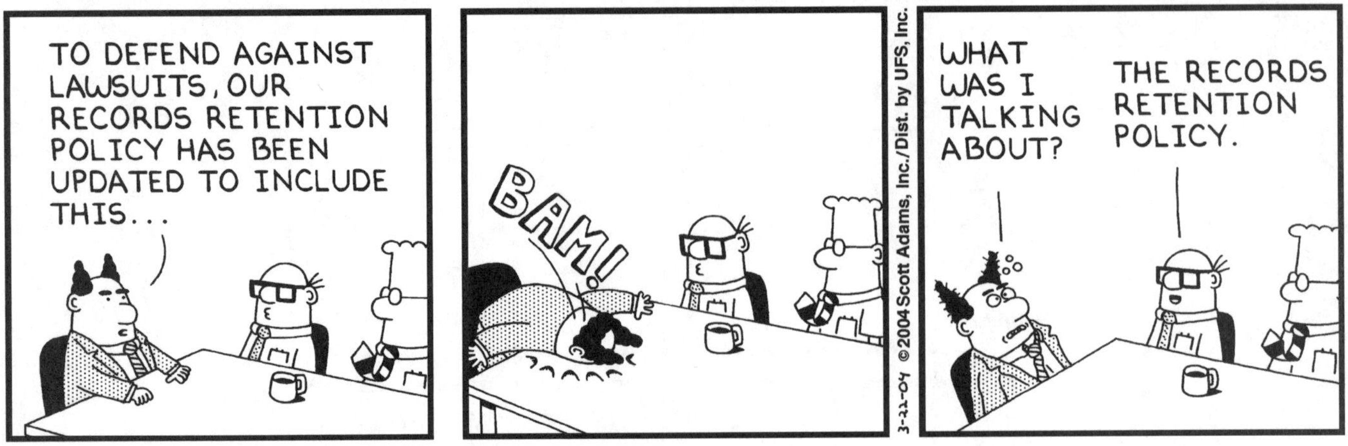
TO DEFEND AGAINST LAWSUITS, OUR RECORDS RETENTION POLICY HAS BEEN UPDATED TO INCLUDE THIS...
BAM!
3-22-04 ©2004 Scott Adams, Inc./Dist. by UFS, Inc.
WHAT WAS I TALKING ABOUT?
THE RECORDS RETENTION POLICY.

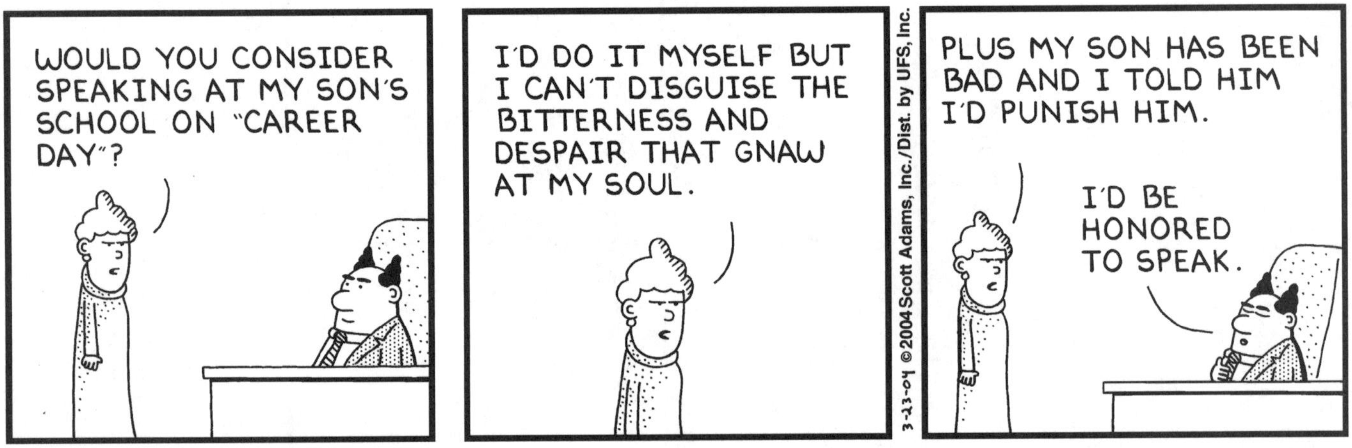
WOULD YOU CONSIDER SPEAKING AT MY SON'S SCHOOL ON "CAREER DAY"?
I'D DO IT MYSELF BUT I CAN'T DISGUISE THE BITTERNESS AND DESPAIR THAT GNAW AT MY SOUL.
3-23-04 ©2004 Scott Adams, Inc./Dist. by UFS, Inc.
PLUS MY SON HAS BEEN BAD AND I TOLD HIM I'D PUNISH HIM.
I'D BE HONORED TO SPEAK.

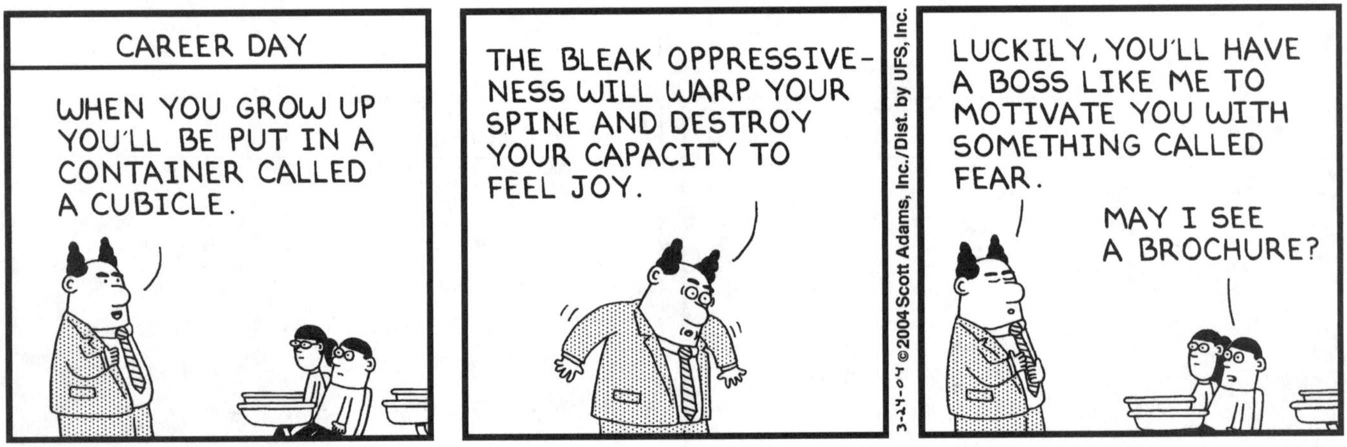
CAREER DAY
WHEN YOU GROW UP YOU'LL BE PUT IN A CONTAINER CALLED A CUBICLE.
THE BLEAK OPPRESSIVE-NESS WILL WARP YOUR SPINE AND DESTROY YOUR CAPACITY TO FEEL JOY.
3-24-04 ©2004 Scott Adams, Inc./Dist. by UFS, Inc.
LUCKILY, YOU'LL HAVE A BOSS LIKE ME TO MOTIVATE YOU WITH SOMETHING CALLED FEAR.
MAY I SEE A BROCHURE?

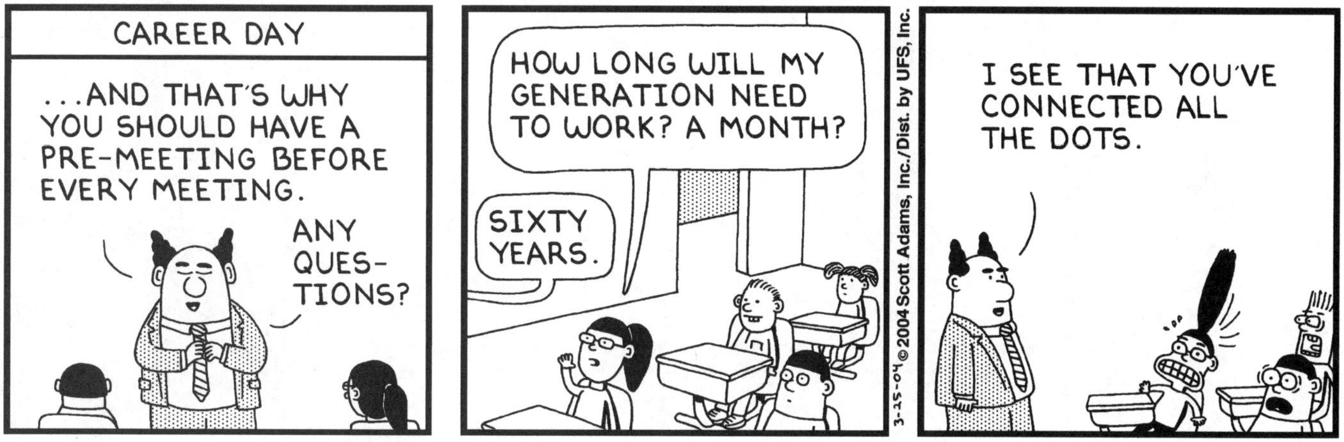
CAREER DAY
...AND THAT'S WHY YOU SHOULD HAVE A PRE-MEETING BEFORE EVERY MEETING.
ANY QUES-TIONS?
HOW LONG WILL MY GENERATION NEED TO WORK? A MONTH?
SIXTY YEARS.
3-25-04 ©2004 Scott Adams, Inc./Dist. by UFS, Inc.
I SEE THAT YOU'VE CONNECTED ALL THE DOTS.

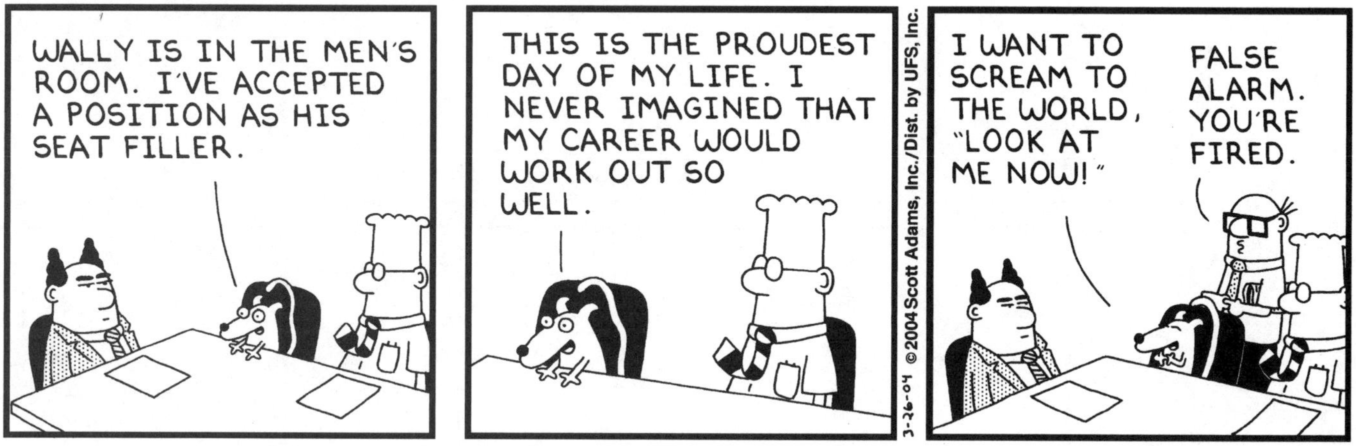
WALLY IS IN THE MEN'S ROOM. I'VE ACCEPTED A POSITION AS HIS SEAT FILLER.
THIS IS THE PROUDEST DAY OF MY LIFE. I NEVER IMAGINED THAT MY CAREER WOULD WORK OUT SO WELL.
3-26-04 ©2004 Scott Adams, Inc./Dist. by UFS, Inc.
I WANT TO SCREAM TO THE WORLD, "LOOK AT ME NOW!"
FALSE ALARM. YOU'RE FIRED.

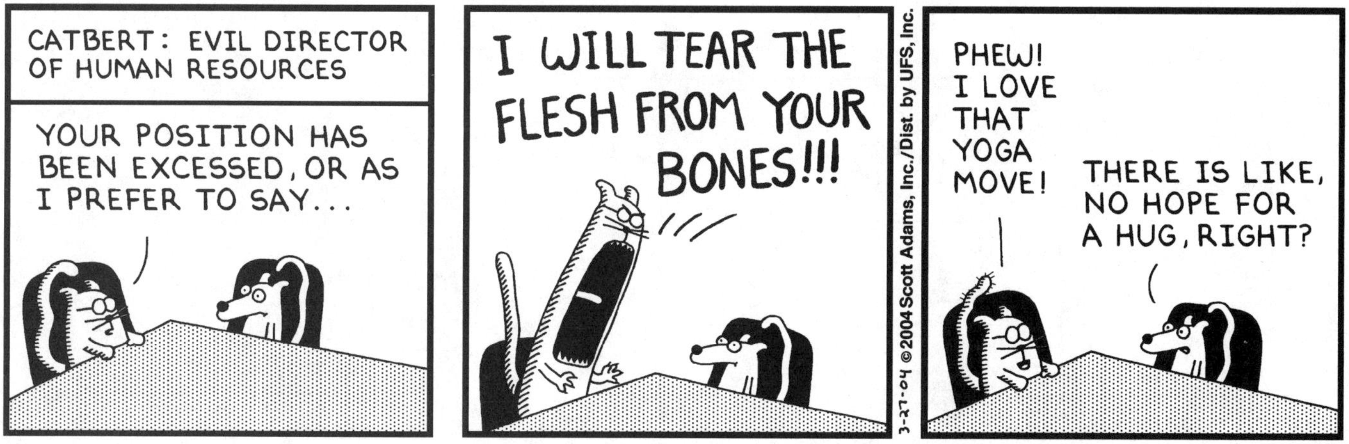
CATBERT: EVIL DIRECTOR OF HUMAN RESOURCES
YOUR POSITION HAS BEEN EXCESSED, OR AS I PREFER TO SAY...
I WILL TEAR THE FLESH FROM YOUR BONES!!!
3-27-04 ©2004 Scott Adams, Inc./Dist. by UFS, Inc.
PHEW! I LOVE THAT YOGA MOVE!
THERE IS LIKE, NO HOPE FOR A HUG, RIGHT?

REMEMBER, QUALITY IS OUR TOP PRIORITY.
QUALITY
QUESTION: IS IT MORE IMPORTANT THAN SAFETY?
OOH...I FORGOT ABOUT THAT ONE.
QUESTION: IS QUALITY MORE IMPORTANT THAN OBEYING THE LAW?
WELL, PROBABLY NOT.
IF WE COULD MAXIMIZE SHAREHOLDER VALUE BY SELLING LOWER QUALITY ITEMS...
...WOULDN'T WE HAVE A FIDUCIARY RESPONSIBILITY TO DO IT?
HMM
I'M SURE IT'S IN THE TOP FOUR.
QUALITY
WHAT IF WE HAD TO LIE TO ACHIEVE QUALITY?
©2004 Scott Adams, Inc./Dist. by UFS, Inc.
3-28-04

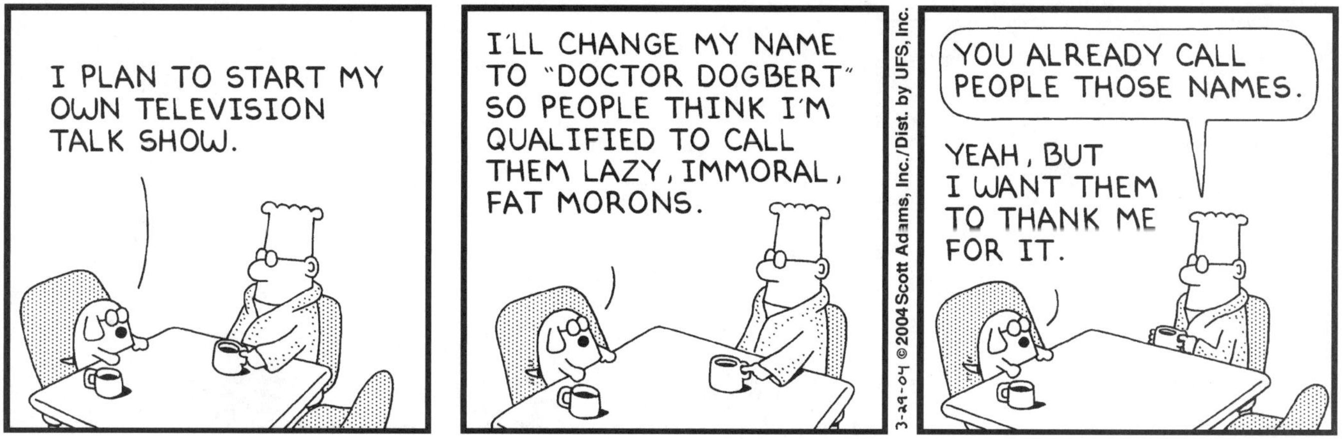
I PLAN TO START MY OWN TELEVISION TALK SHOW.
I'LL CHANGE MY NAME TO "DOCTOR DOGBERT" SO PEOPLE THINK I'M QUALIFIED TO CALL THEM LAZY, IMMORAL, FAT MORONS.
YOU ALREADY CALL PEOPLE THOSE NAMES.
YEAH, BUT I WANT THEM TO THANK ME FOR IT.
3-29-04 ©2004 Scott Adams, Inc./Dist. by UFS, Inc.

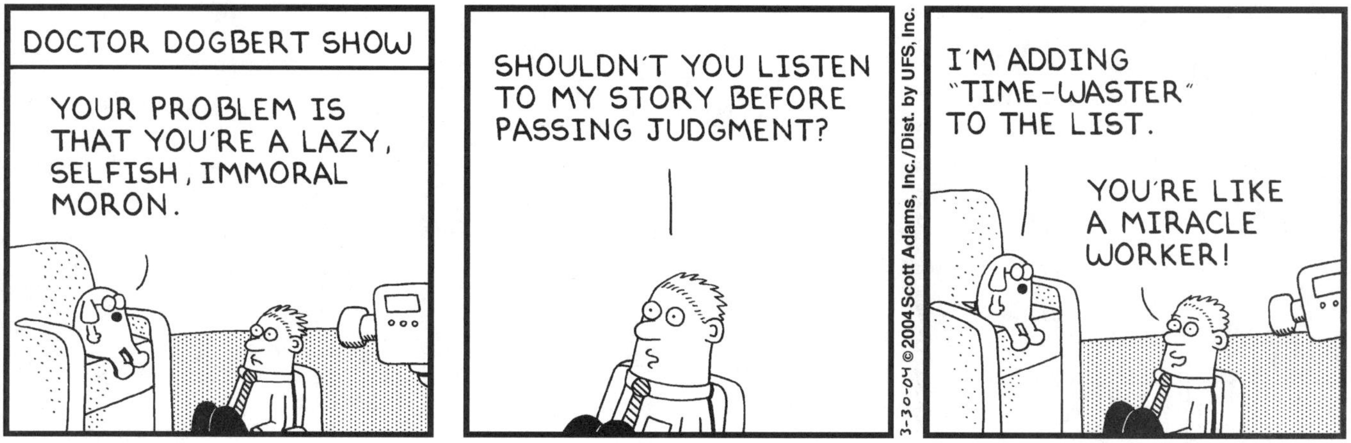
DOCTOR DOGBERT SHOW
YOUR PROBLEM IS THAT YOU'RE A LAZY, SELFISH, IMMORAL MORON.
SHOULDN'T YOU LISTEN TO MY STORY BEFORE PASSING JUDGMENT?
I'M ADDING "TIME-WASTER" TO THE LIST.
YOU'RE LIKE A MIRACLE WORKER!
3-30-04 ©2004 Scott Adams, Inc./Dist. by UFS, Inc.

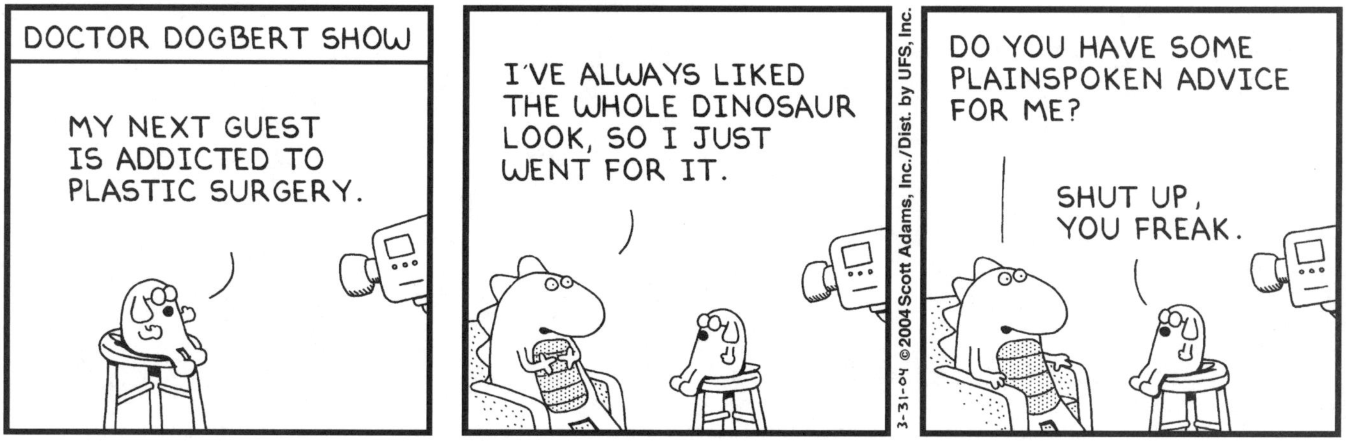
DOCTOR DOGBERT SHOW
MY NEXT GUEST IS ADDICTED TO PLASTIC SURGERY.
I'VE ALWAYS LIKED THE WHOLE DINOSAUR LOOK, SO I JUST WENT FOR IT.
DO YOU HAVE SOME PLAINSPOKEN ADVICE FOR ME?
SHUT UP, YOU FREAK.
3-31-04 ©2004 Scott Adams, Inc./Dist. by UFS, Inc.

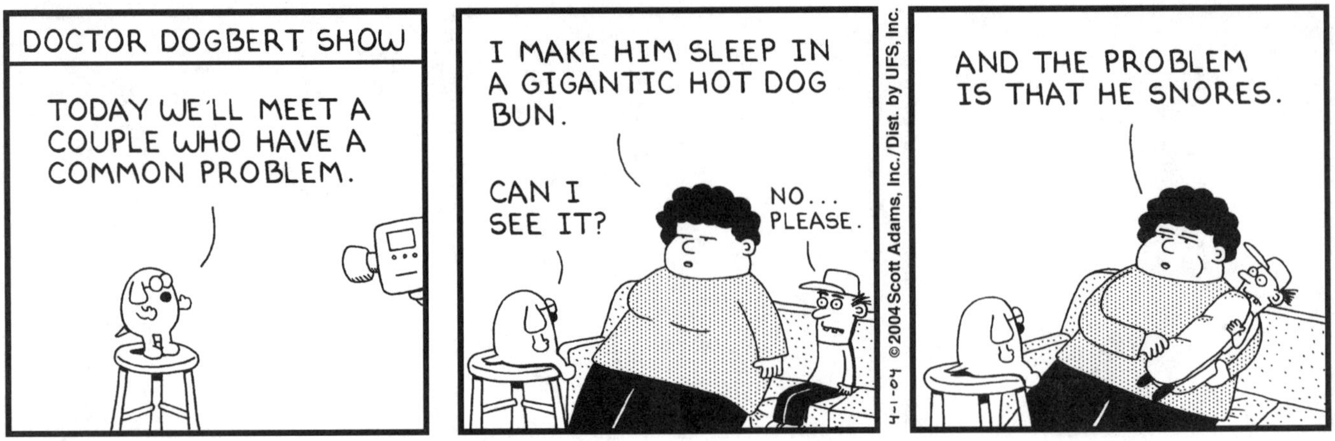
DOCTOR DOGBERT SHOW
TODAY WE'LL MEET A COUPLE WHO HAVE A COMMON PROBLEM.
I MAKE HIM SLEEP IN A GIGANTIC HOT DOG BUN.
CAN I SEE IT?
NO... PLEASE.
4-1-04 © 2004 Scott Adams, Inc./Dist. by UFS, Inc.
AND THE PROBLEM IS THAT HE SNORES.

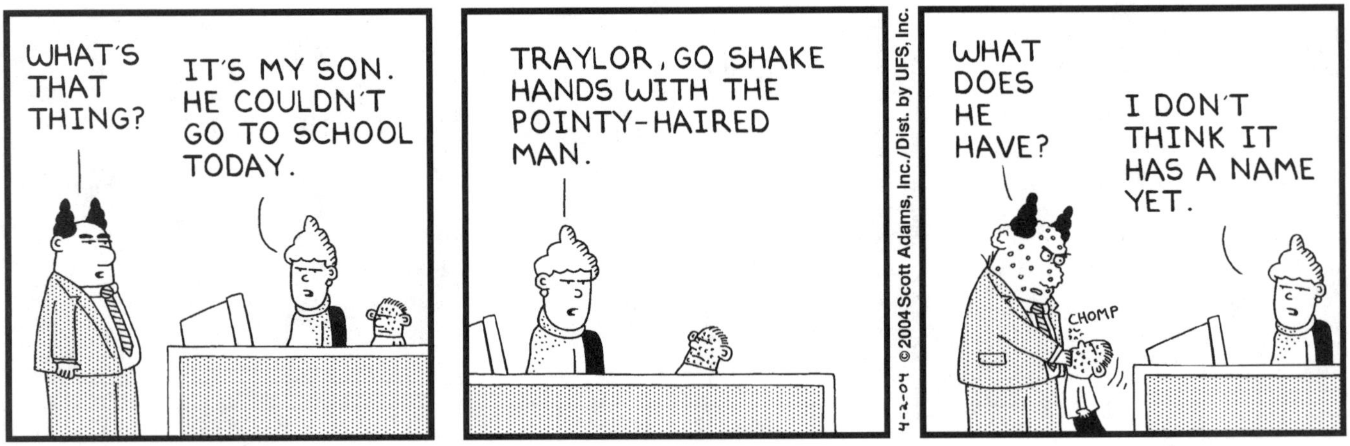
WHAT'S THAT THING?
IT'S MY SON. HE COULDN'T GO TO SCHOOL TODAY.
TRAYLOR, GO SHAKE HANDS WITH THE POINTY-HAIRED MAN.
4-2-04 © 2004 Scott Adams, Inc./Dist. by UFS, Inc.
WHAT DOES HE HAVE?
CHOMP
I DON'T THINK IT HAS A NAME YET.

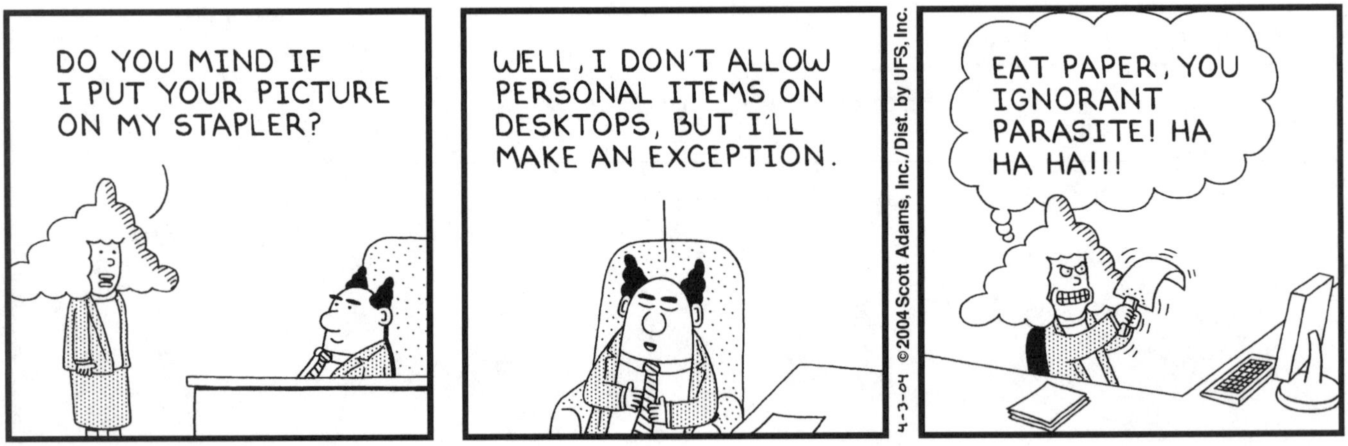
DO YOU MIND IF I PUT YOUR PICTURE ON MY STAPLER?
WELL, I DON'T ALLOW PERSONAL ITEMS ON DESKTOPS, BUT I'LL MAKE AN EXCEPTION.
4-3-04 © 2004 Scott Adams, Inc./Dist. by UFS, Inc.
EAT PAPER, YOU IGNORANT PARASITE! HA HA HA!!!

THIS WAS A PRODUCTIVE FOUR-HOUR LEADERSHIP MEETING.
I'D LIKE ONE OF YOU TO TYPE UP YOUR NOTES AND SEND AN E-MAIL TO THE ENTIRE COMPANY.
©2004 Scott Adams, Inc. /Dist. by UFS, Inc.
NO ONE TOOK NOTES?
I DIDN'T HAVE A PEN.
OKAY, NO PROBLEM. DOES ANYONE REMEMBER WHAT WE DECIDED?
4-4-04
WE AGREED TO INCREASE... SOMETHING.
NO, DECREASE SOMETHING.
NEVER MIND. LET'S TRY IT AGAIN ON THURSDAY AT 8 A.M.
WHEN IS THE NEXT LEADERSHIP MEETING?
I SHOULD HAVE WRITTEN THAT DOWN.

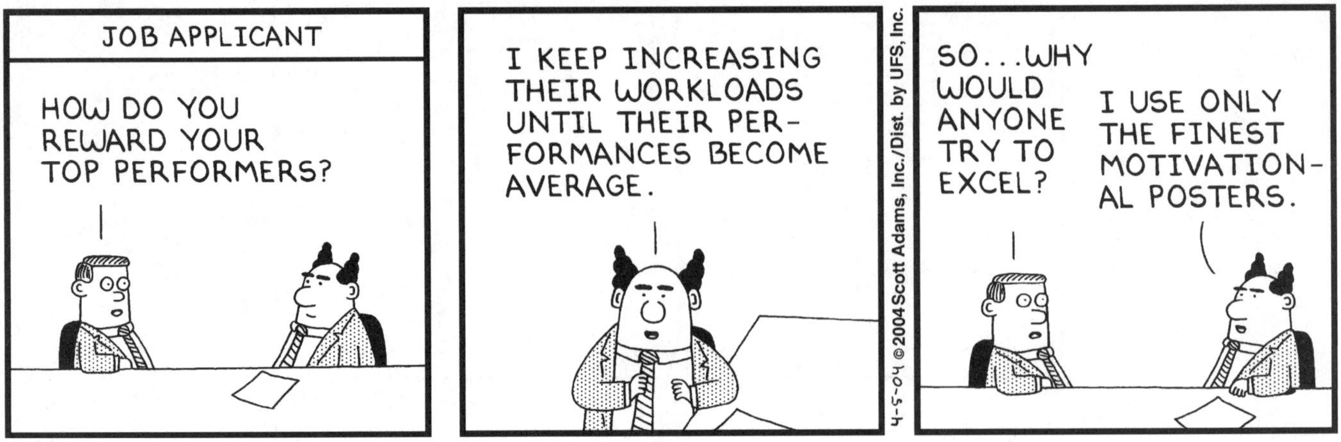
JOB APPLICANT
HOW DO YOU REWARD YOUR TOP PERFORMERS?
I KEEP INCREASING THEIR WORKLOADS UNTIL THEIR PERFORMANCES BECOME AVERAGE.
4-5-04 ©2004 Scott Adams, Inc./Dist. by UFS, Inc.
SO...WHY WOULD ANYONE TRY TO EXCEL?
I USE ONLY THE FINEST MOTIVATIONAL POSTERS.

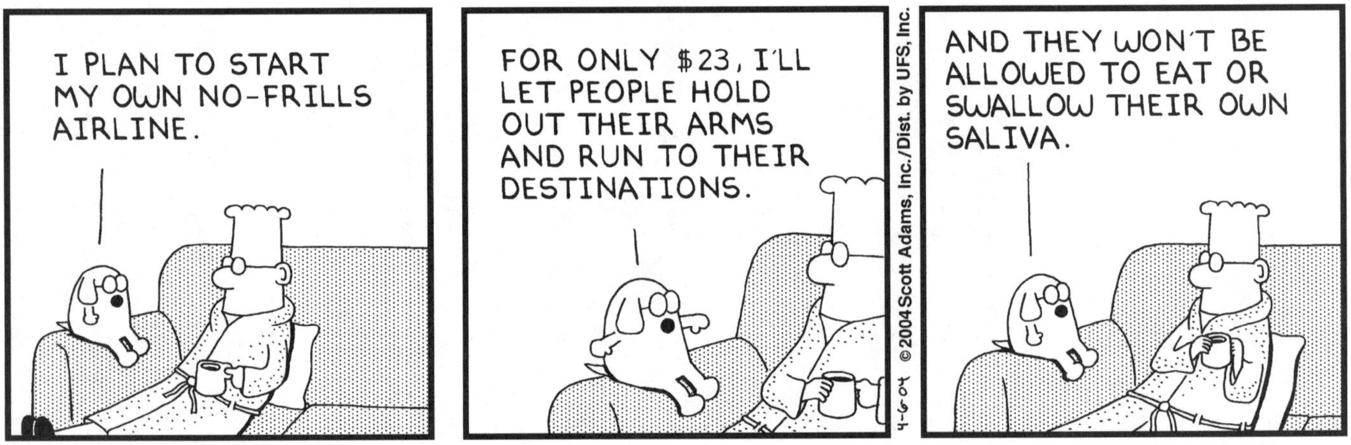
I PLAN TO START MY OWN NO-FRILLS AIRLINE.
FOR ONLY $23, I'LL LET PEOPLE HOLD OUT THEIR ARMS AND RUN TO THEIR DESTINATIONS.
4-6-04 ©2004 Scott Adams, Inc./Dist. by UFS, Inc.
AND THEY WON'T BE ALLOWED TO EAT OR SWALLOW THEIR OWN SALIVA.

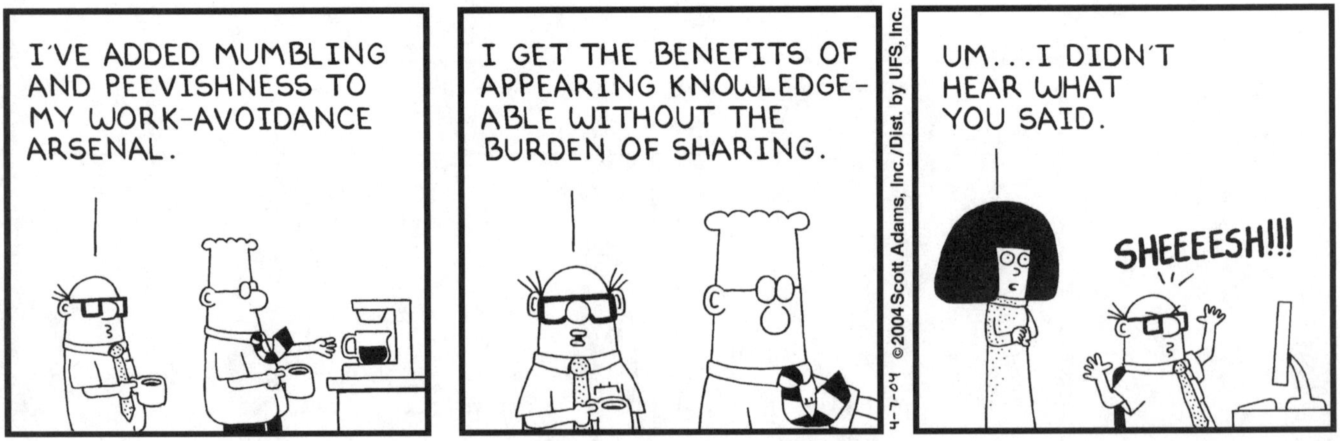
I'VE ADDED MUMBLING AND PEEVISHNESS TO MY WORK-AVOIDANCE ARSENAL.
I GET THE BENEFITS OF APPEARING KNOWLEDGEABLE WITHOUT THE BURDEN OF SHARING.
4-7-04 ©2004 Scott Adams, Inc./Dist. by UFS, Inc.
UM...I DIDN'T HEAR WHAT YOU SAID.
SHEEEESH!!!

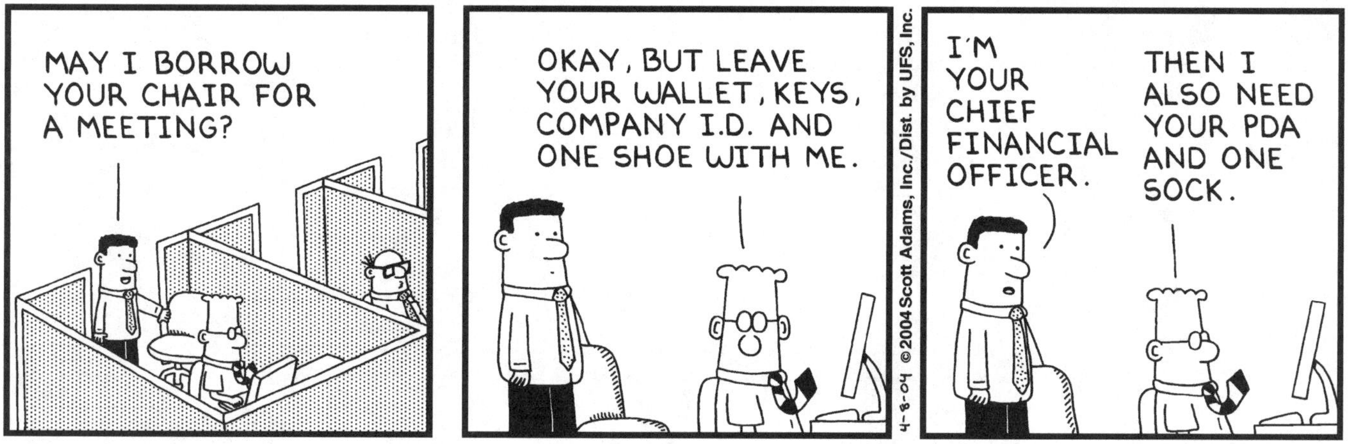
MAY I BORROW YOUR CHAIR FOR A MEETING?
OKAY, BUT LEAVE YOUR WALLET, KEYS, COMPANY I.D. AND ONE SHOE WITH ME.
4-8-04 ©2004 Scott Adams, Inc./Dist. by UFS, Inc.
I'M YOUR CHIEF FINANCIAL OFFICER.
THEN I ALSO NEED YOUR PDA AND ONE SOCK.

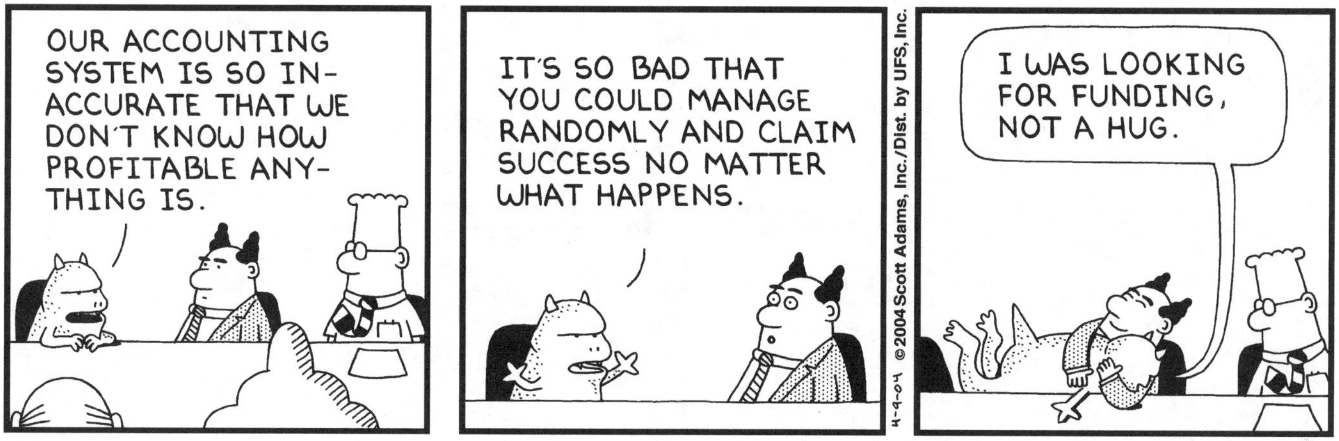
OUR ACCOUNTING SYSTEM IS SO IN-ACCURATE THAT WE DON'T KNOW HOW PROFITABLE ANY-THING IS.
IT'S SO BAD THAT YOU COULD MANAGE RANDOMLY AND CLAIM SUCCESS NO MATTER WHAT HAPPENS.
4-9-04 ©2004 Scott Adams, Inc./Dist. by UFS, Inc.
I WAS LOOKING FOR FUNDING, NOT A HUG.

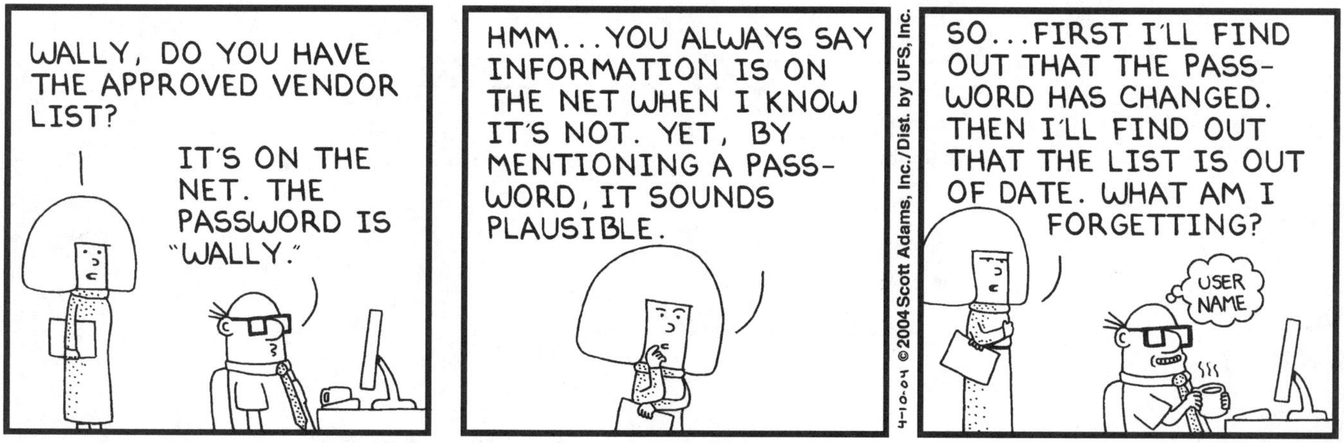
WALLY, DO YOU HAVE THE APPROVED VENDOR LIST?
IT'S ON THE NET. THE PASSWORD IS "WALLY."
HMM...YOU ALWAYS SAY INFORMATION IS ON THE NET WHEN I KNOW IT'S NOT. YET, BY MENTIONING A PASS-WORD, IT SOUNDS PLAUSIBLE.
4-10-04 ©2004 Scott Adams, Inc./Dist. by UFS, Inc.
SO...FIRST I'LL FIND OUT THAT THE PASS-WORD HAS CHANGED. THEN I'LL FIND OUT THAT THE LIST IS OUT OF DATE. WHAT AM I FORGETTING?
USER NAME

YOUR PAY WILL BE CALCULATED A NEW WAY.
THEN I SAID, "TEAL ISN'T A COLOR."
SHHH! NO SIDE CONVERSATIONS.
...MULTIPLIED BY THE BASE SALARY...
I THINK IT'S A SPICE.
NO SIDE CONVERSATIONS!!!
IT'S LIKE CILANTRO.
I CAN'T HELP IT. I'M THE KIND OF GUY WHO NEEDS TO TALK OR ELSE IT FEELS LIKE MY HEAD WILL EXPLODE.
LET'S TEST THAT THEORY.
MMPH!
WOW! THAT WORKED OUT BETTER THAN I'D HOPED.
© 2004 Scott Adams, Inc./Dist. by UFS, Inc.
4-11-04

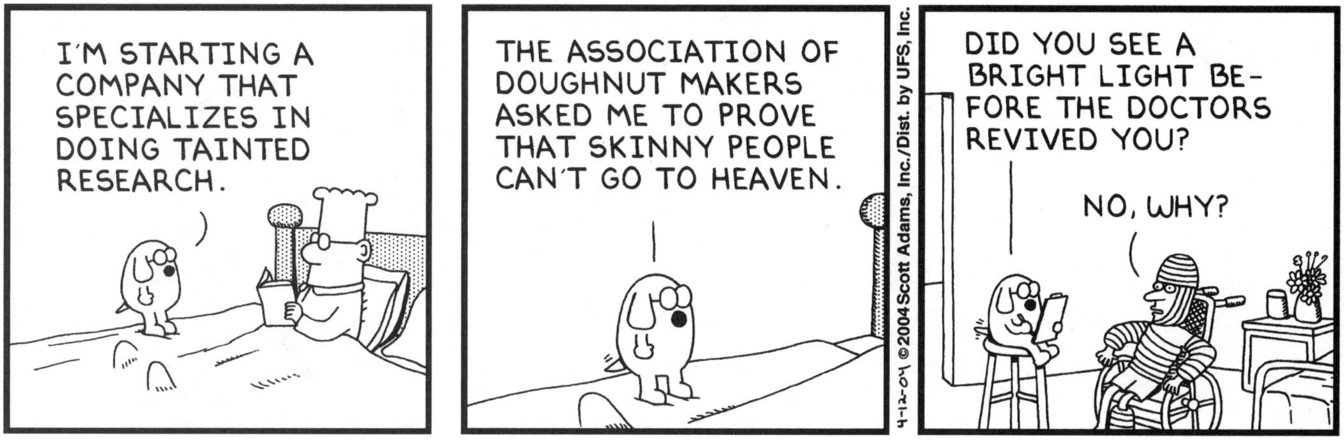
I'M STARTING A COMPANY THAT SPECIALIZES IN DOING TAINTED RESEARCH.
THE ASSOCIATION OF DOUGHNUT MAKERS ASKED ME TO PROVE THAT SKINNY PEOPLE CAN'T GO TO HEAVEN.
4-12-04 ©2004 Scott Adams, Inc./Dist. by UFS, Inc.
DID YOU SEE A BRIGHT LIGHT BEFORE THE DOCTORS REVIVED YOU?
NO, WHY?

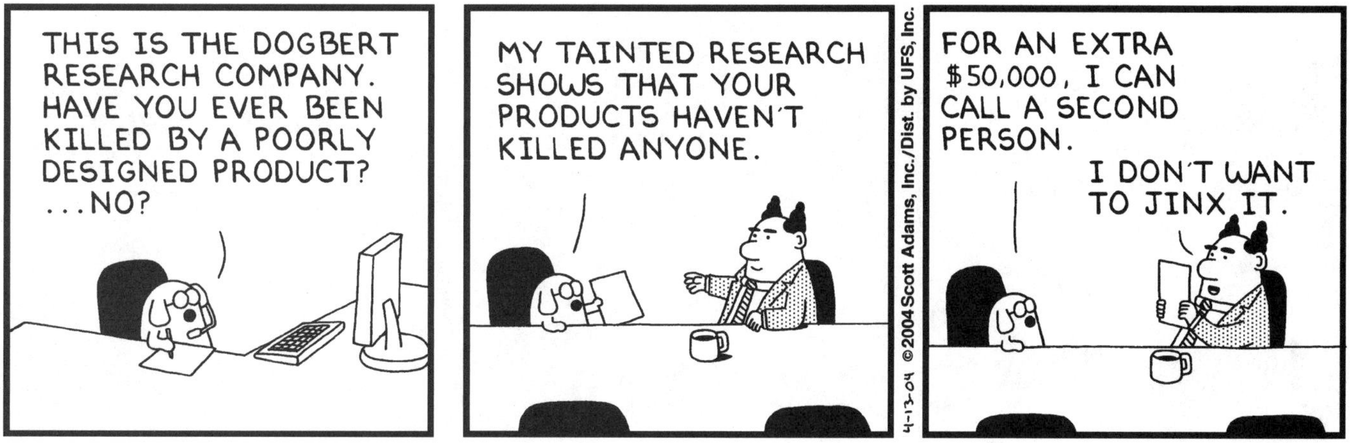
THIS IS THE DOGBERT RESEARCH COMPANY. HAVE YOU EVER BEEN KILLED BY A POORLY DESIGNED PRODUCT? ...NO?
MY TAINTED RESEARCH SHOWS THAT YOUR PRODUCTS HAVEN'T KILLED ANYONE.
4-13-04 ©2004 Scott Adams, Inc./Dist. by UFS, Inc.
FOR AN EXTRA $50,000, I CAN CALL A SECOND PERSON.
I DON'T WANT TO JINX IT.

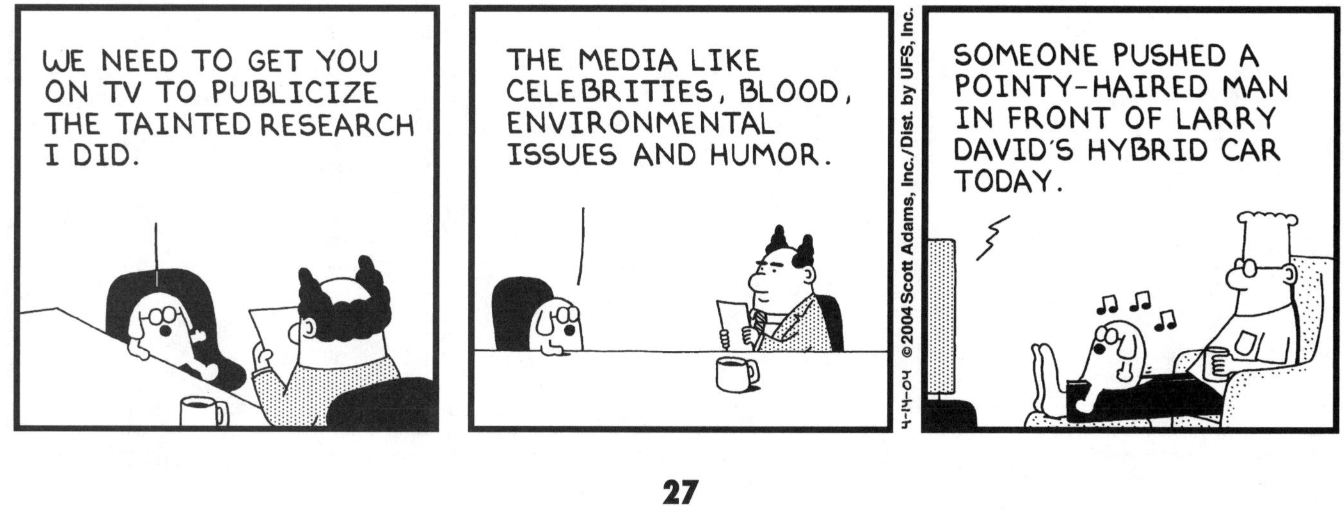
WE NEED TO GET YOU ON TV TO PUBLICIZE THE TAINTED RESEARCH I DID.
THE MEDIA LIKE CELEBRITIES, BLOOD, ENVIRONMENTAL ISSUES AND HUMOR.
4-14-04 ©2004 Scott Adams, Inc./Dist. by UFS, Inc.
SOMEONE PUSHED A POINTY-HAIRED MAN IN FRONT OF LARRY DAVID'S HYBRID CAR TODAY.

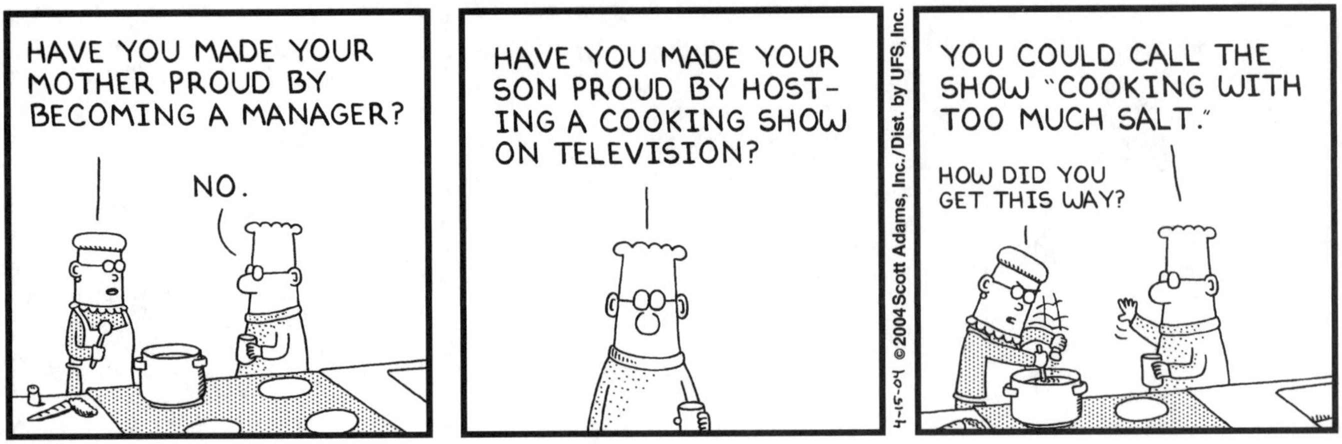
HAVE YOU MADE YOUR MOTHER PROUD BY BECOMING A MANAGER?
NO.
HAVE YOU MADE YOUR SON PROUD BY HOSTING A COOKING SHOW ON TELEVISION?
YOU COULD CALL THE SHOW "COOKING WITH TOO MUCH SALT."
HOW DID YOU GET THIS WAY?
4-15-04 © 2004 Scott Adams, Inc./Dist. by UFS, Inc.

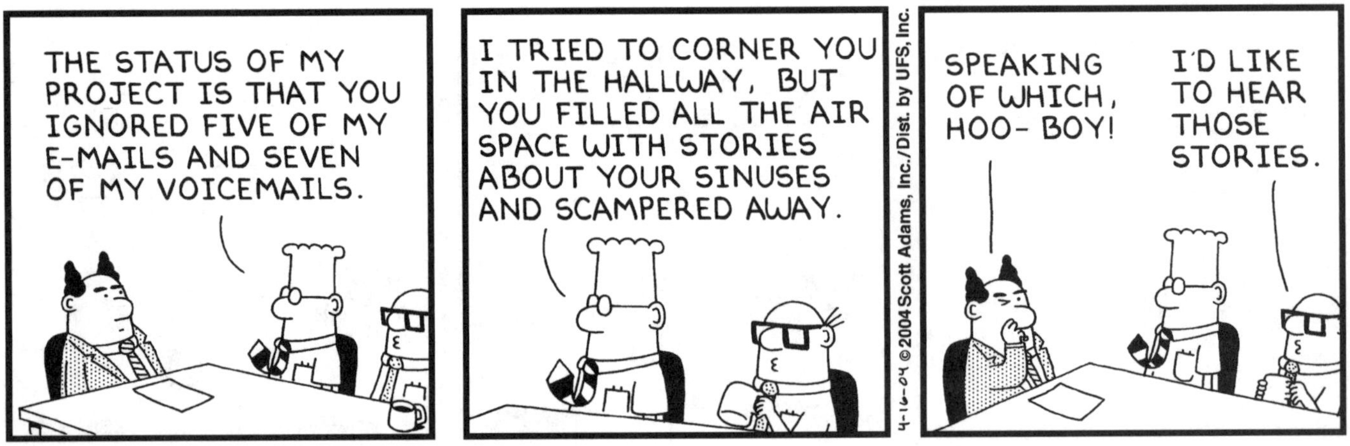
THE STATUS OF MY PROJECT IS THAT YOU IGNORED FIVE OF MY E-MAILS AND SEVEN OF MY VOICEMAILS.
I TRIED TO CORNER YOU IN THE HALLWAY, BUT YOU FILLED ALL THE AIR SPACE WITH STORIES ABOUT YOUR SINUSES AND SCAMPERED AWAY.
SPEAKING OF WHICH, HOO-BOY!
I'D LIKE TO HEAR THOSE STORIES.
4-16-04 © 2004 Scott Adams, Inc./Dist. by UFS, Inc.

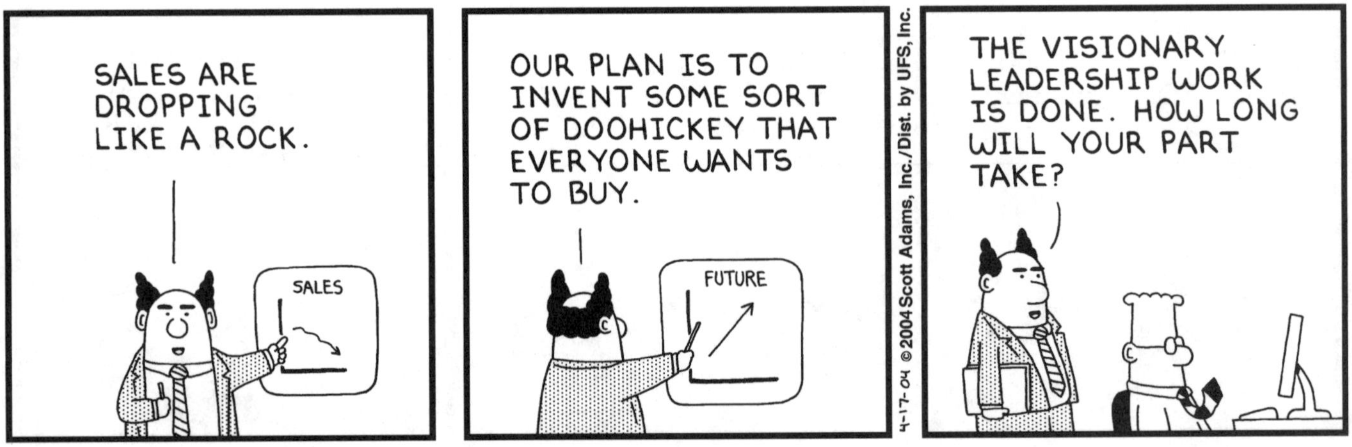
SALES ARE DROPPING LIKE A ROCK.
SALES
OUR PLAN IS TO INVENT SOME SORT OF DOOHICKEY THAT EVERYONE WANTS TO BUY.
FUTURE
THE VISIONARY LEADERSHIP WORK IS DONE. HOW LONG WILL YOUR PART TAKE?
4-17-04 © 2004 Scott Adams, Inc./Dist. by UFS, Inc.

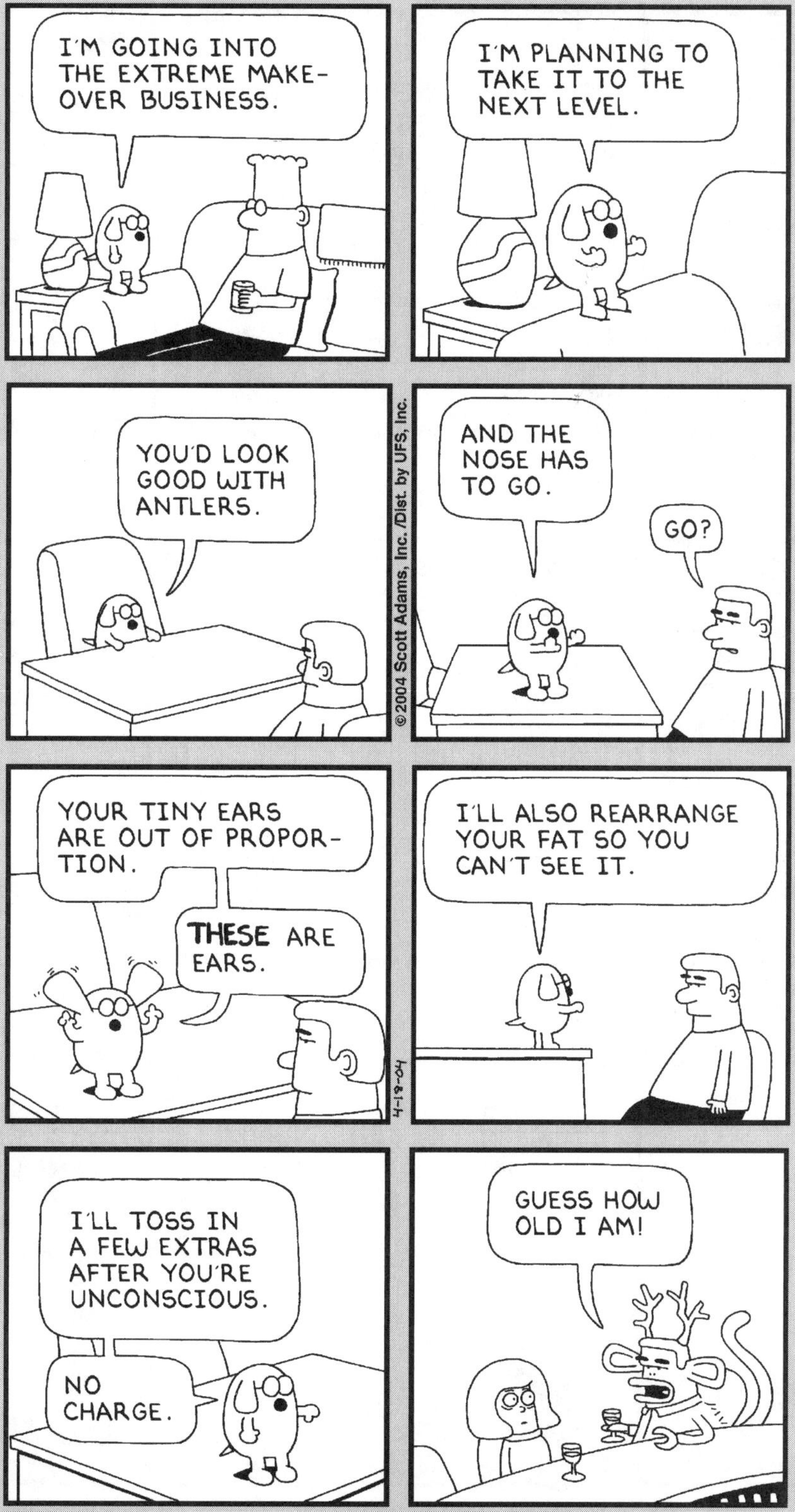
I'M GOING INTO THE EXTREME MAKE-OVER BUSINESS.
I'M PLANNING TO TAKE IT TO THE NEXT LEVEL.
YOU'D LOOK GOOD WITH ANTLERS.
AND THE NOSE HAS TO GO.
GO?
YOUR TINY EARS ARE OUT OF PROPOR-TION.
THESE ARE EARS.
I'LL ALSO REARRANGE YOUR FAT SO YOU CAN'T SEE IT.
I'LL TOSS IN A FEW EXTRAS AFTER YOU'RE UNCONSCIOUS.
NO CHARGE.
GUESS HOW OLD I AM!
©2004 Scott Adams, Inc./Dist. by UFS, Inc.
4-19-04

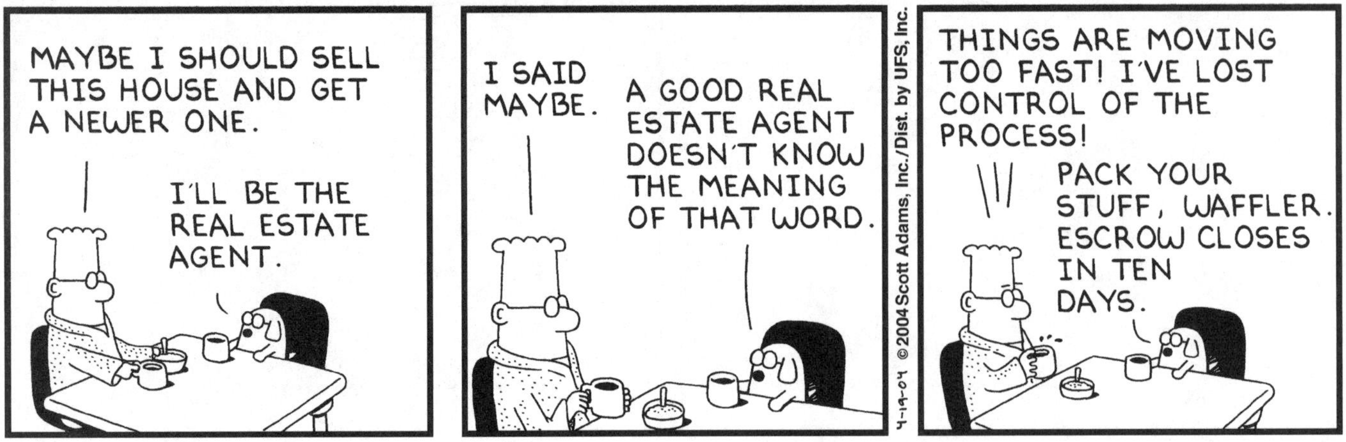
MAYBE I SHOULD SELL THIS HOUSE AND GET A NEWER ONE.
I'LL BE THE REAL ESTATE AGENT.
I SAID MAYBE.
A GOOD REAL ESTATE AGENT DOESN'T KNOW THE MEANING OF THAT WORD.
4-19-04 ©2004 Scott Adams, Inc./Dist. by UFS, Inc.
THINGS ARE MOVING TOO FAST! I'VE LOST CONTROL OF THE PROCESS!
PACK YOUR STUFF, WAFFLER. ESCROW CLOSES IN TEN DAYS.

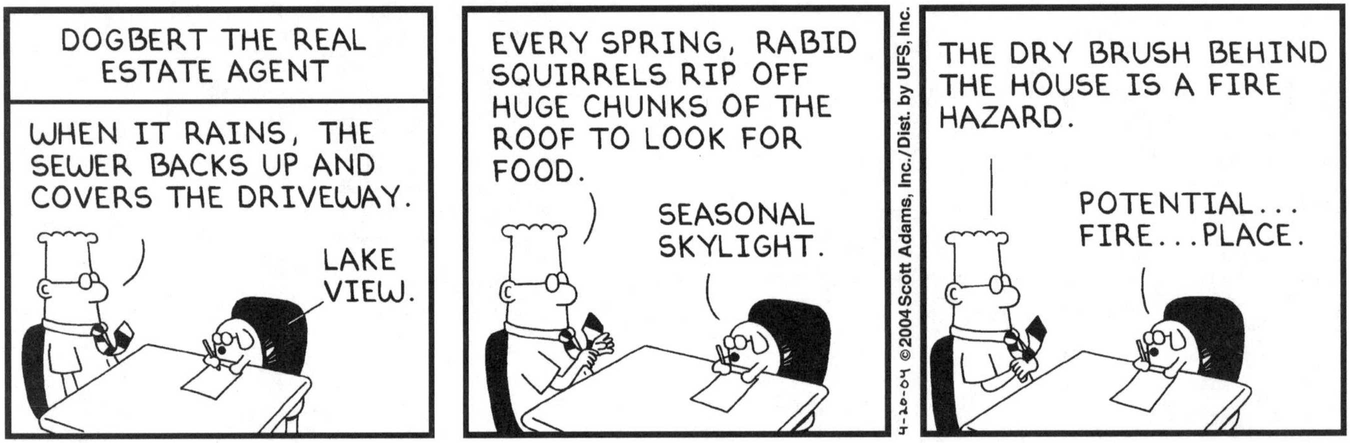
DOGBERT THE REAL ESTATE AGENT
WHEN IT RAINS, THE SEWER BACKS UP AND COVERS THE DRIVEWAY.
LAKE VIEW.
EVERY SPRING, RABID SQUIRRELS RIP OFF HUGE CHUNKS OF THE ROOF TO LOOK FOR FOOD.
SEASONAL SKYLIGHT.
4-20-04 ©2004 Scott Adams, Inc./Dist. by UFS, Inc.
THE DRY BRUSH BEHIND THE HOUSE IS A FIRE HAZARD.
POTENTIAL... FIRE... PLACE.

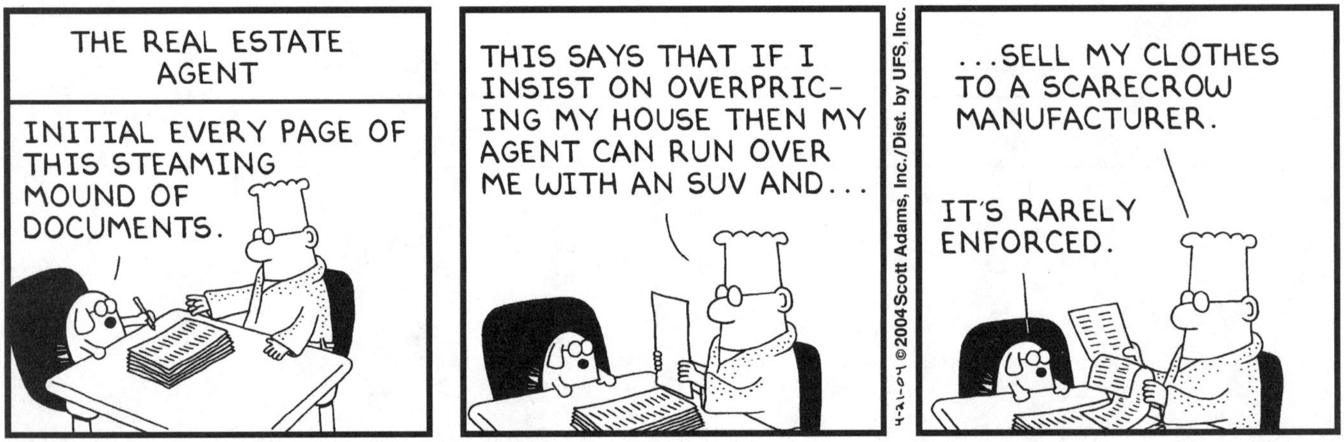
THE REAL ESTATE AGENT
INITIAL EVERY PAGE OF THIS STEAMING MOUND OF DOCUMENTS.
THIS SAYS THAT IF I INSIST ON OVERPRIC-ING MY HOUSE THEN MY AGENT CAN RUN OVER ME WITH AN SUV AND...
4-21-04 ©2004 Scott Adams, Inc./Dist. by UFS, Inc.
...SELL MY CLOTHES TO A SCARECROW MANUFACTURER.
IT'S RARELY ENFORCED.

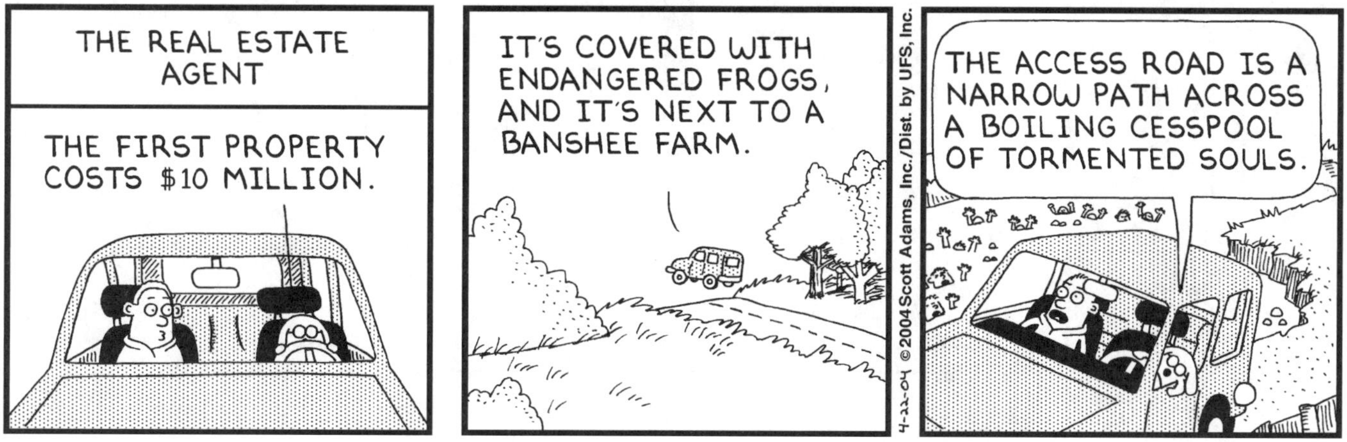
THE REAL ESTATE AGENT
THE FIRST PROPERTY COSTS $10 MILLION.
IT'S COVERED WITH ENDANGERED FROGS, AND IT'S NEXT TO A BANSHEE FARM.
THE ACCESS ROAD IS A NARROW PATH ACROSS A BOILING CESSPOOL OF TORMENTED SOULS.
4-22-04 © 2004 Scott Adams, Inc./Dist. by UFS, Inc.

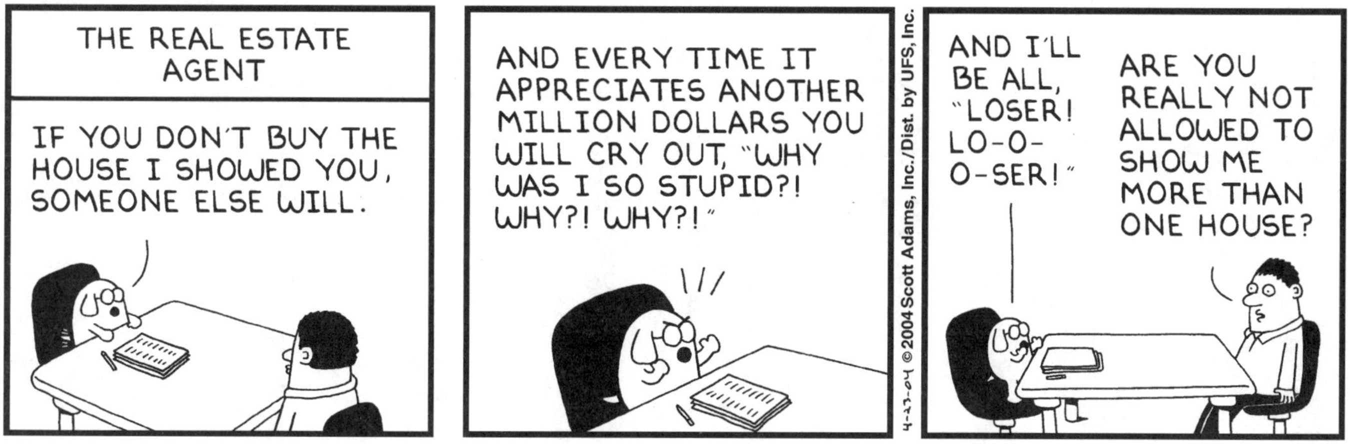
THE REAL ESTATE AGENT
IF YOU DON'T BUY THE HOUSE I SHOWED YOU, SOMEONE ELSE WILL.
AND EVERY TIME IT APPRECIATES ANOTHER MILLION DOLLARS YOU WILL CRY OUT, "WHY WAS I SO STUPID?! WHY?! WHY?!"
AND I'LL BE ALL, "LOSER! LO-O-O-SER!"
ARE YOU REALLY NOT ALLOWED TO SHOW ME MORE THAN ONE HOUSE?
4-23-04 © 2004 Scott Adams, Inc./Dist. by UFS, Inc.

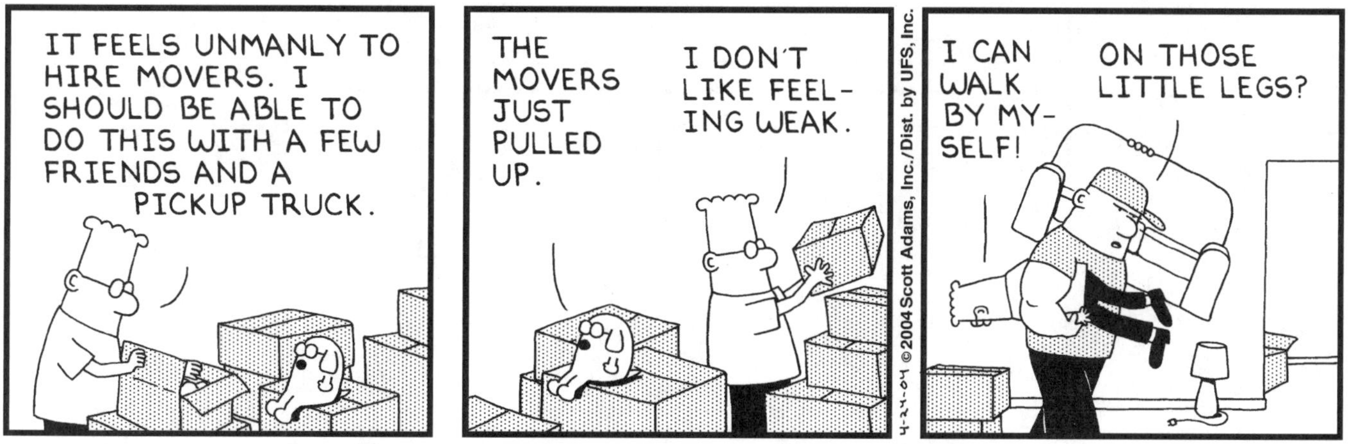
IT FEELS UNMANLY TO HIRE MOVERS. I SHOULD BE ABLE TO DO THIS WITH A FEW FRIENDS AND A PICKUP TRUCK.
THE MOVERS JUST PULLED UP.
I DON'T LIKE FEEL-ING WEAK.
I CAN WALK BY MY-SELF!
ON THOSE LITTLE LEGS?
4-24-04 © 2004 Scott Adams, Inc./Dist. by UFS, Inc.

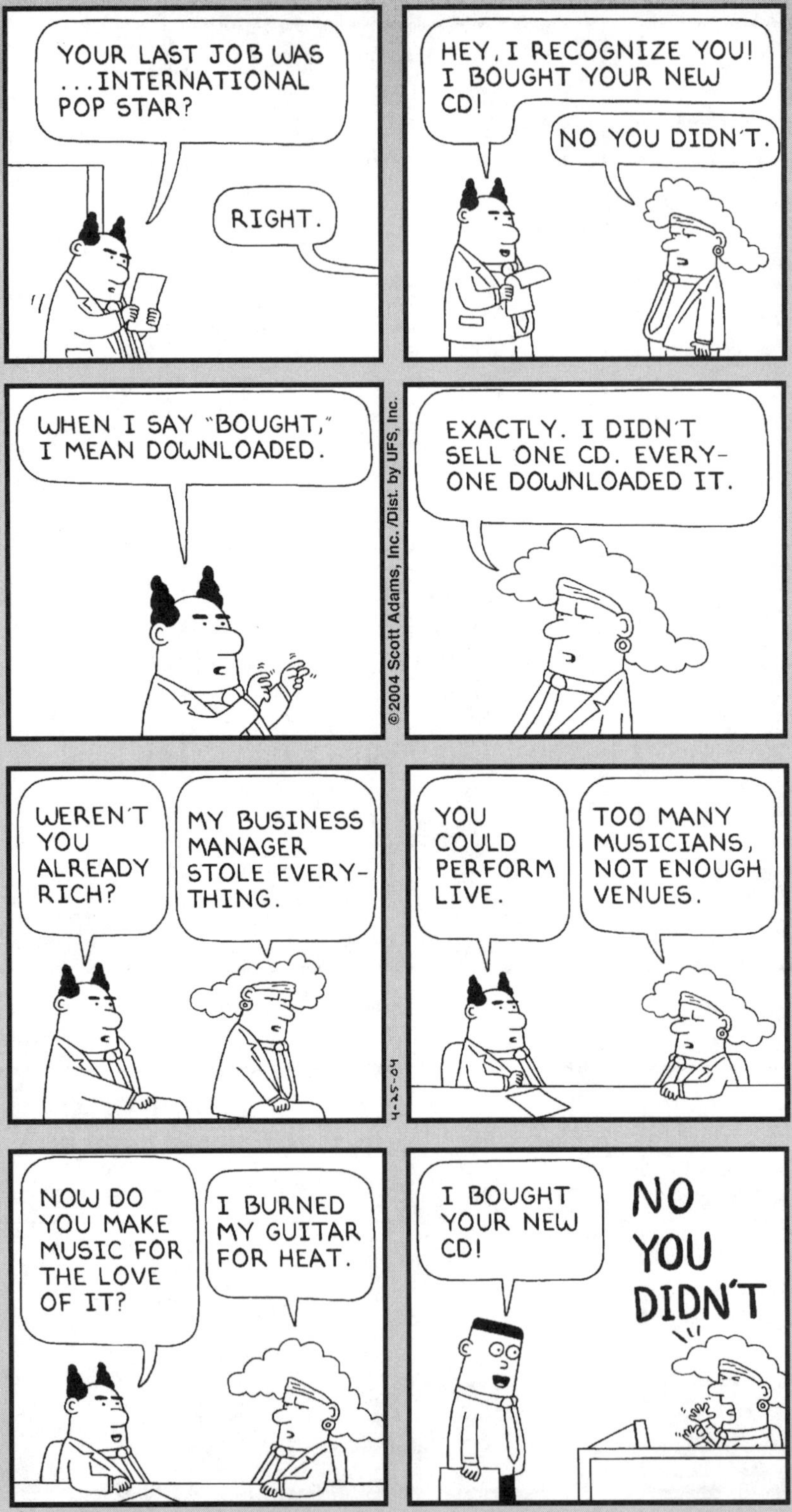
YOUR LAST JOB WAS ...INTERNATIONAL POP STAR?
RIGHT.
HEY, I RECOGNIZE YOU! I BOUGHT YOUR NEW CD!
NO YOU DIDN'T.
WHEN I SAY "BOUGHT," I MEAN DOWNLOADED.
©2004 Scott Adams, Inc. /Dist. by UFS, Inc.
EXACTLY. I DIDN'T SELL ONE CD. EVERYONE DOWNLOADED IT.
WEREN'T YOU ALREADY RICH?
MY BUSINESS MANAGER STOLE EVERYTHING.
4-25-04
YOU COULD PERFORM LIVE.
TOO MANY MUSICIANS, NOT ENOUGH VENUES.
NOW DO YOU MAKE MUSIC FOR THE LOVE OF IT?
I BURNED MY GUITAR FOR HEAT.
I BOUGHT YOUR NEW CD!
NO YOU DIDN'T

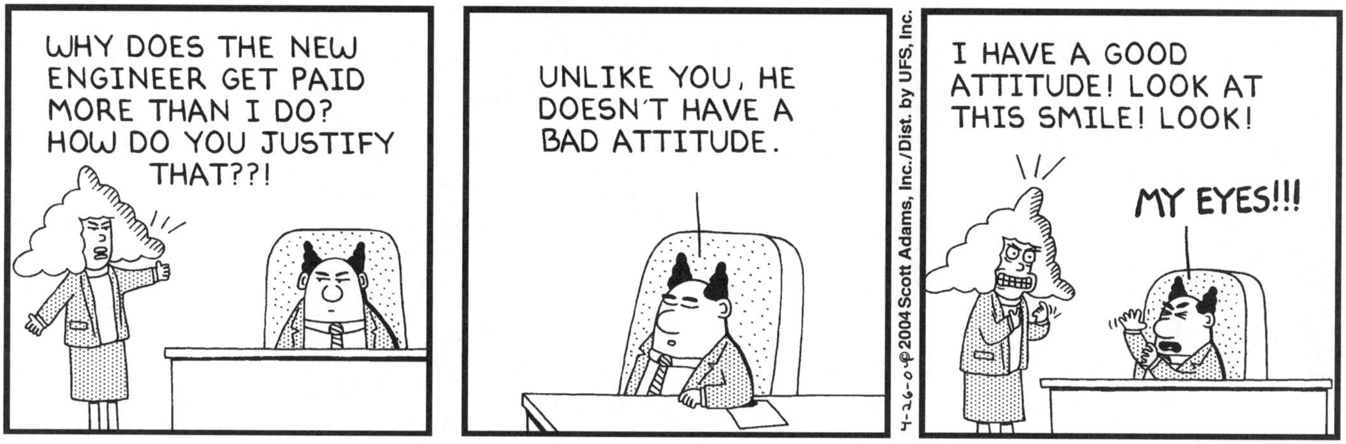
WHY DOES THE NEW ENGINEER GET PAID MORE THAN I DO? HOW DO YOU JUSTIFY THAT??!
UNLIKE YOU, HE DOESN'T HAVE A BAD ATTITUDE.
©2004 Scott Adams, Inc./Dist. by UFS, Inc.
I HAVE A GOOD ATTITUDE! LOOK AT THIS SMILE! LOOK!
MY EYES!!!

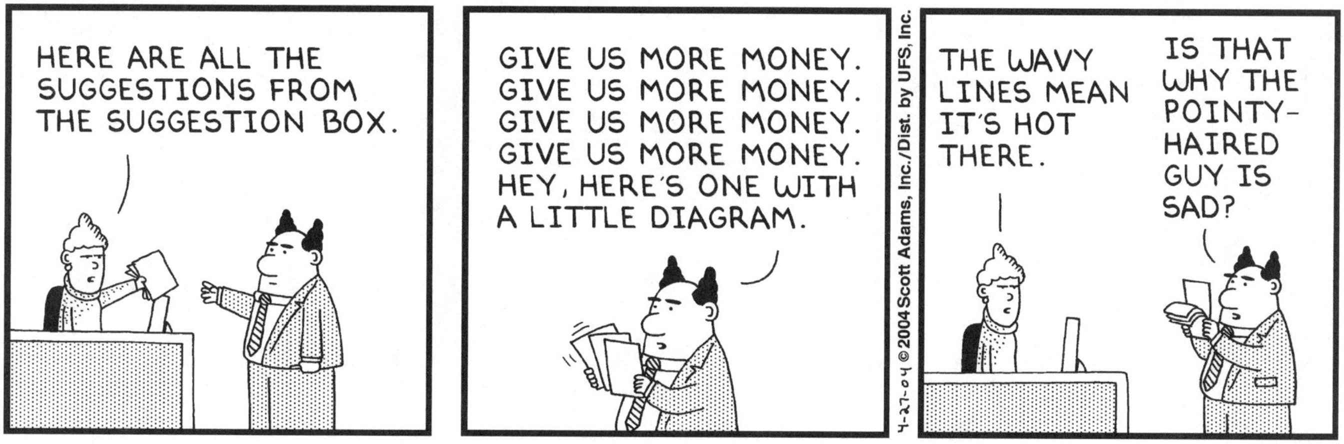
HERE ARE ALL THE SUGGESTIONS FROM THE SUGGESTION BOX.
GIVE US MORE MONEY. GIVE US MORE MONEY. GIVE US MORE MONEY. GIVE US MORE MONEY. HEY, HERE'S ONE WITH A LITTLE DIAGRAM.
©2004 Scott Adams, Inc./Dist. by UFS, Inc.
THE WAVY LINES MEAN IT'S HOT THERE.
IS THAT WHY THE POINTY-HAIRED GUY IS SAD?

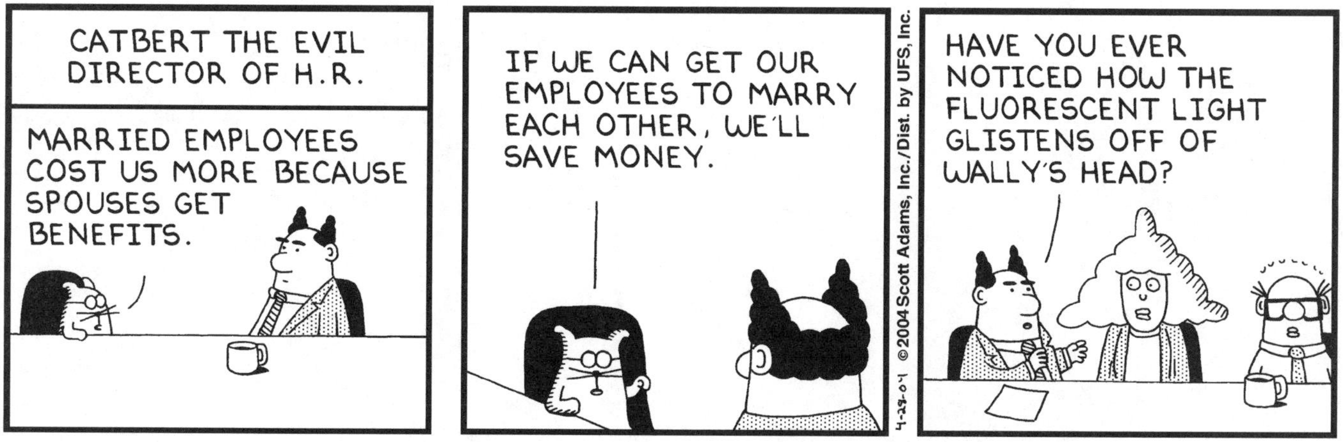
CATBERT THE EVIL DIRECTOR OF H.R.
MARRIED EMPLOYEES COST US MORE BECAUSE SPOUSES GET BENEFITS.
IF WE CAN GET OUR EMPLOYEES TO MARRY EACH OTHER, WE'LL SAVE MONEY.
©2004 Scott Adams, Inc./Dist. by UFS, Inc.
HAVE YOU EVER NOTICED HOW THE FLUORESCENT LIGHT GLISTENS OFF OF WALLY'S HEAD?

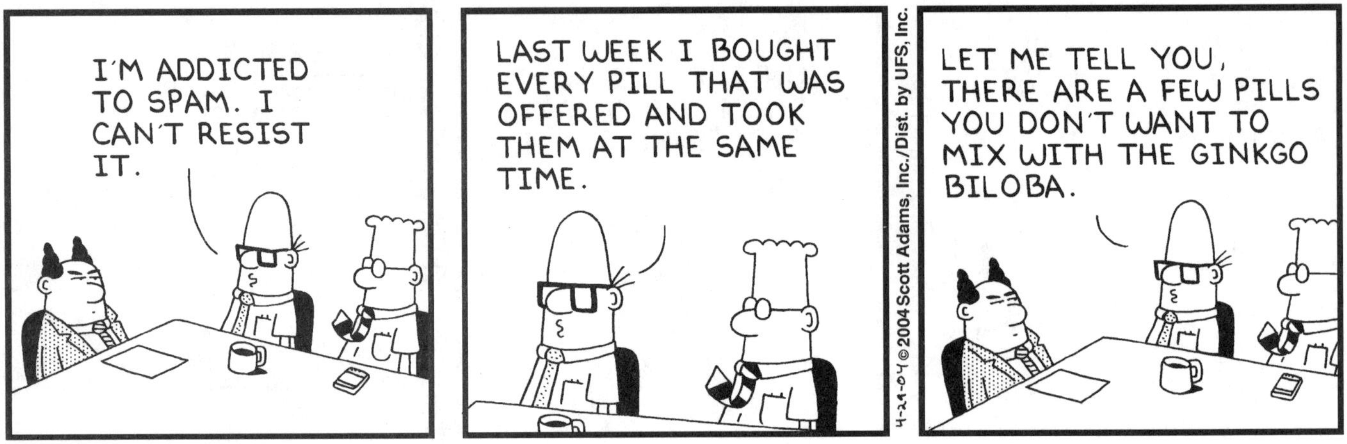
I'M ADDICTED TO SPAM. I CAN'T RESIST IT.
LAST WEEK I BOUGHT EVERY PILL THAT WAS OFFERED AND TOOK THEM AT THE SAME TIME.
4-29-04 ©2004 Scott Adams, Inc./Dist. by UFS, Inc.
LET ME TELL YOU, THERE ARE A FEW PILLS YOU DON'T WANT TO MIX WITH THE GINKGO BILOBA.

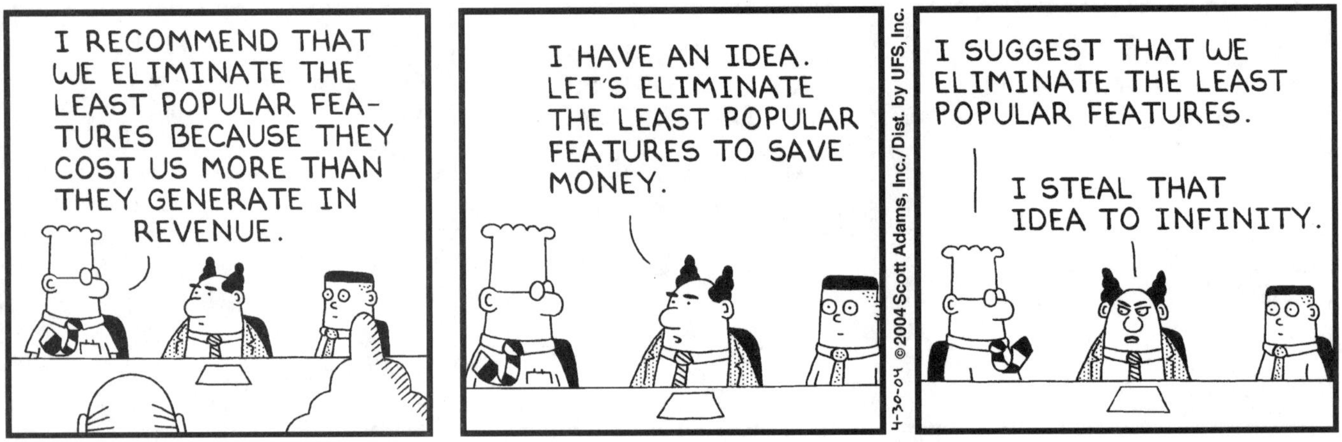
I RECOMMEND THAT WE ELIMINATE THE LEAST POPULAR FEA-TURES BECAUSE THEY COST US MORE THAN THEY GENERATE IN REVENUE.
I HAVE AN IDEA. LET'S ELIMINATE THE LEAST POPULAR FEATURES TO SAVE MONEY.
4-30-04 ©2004 Scott Adams, Inc./Dist. by UFS, Inc.
I SUGGEST THAT WE ELIMINATE THE LEAST POPULAR FEATURES.
I STEAL THAT IDEA TO INFINITY.

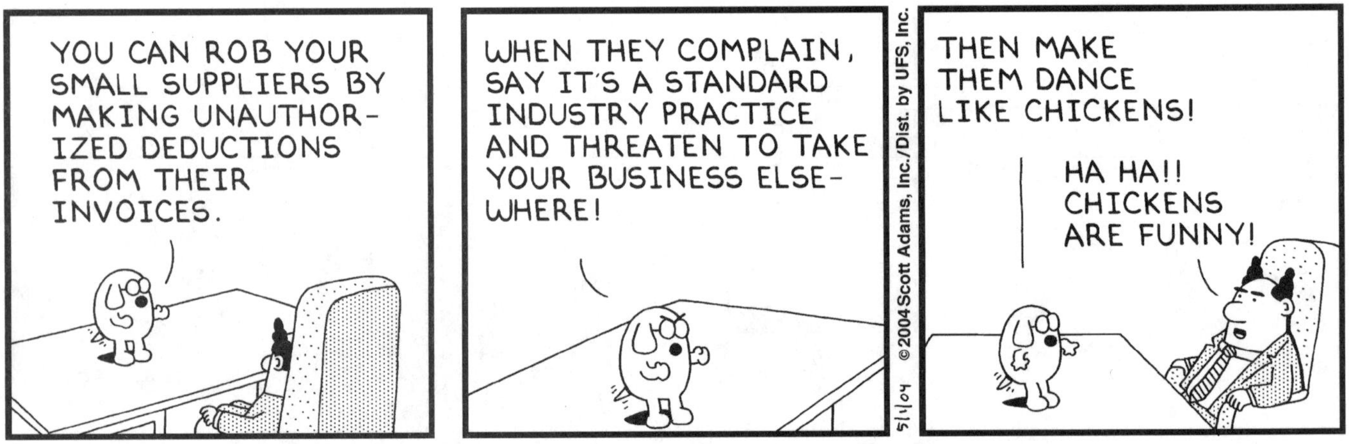
YOU CAN ROB YOUR SMALL SUPPLIERS BY MAKING UNAUTHOR-IZED DEDUCTIONS FROM THEIR INVOICES.
WHEN THEY COMPLAIN, SAY IT'S A STANDARD INDUSTRY PRACTICE AND THREATEN TO TAKE YOUR BUSINESS ELSE-WHERE!
5/1/04 ©2004 Scott Adams, Inc./Dist. by UFS, Inc.
THEN MAKE THEM DANCE LIKE CHICKENS!
HA HA!! CHICKENS ARE FUNNY!

DOGBERT EXPLAINS STOCK INVESTING
PAY ATTENTION.
FIRST, EMPLOYEES PROVIDE VALUABLE DATA.
IS YOUR PROJECT ON SCHEDULE?
I DIDN'T KNOW I HAD A PROJECT.
A MANAGER REFINES THE DATA.
WE'RE ON SCHEDULE.
THE CEO GIVES "VISIBILITY" TO ANALYSTS.
NO PROBLEMS WHATSOEVER.
©2004 Scott Adams, Inc./Dist. by UFS, Inc.
ACCOUNTANTS PUBLISH BAD NEWS IN FOOTNOTES USING A COMBINATION OF NANOTECHNOLOGY AND GIBBERISH.
STILL TOO OBVIOUS.
DISCOUNT BROKERAGE FIRMS TELL YOU THAT YOU'RE SMART.
USE YOUR OWN IDEAS!
INVESTORS DO THEIR OWN RESEARCH.
BUY IT BECAUSE I DID.
THANK YOU, UNBIASED STRANGER!
A SECRET SOCIETY OF DONALD TRUMP LOOK-ALIKES END UP WITH ALL YOUR MONEY.
YOU'RE FIRED.
YOU ARE!

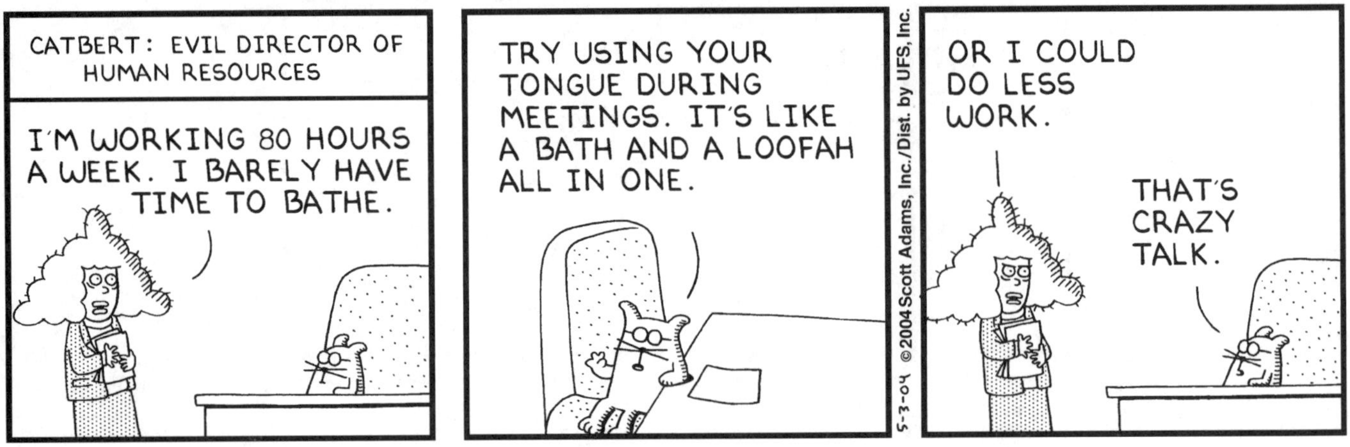
CATBERT: EVIL DIRECTOR OF HUMAN RESOURCES
I'M WORKING 80 HOURS A WEEK. I BARELY HAVE TIME TO BATHE.
TRY USING YOUR TONGUE DURING MEETINGS. IT'S LIKE A BATH AND A LOOFAH ALL IN ONE.
5-3-04 © 2004 Scott Adams, Inc./Dist. by UFS, Inc.
OR I COULD DO LESS WORK.
THAT'S CRAZY TALK.

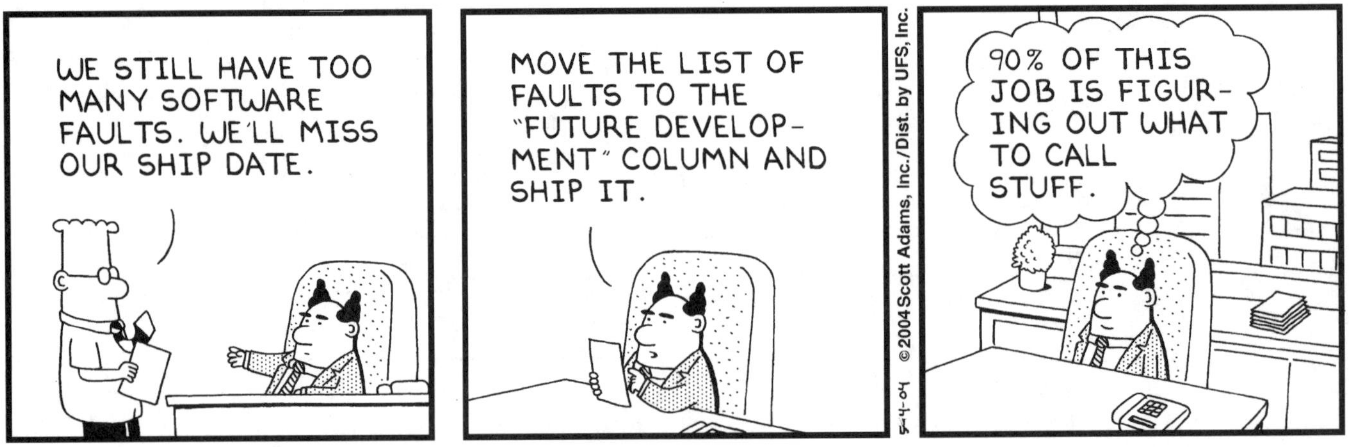
WE STILL HAVE TOO MANY SOFTWARE FAULTS. WE'LL MISS OUR SHIP DATE.
MOVE THE LIST OF FAULTS TO THE "FUTURE DEVELOPMENT" COLUMN AND SHIP IT.
5-4-04 © 2004 Scott Adams, Inc./Dist. by UFS, Inc.
90% OF THIS JOB IS FIGURING OUT WHAT TO CALL STUFF.

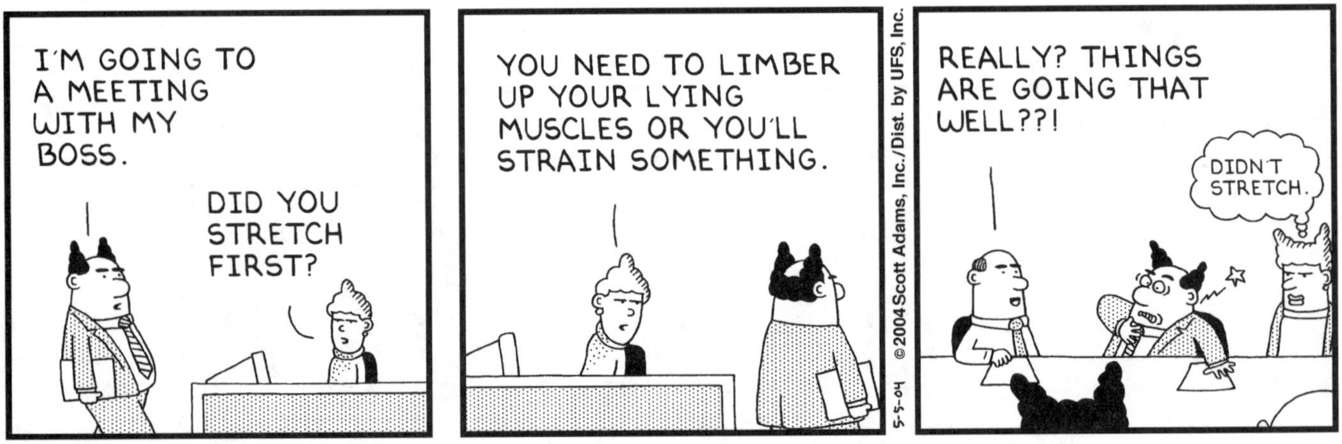
I'M GOING TO A MEETING WITH MY BOSS.
DID YOU STRETCH FIRST?
YOU NEED TO LIMBER UP YOUR LYING MUSCLES OR YOU'LL STRAIN SOMETHING.
5-5-04 © 2004 Scott Adams, Inc./Dist. by UFS, Inc.
REALLY? THINGS ARE GOING THAT WELL??!
DIDN'T STRETCH.

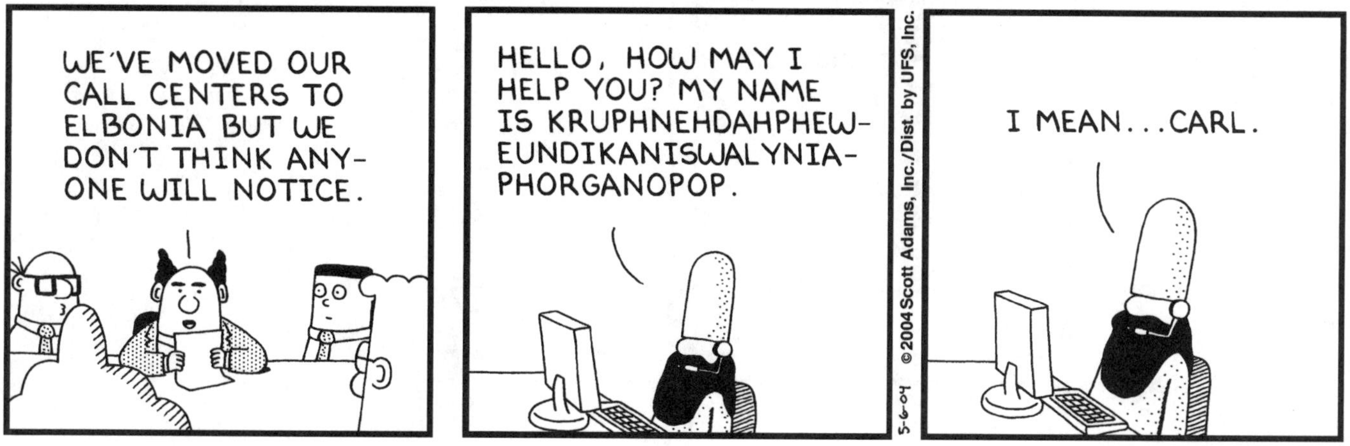
WE'VE MOVED OUR CALL CENTERS TO ELBONIA BUT WE DON'T THINK ANY-ONE WILL NOTICE.
HELLO, HOW MAY I HELP YOU? MY NAME IS KRUPHNEHDAHPHEW-EUNDIKANISWALYNIA-PHORGANOPOP.
I MEAN...CARL.
5-6-04 © 2004 Scott Adams, Inc./Dist. by UFS, Inc.

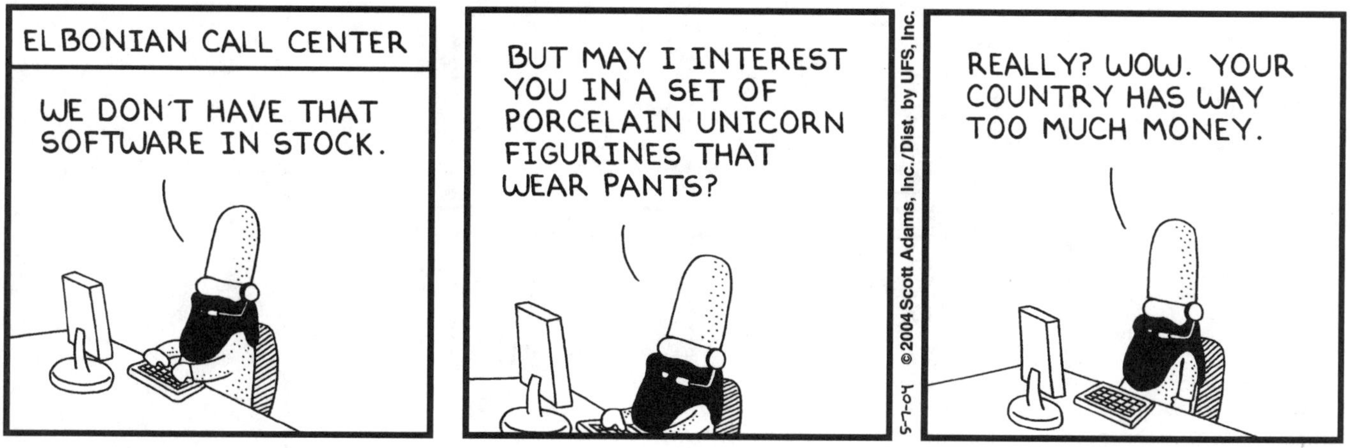
ELBONIAN CALL CENTER
WE DON'T HAVE THAT SOFTWARE IN STOCK.
BUT MAY I INTEREST YOU IN A SET OF PORCELAIN UNICORN FIGURINES THAT WEAR PANTS?
REALLY? WOW. YOUR COUNTRY HAS WAY TOO MUCH MONEY.
5-7-04 © 2004 Scott Adams, Inc./Dist. by UFS, Inc.

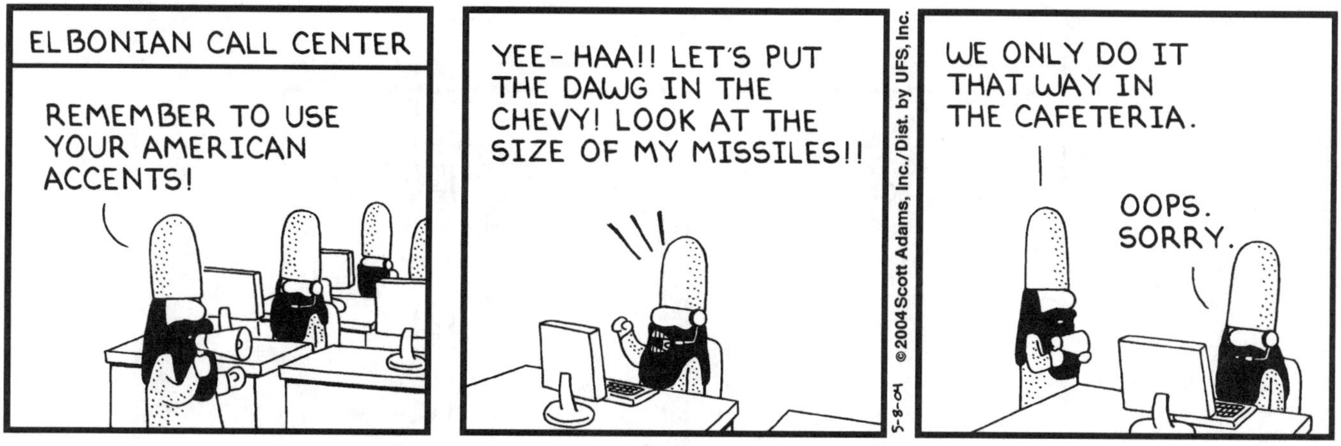
ELBONIAN CALL CENTER
REMEMBER TO USE YOUR AMERICAN ACCENTS!
YEE-HAA!! LET'S PUT THE DAWG IN THE CHEVY! LOOK AT THE SIZE OF MY MISSILES!!
WE ONLY DO IT THAT WAY IN THE CAFETERIA.
OOPS. SORRY.
5-8-04 © 2004 Scott Adams, Inc./Dist. by UFS, Inc.

CAN I TALK TO YOU AFTER THE MANDATORY MEETING?
WHOA! WHOA! I DIDN'T GIVE YOU APPROVAL TO ATTEND THAT MEETING.
THE MEETING IS MANDATORY.
APPROVAL IS MANDATORY, TOO.
©2004 Scott Adams, Inc./Dist. by UFS, Inc.
OKAY, WHATEVER.
MAY I GO TO THE MANDATORY MEETING?
ALL REQUESTS MUST BE IN WRITING.
5-9-04
IT'S MANDATORY!!!
MAN-DUH-TORY!!!
IF PEOPLE START BENDING THE RULES, BEFORE LONG, MURDER WILL BE LEGAL.
THAT WAS THE FINEST MANDATORY MEETING I'VE EVER ATTENDED! THEY HANDED OUT CASH!
SHUT UP.
$

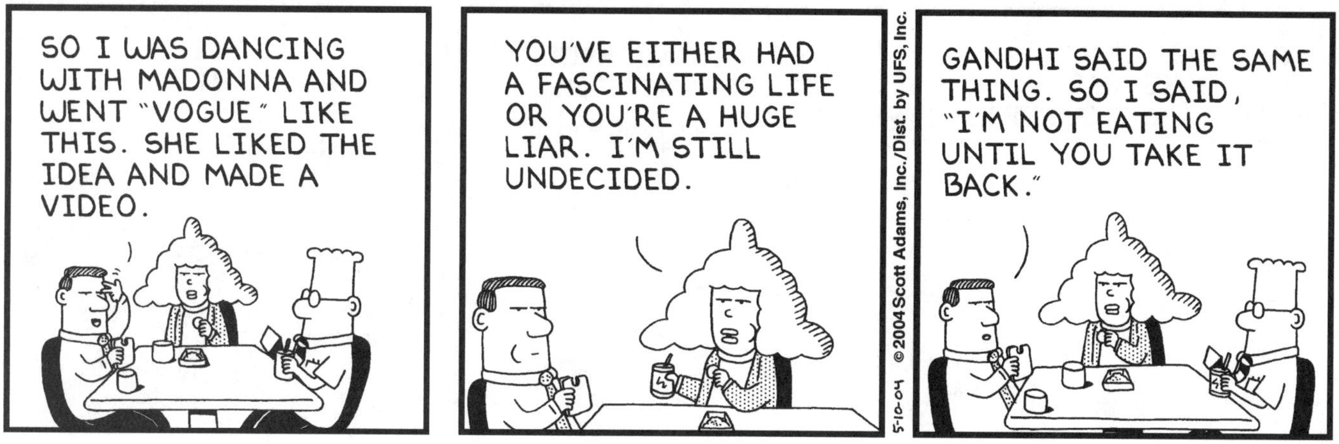
SO I WAS DANCING WITH MADONNA AND WENT "VOGUE" LIKE THIS. SHE LIKED THE IDEA AND MADE A VIDEO.
YOU'VE EITHER HAD A FASCINATING LIFE OR YOU'RE A HUGE LIAR. I'M STILL UNDECIDED.
GANDHI SAID THE SAME THING. SO I SAID, "I'M NOT EATING UNTIL YOU TAKE IT BACK."
5-10-04

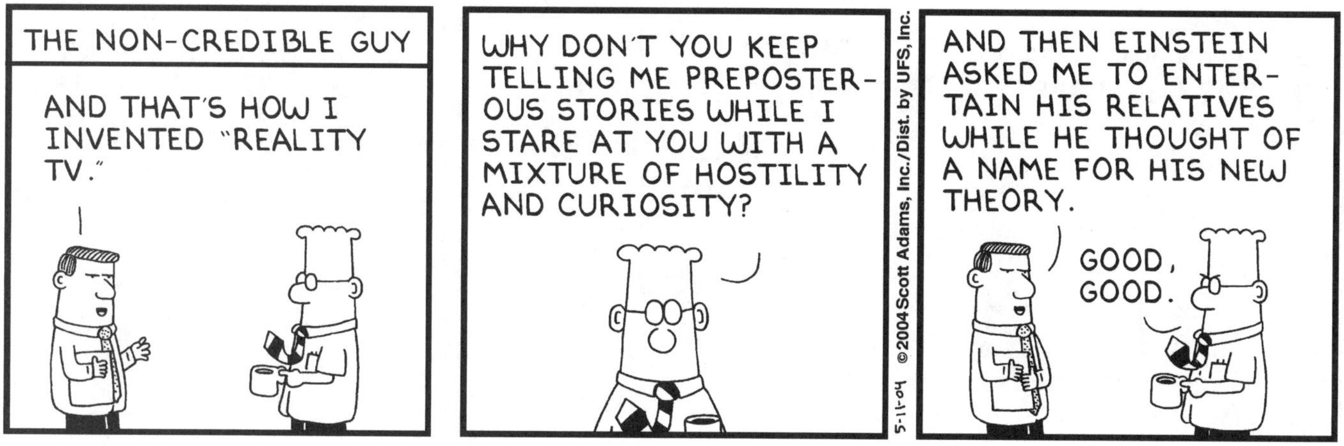
THE NON-CREDIBLE GUY
AND THAT'S HOW I INVENTED "REALITY TV."
WHY DON'T YOU KEEP TELLING ME PREPOSTER-OUS STORIES WHILE I STARE AT YOU WITH A MIXTURE OF HOSTILITY AND CURIOSITY?
AND THEN EINSTEIN ASKED ME TO ENTER-TAIN HIS RELATIVES WHILE HE THOUGHT OF A NAME FOR HIS NEW THEORY.
GOOD, GOOD.
5-11-04

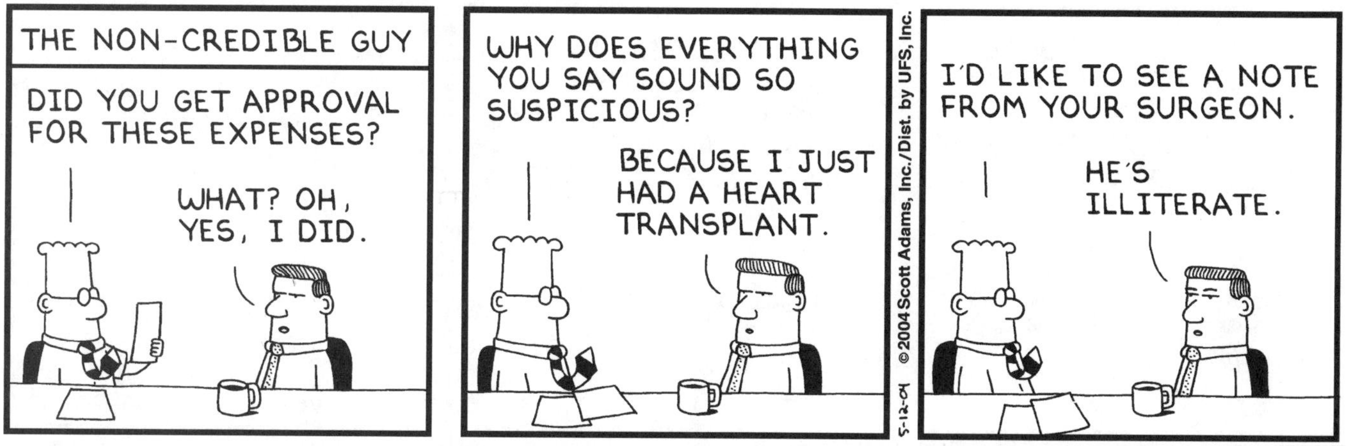
THE NON-CREDIBLE GUY
DID YOU GET APPROVAL FOR THESE EXPENSES?
WHAT? OH, YES, I DID.
WHY DOES EVERYTHING YOU SAY SOUND SO SUSPICIOUS?
BECAUSE I JUST HAD A HEART TRANSPLANT.
I'D LIKE TO SEE A NOTE FROM YOUR SURGEON.
HE'S ILLITERATE.
5-12-04

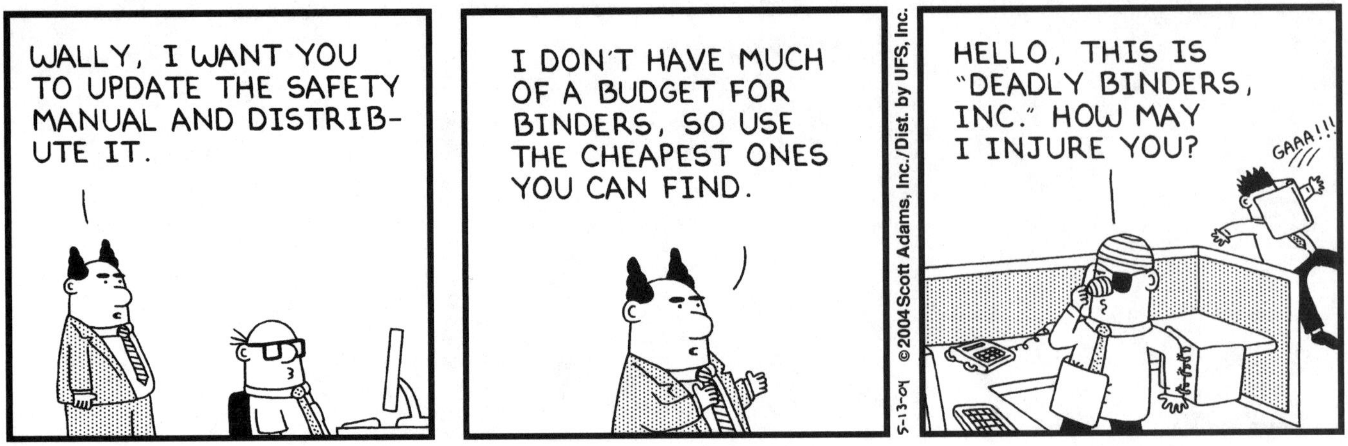
WALLY, I WANT YOU TO UPDATE THE SAFETY MANUAL AND DISTRIB-UTE IT.
I DON'T HAVE MUCH OF A BUDGET FOR BINDERS, SO USE THE CHEAPEST ONES YOU CAN FIND.
5-13-04 ©2004 Scott Adams, Inc./Dist. by UFS, Inc.
HELLO, THIS IS "DEADLY BINDERS, INC." HOW MAY I INJURE YOU?
GAAA!!!

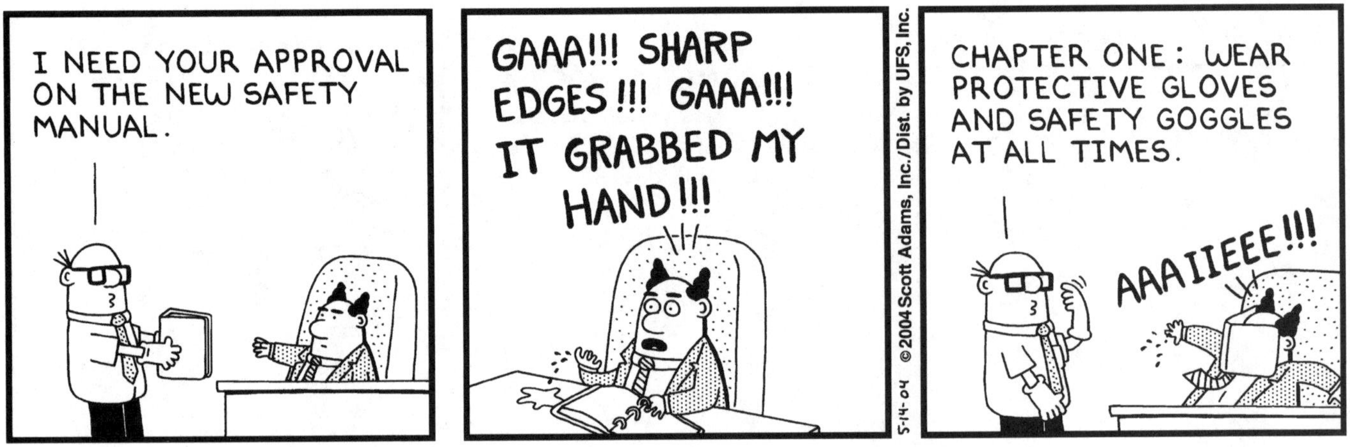
I NEED YOUR APPROVAL ON THE NEW SAFETY MANUAL.
GAAA!!! SHARP EDGES!!! GAAA!!! IT GRABBED MY HAND!!!
5-14-04 ©2004 Scott Adams, Inc./Dist. by UFS, Inc.
CHAPTER ONE: WEAR PROTECTIVE GLOVES AND SAFETY GOGGLES AT ALL TIMES.
AAAIIEEE!!!

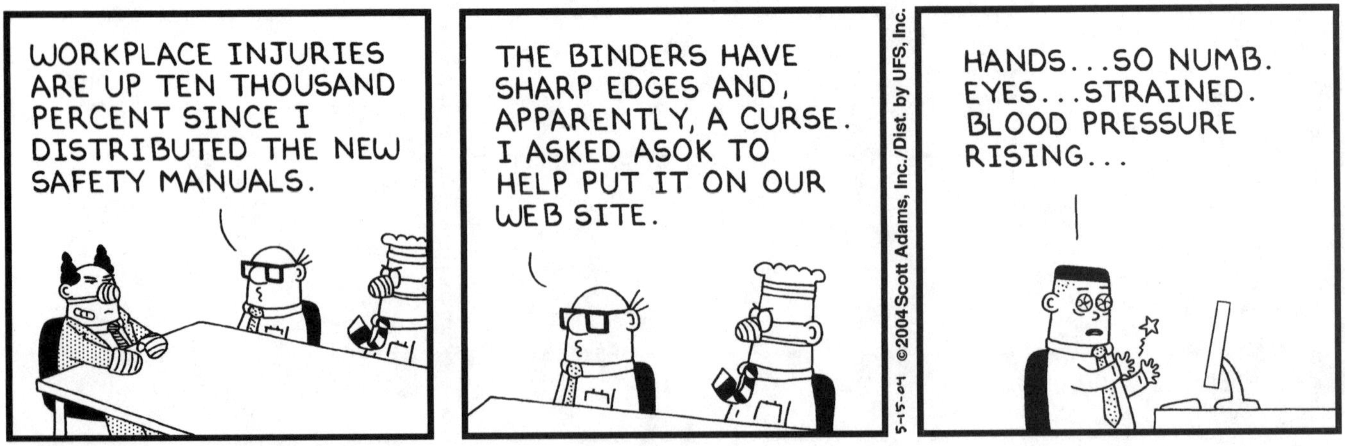
WORKPLACE INJURIES ARE UP TEN THOUSAND PERCENT SINCE I DISTRIBUTED THE NEW SAFETY MANUALS.
THE BINDERS HAVE SHARP EDGES AND, APPARENTLY, A CURSE. I ASKED ASOK TO HELP PUT IT ON OUR WEB SITE.
5-15-04 ©2004 Scott Adams, Inc./Dist. by UFS, Inc.
HANDS...SO NUMB. EYES...STRAINED. BLOOD PRESSURE RISING...

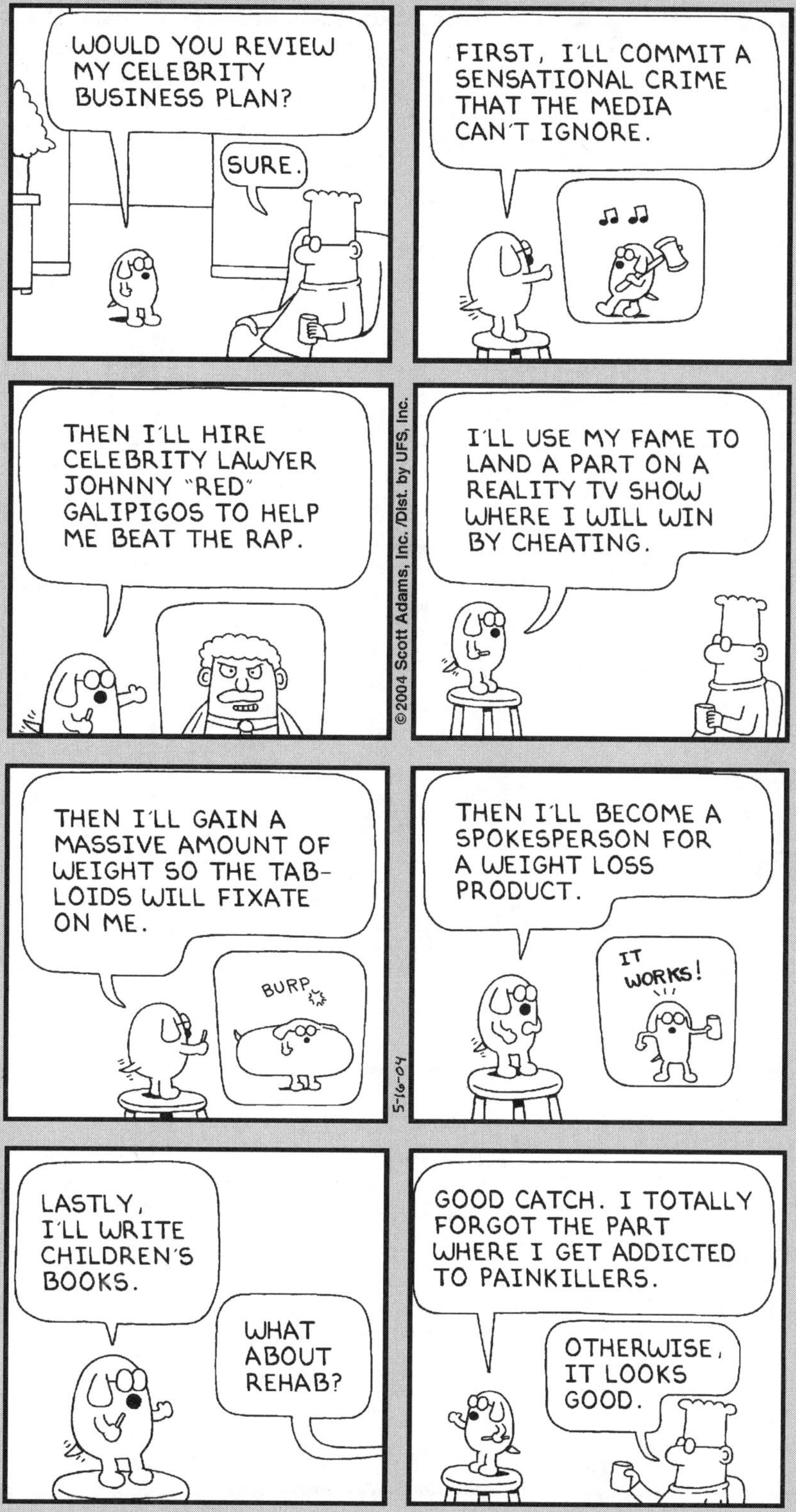
WOULD YOU REVIEW MY CELEBRITY BUSINESS PLAN?
SURE.
FIRST, I'LL COMMIT A SENSATIONAL CRIME THAT THE MEDIA CAN'T IGNORE.
THEN I'LL HIRE CELEBRITY LAWYER JOHNNY "RED" GALIPIGOS TO HELP ME BEAT THE RAP.
I'LL USE MY FAME TO LAND A PART ON A REALITY TV SHOW WHERE I WILL WIN BY CHEATING.
THEN I'LL GAIN A MASSIVE AMOUNT OF WEIGHT SO THE TAB-LOIDS WILL FIXATE ON ME.
BURP
THEN I'LL BECOME A SPOKESPERSON FOR A WEIGHT LOSS PRODUCT.
IT WORKS!
LASTLY, I'LL WRITE CHILDREN'S BOOKS.
WHAT ABOUT REHAB?
GOOD CATCH. I TOTALLY FORGOT THE PART WHERE I GET ADDICTED TO PAINKILLERS.
OTHERWISE, IT LOOKS GOOD.
5-16-04

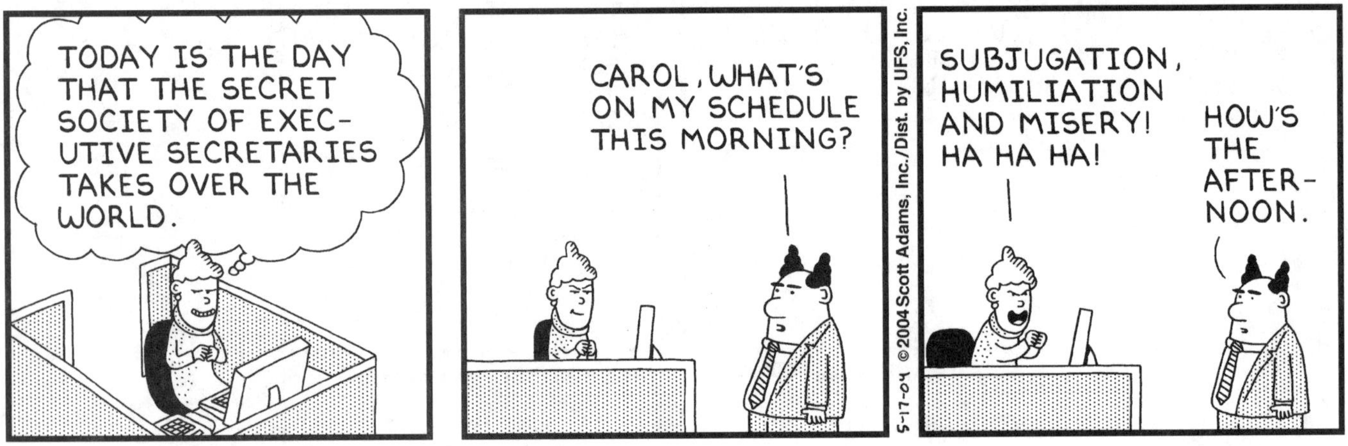
TODAY IS THE DAY THAT THE SECRET SOCIETY OF EXEC-UTIVE SECRETARIES TAKES OVER THE WORLD.
CAROL, WHAT'S ON MY SCHEDULE THIS MORNING?
5-17-04 © 2004 Scott Adams, Inc./Dist. by UFS, Inc.
SUBJUGATION, HUMILIATION AND MISERY! HA HA HA!
HOW'S THE AFTER-NOON.

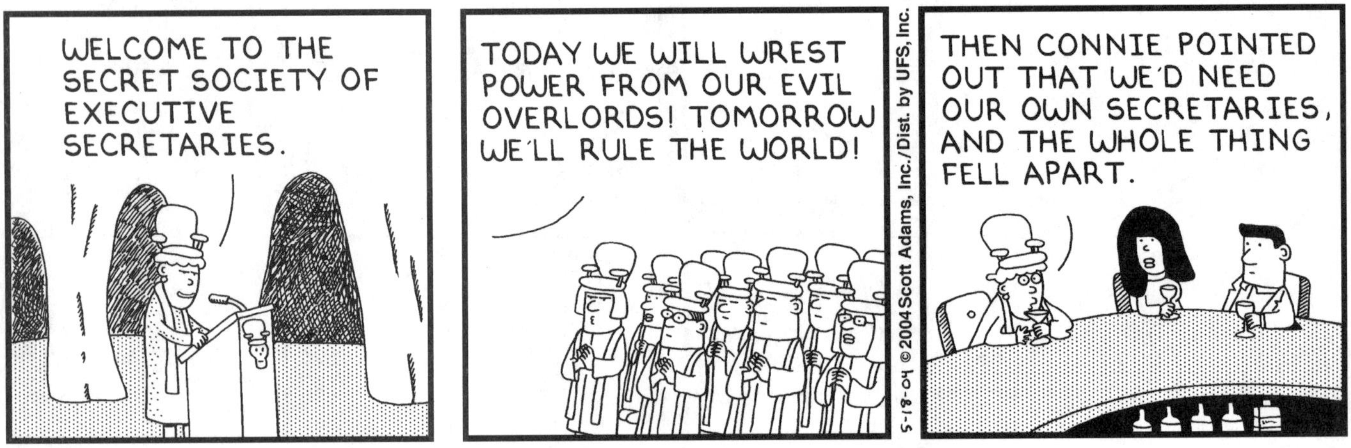
WELCOME TO THE SECRET SOCIETY OF EXECUTIVE SECRETARIES.
TODAY WE WILL WREST POWER FROM OUR EVIL OVERLORDS! TOMORROW WE'LL RULE THE WORLD!
5-18-04 © 2004 Scott Adams, Inc./Dist. by UFS, Inc.
THEN CONNIE POINTED OUT THAT WE'D NEED OUR OWN SECRETARIES, AND THE WHOLE THING FELL APART.

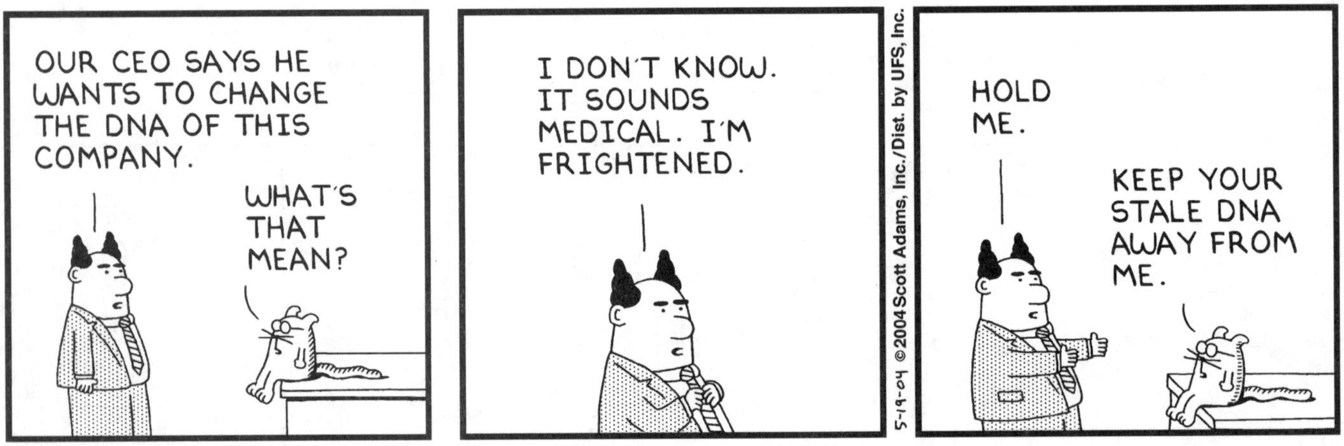
OUR CEO SAYS HE WANTS TO CHANGE THE DNA OF THIS COMPANY.
WHAT'S THAT MEAN?
I DON'T KNOW. IT SOUNDS MEDICAL. I'M FRIGHTENED.
5-19-04 © 2004 Scott Adams, Inc./Dist. by UFS, Inc.
HOLD ME.
KEEP YOUR STALE DNA AWAY FROM ME.

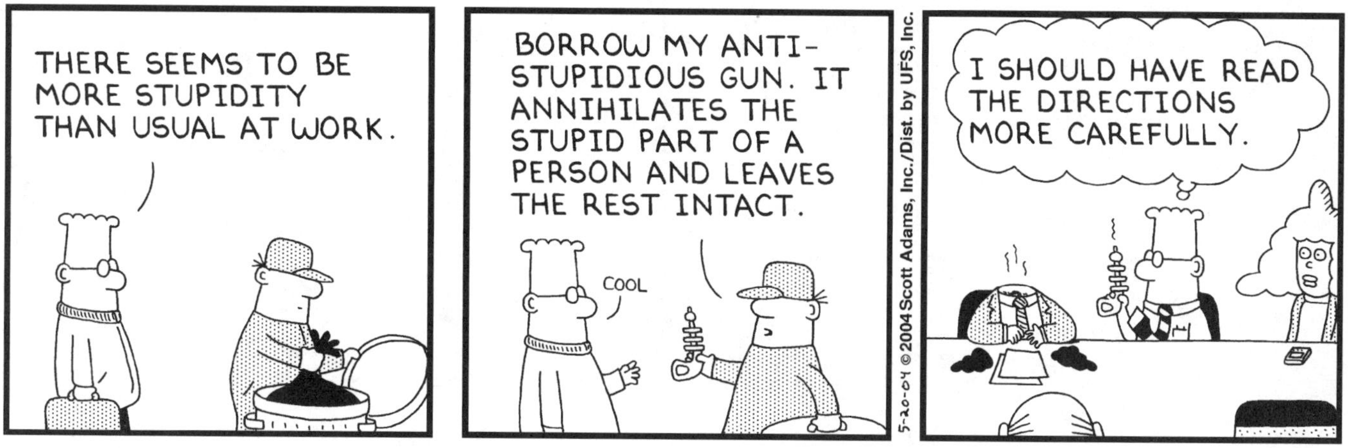
THERE SEEMS TO BE MORE STUPIDITY THAN USUAL AT WORK.
BORROW MY ANTI-STUPIDIOUS GUN. IT ANNIHILATES THE STUPID PART OF A PERSON AND LEAVES THE REST INTACT.
COOL
5-20-04 © 2004 Scott Adams, Inc./Dist. by UFS, Inc.
I SHOULD HAVE READ THE DIRECTIONS MORE CAREFULLY.

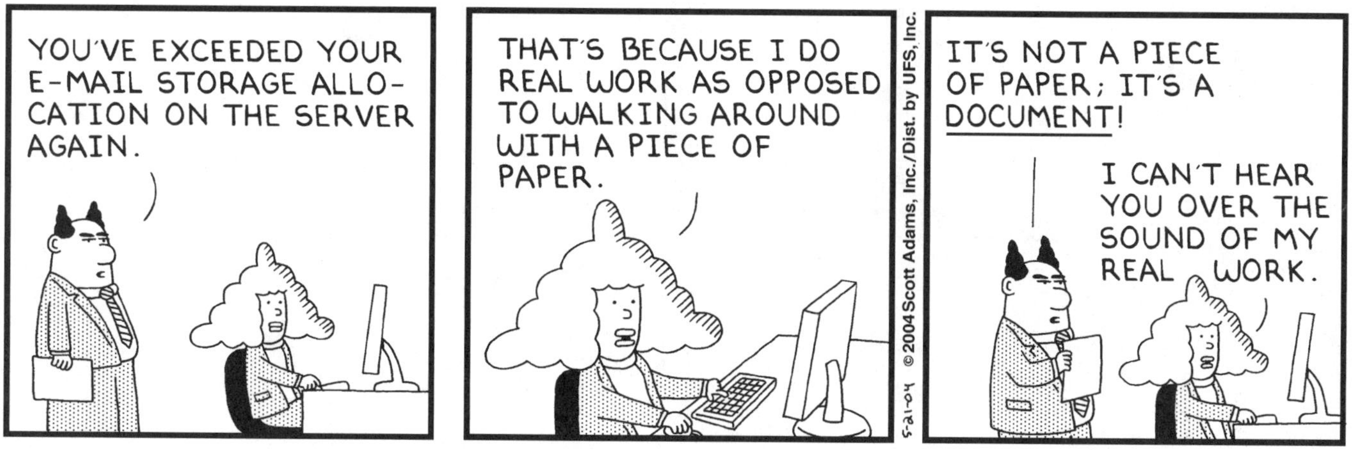
YOU'VE EXCEEDED YOUR E-MAIL STORAGE ALLO-CATION ON THE SERVER AGAIN.
THAT'S BECAUSE I DO REAL WORK AS OPPOSED TO WALKING AROUND WITH A PIECE OF PAPER.
5-21-04 © 2004 Scott Adams, Inc./Dist. by UFS, Inc.
IT'S NOT A PIECE OF PAPER; IT'S A DOCUMENT!
I CAN'T HEAR YOU OVER THE SOUND OF MY REAL WORK.

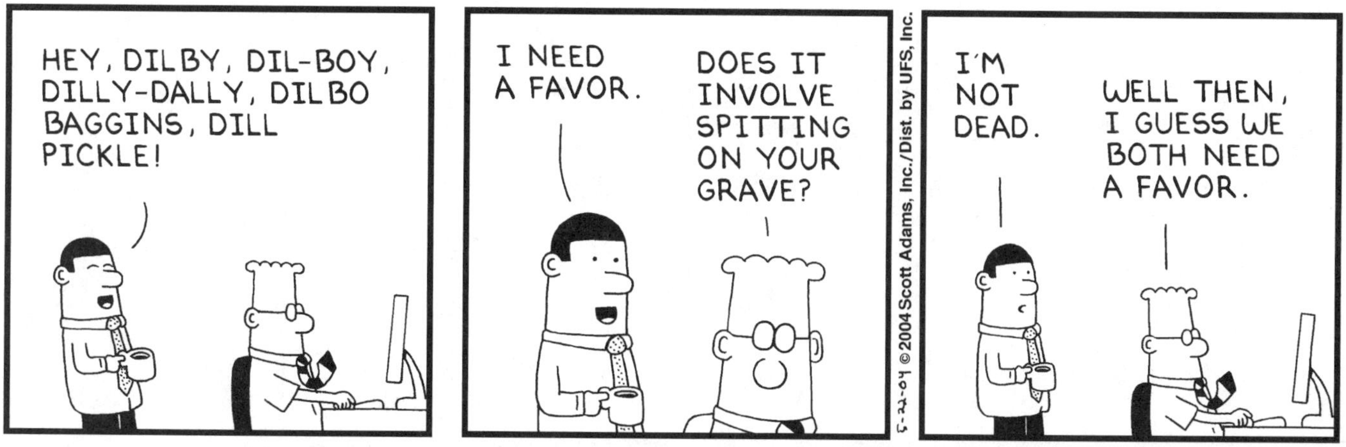
HEY, DILBY, DIL-BOY, DILLY-DALLY, DILBO BAGGINS, DILL PICKLE!
I NEED A FAVOR.
DOES IT INVOLVE SPITTING ON YOUR GRAVE?
5-22-04 © 2004 Scott Adams, Inc./Dist. by UFS, Inc.
I'M NOT DEAD.
WELL THEN, I GUESS WE BOTH NEED A FAVOR.

PERFORMANCE REVIEW
PEOPLE SAY YOU'RE TOO NEGATIVE IN MEETINGS.
NEGATIVE?
WHEN?
ACCORDING TO THE MARKETING DEPART-MENT. YOU POO-POOED A NUMBER OF THEIR IDEAS...
...THE COLD FUSION SCOOTER, PERPETUAL MOTION CLOTHES DRYER, ANTIGRAVITY PANTS, MRI VENDING MACHINE, AND THE LIST GOES ON.
THOSE ARE TERRIBLE IDEAS!
NEGATIVE ATTITUDE!!! GOTTCHA!!!
OKAY, YOU'RE RIGHT. FROM NOW ON, I WILL SUPPORT ALL TERRIBLE IDEAS.
GOOD.
IT'S A TONGUE SCRAPER AND A FROZEN FLAG-POLE!
CAN IT BE ELECTRIFIED?
©2004 Scott Adams, Inc./Dist. by UFS, Inc.
5-23-04

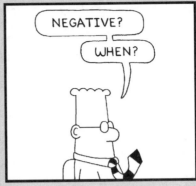

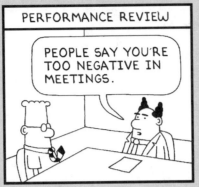

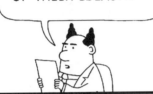

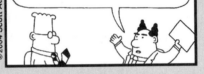

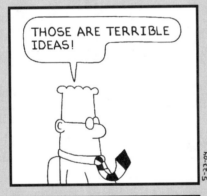

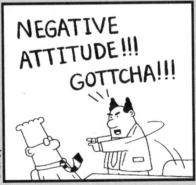

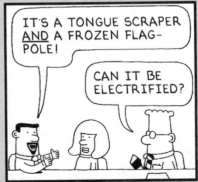

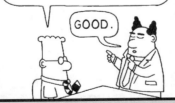

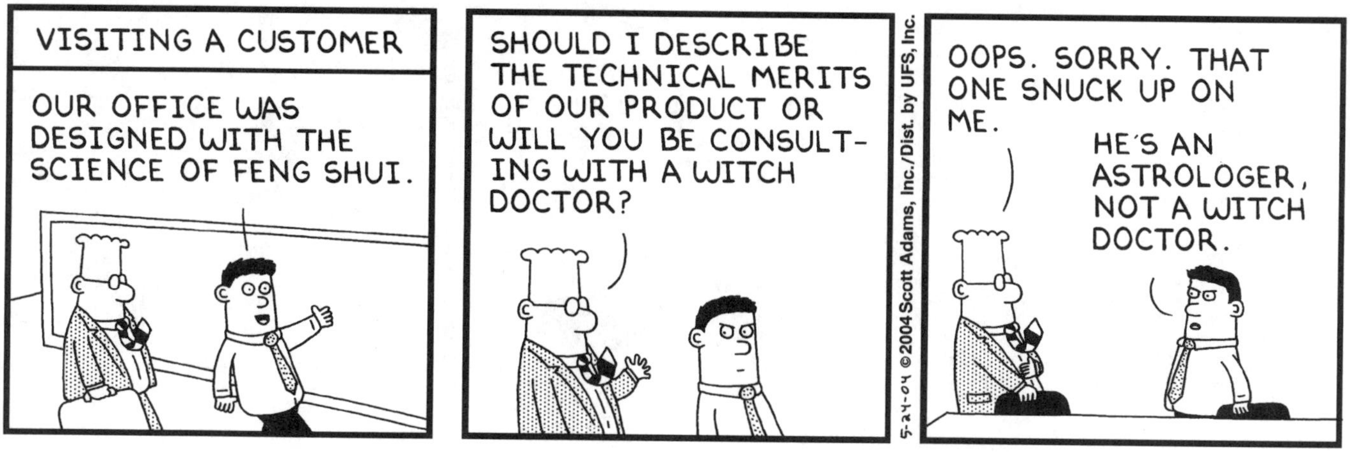
VISITING A CUSTOMER
OUR OFFICE WAS DESIGNED WITH THE SCIENCE OF FENG SHUI.
SHOULD I DESCRIBE THE TECHNICAL MERITS OF OUR PRODUCT OR WILL YOU BE CONSULTING WITH A WITCH DOCTOR?
5-24-04 ©2004 Scott Adams, Inc./Dist. by UFS, Inc.
OOPS. SORRY. THAT ONE SNUCK UP ON ME.
HE'S AN ASTROLOGER, NOT A WITCH DOCTOR.

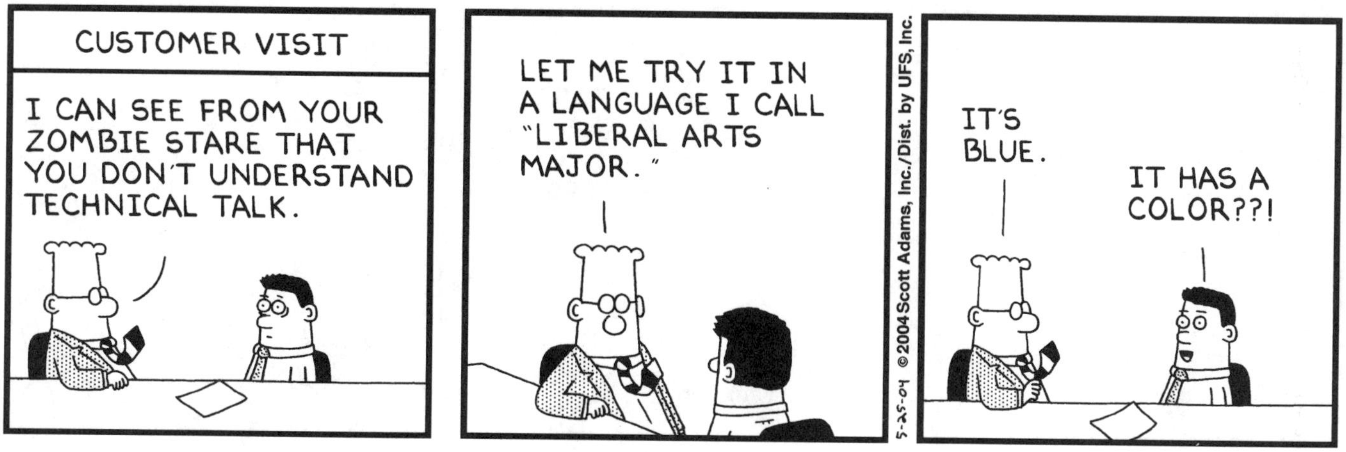
CUSTOMER VISIT
I CAN SEE FROM YOUR ZOMBIE STARE THAT YOU DON'T UNDERSTAND TECHNICAL TALK.
LET ME TRY IT IN A LANGUAGE I CALL "LIBERAL ARTS MAJOR."
5-25-04 ©2004 Scott Adams, Inc./Dist. by UFS, Inc.
IT'S BLUE.
IT HAS A COLOR??!

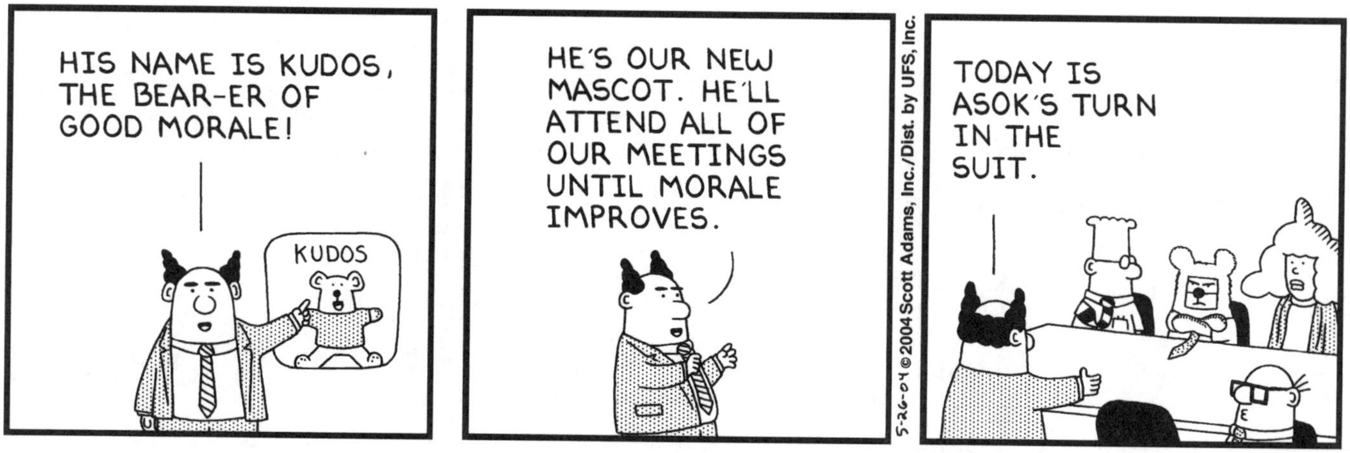
HIS NAME IS KUDOS, THE BEAR-ER OF GOOD MORALE!
KUDOS
HE'S OUR NEW MASCOT. HE'LL ATTEND ALL OF OUR MEETINGS UNTIL MORALE IMPROVES.
5-26-04 ©2004 Scott Adams, Inc./Dist. by UFS, Inc.
TODAY IS ASOK'S TURN IN THE SUIT.

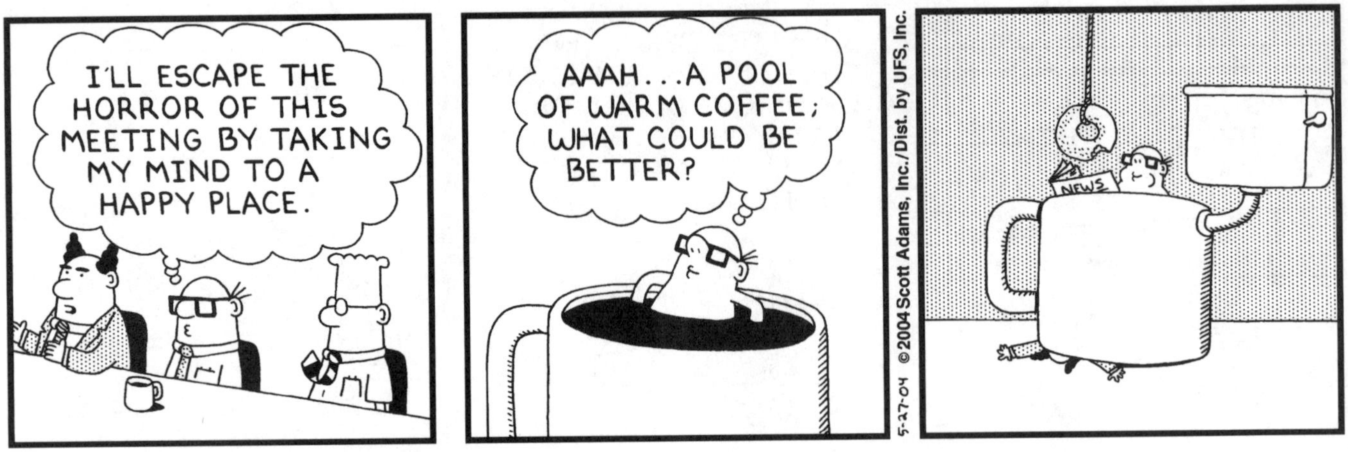
I'LL ESCAPE THE HORROR OF THIS MEETING BY TAKING MY MIND TO A HAPPY PLACE.
AAAH...A POOL OF WARM COFFEE; WHAT COULD BE BETTER?
5-27-04 © 2004 Scott Adams, Inc./Dist. by UFS, Inc.
NEWS

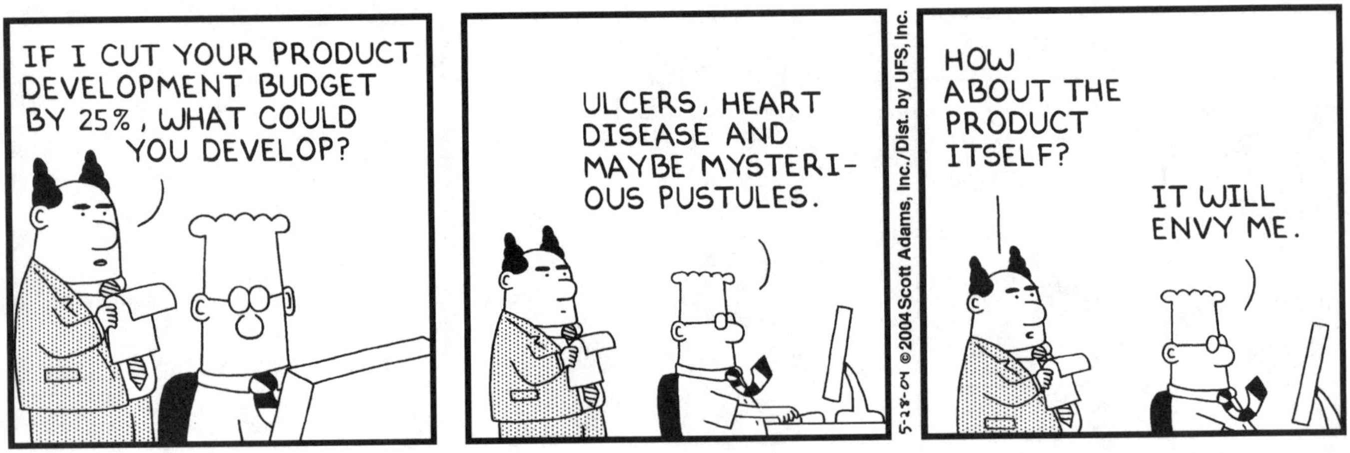
IF I CUT YOUR PRODUCT DEVELOPMENT BUDGET BY 25%, WHAT COULD YOU DEVELOP?
ULCERS, HEART DISEASE AND MAYBE MYSTERIOUS PUSTULES.
5-28-04 © 2004 Scott Adams, Inc./Dist. by UFS, Inc.
HOW ABOUT THE PRODUCT ITSELF?
IT WILL ENVY ME.

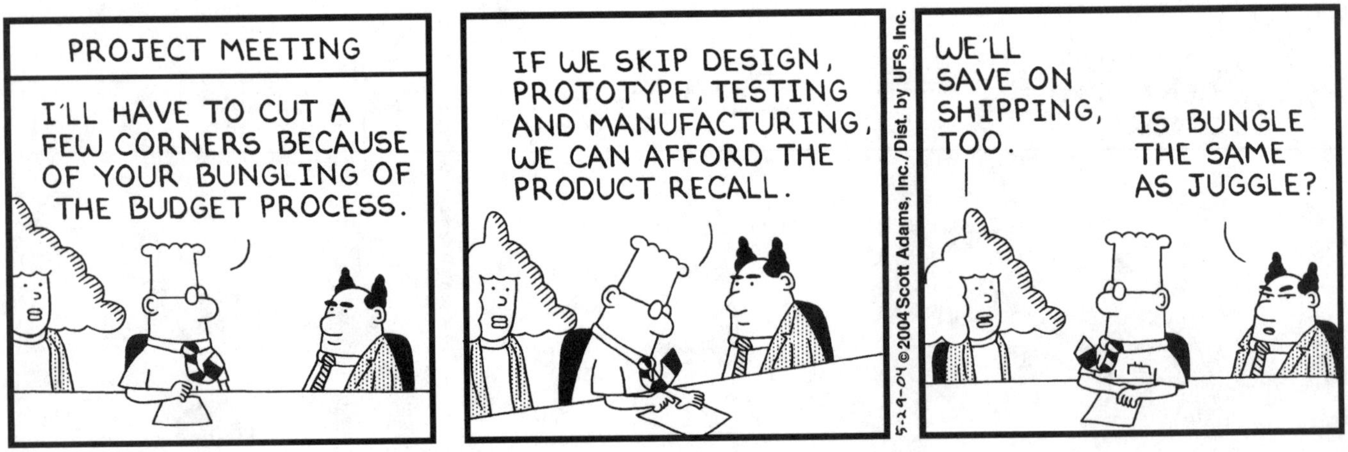
PROJECT MEETING
I'LL HAVE TO CUT A FEW CORNERS BECAUSE OF YOUR BUNGLING OF THE BUDGET PROCESS.
IF WE SKIP DESIGN, PROTOTYPE, TESTING AND MANUFACTURING, WE CAN AFFORD THE PRODUCT RECALL.
5-29-04 © 2004 Scott Adams, Inc./Dist. by UFS, Inc.
WE'LL SAVE ON SHIPPING, TOO.
IS BUNGLE THE SAME AS JUGGLE?

YESTERDAY, SOMEONE IN THIS ROOM GAVE ME A DOCUMENT WITH A YELLOW PAPER CLIP.
I KNOW THAT MULTI-COLORED PAPER CLIPS LOOK "PRETTY."
BUT I REMIND YOU THAT WE ARE ON A TIGHT BUDGET!
WE CAN'T BE THROWING AWAY ALL OUR MONEY ON COLORFUL PAPER CLIPS.
©2004 Scott Adams, Inc./Dist. by UFS, Inc.
DO I MAKE MYSELF CLEAR?!!
I SALVAGED THAT PAPER CLIP FROM INCOMING MAIL.
5-30-04
NOW EXCUSE ME WHILE I STARE AT MY WATCH AND WONDER HOW MUCH YOU'RE PAID PER HOUR.
I'M SURE YOU'VE DONE INEFFICIENT THINGS THAT I DON'T KNOW ABOUT.
TWO MINUTES IS... $5.

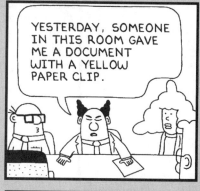

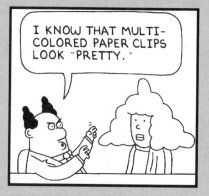

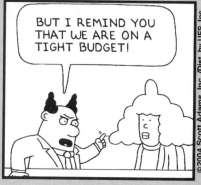

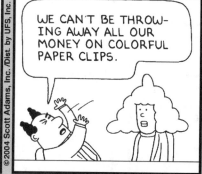

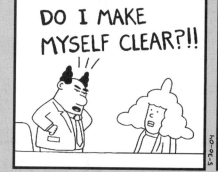

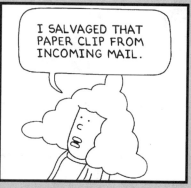

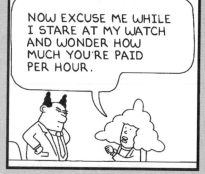

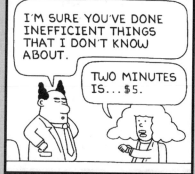

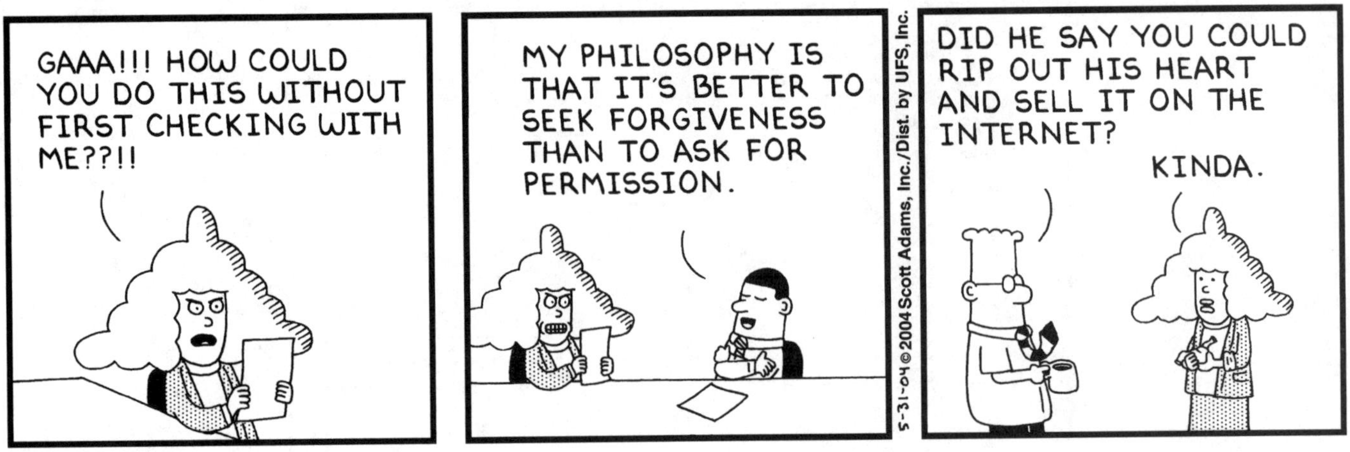
GAAA!!! HOW COULD YOU DO THIS WITHOUT FIRST CHECKING WITH ME??!!
MY PHILOSOPHY IS THAT IT'S BETTER TO SEEK FORGIVENESS THAN TO ASK FOR PERMISSION.
5-31-04 © 2004 Scott Adams, Inc./Dist. by UFS, Inc.
DID HE SAY YOU COULD RIP OUT HIS HEART AND SELL IT ON THE INTERNET?
KINDA.

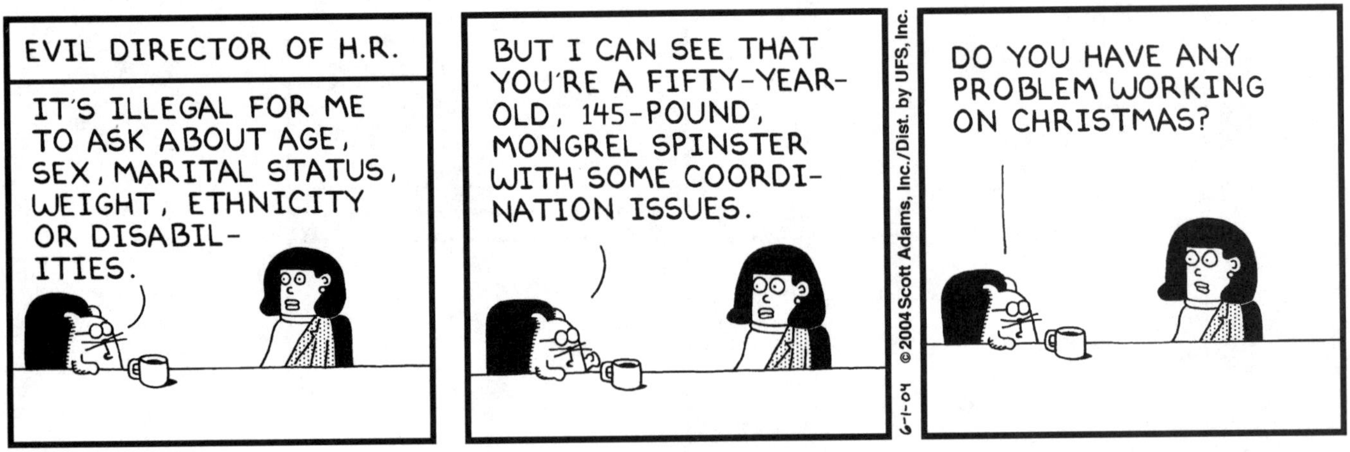
EVIL DIRECTOR OF H.R.
IT'S ILLEGAL FOR ME TO ASK ABOUT AGE, SEX, MARITAL STATUS, WEIGHT, ETHNICITY OR DISABIL-ITIES.
BUT I CAN SEE THAT YOU'RE A FIFTY-YEAR-OLD, 145-POUND, MONGREL SPINSTER WITH SOME COORDI-NATION ISSUES.
6-1-04 © 2004 Scott Adams, Inc./Dist. by UFS, Inc.
DO YOU HAVE ANY PROBLEM WORKING ON CHRISTMAS?

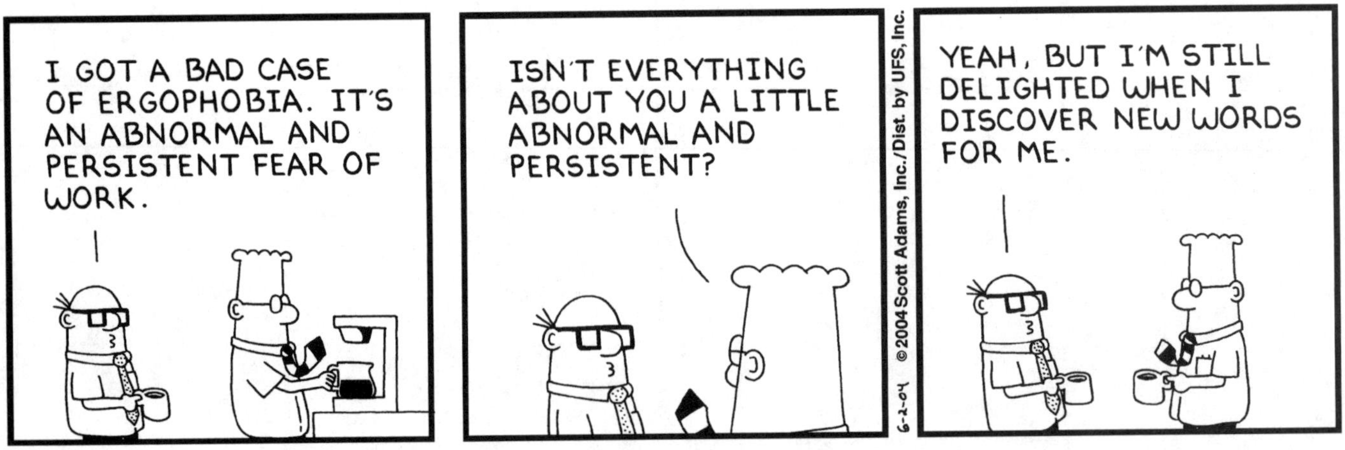
I GOT A BAD CASE OF ERGOPHOBIA. IT'S AN ABNORMAL AND PERSISTENT FEAR OF WORK.
ISN'T EVERYTHING ABOUT YOU A LITTLE ABNORMAL AND PERSISTENT?
6-2-04 © 2004 Scott Adams, Inc./Dist. by UFS, Inc.
YEAH, BUT I'M STILL DELIGHTED WHEN I DISCOVER NEW WORDS FOR ME.

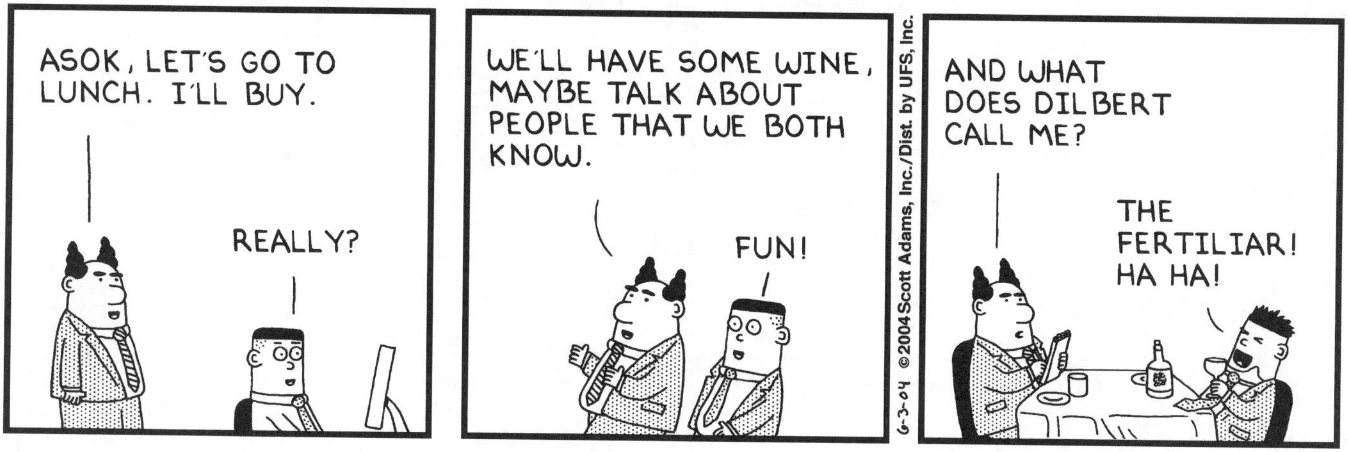
ASOK, LET'S GO TO LUNCH. I'LL BUY.
REALLY?
WE'LL HAVE SOME WINE, MAYBE TALK ABOUT PEOPLE THAT WE BOTH KNOW.
FUN!
6-3-04 ©2004 Scott Adams, Inc./Dist. by UFS, Inc.
AND WHAT DOES DILBERT CALL ME?
THE FERTILIAR! HA HA!

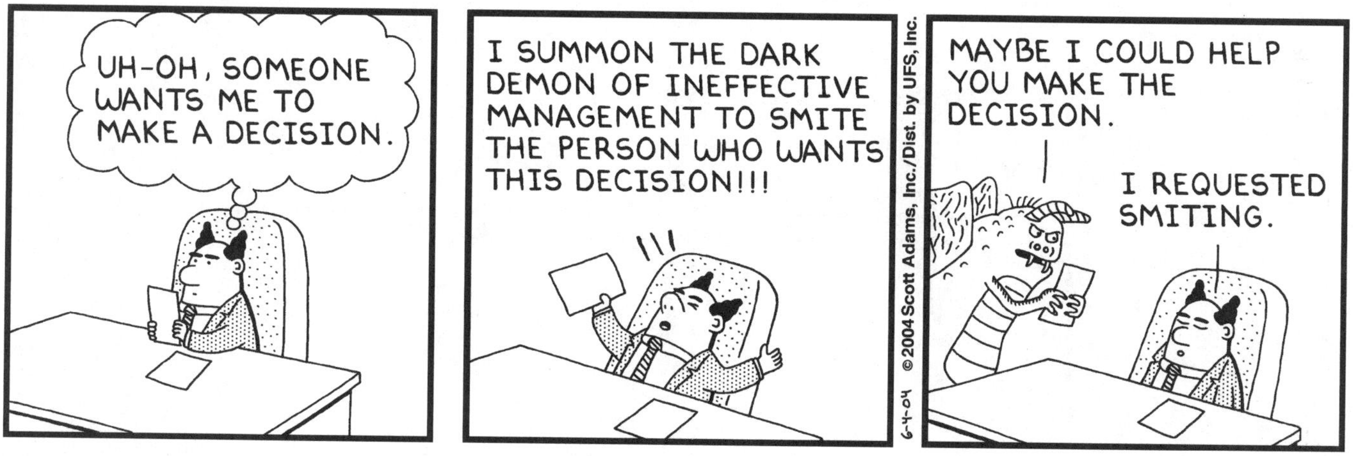
UH-OH, SOMEONE WANTS ME TO MAKE A DECISION.
I SUMMON THE DARK DEMON OF INEFFECTIVE MANAGEMENT TO SMITE THE PERSON WHO WANTS THIS DECISION!!!
6-4-04 ©2004 Scott Adams, Inc./Dist. by UFS, Inc.
MAYBE I COULD HELP YOU MAKE THE DECISION.
I REQUESTED SMITING.

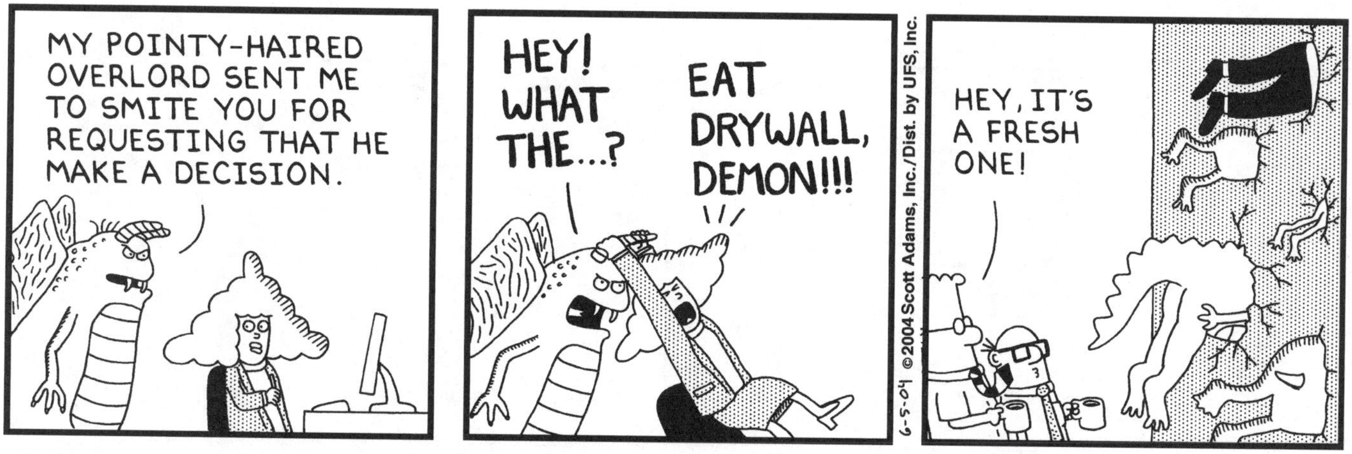
MY POINTY-HAIRED OVERLORD SENT ME TO SMITE YOU FOR REQUESTING THAT HE MAKE A DECISION.
HEY! WHAT THE...?
EAT DRYWALL, DEMON!!!
6-5-04 ©2004 Scott Adams, Inc./Dist. by UFS, Inc.
HEY, IT'S A FRESH ONE!

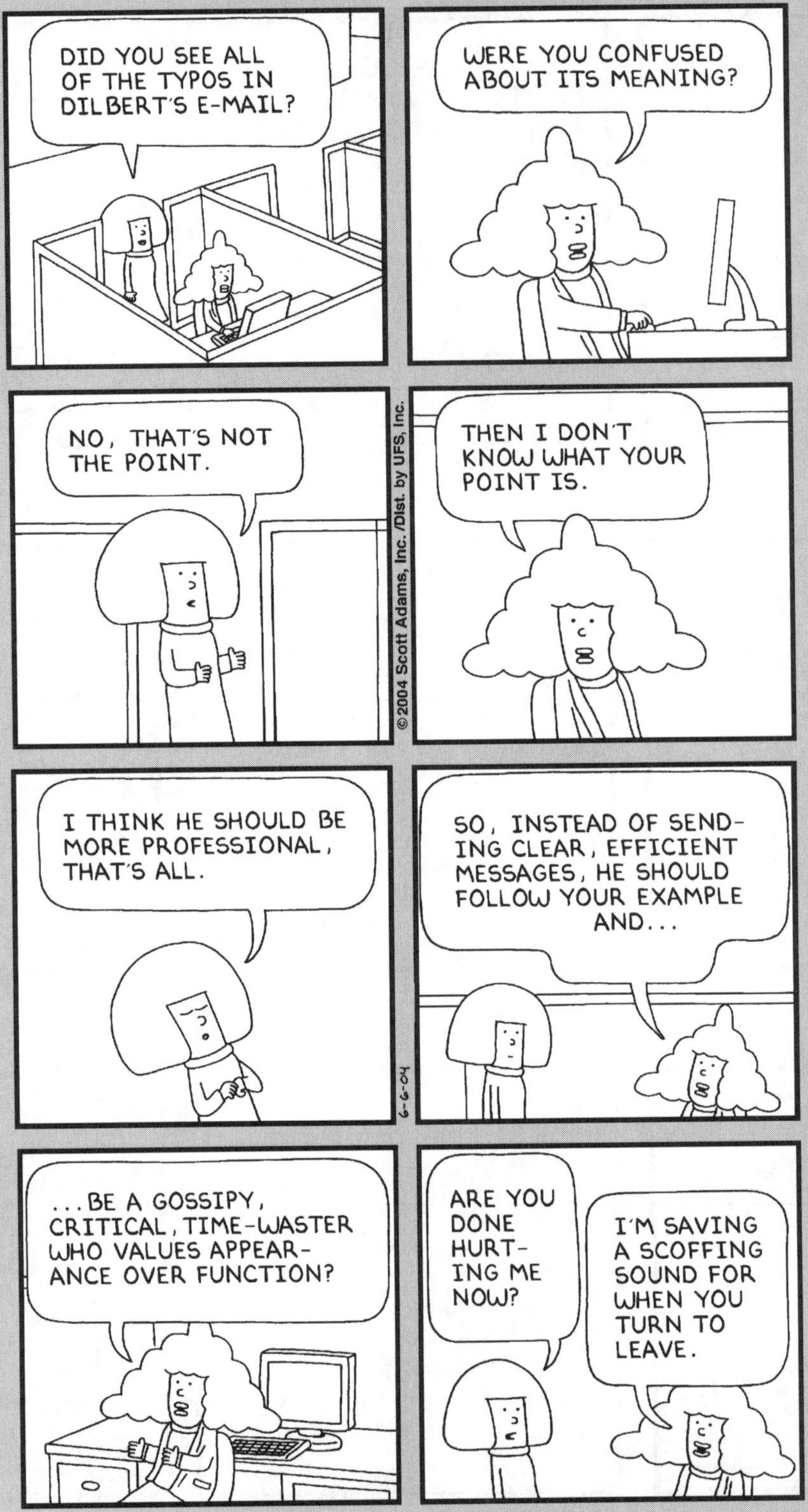
DID YOU SEE ALL OF THE TYPOS IN DILBERT'S E-MAIL?
WERE YOU CONFUSED ABOUT ITS MEANING?
NO, THAT'S NOT THE POINT.
THEN I DON'T KNOW WHAT YOUR POINT IS.
I THINK HE SHOULD BE MORE PROFESSIONAL, THAT'S ALL.
SO, INSTEAD OF SENDING CLEAR, EFFICIENT MESSAGES, HE SHOULD FOLLOW YOUR EXAMPLE AND...
...BE A GOSSIPY, CRITICAL, TIME-WASTER WHO VALUES APPEARANCE OVER FUNCTION?
ARE YOU DONE HURTING ME NOW?
I'M SAVING A SCOFFING SOUND FOR WHEN YOU TURN TO LEAVE.
©2004 Scott Adams, Inc./Dist. by UFS, Inc.
6-6-04

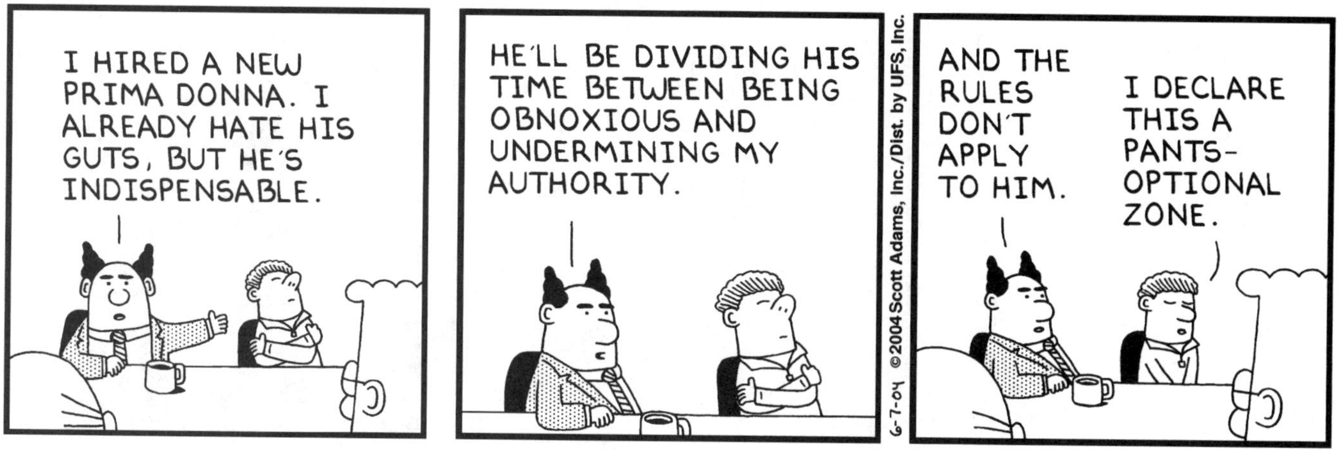
I HIRED A NEW PRIMA DONNA. I ALREADY HATE HIS GUTS, BUT HE'S INDISPENSABLE.
HE'LL BE DIVIDING HIS TIME BETWEEN BEING OBNOXIOUS AND UNDERMINING MY AUTHORITY.
6-7-04 ©2004 Scott Adams, Inc./Dist. by UFS, Inc.
AND THE RULES DON'T APPLY TO HIM.
I DECLARE THIS A PANTS-OPTIONAL ZONE.

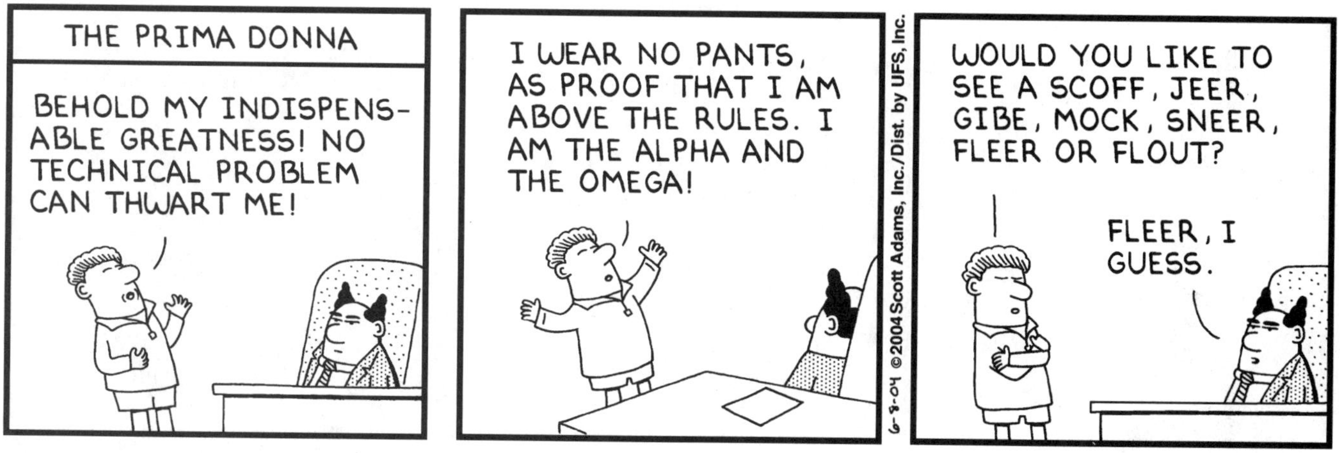
THE PRIMA DONNA
BEHOLD MY INDISPENS-ABLE GREATNESS! NO TECHNICAL PROBLEM CAN THWART ME!
I WEAR NO PANTS, AS PROOF THAT I AM ABOVE THE RULES. I AM THE ALPHA AND THE OMEGA!
6-8-04 ©2004 Scott Adams, Inc./Dist. by UFS, Inc.
WOULD YOU LIKE TO SEE A SCOFF, JEER, GIBE, MOCK, SNEER, FLEER OR FLOUT?
FLEER, I GUESS.

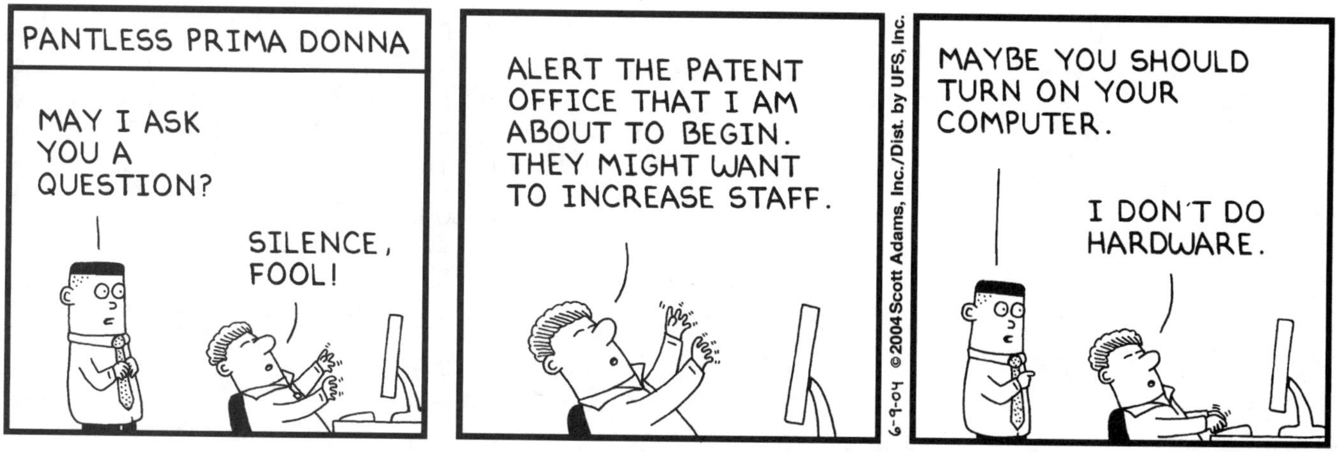
PANTLESS PRIMA DONNA
MAY I ASK YOU A QUESTION?
SILENCE, FOOL!
ALERT THE PATENT OFFICE THAT I AM ABOUT TO BEGIN. THEY MIGHT WANT TO INCREASE STAFF.
6-9-04 ©2004 Scott Adams, Inc./Dist. by UFS, Inc.
MAYBE YOU SHOULD TURN ON YOUR COMPUTER.
I DON'T DO HARDWARE.

PANTLESS PRIMA DONNA

I DEMAND AN ASSISTANT TO DOCUMENT MY MIRACLES.

THAT WHICH I TOUCH WILL BE TAGGED FOR THE SMITHSONIAN. THAT WHICH I CREATE WILL BE FRAMED FOR THE LOUVRE.

REALLY? AN EXCITING ASSIGNMENT? WHAT IS IT?

ASOK, I WANT YOU TO WORK FOR THE PRIMA DONNA. DO WHATEVER HE TELLS YOU.

MAY I POINT OUT THAT HE HAS NEVER PRODUCED ANYTHING EXCEPT ARROGANCE AND NOISE?

YOU WILL STAND BEHIND ME, AND WHEN I END A SENTENCE, YOU WILL EITHER SAY, "TA-DA" OR "CASE CLOSED."

TA-DA

TINA, WHY DID YOU CALL ME A FLAMING #$%!!?

I'M SO SORRY.

THAT WAS MY E-MAIL PERSONALITY. MY REAL-TIME PERSONALITY IS KIND AND GENTLE.

OH. OKAY.

NEVER SPEAK TO ME AGAIN, YOU MISERABLE CLUMP OF DECAYING COMPOST!

?
EXCUSE ME. MAY I ASK A QUESTION?
YOU'RE BLASTING YOUR MUSIC WHILE YOUR WINDOW IS OPEN, SO I'M WONDERING...
ARE YOU THINKING THAT THE PEOPLE AROUND YOU ARE ENJOYING YOUR MUSICAL CHOICES?
OR ARE YOU A PSYCHO-PATH, PRONE TO EGO-CENTRIC, ANTISOCIAL BEHAVIOR?
OR IS IT A DESPERATE, MISGUIDED ATTEMPT TO IMPROVE YOUR ODDS OF FINDING A MATE?
IT'S ACTUALLY A SIMPLE CASE OF PEER IMITA-TION AND COGNITIVE DISSONANCE THAT CAUSES ME TO SELEC-TIVELY FILTER MY PERCEPTIONS.
I LIKE THAT SONG.
GREAT! NOW I SUDDENLY HATE IT! YOU RUINED EVERYTHING!
©2004 Scott Adams, Inc./Dist. by UFS, Inc.
6-13-04

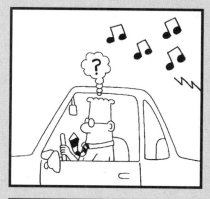

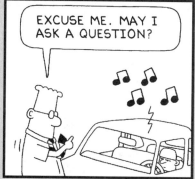

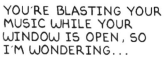

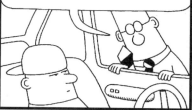

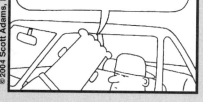

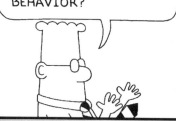

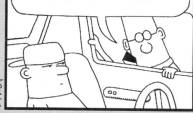

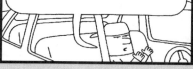

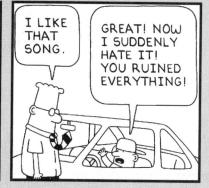

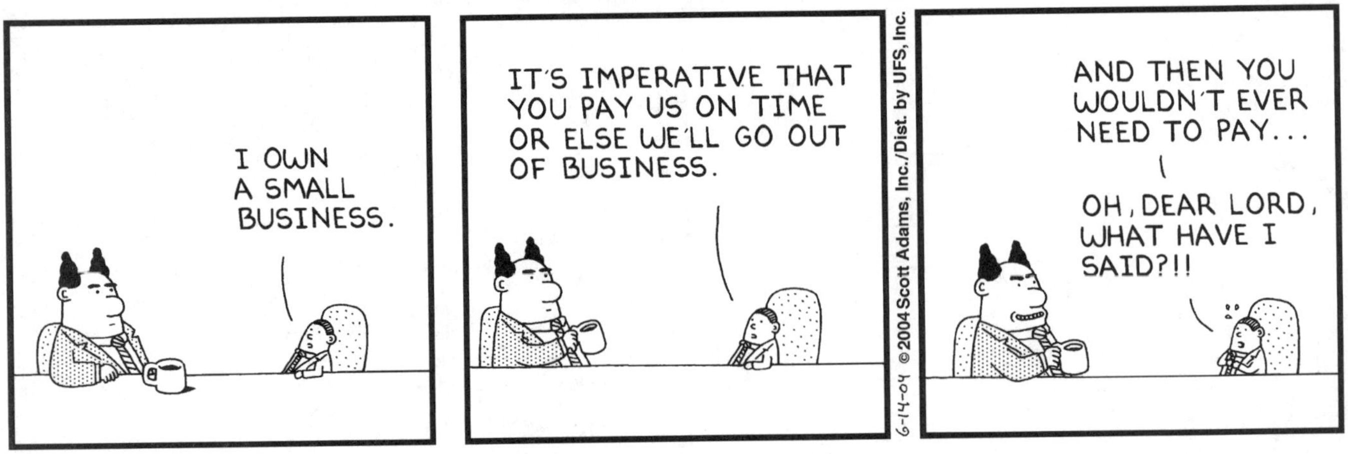
I OWN A SMALL BUSINESS.
IT'S IMPERATIVE THAT YOU PAY US ON TIME OR ELSE WE'LL GO OUT OF BUSINESS.
6-14-04 ©2004 Scott Adams, Inc./Dist. by UFS, Inc.
AND THEN YOU WOULDN'T EVER NEED TO PAY...
OH, DEAR LORD, WHAT HAVE I SAID?!!

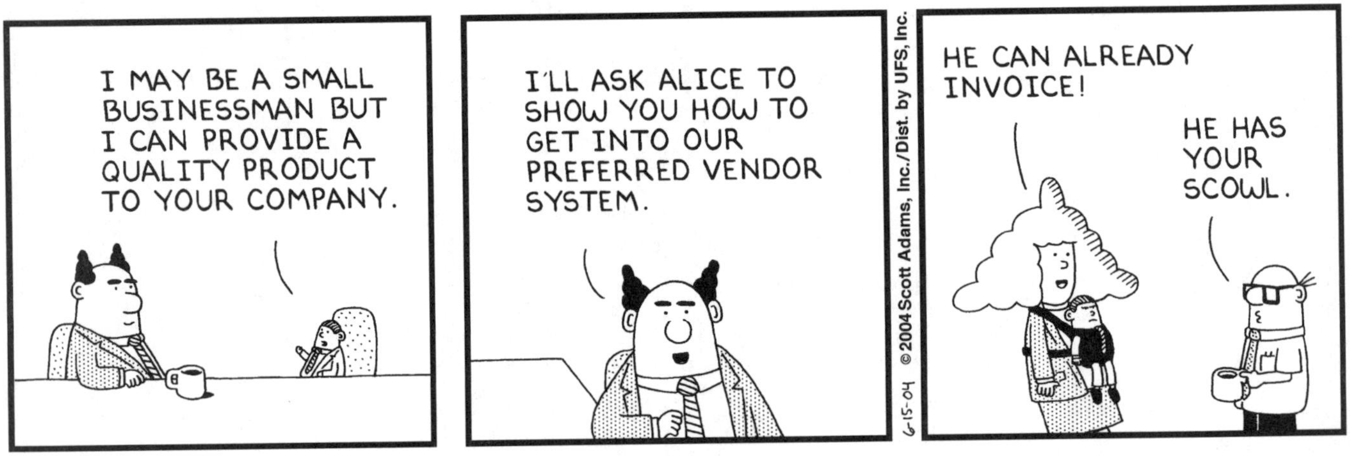
I MAY BE A SMALL BUSINESSMAN BUT I CAN PROVIDE A QUALITY PRODUCT TO YOUR COMPANY.
I'LL ASK ALICE TO SHOW YOU HOW TO GET INTO OUR PREFERRED VENDOR SYSTEM.
6-15-04 ©2004 Scott Adams, Inc./Dist. by UFS, Inc.
HE CAN ALREADY INVOICE!
HE HAS YOUR SCOWL.

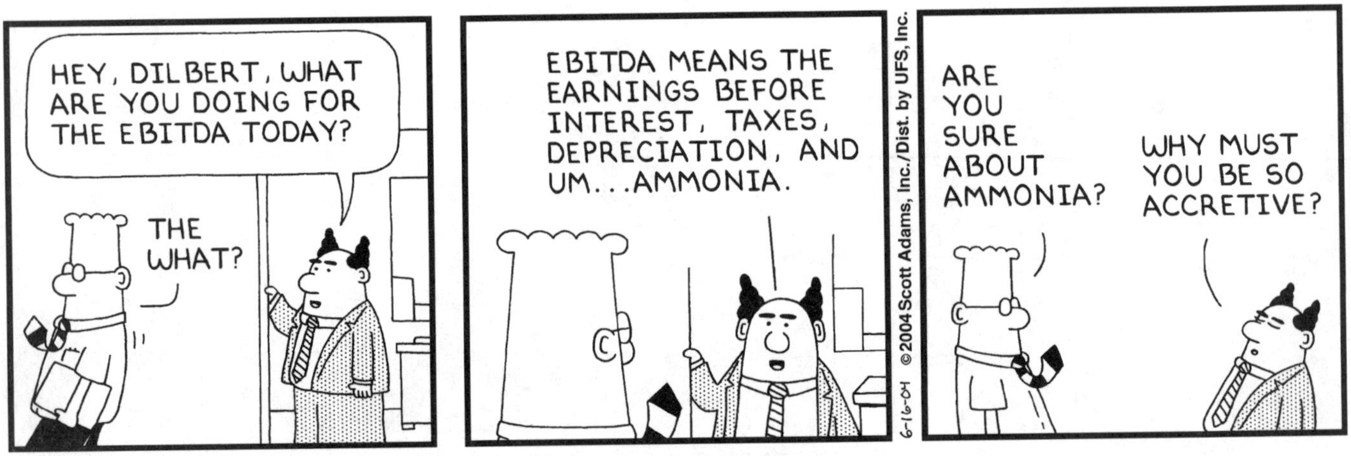
HEY, DILBERT, WHAT ARE YOU DOING FOR THE EBITDA TODAY?
THE WHAT?
EBITDA MEANS THE EARNINGS BEFORE INTEREST, TAXES, DEPRECIATION, AND UM...AMMONIA.
6-16-04 ©2004 Scott Adams, Inc./Dist. by UFS, Inc.
ARE YOU SURE ABOUT AMMONIA?
WHY MUST YOU BE SO ACCRETIVE?

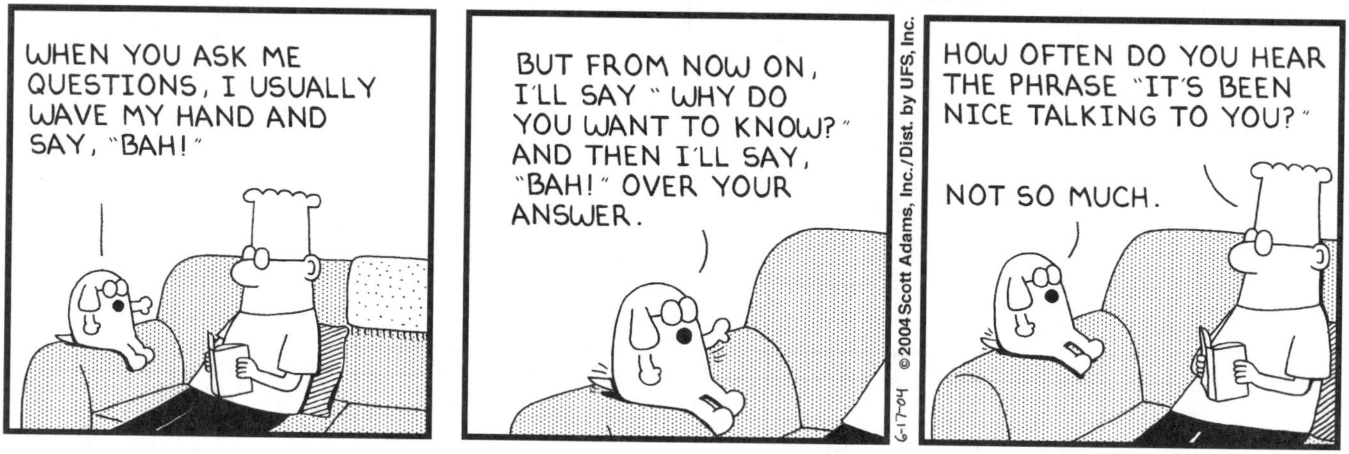
WHEN YOU ASK ME QUESTIONS, I USUALLY WAVE MY HAND AND SAY, "BAH!"
BUT FROM NOW ON, I'LL SAY "WHY DO YOU WANT TO KNOW?" AND THEN I'LL SAY, "BAH!" OVER YOUR ANSWER.
HOW OFTEN DO YOU HEAR THE PHRASE "IT'S BEEN NICE TALKING TO YOU?"
NOT SO MUCH.
© 2004 Scott Adams, Inc./Dist. by UFS, Inc.
6-17-04

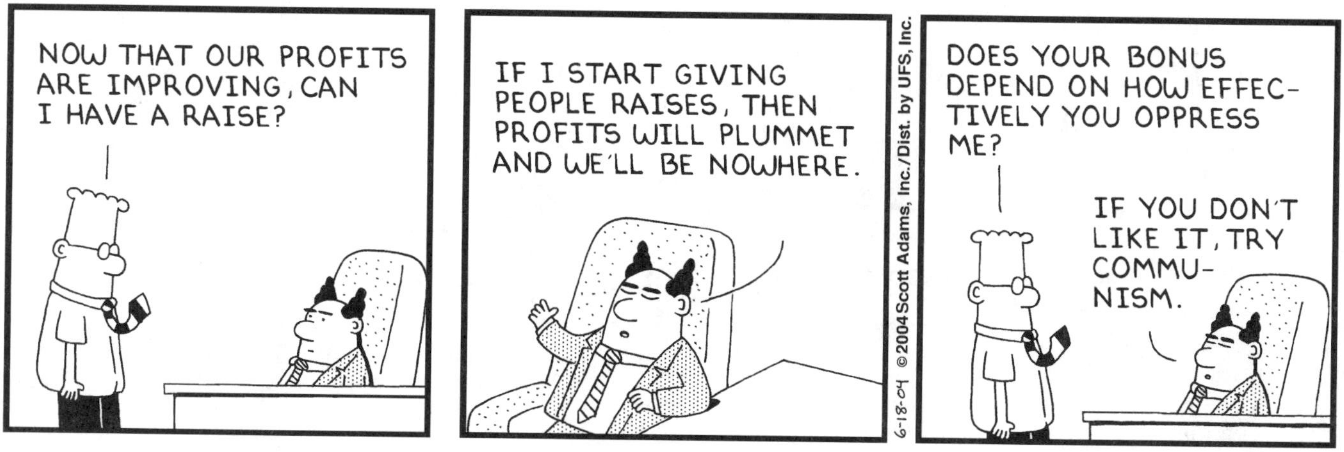
NOW THAT OUR PROFITS ARE IMPROVING, CAN I HAVE A RAISE?
IF I START GIVING PEOPLE RAISES, THEN PROFITS WILL PLUMMET AND WE'LL BE NOWHERE.
DOES YOUR BONUS DEPEND ON HOW EFFECTIVELY YOU OPPRESS ME?
IF YOU DON'T LIKE IT, TRY COMMUNISM.
© 2004 Scott Adams, Inc./Dist. by UFS, Inc.
6-18-04

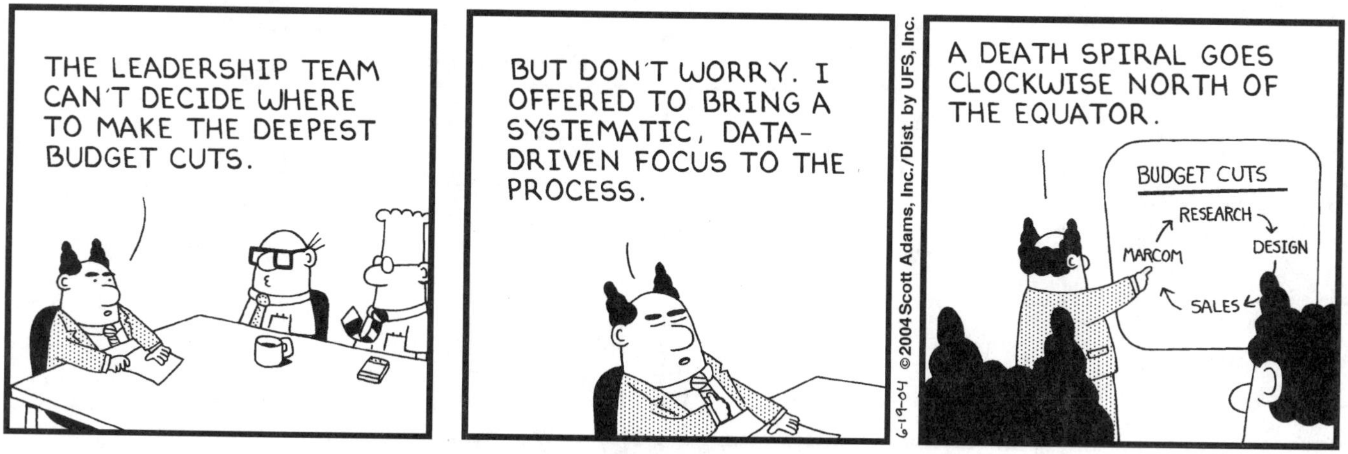
THE LEADERSHIP TEAM CAN'T DECIDE WHERE TO MAKE THE DEEPEST BUDGET CUTS.
BUT DON'T WORRY. I OFFERED TO BRING A SYSTEMATIC, DATA-DRIVEN FOCUS TO THE PROCESS.
A DEATH SPIRAL GOES CLOCKWISE NORTH OF THE EQUATOR.
BUDGET CUTS
RESEARCH
DESIGN
SALES
MARCOM
© 2004 Scott Adams, Inc./Dist. by UFS, Inc.
6-19-04

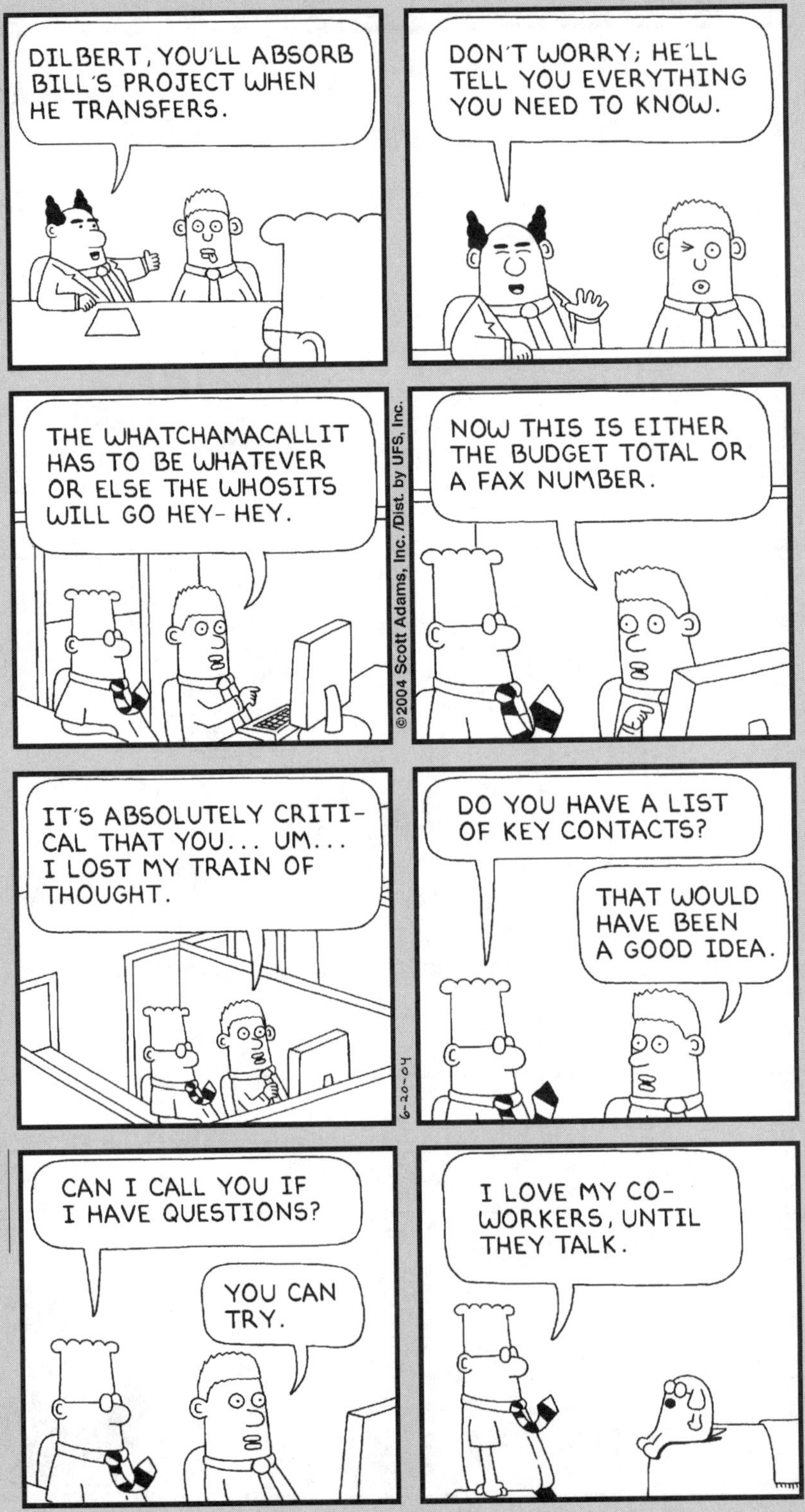
DILBERT, YOU'LL ABSORB BILL'S PROJECT WHEN HE TRANSFERS.
DON'T WORRY; HE'LL TELL YOU EVERYTHING YOU NEED TO KNOW.
THE WHATCHAMACALLIT HAS TO BE WHATEVER OR ELSE THE WHOSITS WILL GO HEY-HEY.
NOW THIS IS EITHER THE BUDGET TOTAL OR A FAX NUMBER.
©2004 Scott Adams, Inc./Dist. by UFS, Inc.
IT'S ABSOLUTELY CRITICAL THAT YOU... UM... I LOST MY TRAIN OF THOUGHT.
DO YOU HAVE A LIST OF KEY CONTACTS?
THAT WOULD HAVE BEEN A GOOD IDEA.
6-20-04
CAN I CALL YOU IF I HAVE QUESTIONS?
YOU CAN TRY.
I LOVE MY CO-WORKERS, UNTIL THEY TALK.

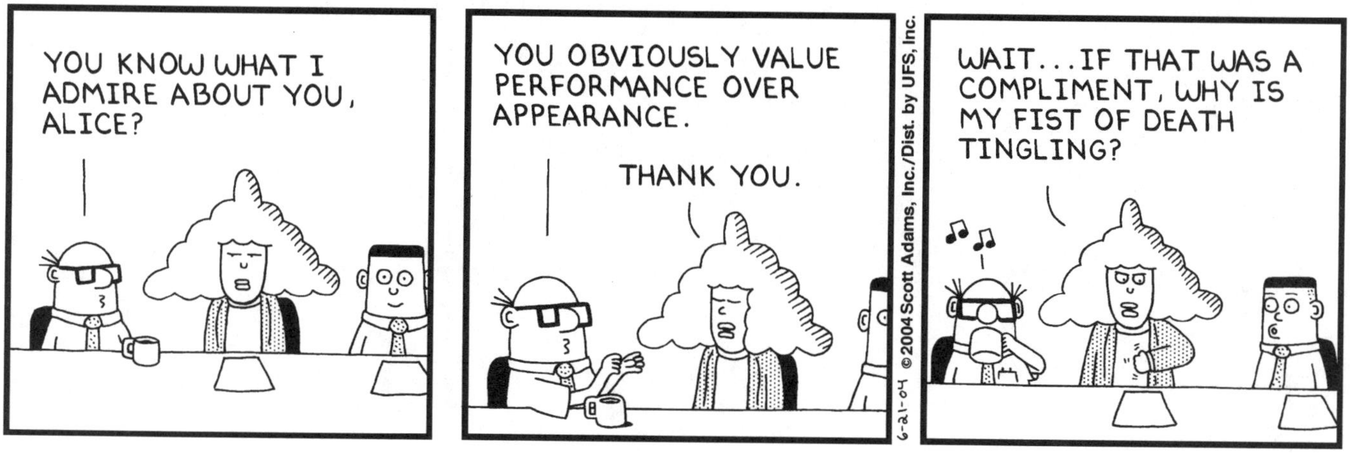
YOU KNOW WHAT I ADMIRE ABOUT YOU, ALICE?
YOU OBVIOUSLY VALUE PERFORMANCE OVER APPEARANCE.
THANK YOU.
6-21-04 © 2004 Scott Adams, Inc./Dist. by UFS, Inc.
WAIT...IF THAT WAS A COMPLIMENT, WHY IS MY FIST OF DEATH TINGLING?

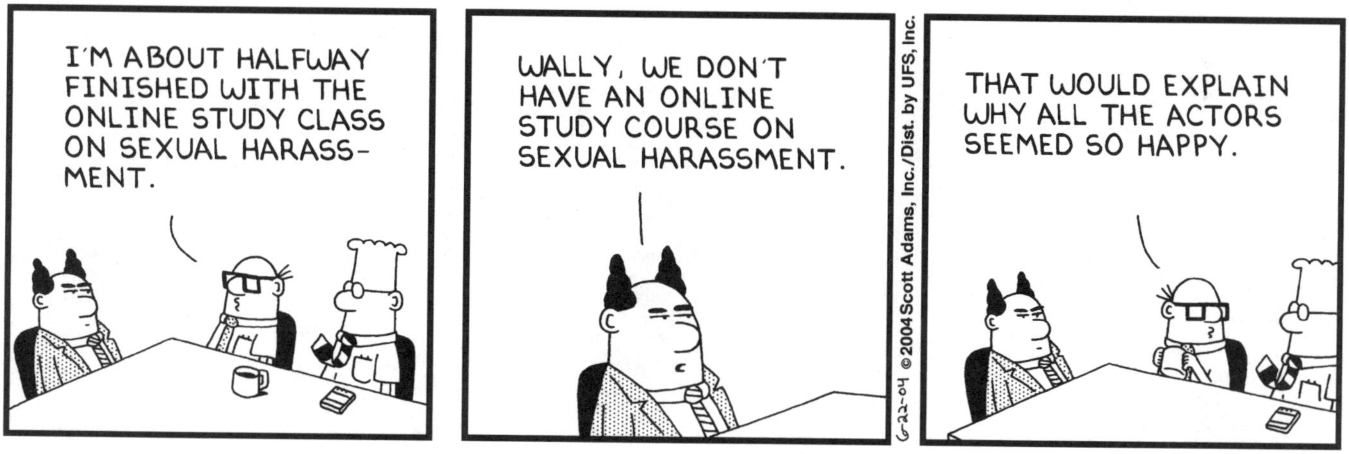
I'M ABOUT HALFWAY FINISHED WITH THE ONLINE STUDY CLASS ON SEXUAL HARASS-MENT.
WALLY, WE DON'T HAVE AN ONLINE STUDY COURSE ON SEXUAL HARASSMENT.
6-22-04 © 2004 Scott Adams, Inc./Dist. by UFS, Inc.
THAT WOULD EXPLAIN WHY ALL THE ACTORS SEEMED SO HAPPY.

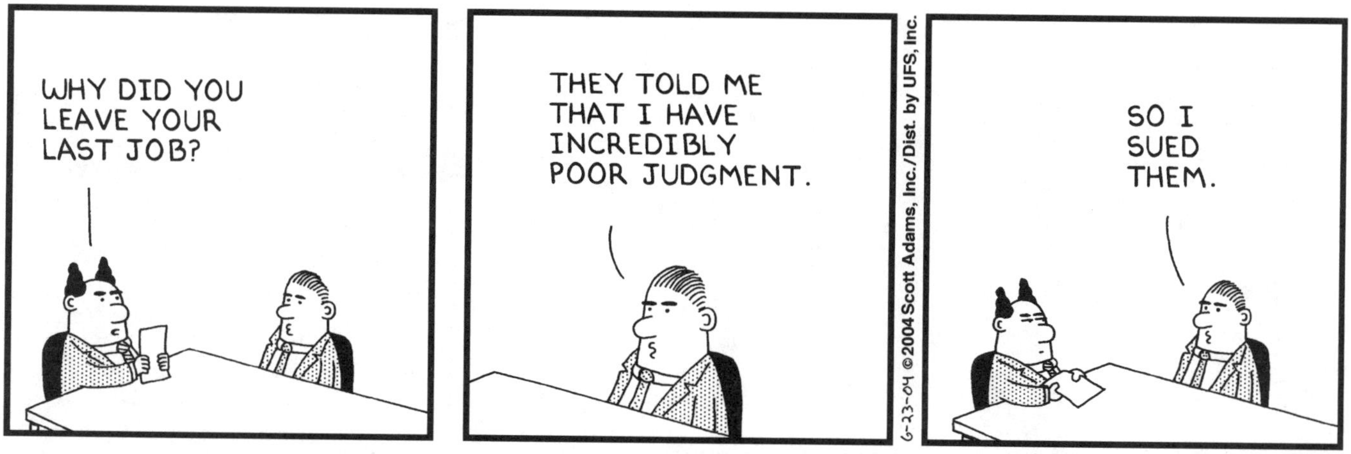
WHY DID YOU LEAVE YOUR LAST JOB?
THEY TOLD ME THAT I HAVE INCREDIBLY POOR JUDGMENT.
6-23-04 © 2004 Scott Adams, Inc./Dist. by UFS, Inc.
SO I SUED THEM.

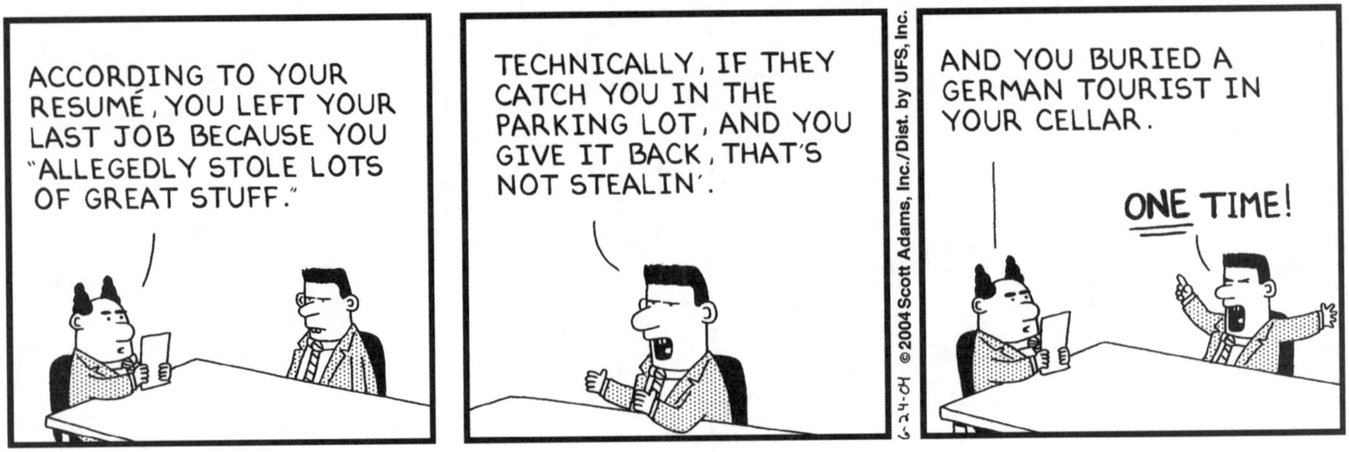
ACCORDING TO YOUR RESUMÉ, YOU LEFT YOUR LAST JOB BECAUSE YOU "ALLEGEDLY STOLE LOTS OF GREAT STUFF."
TECHNICALLY, IF THEY CATCH YOU IN THE PARKING LOT, AND YOU GIVE IT BACK, THAT'S NOT STEALIN'.
AND YOU BURIED A GERMAN TOURIST IN YOUR CELLAR.
ONE TIME!
6-24-04

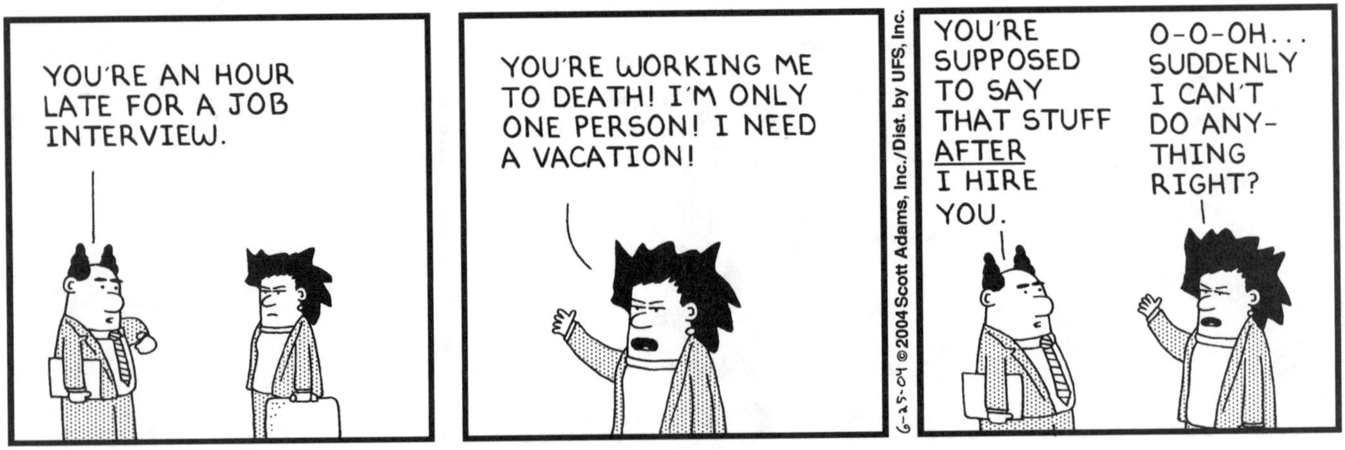
YOU'RE AN HOUR LATE FOR A JOB INTERVIEW.
YOU'RE WORKING ME TO DEATH! I'M ONLY ONE PERSON! I NEED A VACATION!
YOU'RE SUPPOSED TO SAY THAT STUFF AFTER I HIRE YOU.
O-O-OH... SUDDENLY I CAN'T DO ANYTHING RIGHT?
6-25-04

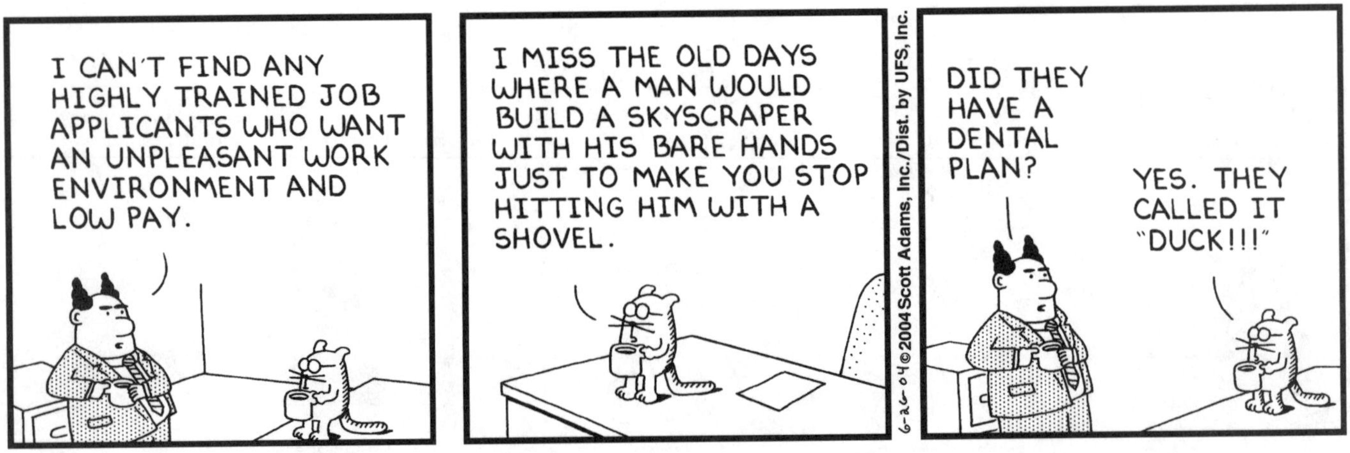
I CAN'T FIND ANY HIGHLY TRAINED JOB APPLICANTS WHO WANT AN UNPLEASANT WORK ENVIRONMENT AND LOW PAY.
I MISS THE OLD DAYS WHERE A MAN WOULD BUILD A SKYSCRAPER WITH HIS BARE HANDS JUST TO MAKE YOU STOP HITTING HIM WITH A SHOVEL.
DID THEY HAVE A DENTAL PLAN?
YES. THEY CALLED IT "DUCK!!!"
6-26-04

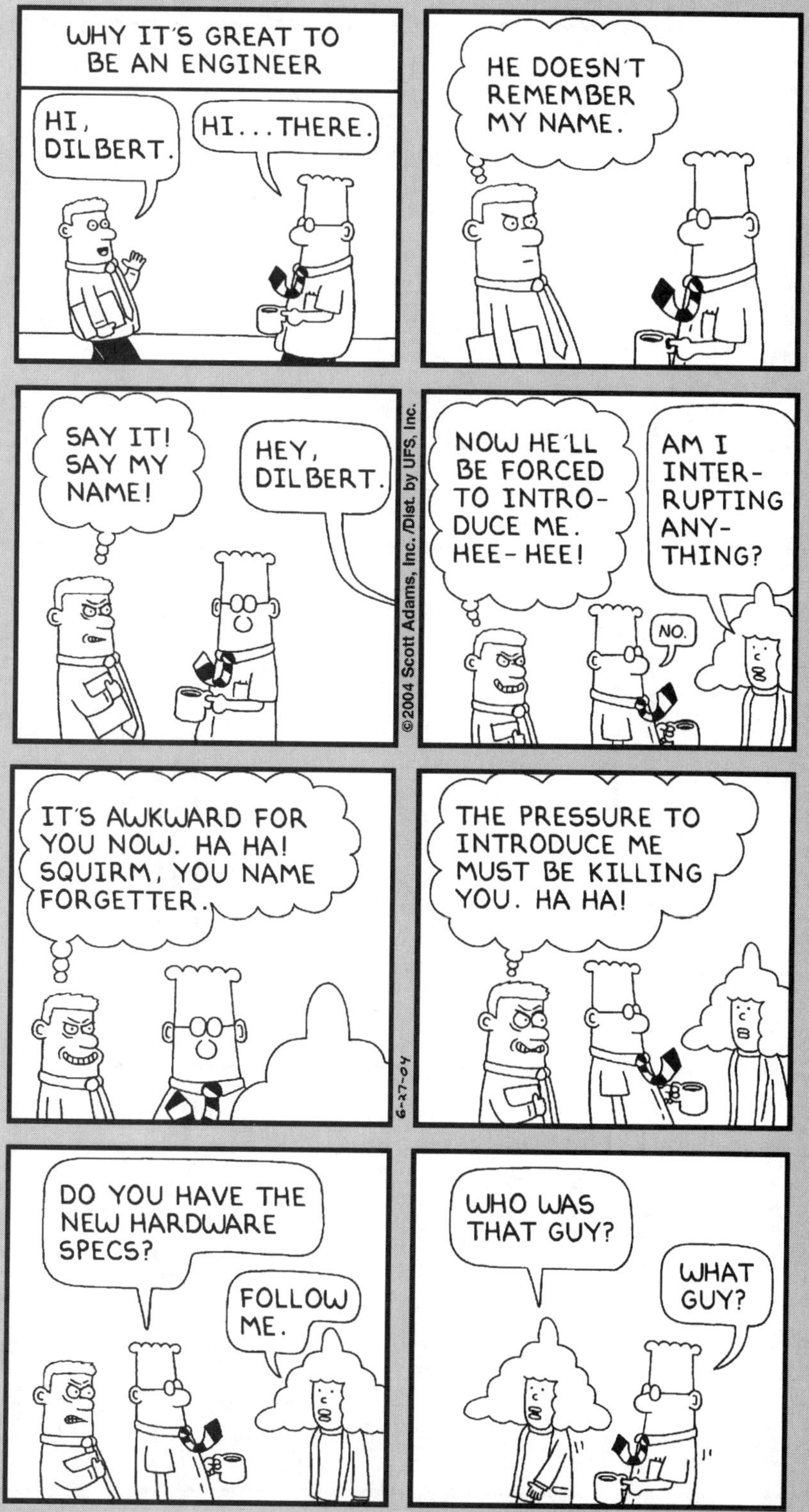
WHY IT'S GREAT TO BE AN ENGINEER
HI, DILBERT.
HI... THERE.
HE DOESN'T REMEMBER MY NAME.
SAY IT! SAY MY NAME!
HEY, DILBERT.
©2004 Scott Adams, Inc./Dist. by UFS, Inc.
NOW HE'LL BE FORCED TO INTRO- DUCE ME. HEE-HEE!
AM I INTER- RUPTING ANY- THING?
NO.
IT'S AWKWARD FOR YOU NOW. HA HA! SQUIRM, YOU NAME FORGETTER.
6-27-04
THE PRESSURE TO INTRODUCE ME MUST BE KILLING YOU. HA HA!
DO YOU HAVE THE NEW HARDWARE SPECS?
FOLLOW ME.
WHO WAS THAT GUY?
WHAT GUY?

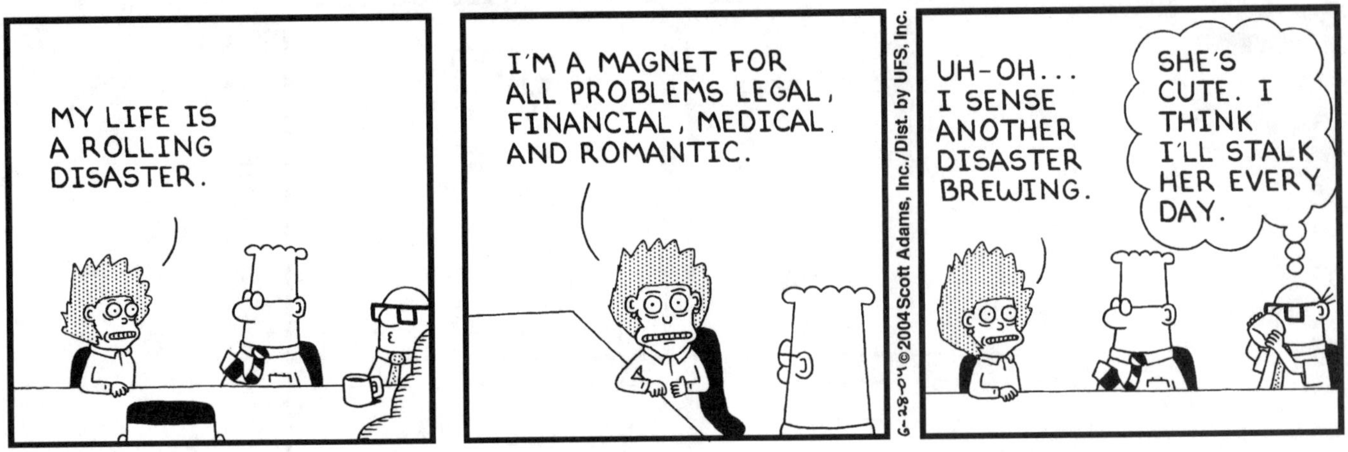
MY LIFE IS A ROLLING DISASTER.
I'M A MAGNET FOR ALL PROBLEMS LEGAL, FINANCIAL, MEDICAL AND ROMANTIC.
UH-OH... I SENSE ANOTHER DISASTER BREWING.
SHE'S CUTE. I THINK I'LL STALK HER EVERY DAY.
6-28-04 © 2004 Scott Adams, Inc./Dist. by UFS, Inc.

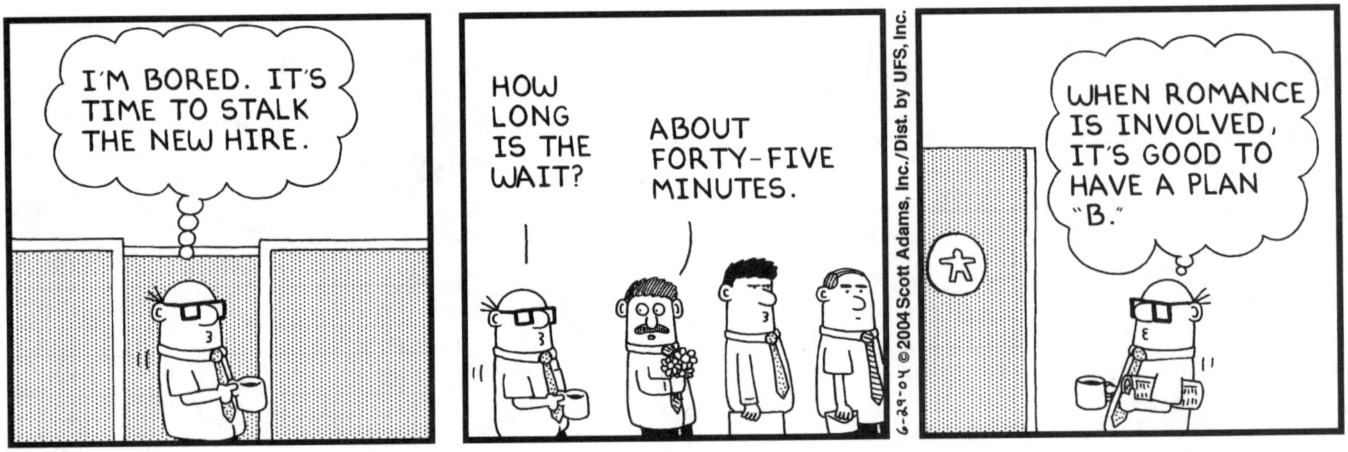
I'M BORED. IT'S TIME TO STALK THE NEW HIRE.
HOW LONG IS THE WAIT?
ABOUT FORTY-FIVE MINUTES.
WHEN ROMANCE IS INVOLVED, IT'S GOOD TO HAVE A PLAN "B."
6-29-04 © 2004 Scott Adams, Inc./Dist. by UFS, Inc.

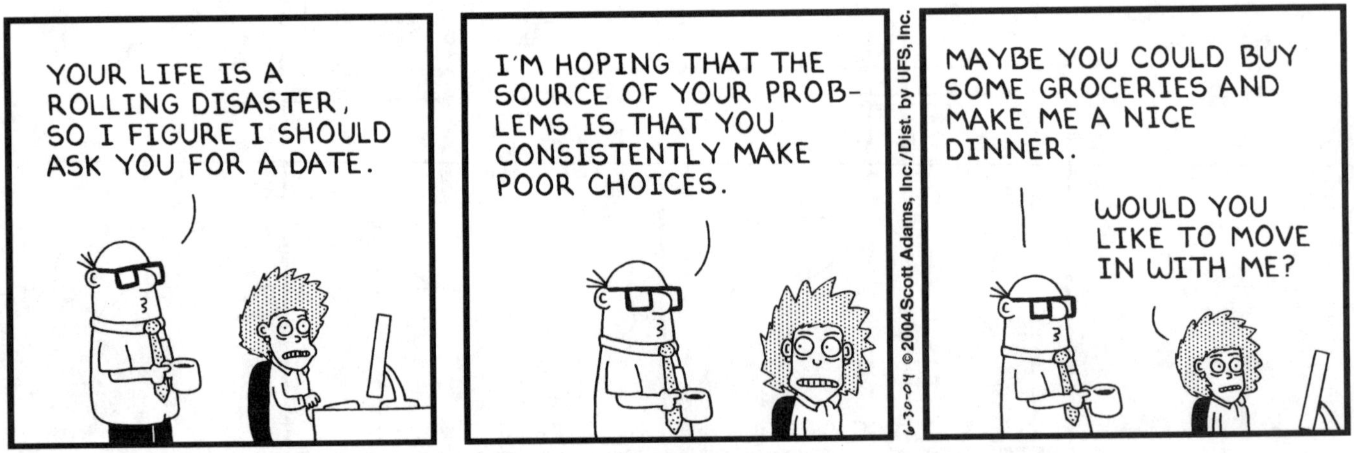
YOUR LIFE IS A ROLLING DISASTER, SO I FIGURE I SHOULD ASK YOU FOR A DATE.
I'M HOPING THAT THE SOURCE OF YOUR PROBLEMS IS THAT YOU CONSISTENTLY MAKE POOR CHOICES.
MAYBE YOU COULD BUY SOME GROCERIES AND MAKE ME A NICE DINNER.
WOULD YOU LIKE TO MOVE IN WITH ME?
6-30-04 © 2004 Scott Adams, Inc./Dist. by UFS, Inc.

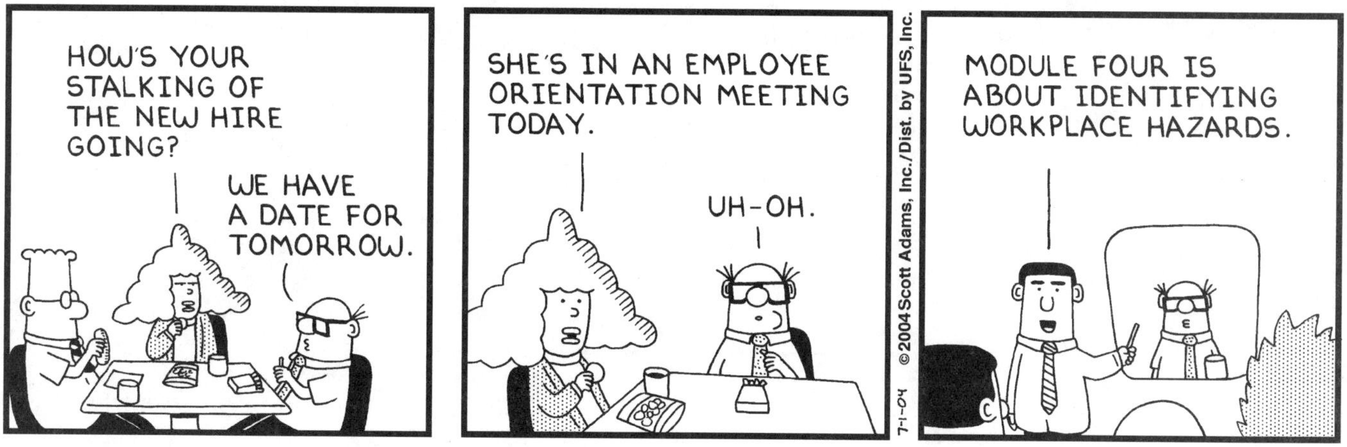
HOW'S YOUR STALKING OF THE NEW HIRE GOING?
WE HAVE A DATE FOR TOMORROW.
SHE'S IN AN EMPLOYEE ORIENTATION MEETING TODAY.
UH-OH.
7-1-04 © 2004 Scott Adams, Inc./Dist. by UFS, Inc.
MODULE FOUR IS ABOUT IDENTIFYING WORKPLACE HAZARDS.

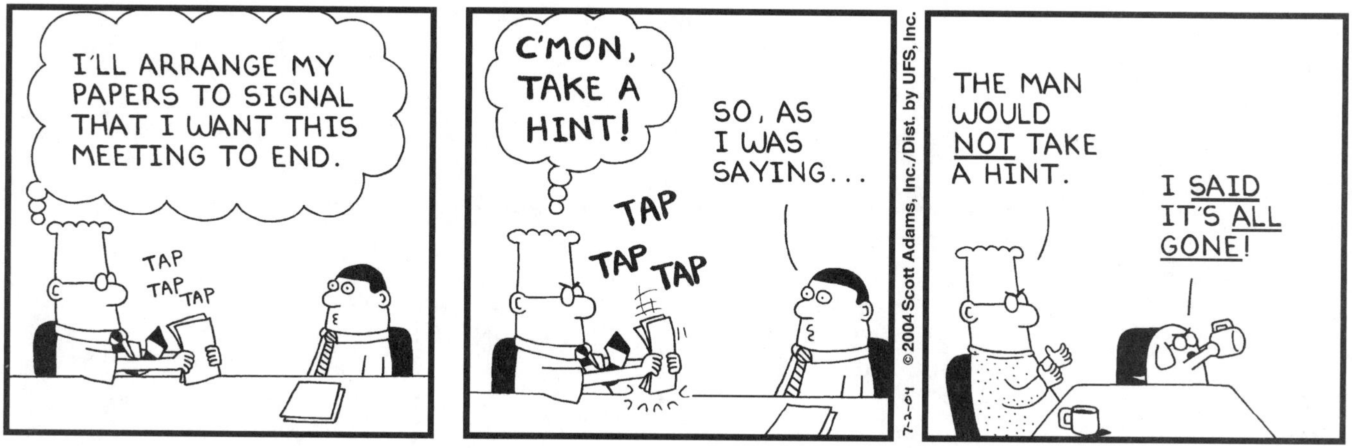
I'LL ARRANGE MY PAPERS TO SIGNAL THAT I WANT THIS MEETING TO END.
TAP TAP TAP
C'MON, TAKE A HINT!
TAP TAP TAP
SO, AS I WAS SAYING...
7-2-04 © 2004 Scott Adams, Inc./Dist. by UFS, Inc.
THE MAN WOULD NOT TAKE A HINT.
I SAID IT'S ALL GONE!

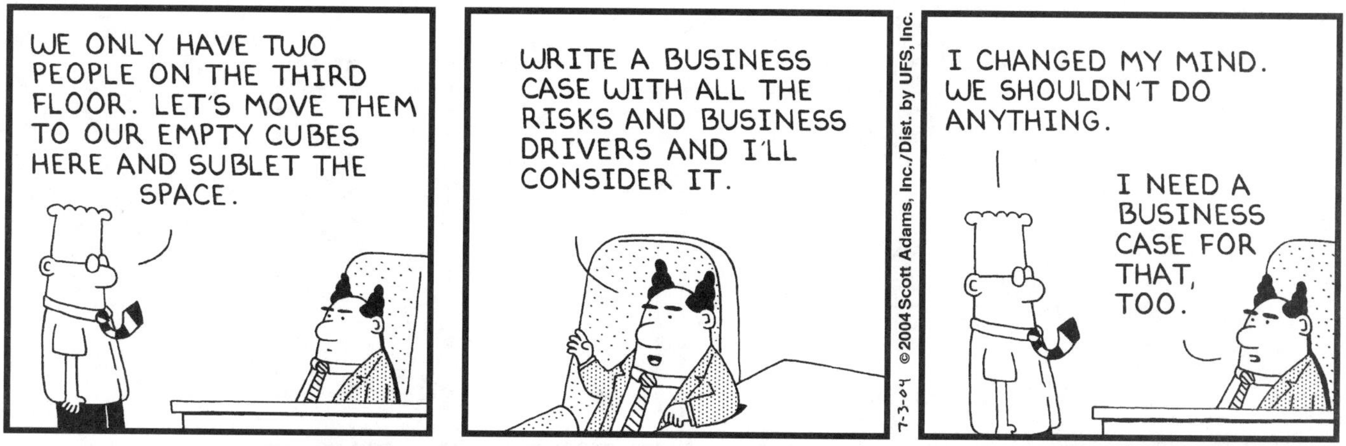
WE ONLY HAVE TWO PEOPLE ON THE THIRD FLOOR. LET'S MOVE THEM TO OUR EMPTY CUBES HERE AND SUBLET THE SPACE.
WRITE A BUSINESS CASE WITH ALL THE RISKS AND BUSINESS DRIVERS AND I'LL CONSIDER IT.
7-3-04 © 2004 Scott Adams, Inc./Dist. by UFS, Inc.
I CHANGED MY MIND. WE SHOULDN'T DO ANYTHING.
I NEED A BUSINESS CASE FOR THAT, TOO.

CAROL, I NEED TEN MINUTES ON THE POINTY-HAIRED BOSS' SCHEDULE.
I DON'T LET HIM HAVE MEETINGS ANYMORE.
WHAT?
EVERY TIME HE HAD A MEETING IT JUST CREATED MORE WORK FOR ME.
IT WAS ALWAYS "CAROL, GET ME A FILE," AND "CAROL, SCHEDULE ANOTHER MEETING."
OBVIOUSLY I HAD TO PUT AN END TO THE MADNESS.
I GUESS I COULD E-MAIL HIM.
YOU COULD TRY.
©2004 Scott Adams, Inc. /Dist. by UFS, Inc.
7/4/04

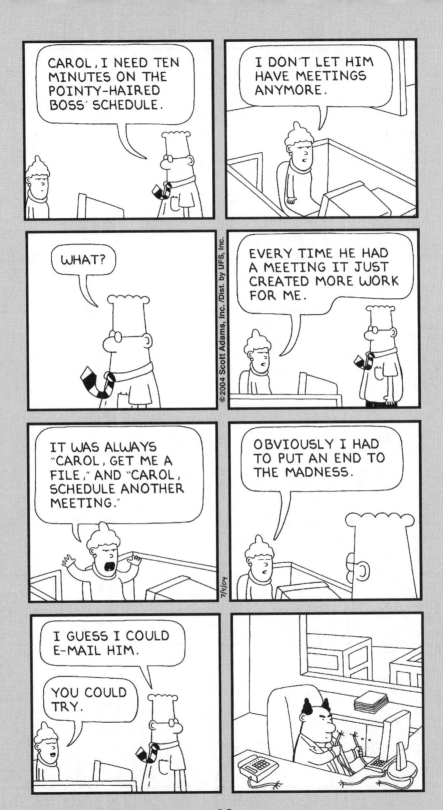

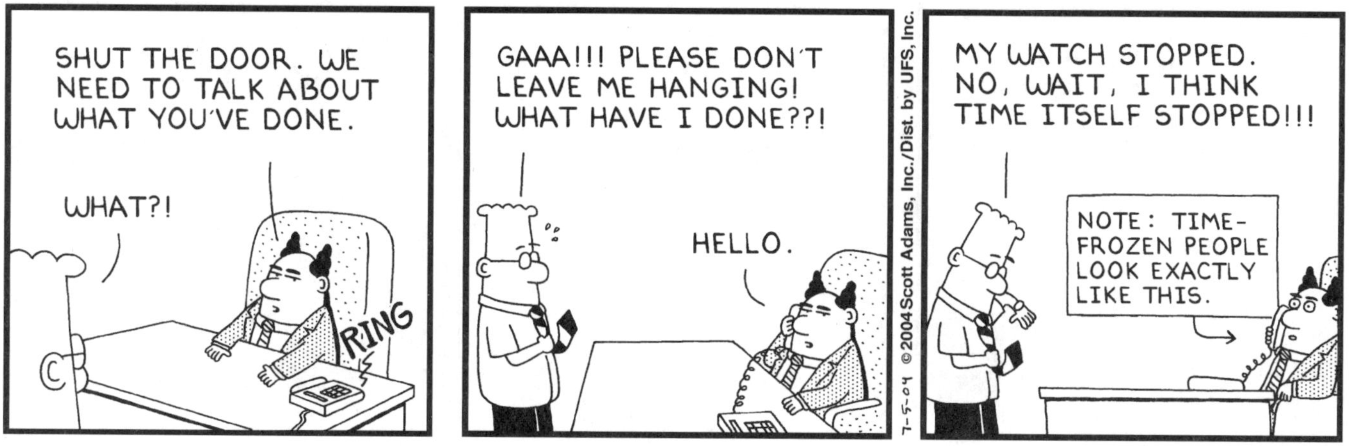
SHUT THE DOOR. WE NEED TO TALK ABOUT WHAT YOU'VE DONE.
WHAT?!
RING
GAAA!!! PLEASE DON'T LEAVE ME HANGING! WHAT HAVE I DONE??!
HELLO.
7-5-04 © 2004 Scott Adams, Inc./Dist. by UFS, Inc.
MY WATCH STOPPED. NO, WAIT, I THINK TIME ITSELF STOPPED!!!
NOTE: TIME-FROZEN PEOPLE LOOK EXACTLY LIKE THIS.

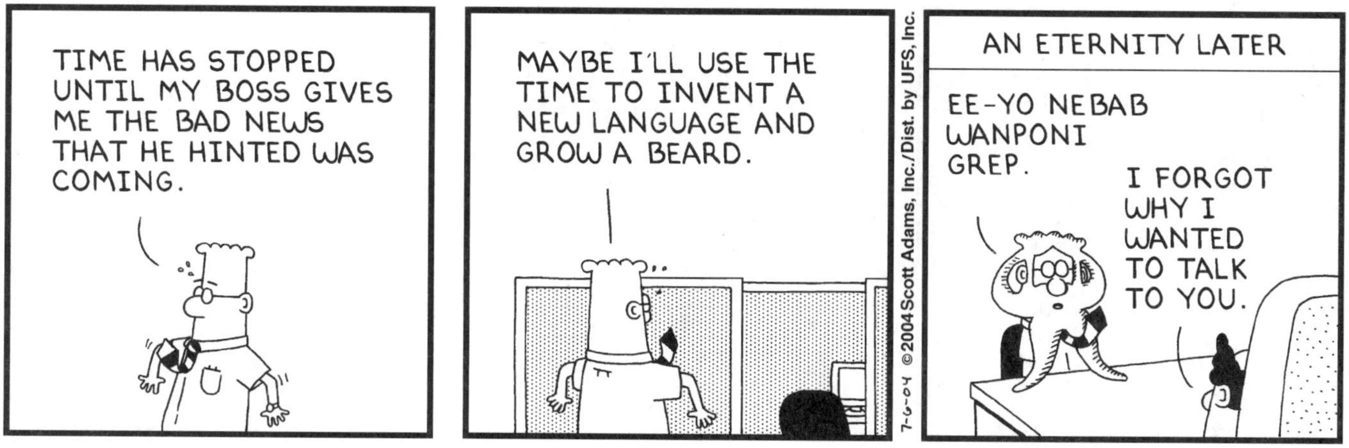
TIME HAS STOPPED UNTIL MY BOSS GIVES ME THE BAD NEWS THAT HE HINTED WAS COMING.
MAYBE I'LL USE THE TIME TO INVENT A NEW LANGUAGE AND GROW A BEARD.
7-6-04 © 2004 Scott Adams, Inc./Dist. by UFS, Inc.
AN ETERNITY LATER
EE-YO NEBAB WANPONI GREP.
I FORGOT WHY I WANTED TO TALK TO YOU.

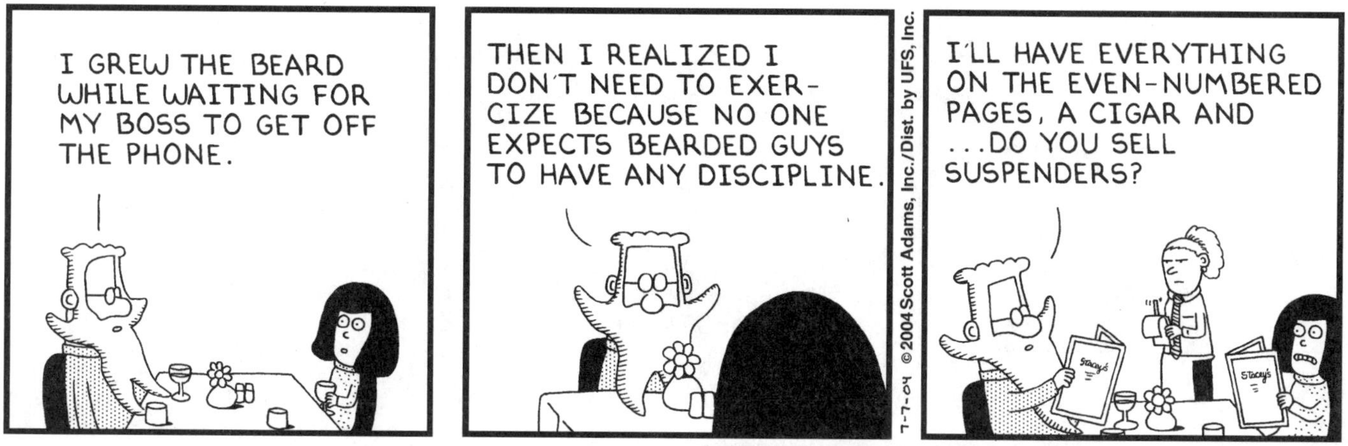
I GREW THE BEARD WHILE WAITING FOR MY BOSS TO GET OFF THE PHONE.
THEN I REALIZED I DON'T NEED TO EXER-CIZE BECAUSE NO ONE EXPECTS BEARDED GUYS TO HAVE ANY DISCIPLINE.
7-7-04 © 2004 Scott Adams, Inc./Dist. by UFS, Inc.
I'LL HAVE EVERYTHING ON THE EVEN-NUMBERED PAGES, A CIGAR AND ...DO YOU SELL SUSPENDERS?
Stacy's
Stacy's

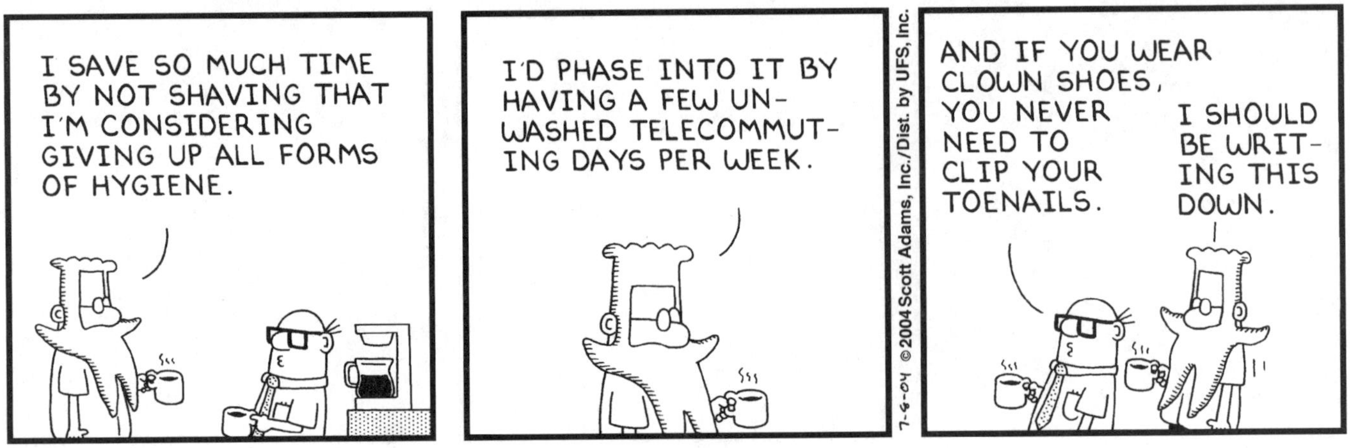
I SAVE SO MUCH TIME BY NOT SHAVING THAT I'M CONSIDERING GIVING UP ALL FORMS OF HYGIENE.
I'D PHASE INTO IT BY HAVING A FEW UN-WASHED TELECOMMUT-ING DAYS PER WEEK.
7-6-04 ©2004 Scott Adams, Inc./Dist. by UFS, Inc.
AND IF YOU WEAR CLOWN SHOES, YOU NEVER NEED TO CLIP YOUR TOENAILS.
I SHOULD BE WRIT-ING THIS DOWN.

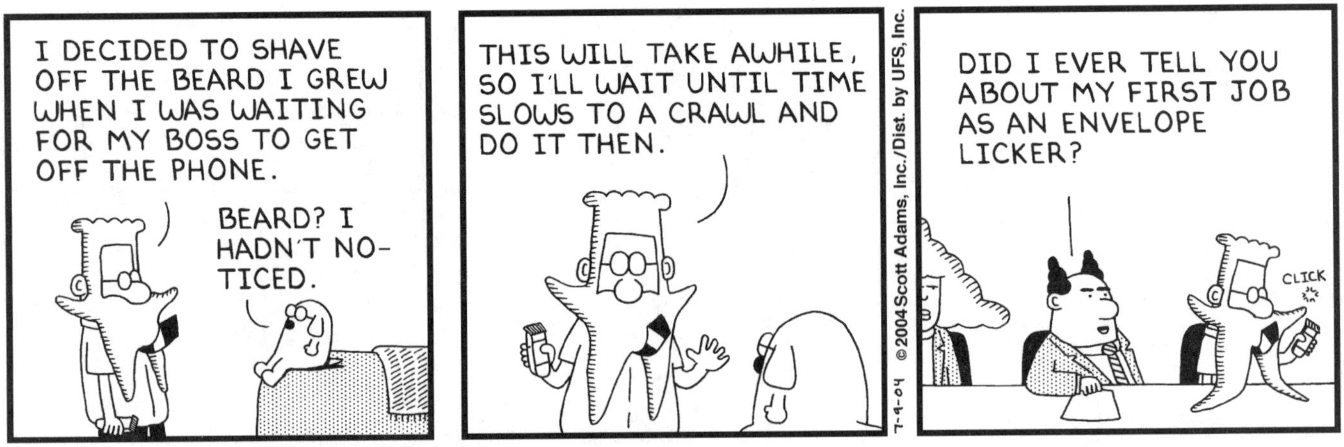
I DECIDED TO SHAVE OFF THE BEARD I GREW WHEN I WAS WAITING FOR MY BOSS TO GET OFF THE PHONE.
BEARD? I HADN'T NO-TICED.
THIS WILL TAKE AWHILE, SO I'LL WAIT UNTIL TIME SLOWS TO A CRAWL AND DO IT THEN.
7-9-04 ©2004 Scott Adams, Inc./Dist. by UFS, Inc.
DID I EVER TELL YOU ABOUT MY FIRST JOB AS AN ENVELOPE LICKER?
CLICK

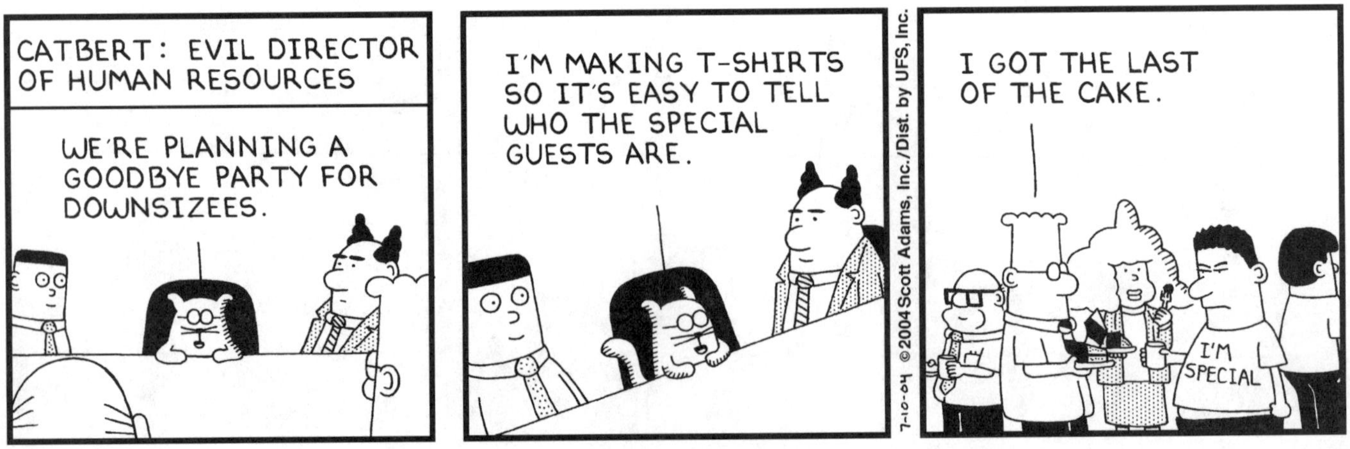
CATBERT: EVIL DIRECTOR OF HUMAN RESOURCES
WE'RE PLANNING A GOODBYE PARTY FOR DOWNSIZEES.
I'M MAKING T-SHIRTS SO IT'S EASY TO TELL WHO THE SPECIAL GUESTS ARE.
7-10-04 ©2004 Scott Adams, Inc./Dist. by UFS, Inc.
I GOT THE LAST OF THE CAKE.
I'M SPECIAL

DILBERT, THIS IS PROXIS. I RECRUITED HIM FROM THE GULLIBLE NEBULA.
I CONVINCED HIM TO RELOCATE HIS FAMILY.
HELLO.
MY SPACESHIP WAS DESTROYED DURING THE LANDING, BUT THAT'S NO PROBLEM.
I EXPECT TO WORK HERE FOR THE REST OF MY 300-YEAR LIFESPAN.
THAT REMINDS ME: WE NEED TO TALK.
YOUR JOB FUNCTION HAS BEEN OUTSOURCED. I HAVE TO LET YOU GO.
YOUR SEVERANCE PACKAGE IS: I GRAB YOU BY THE SNOUT AND FLING YOU ONTO THE SIDEWALK.
MAY I USE YOU AS A REFERENCE?
©2004 Scott Adams, Inc. /Dist. by UFS, Inc.
7-11-04

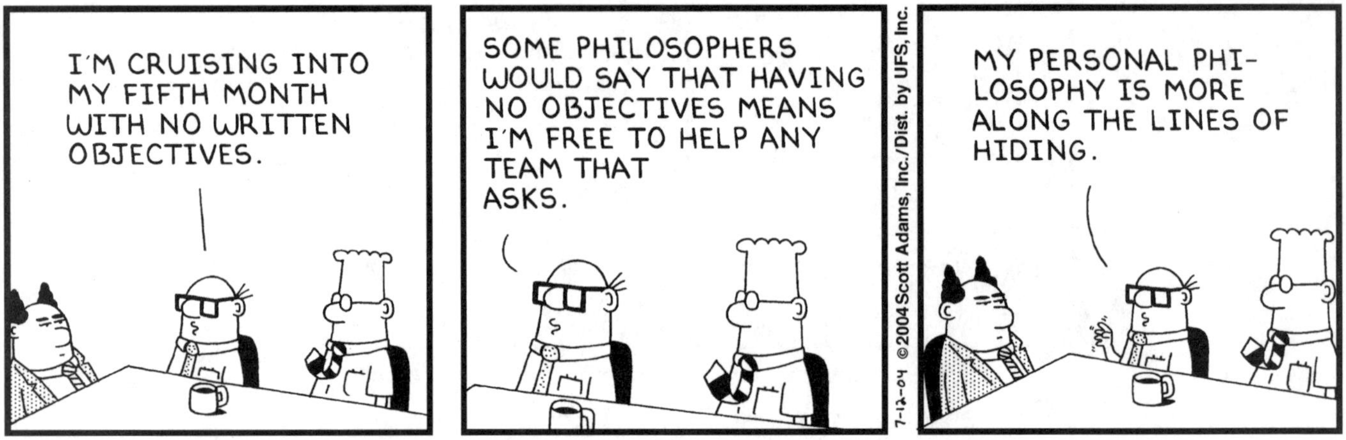
I'M CRUISING INTO MY FIFTH MONTH WITH NO WRITTEN OBJECTIVES.
SOME PHILOSOPHERS WOULD SAY THAT HAVING NO OBJECTIVES MEANS I'M FREE TO HELP ANY TEAM THAT ASKS.
MY PERSONAL PHI-LOSOPHY IS MORE ALONG THE LINES OF HIDING.
7-12-04 ©2004 Scott Adams, Inc./Dist. by UFS, Inc.

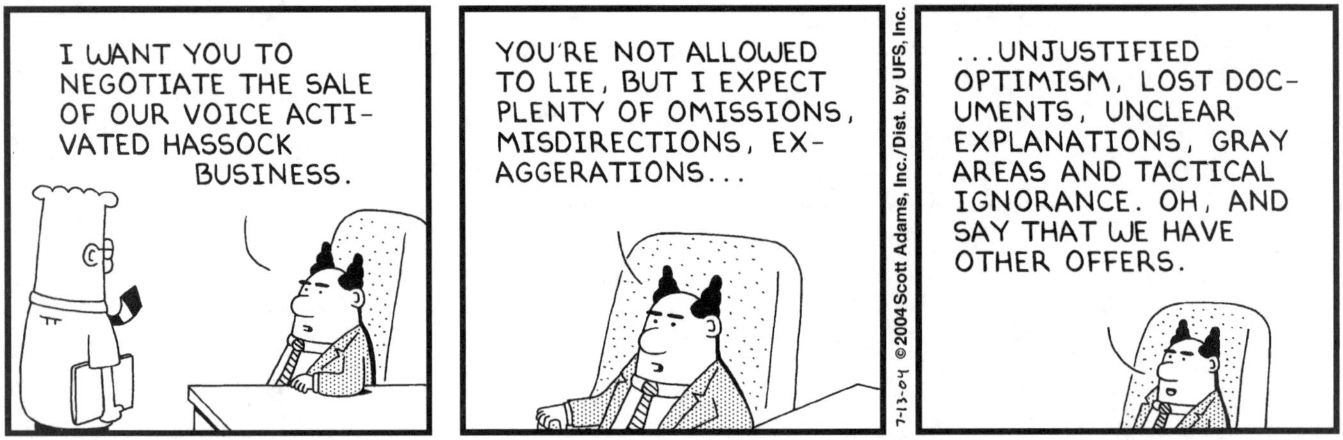
I WANT YOU TO NEGOTIATE THE SALE OF OUR VOICE ACTI-VATED HASSOCK BUSINESS.
YOU'RE NOT ALLOWED TO LIE, BUT I EXPECT PLENTY OF OMISSIONS, MISDIRECTIONS, EX-AGGERATIONS...
...UNJUSTIFIED OPTIMISM, LOST DOC-UMENTS, UNCLEAR EXPLANATIONS, GRAY AREAS AND TACTICAL IGNORANCE. OH, AND SAY THAT WE HAVE OTHER OFFERS.
7-13-04 ©2004 Scott Adams, Inc./Dist. by UFS, Inc.

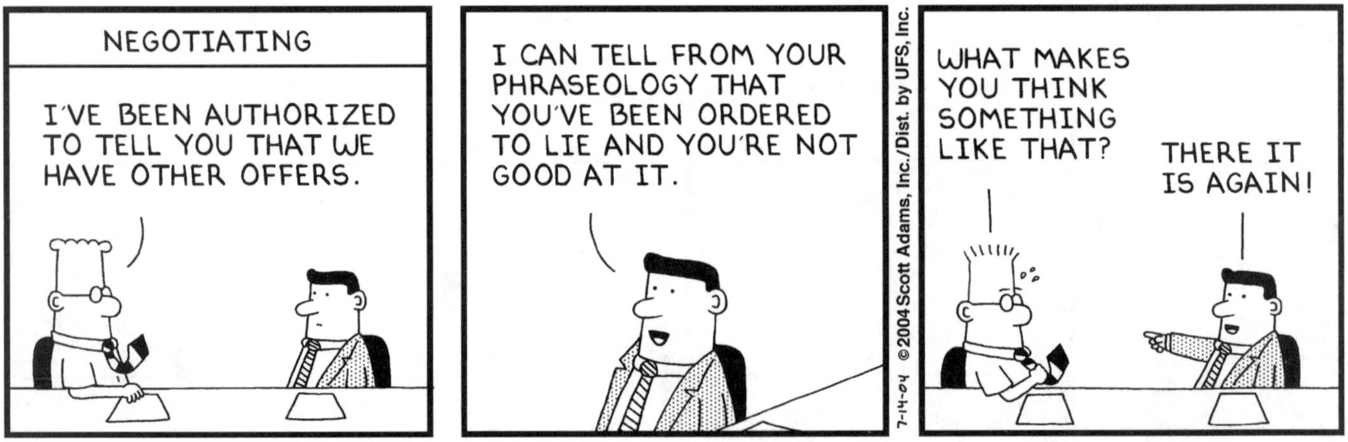
NEGOTIATING
I'VE BEEN AUTHORIZED TO TELL YOU THAT WE HAVE OTHER OFFERS.
I CAN TELL FROM YOUR PHRASEOLOGY THAT YOU'VE BEEN ORDERED TO LIE AND YOU'RE NOT GOOD AT IT.
WHAT MAKES YOU THINK SOMETHING LIKE THAT?
THERE IT IS AGAIN!
7-14-04 ©2004 Scott Adams, Inc./Dist. by UFS, Inc.

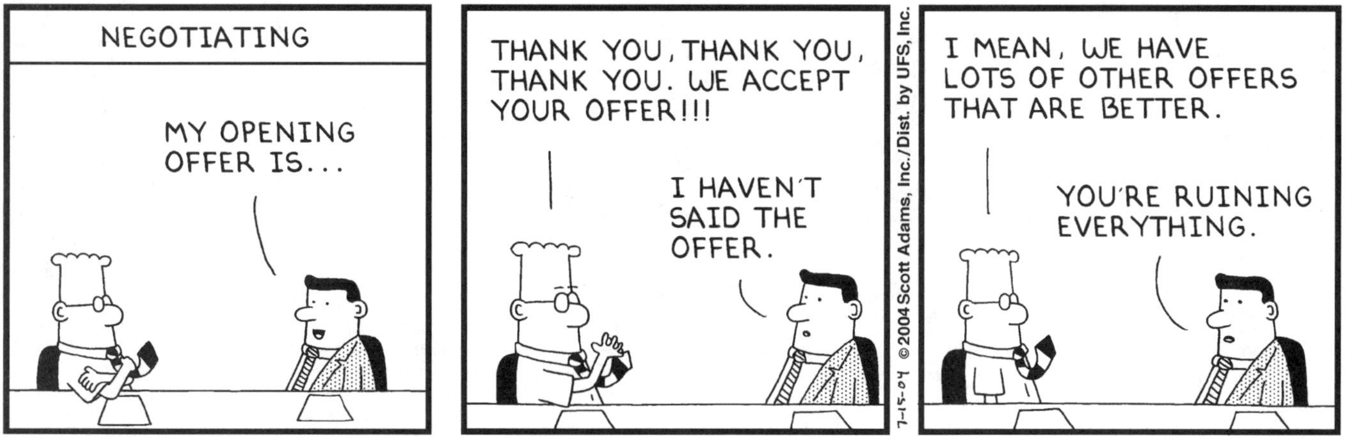
NEGOTIATING
MY OPENING OFFER IS...
THANK YOU, THANK YOU, THANK YOU. WE ACCEPT YOUR OFFER!!!
I HAVEN'T SAID THE OFFER.
7-15-04 ©2004 Scott Adams, Inc./Dist. by UFS, Inc.
I MEAN, WE HAVE LOTS OF OTHER OFFERS THAT ARE BETTER.
YOU'RE RUINING EVERYTHING.

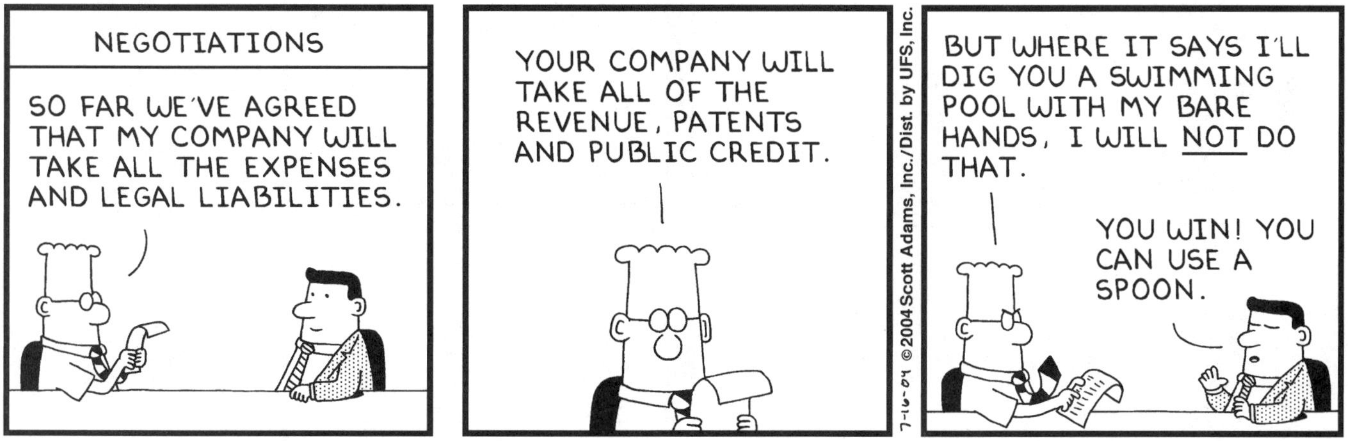
NEGOTIATIONS
SO FAR WE'VE AGREED THAT MY COMPANY WILL TAKE ALL THE EXPENSES AND LEGAL LIABILITIES.
YOUR COMPANY WILL TAKE ALL OF THE REVENUE, PATENTS AND PUBLIC CREDIT.
7-16-04 ©2004 Scott Adams, Inc./Dist. by UFS, Inc.
BUT WHERE IT SAYS I'LL DIG YOU A SWIMMING POOL WITH MY BARE HANDS, I WILL NOT DO THAT.
YOU WIN! YOU CAN USE A SPOON.

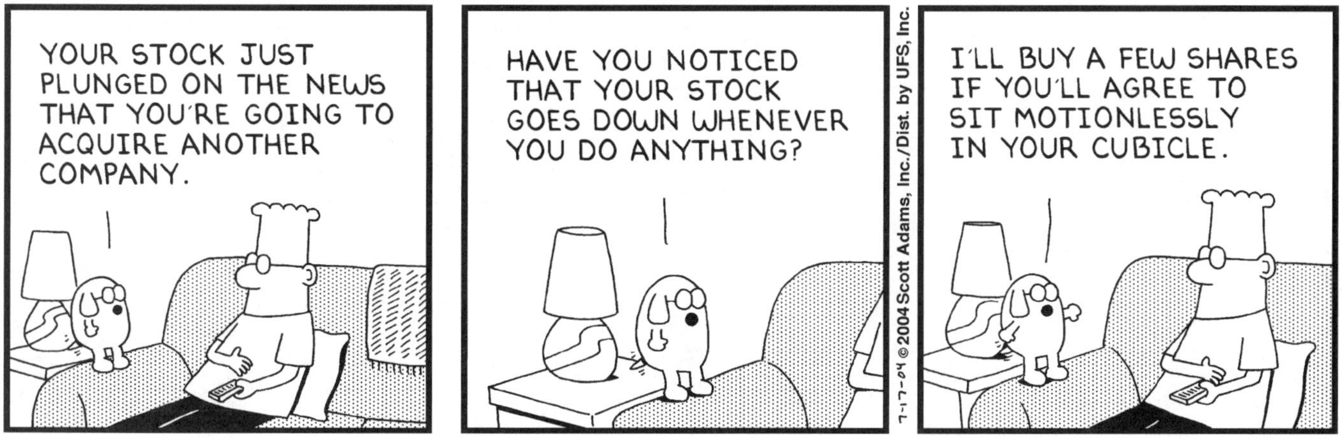
YOUR STOCK JUST PLUNGED ON THE NEWS THAT YOU'RE GOING TO ACQUIRE ANOTHER COMPANY.
HAVE YOU NOTICED THAT YOUR STOCK GOES DOWN WHENEVER YOU DO ANYTHING?
7-17-04 ©2004 Scott Adams, Inc./Dist. by UFS, Inc.
I'LL BUY A FEW SHARES IF YOU'LL AGREE TO SIT MOTIONLESSLY IN YOUR CUBICLE.

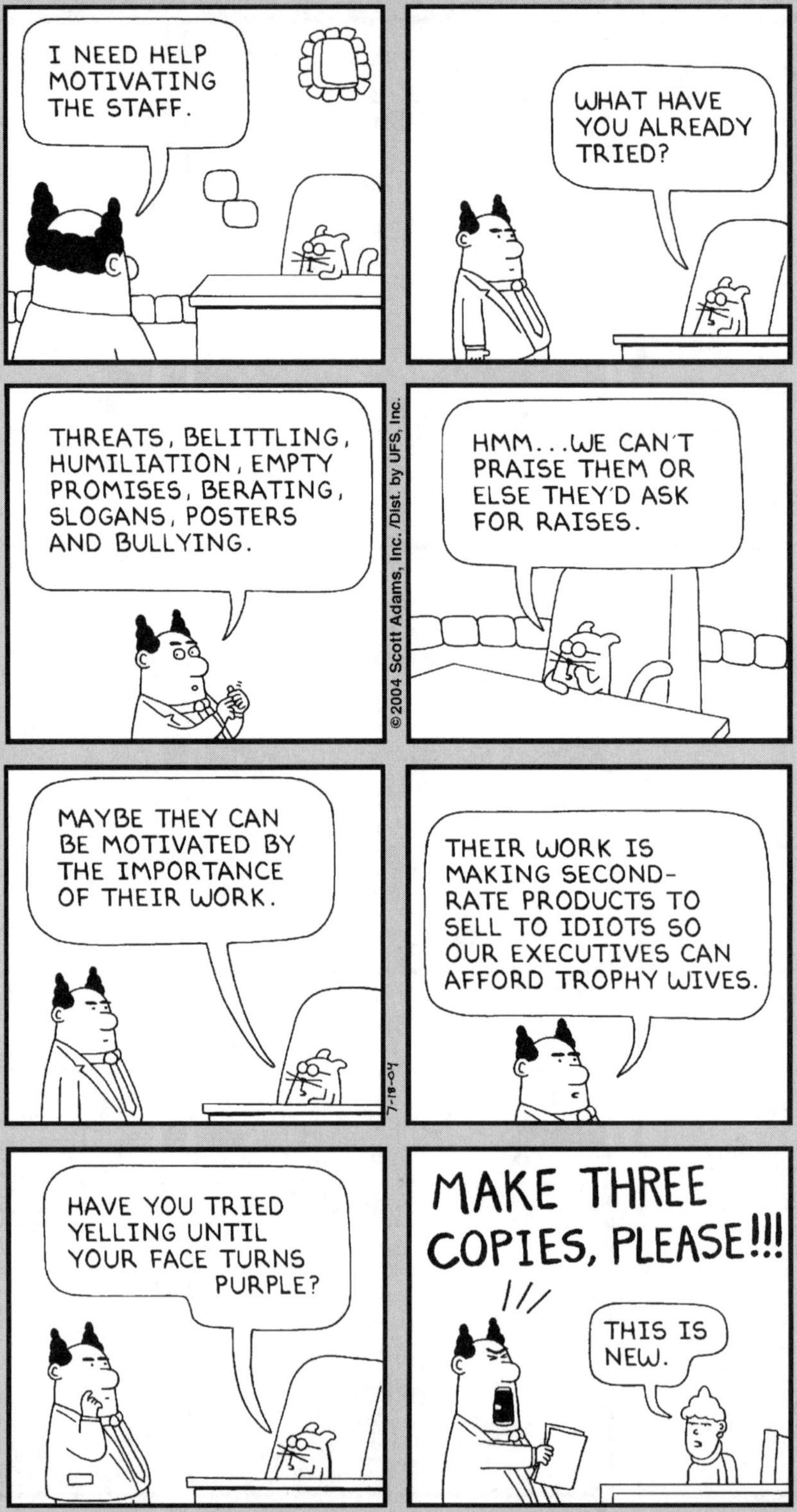
I NEED HELP MOTIVATING THE STAFF.
WHAT HAVE YOU ALREADY TRIED?
THREATS, BELITTLING, HUMILIATION, EMPTY PROMISES, BERATING, SLOGANS, POSTERS AND BULLYING.
HMM...WE CAN'T PRAISE THEM OR ELSE THEY'D ASK FOR RAISES.
MAYBE THEY CAN BE MOTIVATED BY THE IMPORTANCE OF THEIR WORK.
THEIR WORK IS MAKING SECOND-RATE PRODUCTS TO SELL TO IDIOTS SO OUR EXECUTIVES CAN AFFORD TROPHY WIVES.
HAVE YOU TRIED YELLING UNTIL YOUR FACE TURNS PURPLE?
MAKE THREE COPIES, PLEASE!!!
THIS IS NEW.
©2004 Scott Adams, Inc. /Dist. by UFS, Inc.
7-18-04

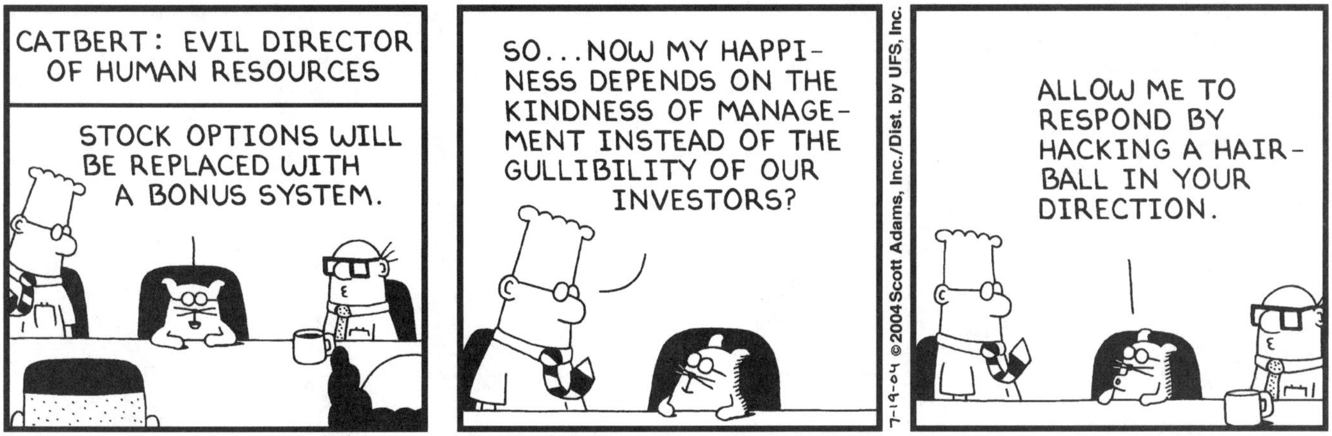
CATBERT: EVIL DIRECTOR OF HUMAN RESOURCES
STOCK OPTIONS WILL BE REPLACED WITH A BONUS SYSTEM.
SO...NOW MY HAPPINESS DEPENDS ON THE KINDNESS OF MANAGEMENT INSTEAD OF THE GULLIBILITY OF OUR INVESTORS?
7-19-04 ©2004 Scott Adams, Inc./Dist. by UFS, Inc.
ALLOW ME TO RESPOND BY HACKING A HAIRBALL IN YOUR DIRECTION.

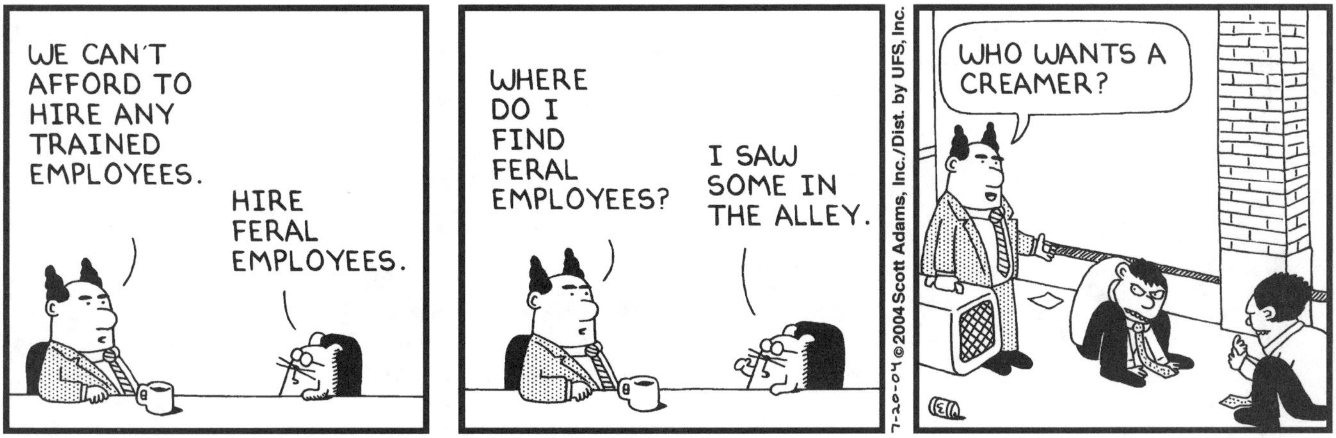
WE CAN'T AFFORD TO HIRE ANY TRAINED EMPLOYEES.
HIRE FERAL EMPLOYEES.
WHERE DO I FIND FERAL EMPLOYEES?
I SAW SOME IN THE ALLEY.
7-20-04 ©2004 Scott Adams, Inc./Dist. by UFS, Inc.
WHO WANTS A CREAMER?

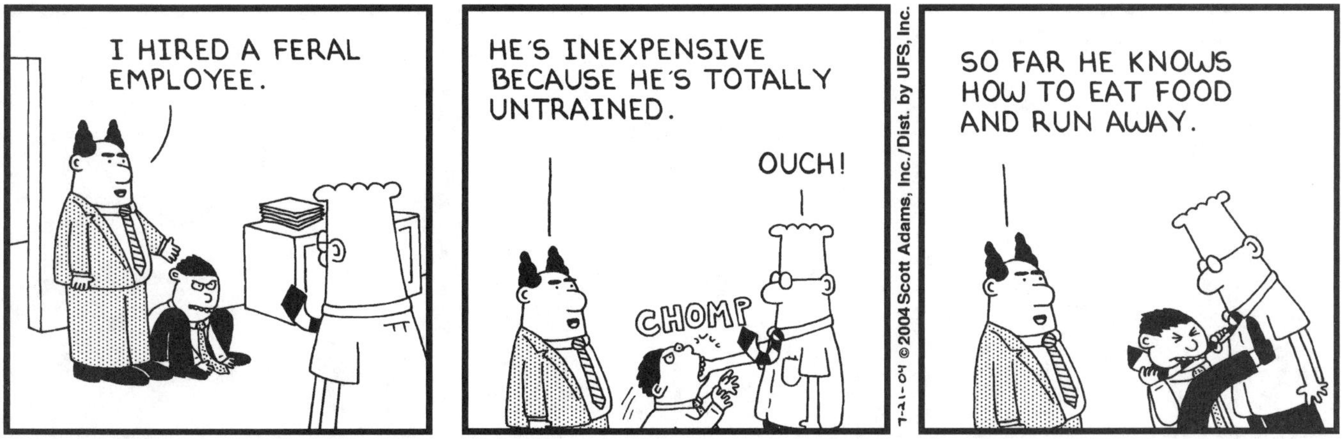
I HIRED A FERAL EMPLOYEE.
HE'S INEXPENSIVE BECAUSE HE'S TOTALLY UNTRAINED.
OUCH!
CHOMP
7-21-04 ©2004 Scott Adams, Inc./Dist. by UFS, Inc.
SO FAR HE KNOWS HOW TO EAT FOOD AND RUN AWAY.

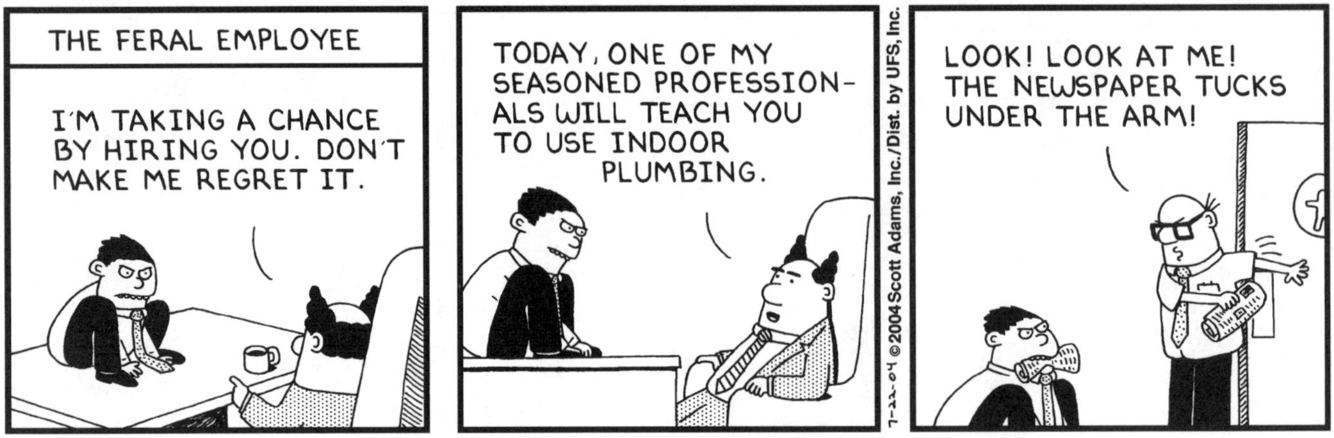
THE FERAL EMPLOYEE
I'M TAKING A CHANCE BY HIRING YOU. DON'T MAKE ME REGRET IT.
TODAY, ONE OF MY SEASONED PROFESSIONALS WILL TEACH YOU TO USE INDOOR PLUMBING.
© 2004 Scott Adams, Inc./Dist. by UFS, Inc.
7-22-04
LOOK! LOOK AT ME! THE NEWSPAPER TUCKS UNDER THE ARM!

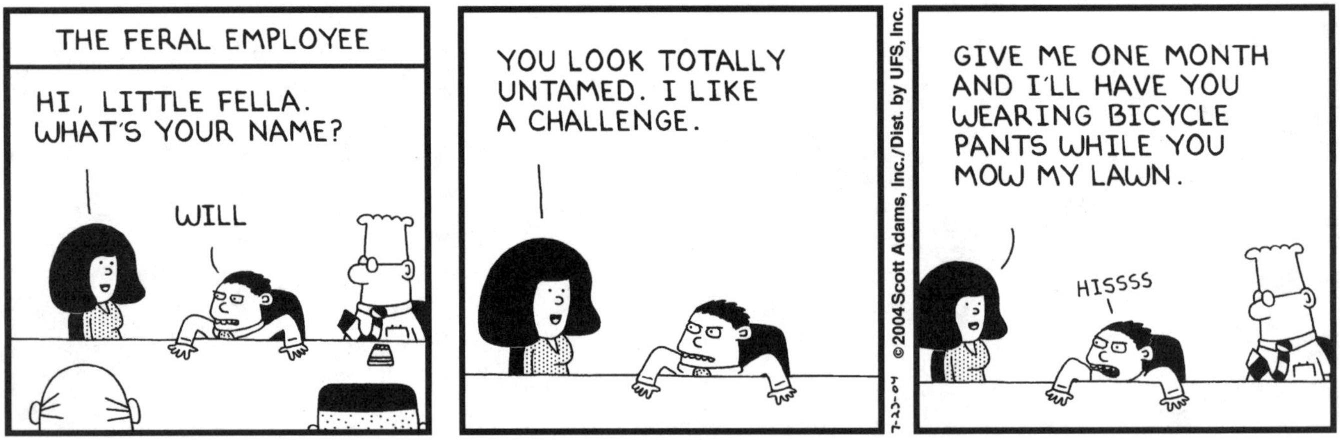
THE FERAL EMPLOYEE
HI, LITTLE FELLA. WHAT'S YOUR NAME?
WILL
YOU LOOK TOTALLY UNTAMED. I LIKE A CHALLENGE.
© 2004 Scott Adams, Inc./Dist. by UFS, Inc.
7-23-04
GIVE ME ONE MONTH AND I'LL HAVE YOU WEARING BICYCLE PANTS WHILE YOU MOW MY LAWN.
HISSSS

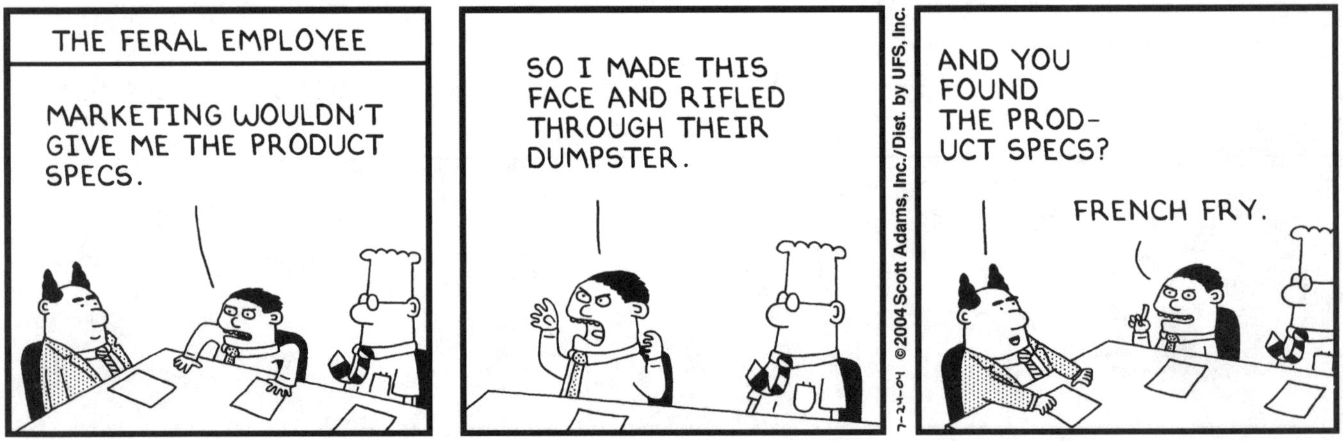
THE FERAL EMPLOYEE
MARKETING WOULDN'T GIVE ME THE PRODUCT SPECS.
SO I MADE THIS FACE AND RIFLED THROUGH THEIR DUMPSTER.
© 2004 Scott Adams, Inc./Dist. by UFS, Inc.
7-24-04
AND YOU FOUND THE PRODUCT SPECS?
FRENCH FRY.

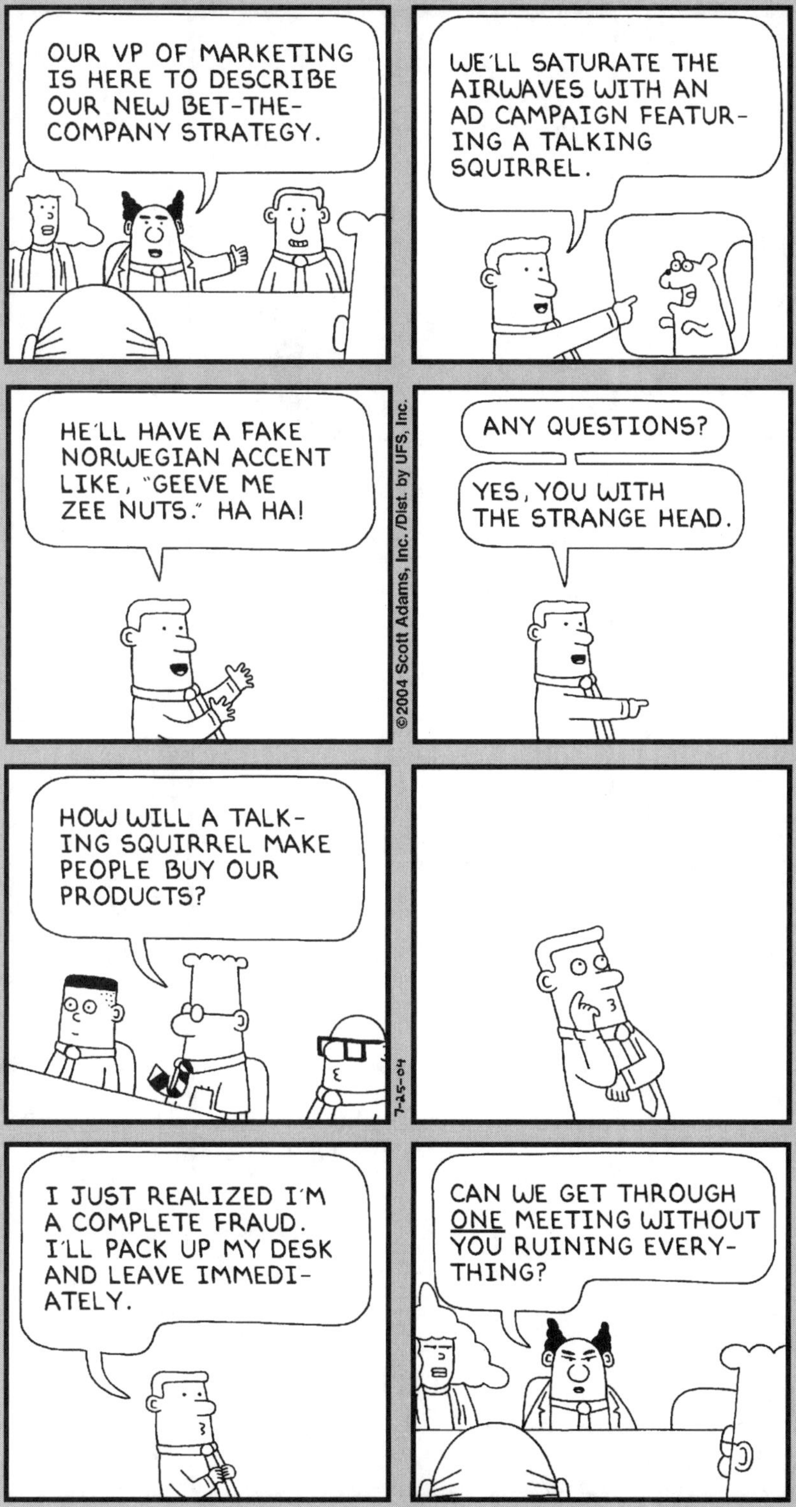

OUR VP OF MARKETING IS HERE TO DESCRIBE OUR NEW BET-THE-COMPANY STRATEGY.
WE'LL SATURATE THE AIRWAVES WITH AN AD CAMPAIGN FEATURING A TALKING SQUIRREL.
HE'LL HAVE A FAKE NORWEGIAN ACCENT LIKE, "GEEVE ME ZEE NUTS." HA HA!
ANY QUESTIONS?
YES, YOU WITH THE STRANGE HEAD.
HOW WILL A TALKING SQUIRREL MAKE PEOPLE BUY OUR PRODUCTS?
I JUST REALIZED I'M A COMPLETE FRAUD. I'LL PACK UP MY DESK AND LEAVE IMMEDIATELY.
CAN WE GET THROUGH ONE MEETING WITHOUT YOU RUINING EVERYTHING?
©2004 Scott Adams, Inc./Dist. by UFS, Inc.
7-25-04

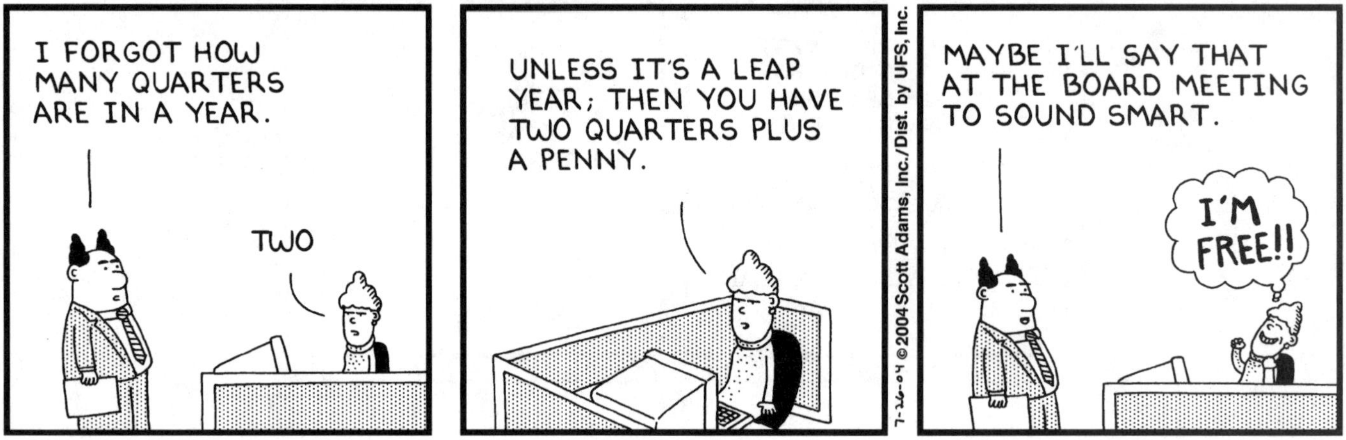
I FORGOT HOW MANY QUARTERS ARE IN A YEAR.
TWO
UNLESS IT'S A LEAP YEAR; THEN YOU HAVE TWO QUARTERS PLUS A PENNY.
MAYBE I'LL SAY THAT AT THE BOARD MEETING TO SOUND SMART.
I'M FREE!!
7-26-04 © 2004 Scott Adams, Inc./Dist. by UFS, Inc.

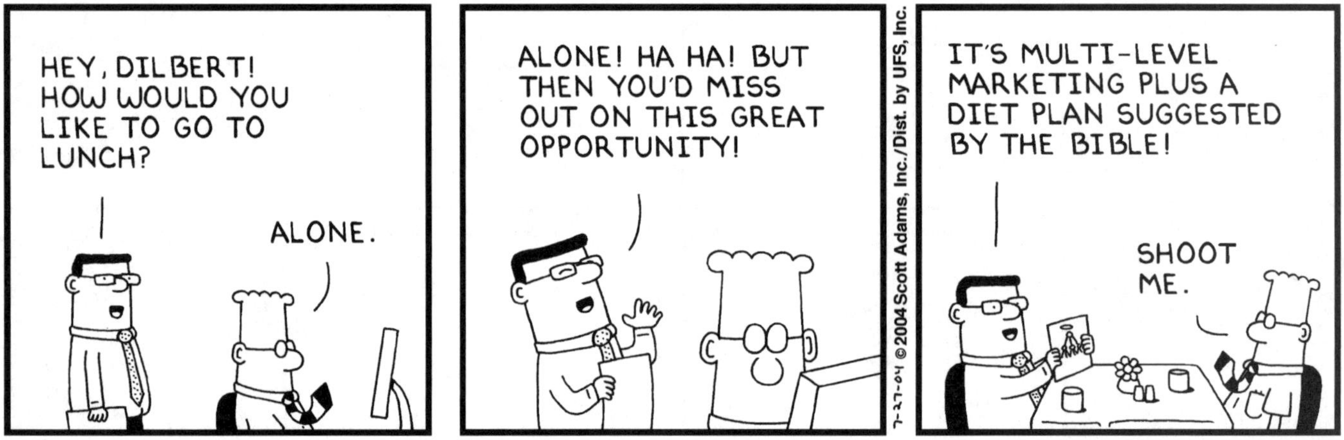
HEY, DILBERT! HOW WOULD YOU LIKE TO GO TO LUNCH?
ALONE.
ALONE! HA HA! BUT THEN YOU'D MISS OUT ON THIS GREAT OPPORTUNITY!
IT'S MULTI-LEVEL MARKETING PLUS A DIET PLAN SUGGESTED BY THE BIBLE!
SHOOT ME.
7-27-04 © 2004 Scott Adams, Inc./Dist. by UFS, Inc.

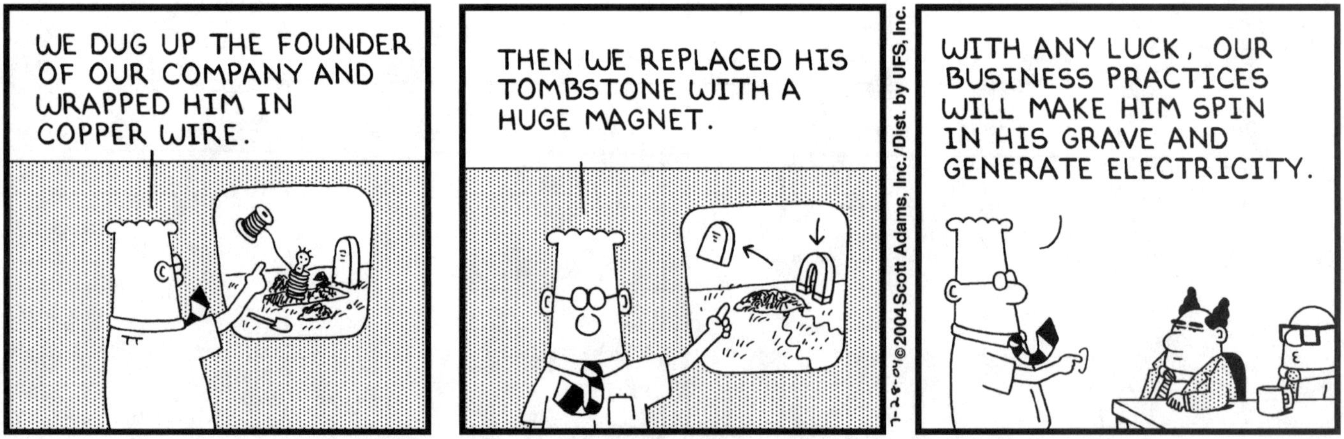
WE DUG UP THE FOUNDER OF OUR COMPANY AND WRAPPED HIM IN COPPER WIRE.
THEN WE REPLACED HIS TOMBSTONE WITH A HUGE MAGNET.
WITH ANY LUCK, OUR BUSINESS PRACTICES WILL MAKE HIM SPIN IN HIS GRAVE AND GENERATE ELECTRICITY.
7-28-04 © 2004 Scott Adams, Inc./Dist. by UFS, Inc.

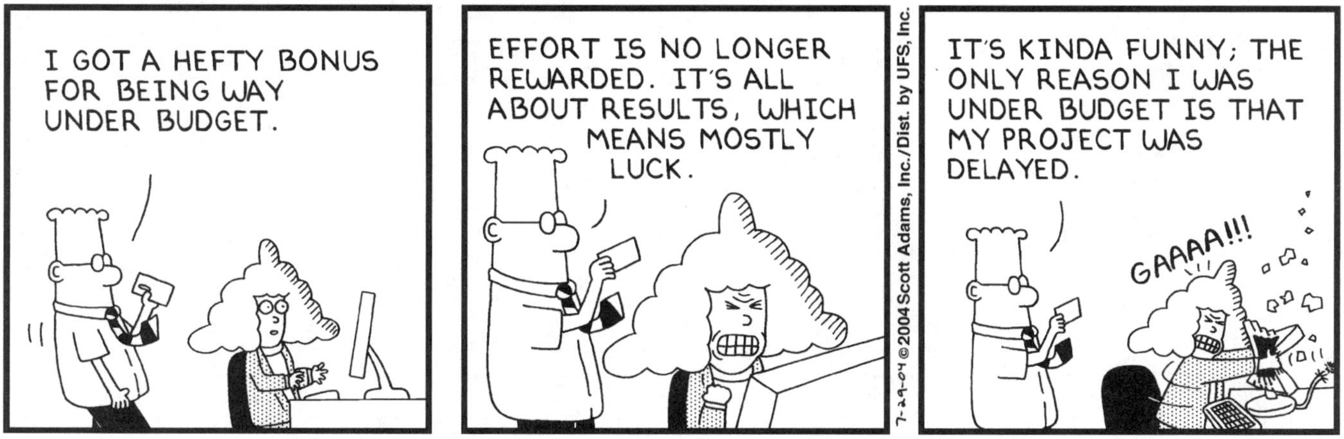
I GOT A HEFTY BONUS FOR BEING WAY UNDER BUDGET.
EFFORT IS NO LONGER REWARDED. IT'S ALL ABOUT RESULTS, WHICH MEANS MOSTLY LUCK.
IT'S KINDA FUNNY; THE ONLY REASON I WAS UNDER BUDGET IS THAT MY PROJECT WAS DELAYED.
GAAAA!!!
7-29-04 ©2004 Scott Adams, Inc./Dist. by UFS, Inc.

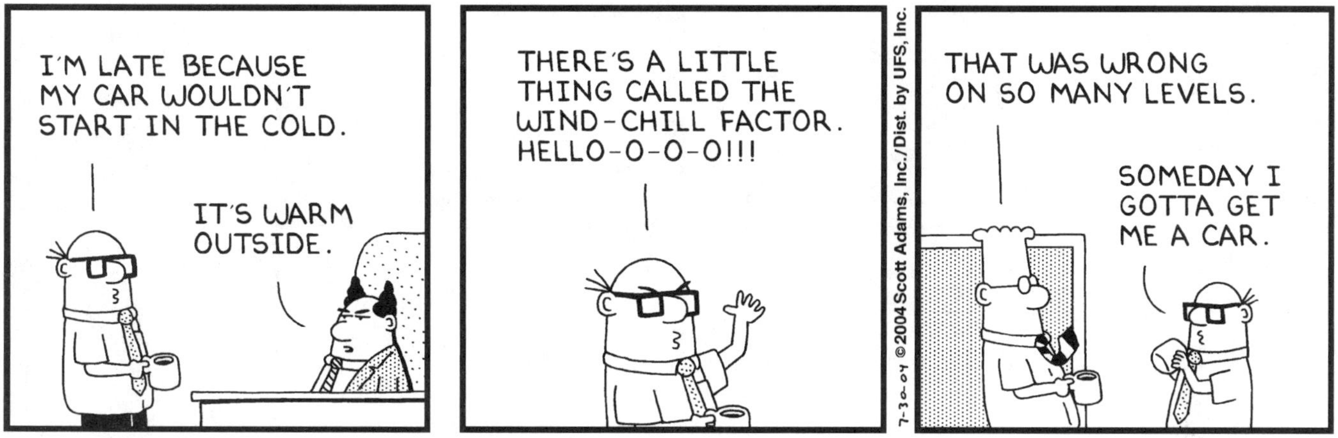
I'M LATE BECAUSE MY CAR WOULDN'T START IN THE COLD.
IT'S WARM OUTSIDE.
THERE'S A LITTLE THING CALLED THE WIND-CHILL FACTOR. HELLO-O-O-O!!!
THAT WAS WRONG ON SO MANY LEVELS.
SOMEDAY I GOTTA GET ME A CAR.
7-30-04 ©2004 Scott Adams, Inc./Dist. by UFS, Inc.

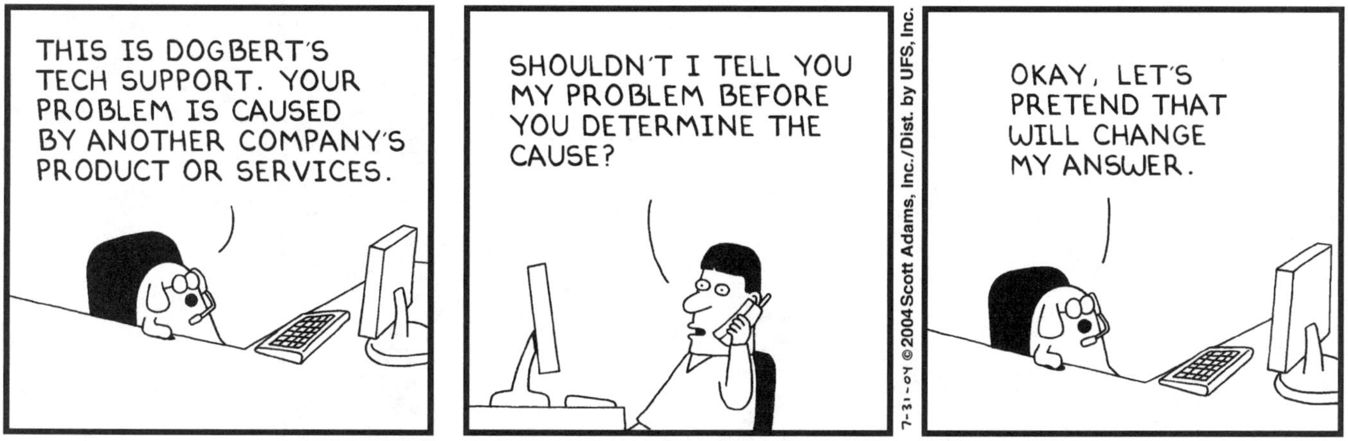
THIS IS DOGBERT'S TECH SUPPORT. YOUR PROBLEM IS CAUSED BY ANOTHER COMPANY'S PRODUCT OR SERVICES.
SHOULDN'T I TELL YOU MY PROBLEM BEFORE YOU DETERMINE THE CAUSE?
OKAY, LET'S PRETEND THAT WILL CHANGE MY ANSWER.
7-31-04 ©2004 Scott Adams, Inc./Dist. by UFS, Inc.

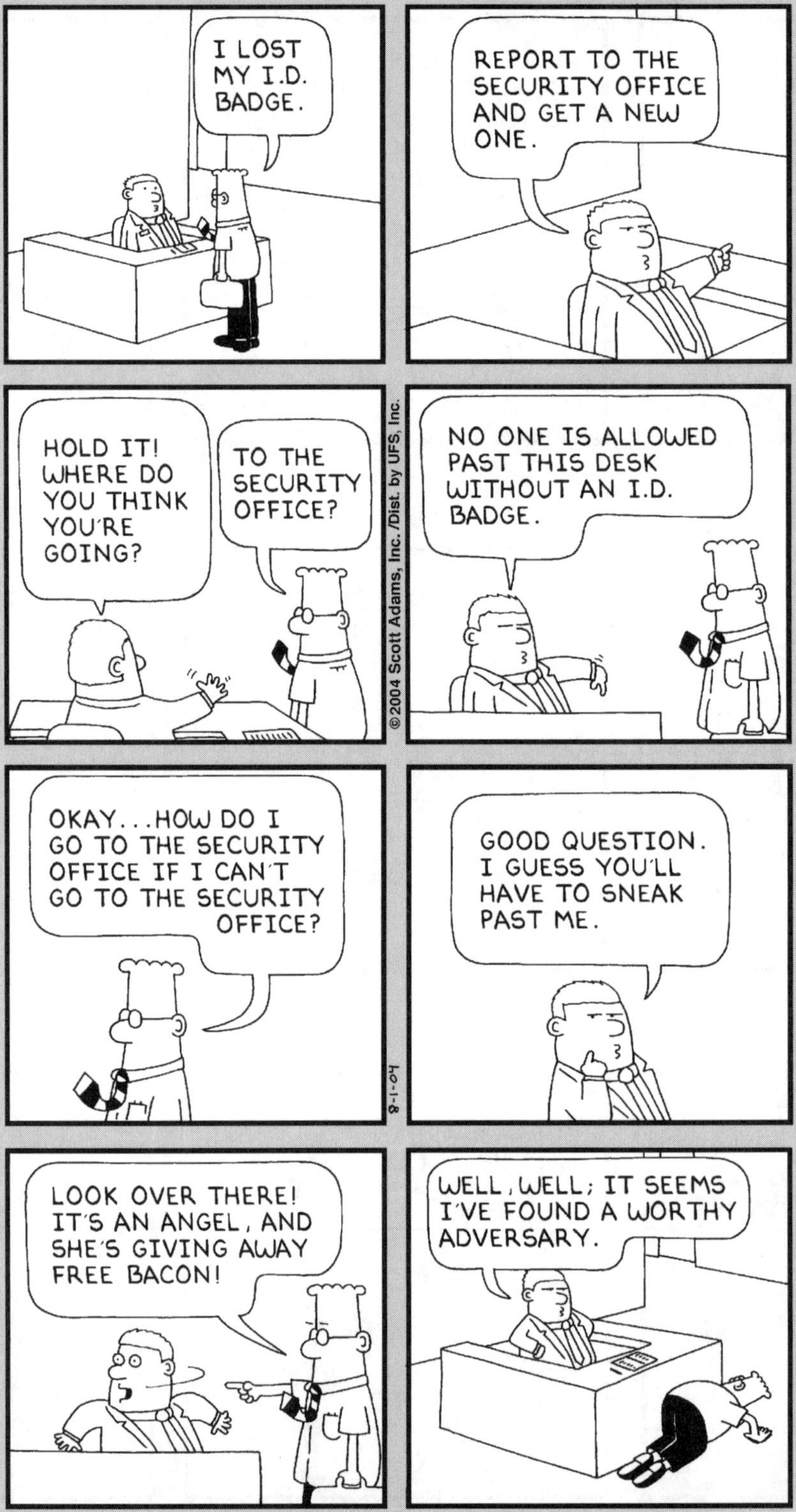
I LOST MY I.D. BADGE.
REPORT TO THE SECURITY OFFICE AND GET A NEW ONE.
HOLD IT! WHERE DO YOU THINK YOU'RE GOING?
TO THE SECURITY OFFICE?
©2004 Scott Adams, Inc. /Dist. by UFS, Inc.
NO ONE IS ALLOWED PAST THIS DESK WITHOUT AN I.D. BADGE.
OKAY...HOW DO I GO TO THE SECURITY OFFICE IF I CAN'T GO TO THE SECURITY OFFICE?
8-1-04
GOOD QUESTION. I GUESS YOU'LL HAVE TO SNEAK PAST ME.
LOOK OVER THERE! IT'S AN ANGEL, AND SHE'S GIVING AWAY FREE BACON!
WELL, WELL; IT SEEMS I'VE FOUND A WORTHY ADVERSARY.

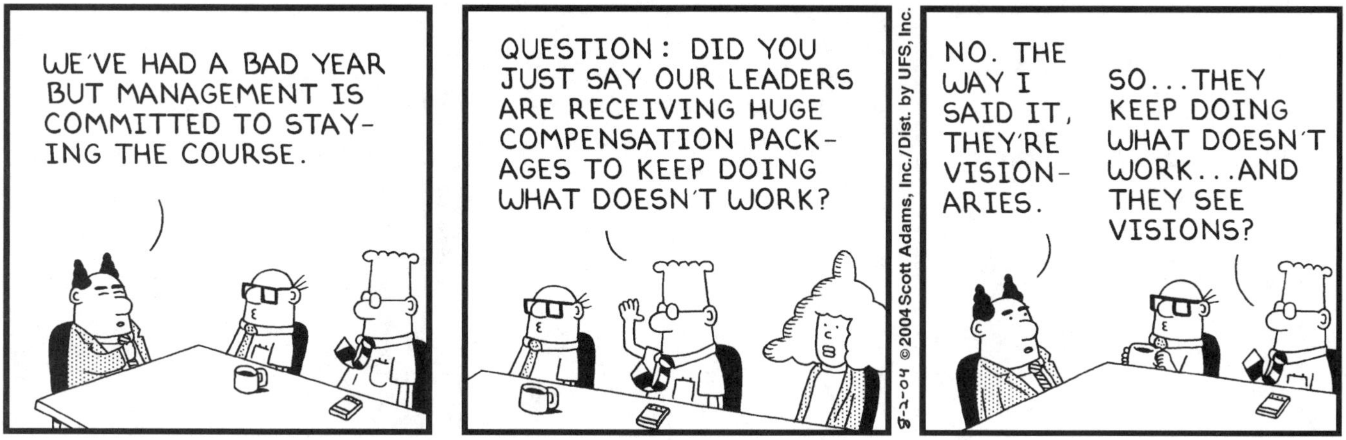
WE'VE HAD A BAD YEAR BUT MANAGEMENT IS COMMITTED TO STAYING THE COURSE.
QUESTION: DID YOU JUST SAY OUR LEADERS ARE RECEIVING HUGE COMPENSATION PACKAGES TO KEEP DOING WHAT DOESN'T WORK?
8-2-04 © 2004 Scott Adams, Inc./Dist. by UFS, Inc.
NO. THE WAY I SAID IT, THEY'RE VISIONARIES.
SO...THEY KEEP DOING WHAT DOESN'T WORK...AND THEY SEE VISIONS?

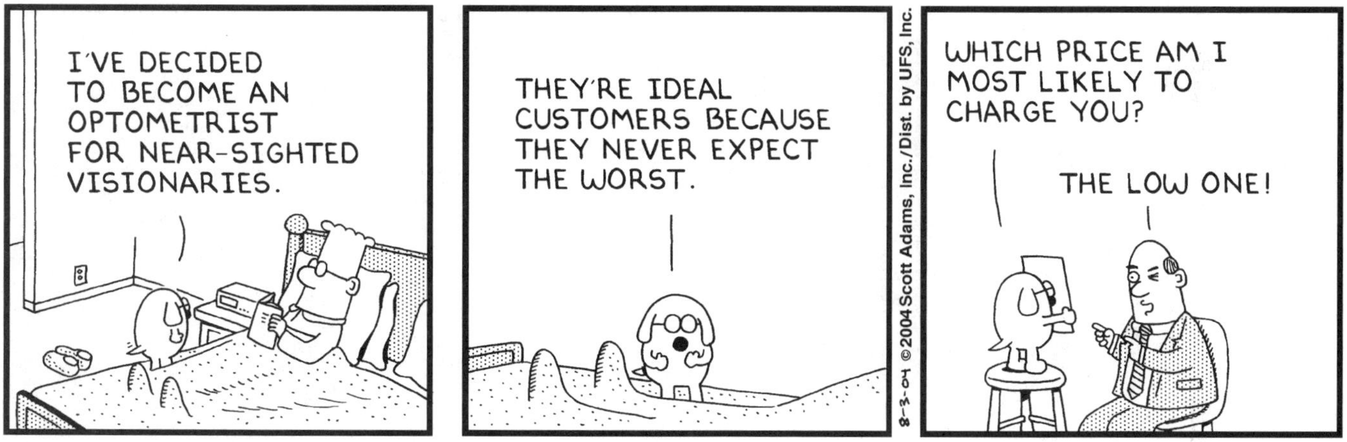
I'VE DECIDED TO BECOME AN OPTOMETRIST FOR NEAR-SIGHTED VISIONARIES.
THEY'RE IDEAL CUSTOMERS BECAUSE THEY NEVER EXPECT THE WORST.
8-3-04 © 2004 Scott Adams, Inc./Dist. by UFS, Inc.
WHICH PRICE AM I MOST LIKELY TO CHARGE YOU?
THE LOW ONE!

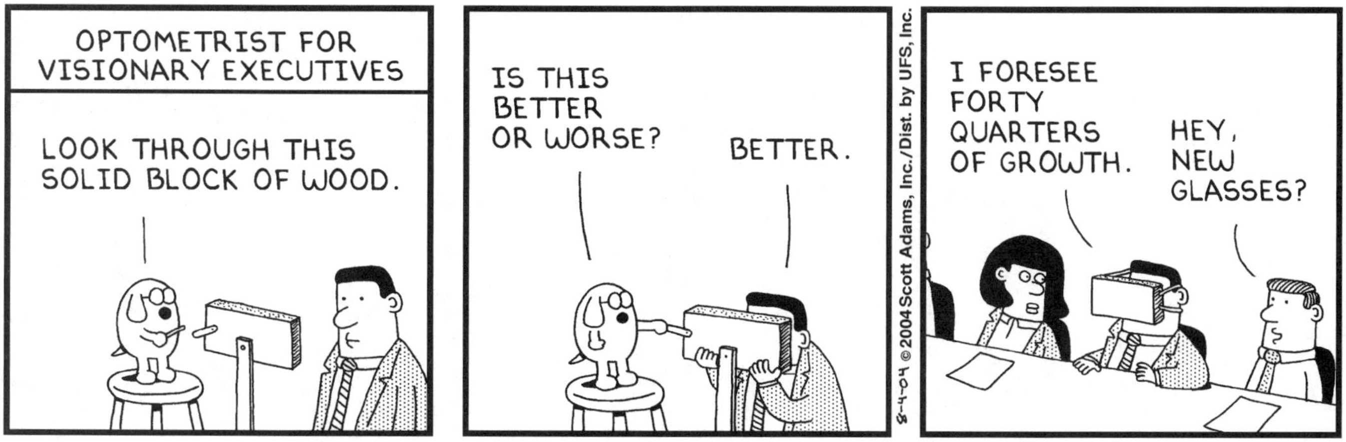
OPTOMETRIST FOR VISIONARY EXECUTIVES
LOOK THROUGH THIS SOLID BLOCK OF WOOD.
IS THIS BETTER OR WORSE?
BETTER.
8-4-04 © 2004 Scott Adams, Inc./Dist. by UFS, Inc.
I FORESEE FORTY QUARTERS OF GROWTH.
HEY, NEW GLASSES?

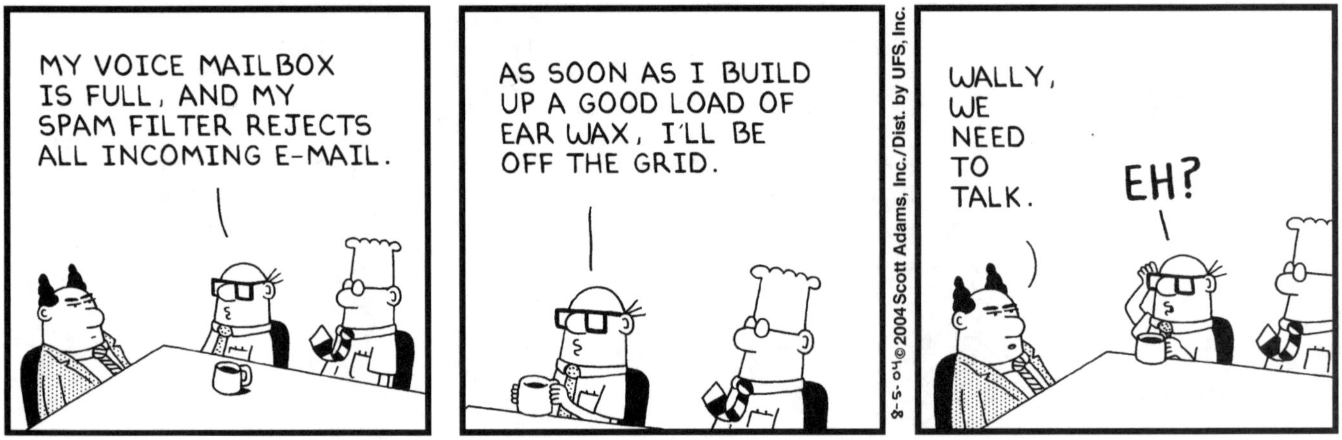
MY VOICE MAILBOX IS FULL, AND MY SPAM FILTER REJECTS ALL INCOMING E-MAIL.
AS SOON AS I BUILD UP A GOOD LOAD OF EAR WAX, I'LL BE OFF THE GRID.
8-5-04 ©2004 Scott Adams, Inc./Dist. by UFS, Inc.
WALLY, WE NEED TO TALK.
EH?

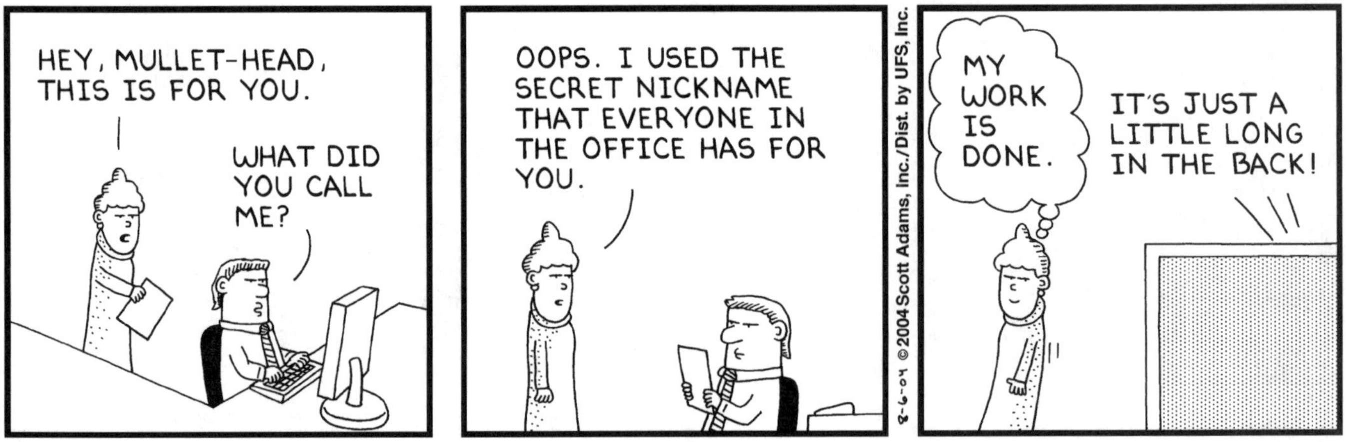
HEY, MULLET-HEAD, THIS IS FOR YOU.
WHAT DID YOU CALL ME?
OOPS. I USED THE SECRET NICKNAME THAT EVERYONE IN THE OFFICE HAS FOR YOU.
8-6-04 ©2004 Scott Adams, Inc./Dist. by UFS, Inc.
MY WORK IS DONE.
IT'S JUST A LITTLE LONG IN THE BACK!

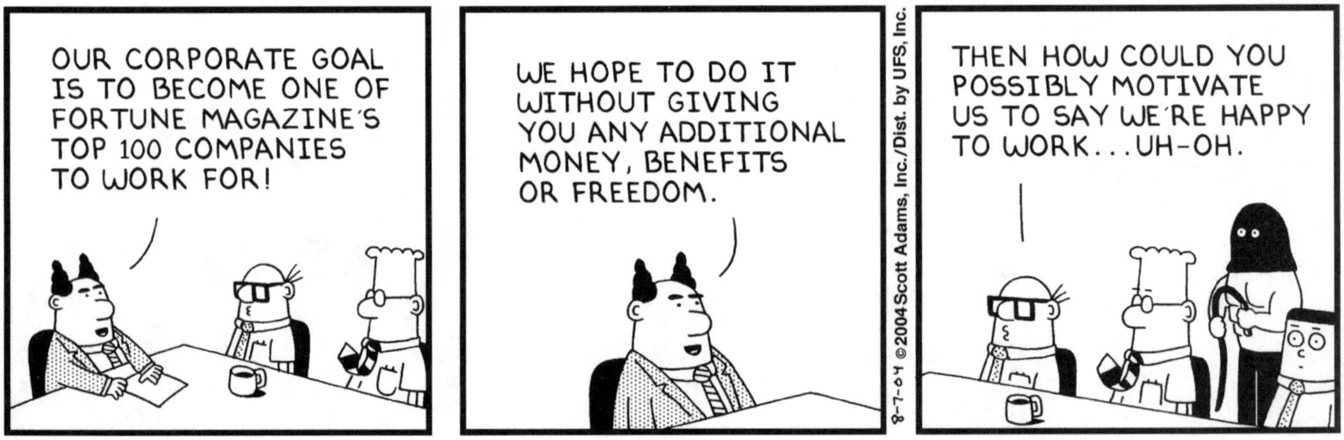
OUR CORPORATE GOAL IS TO BECOME ONE OF FORTUNE MAGAZINE'S TOP 100 COMPANIES TO WORK FOR!
WE HOPE TO DO IT WITHOUT GIVING YOU ANY ADDITIONAL MONEY, BENEFITS OR FREEDOM.
8-7-04 ©2004 Scott Adams, Inc./Dist. by UFS, Inc.
THEN HOW COULD YOU POSSIBLY MOTIVATE US TO SAY WE'RE HAPPY TO WORK...UH-OH.

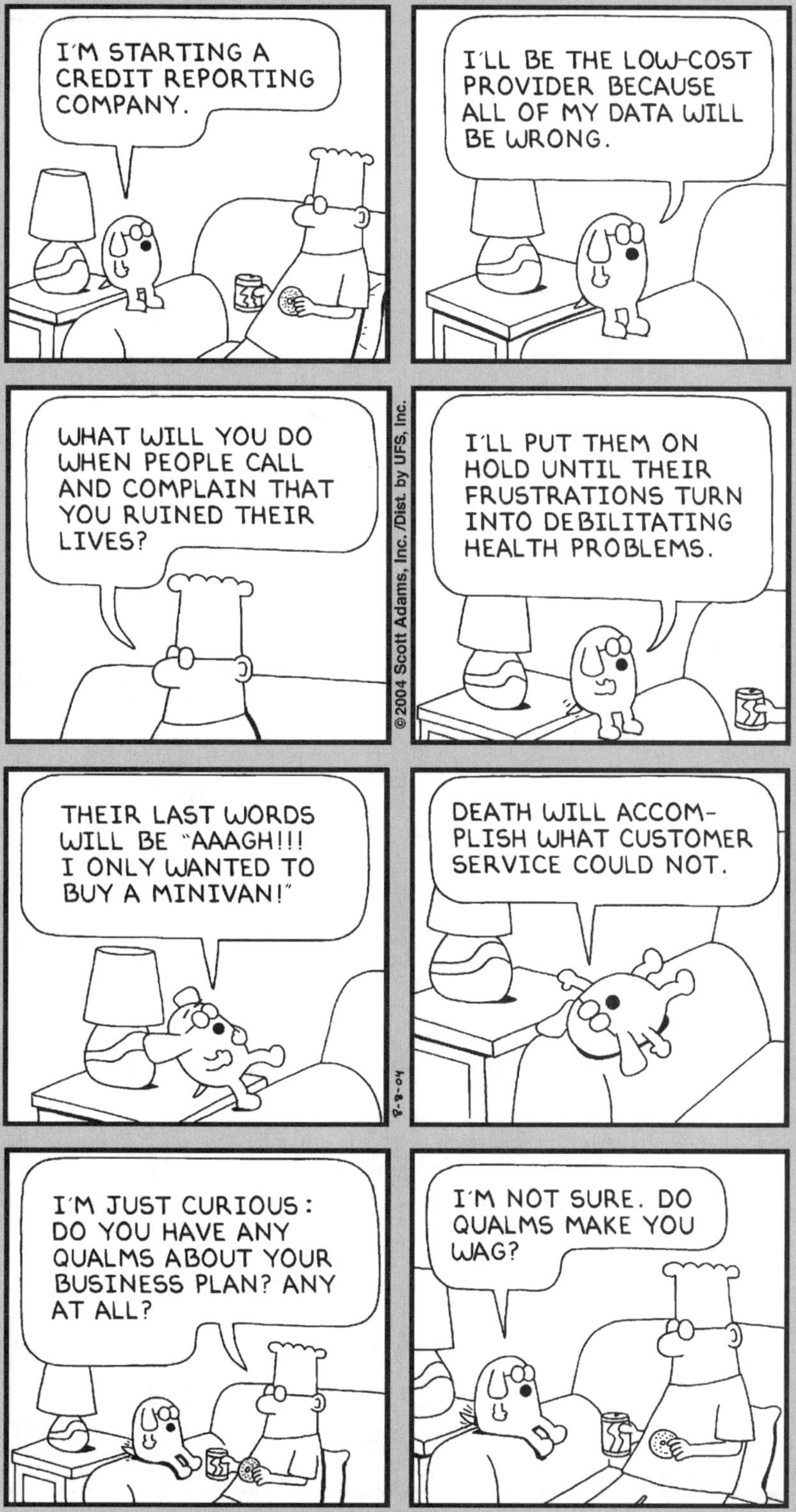
I'M STARTING A CREDIT REPORTING COMPANY.
I'LL BE THE LOW-COST PROVIDER BECAUSE ALL OF MY DATA WILL BE WRONG.
WHAT WILL YOU DO WHEN PEOPLE CALL AND COMPLAIN THAT YOU RUINED THEIR LIVES?
I'LL PUT THEM ON HOLD UNTIL THEIR FRUSTRATIONS TURN INTO DEBILITATING HEALTH PROBLEMS.
THEIR LAST WORDS WILL BE "AAAGH!!! I ONLY WANTED TO BUY A MINIVAN!"
DEATH WILL ACCOM-PLISH WHAT CUSTOMER SERVICE COULD NOT.
I'M JUST CURIOUS: DO YOU HAVE ANY QUALMS ABOUT YOUR BUSINESS PLAN? ANY AT ALL?
I'M NOT SURE. DO QUALMS MAKE YOU WAG?
© 2004 Scott Adams, Inc./Dist. by UFS, Inc.
9-8-04

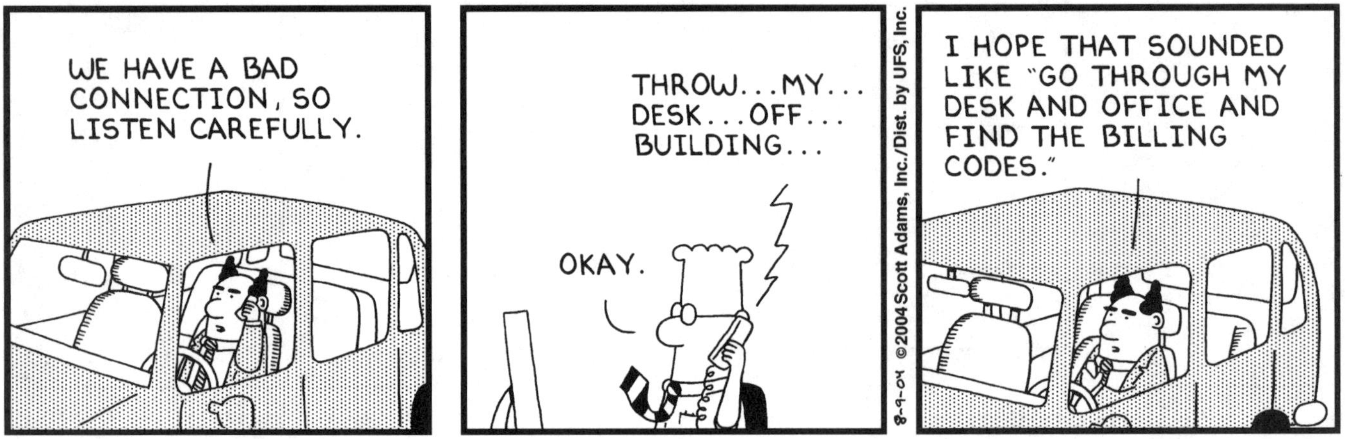
WE HAVE A BAD CONNECTION, SO LISTEN CAREFULLY.
THROW...MY... DESK...OFF... BUILDING...
OKAY.
8-9-04 ©2004 Scott Adams, Inc./Dist. by UFS, Inc.
I HOPE THAT SOUNDED LIKE "GO THROUGH MY DESK AND OFFICE AND FIND THE BILLING CODES."

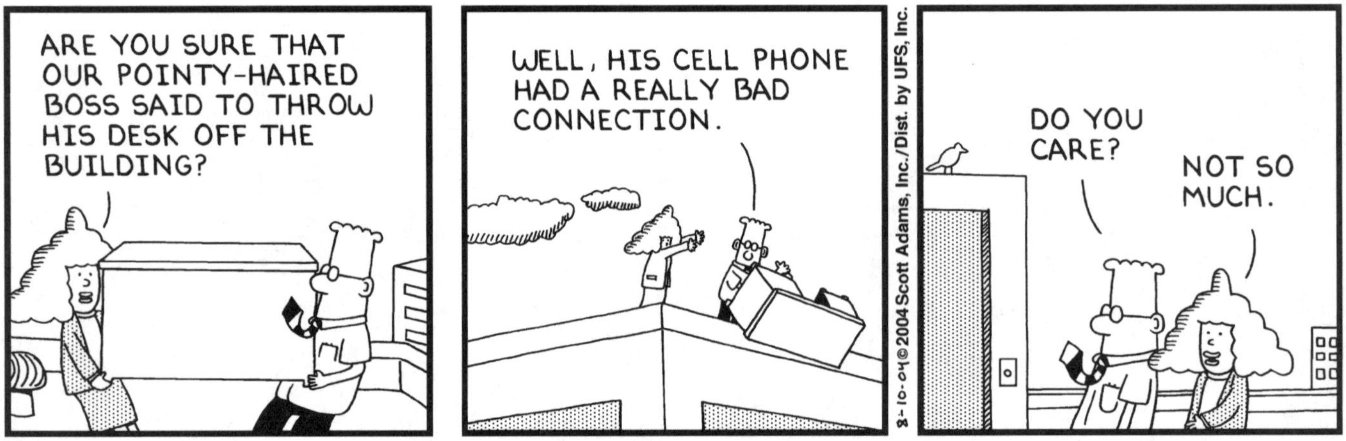
ARE YOU SURE THAT OUR POINTY-HAIRED BOSS SAID TO THROW HIS DESK OFF THE BUILDING?
WELL, HIS CELL PHONE HAD A REALLY BAD CONNECTION.
8-10-04 ©2004 Scott Adams, Inc./Dist. by UFS, Inc.
DO YOU CARE?
NOT SO MUCH.

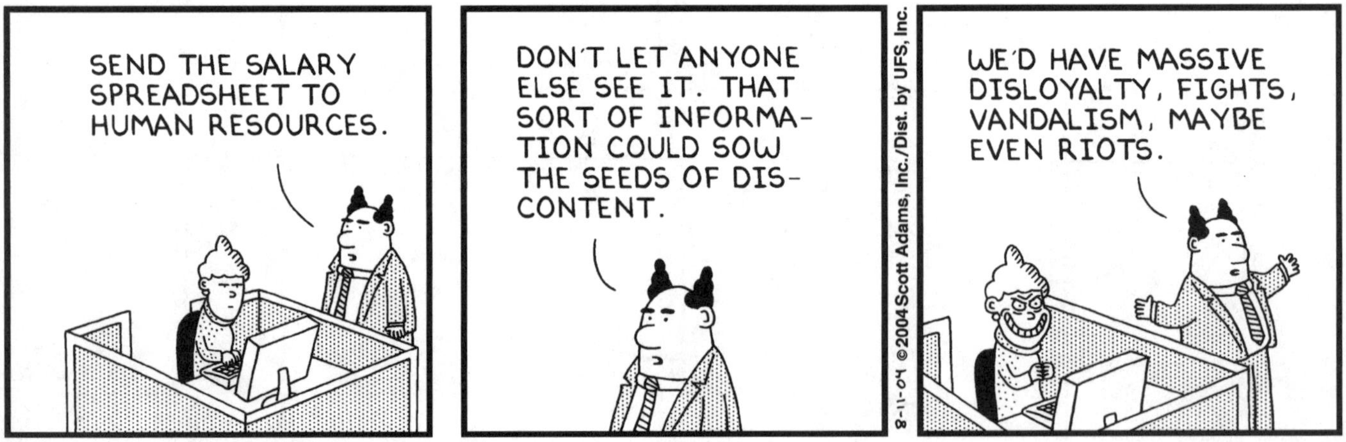
SEND THE SALARY SPREADSHEET TO HUMAN RESOURCES.
DON'T LET ANYONE ELSE SEE IT. THAT SORT OF INFORMA-TION COULD SOW THE SEEDS OF DIS-CONTENT.
8-11-04 ©2004 Scott Adams, Inc./Dist. by UFS, Inc.
WE'D HAVE MASSIVE DISLOYALTY, FIGHTS, VANDALISM, MAYBE EVEN RIOTS.

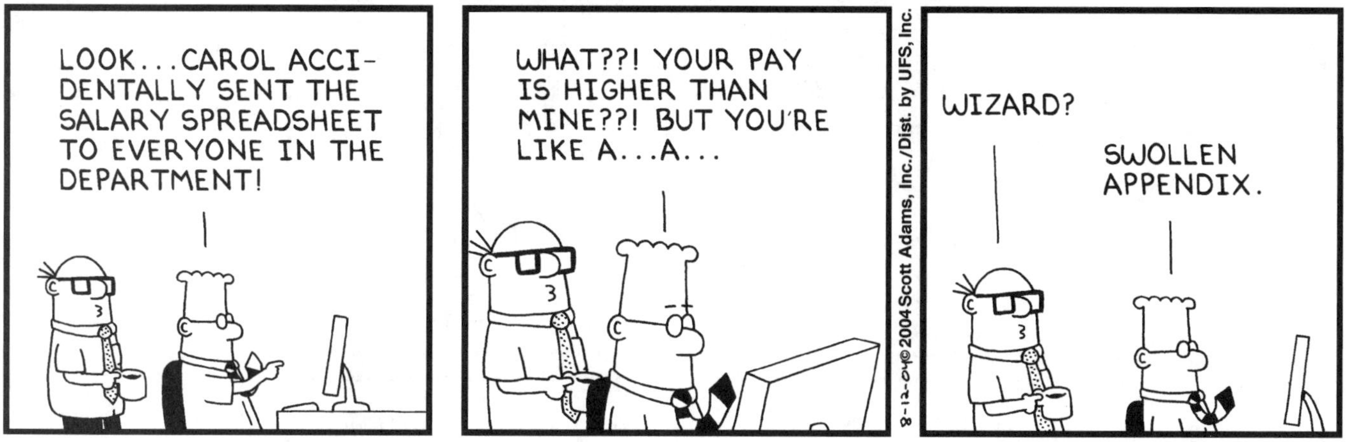
LOOK...CAROL ACCIDENTALLY SENT THE SALARY SPREADSHEET TO EVERYONE IN THE DEPARTMENT!
WHAT??! YOUR PAY IS HIGHER THAN MINE??! BUT YOU'RE LIKE A...A...
8-12-04 © 2004 Scott Adams, Inc./Dist. by UFS, Inc.
WIZARD?
SWOLLEN APPENDIX.

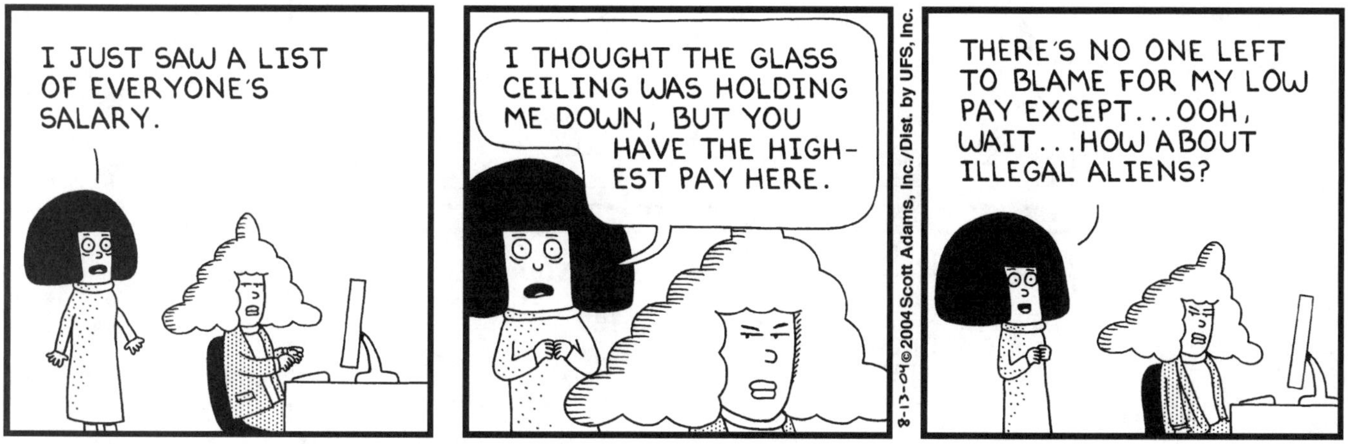
I JUST SAW A LIST OF EVERYONE'S SALARY.
I THOUGHT THE GLASS CEILING WAS HOLDING ME DOWN, BUT YOU HAVE THE HIGHEST PAY HERE.
8-13-04 © 2004 Scott Adams, Inc./Dist. by UFS, Inc.
THERE'S NO ONE LEFT TO BLAME FOR MY LOW PAY EXCEPT...OOH, WAIT...HOW ABOUT ILLEGAL ALIENS?

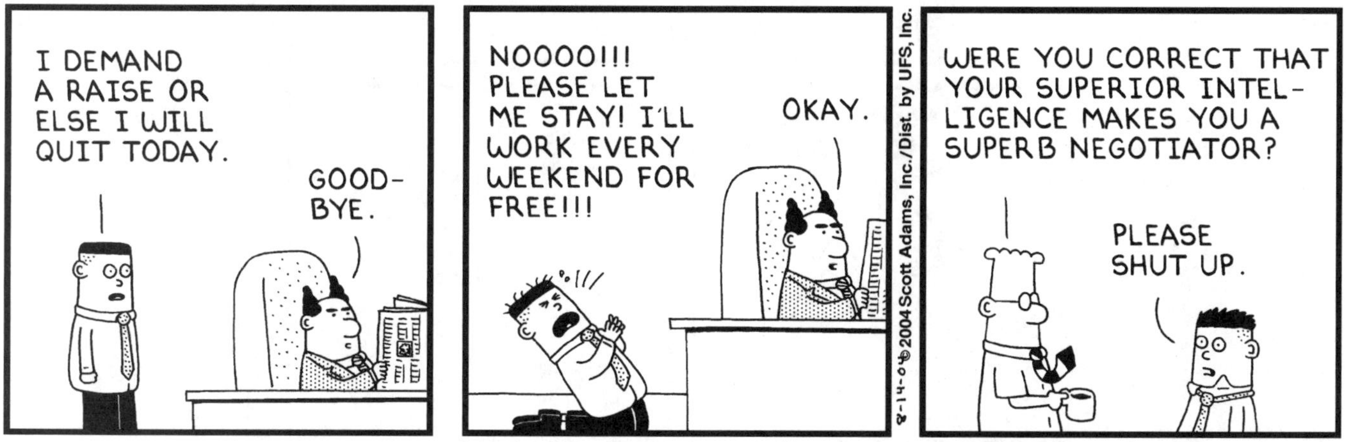
I DEMAND A RAISE OR ELSE I WILL QUIT TODAY.
GOOD-BYE.
NOOOO!!! PLEASE LET ME STAY! I'LL WORK EVERY WEEKEND FOR FREE!!!
OKAY.
8-14-04 © 2004 Scott Adams, Inc./Dist. by UFS, Inc.
WERE YOU CORRECT THAT YOUR SUPERIOR INTELLIGENCE MAKES YOU A SUPERB NEGOTIATOR?
PLEASE SHUT UP.

WE'RE OUTSOURCING OUR SATELLITE LAUNCH PROGRAM TO ELBONIA.
WE BUILT THE BILLION-DOLLAR SATELLITE HERE; THE ELBONIANS WILL PUT IT INTO ORBIT.
DILBERT, I WANT YOU TO BE OUR LIAISON.
AAAAGH!!!
© 2004 Scott Adams, Inc./Dist. by UFS, Inc.
THAT'S OUR INSURANCE COMPANY. THEY'VE BEEN JUMPY LATELY.
IN ELBONIA
OUR PLAN IS TO TEASE A PIG UNTIL HE KICKS THE SATELLITE INTO ORBIT.
8-15-04
THE RISK IS THAT OUR PIG MIGHT PREFER FISTICUFFS.
SLEDGEHAMMER! ABORT! ABORT!
IT WAS HOLLOW.
DON'T MENTION THAT TO OUR INSURANCE COMPANY.

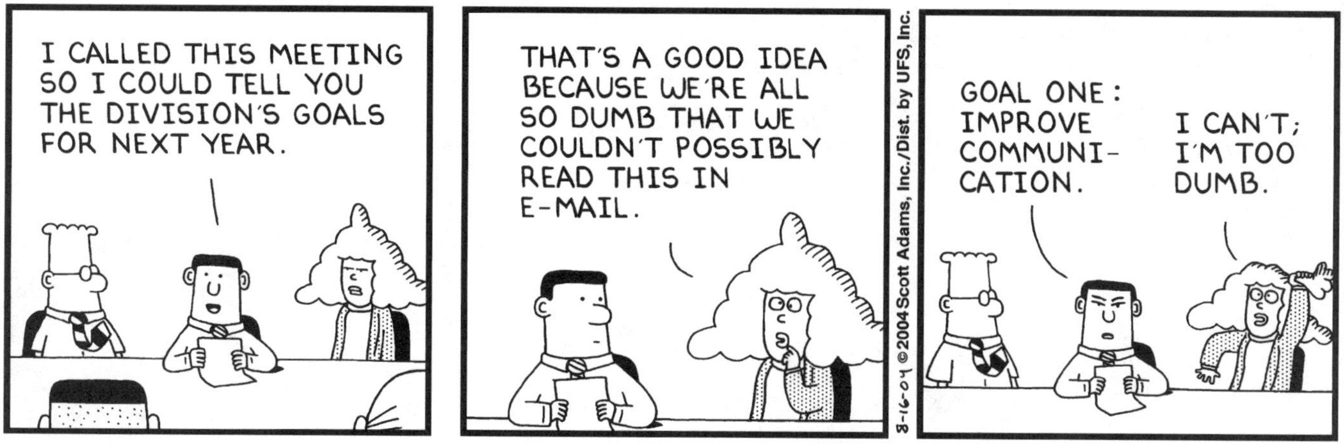
I CALLED THIS MEETING SO I COULD TELL YOU THE DIVISION'S GOALS FOR NEXT YEAR.
THAT'S A GOOD IDEA BECAUSE WE'RE ALL SO DUMB THAT WE COULDN'T POSSIBLY READ THIS IN E-MAIL.
GOAL ONE: IMPROVE COMMUNI-CATION.
I CAN'T; I'M TOO DUMB.
8-16-04 ©2004 Scott Adams, Inc./Dist. by UFS, Inc.

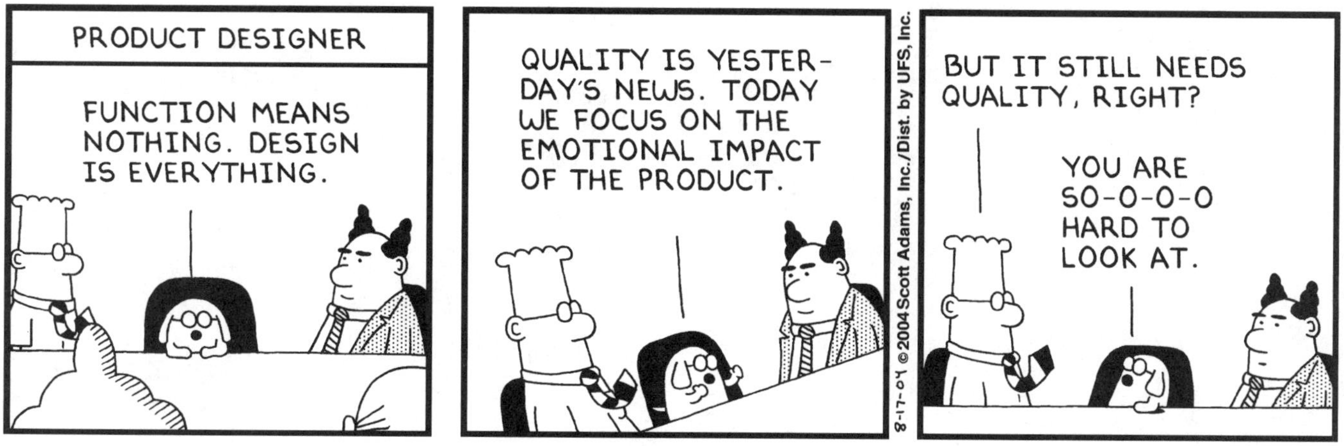
PRODUCT DESIGNER
FUNCTION MEANS NOTHING. DESIGN IS EVERYTHING.
QUALITY IS YESTER-DAY'S NEWS. TODAY WE FOCUS ON THE EMOTIONAL IMPACT OF THE PRODUCT.
BUT IT STILL NEEDS QUALITY, RIGHT?
YOU ARE SO-O-O-O HARD TO LOOK AT.
8-17-04 ©2004 Scott Adams, Inc./Dist. by UFS, Inc.

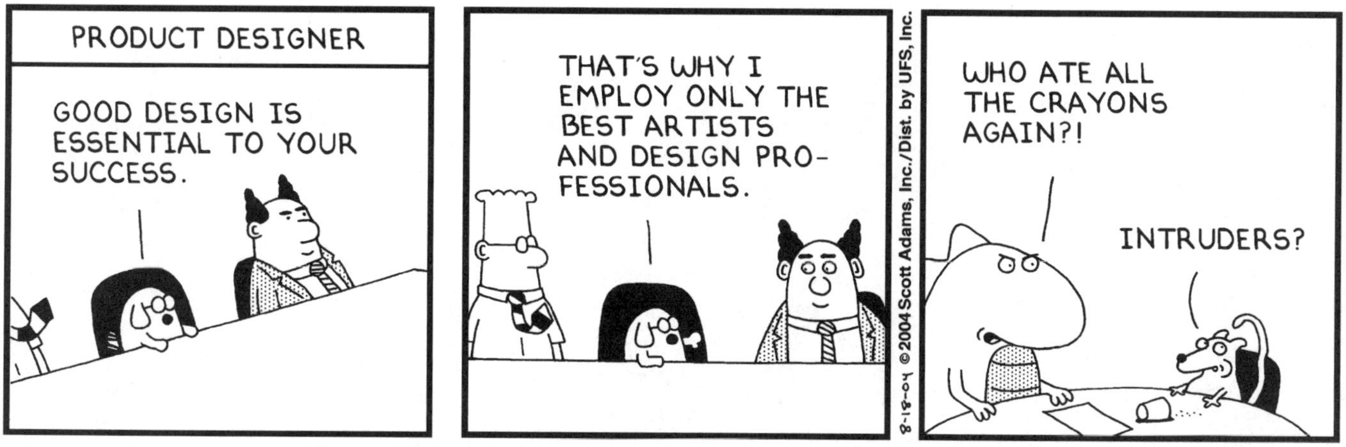
PRODUCT DESIGNER
GOOD DESIGN IS ESSENTIAL TO YOUR SUCCESS.
THAT'S WHY I EMPLOY ONLY THE BEST ARTISTS AND DESIGN PRO-FESSIONALS.
WHO ATE ALL THE CRAYONS AGAIN?!
INTRUDERS?
8-18-04 ©2004 Scott Adams, Inc./Dist. by UFS, Inc.

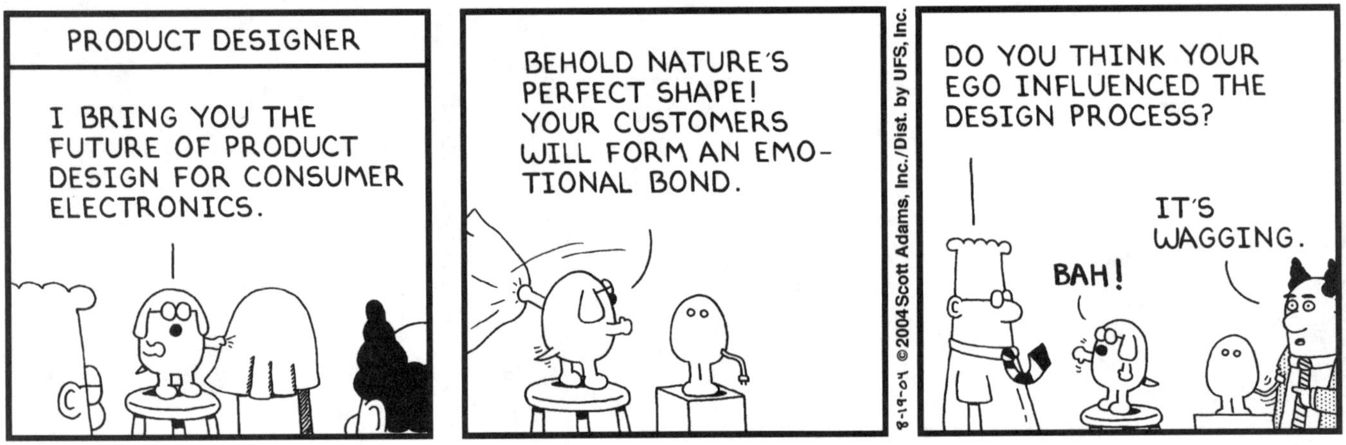
PRODUCT DESIGNER
I BRING YOU THE FUTURE OF PRODUCT DESIGN FOR CONSUMER ELECTRONICS.
BEHOLD NATURE'S PERFECT SHAPE! YOUR CUSTOMERS WILL FORM AN EMO-TIONAL BOND.
8-19-04 © 2004 Scott Adams, Inc./Dist. by UFS, Inc.
DO YOU THINK YOUR EGO INFLUENCED THE DESIGN PROCESS?
BAH!
IT'S WAGGING.

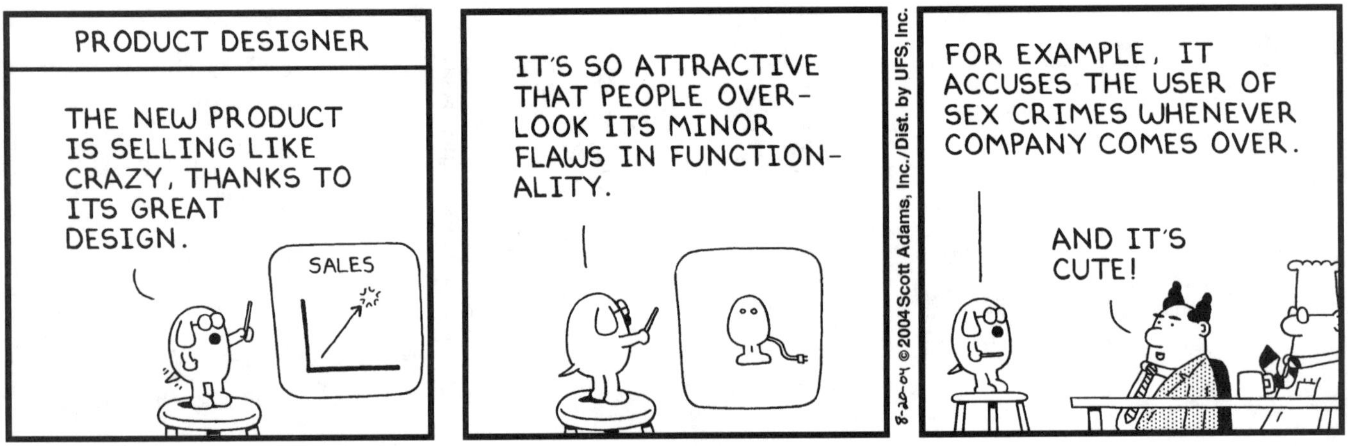
PRODUCT DESIGNER
THE NEW PRODUCT IS SELLING LIKE CRAZY, THANKS TO ITS GREAT DESIGN.
SALES
IT'S SO ATTRACTIVE THAT PEOPLE OVER-LOOK ITS MINOR FLAWS IN FUNCTION-ALITY.
8-20-04 © 2004 Scott Adams, Inc./Dist. by UFS, Inc.
FOR EXAMPLE, IT ACCUSES THE USER OF SEX CRIMES WHENEVER COMPANY COMES OVER.
AND IT'S CUTE!

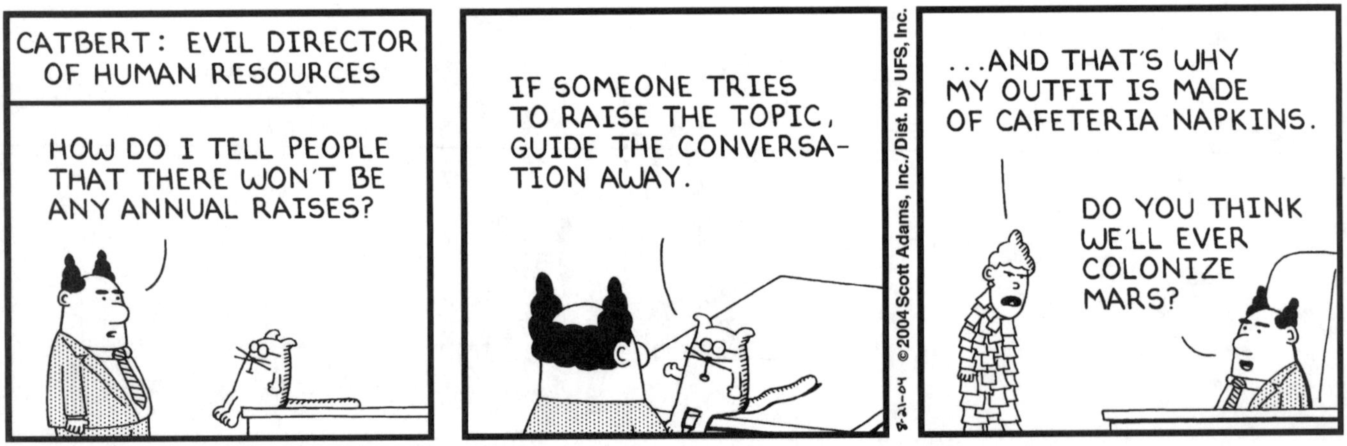
CATBERT: EVIL DIRECTOR OF HUMAN RESOURCES
HOW DO I TELL PEOPLE THAT THERE WON'T BE ANY ANNUAL RAISES?
IF SOMEONE TRIES TO RAISE THE TOPIC, GUIDE THE CONVERSA-TION AWAY.
8-21-04 © 2004 Scott Adams, Inc./Dist. by UFS, Inc.
...AND THAT'S WHY MY OUTFIT IS MADE OF CAFETERIA NAPKINS.
DO YOU THINK WE'LL EVER COLONIZE MARS?

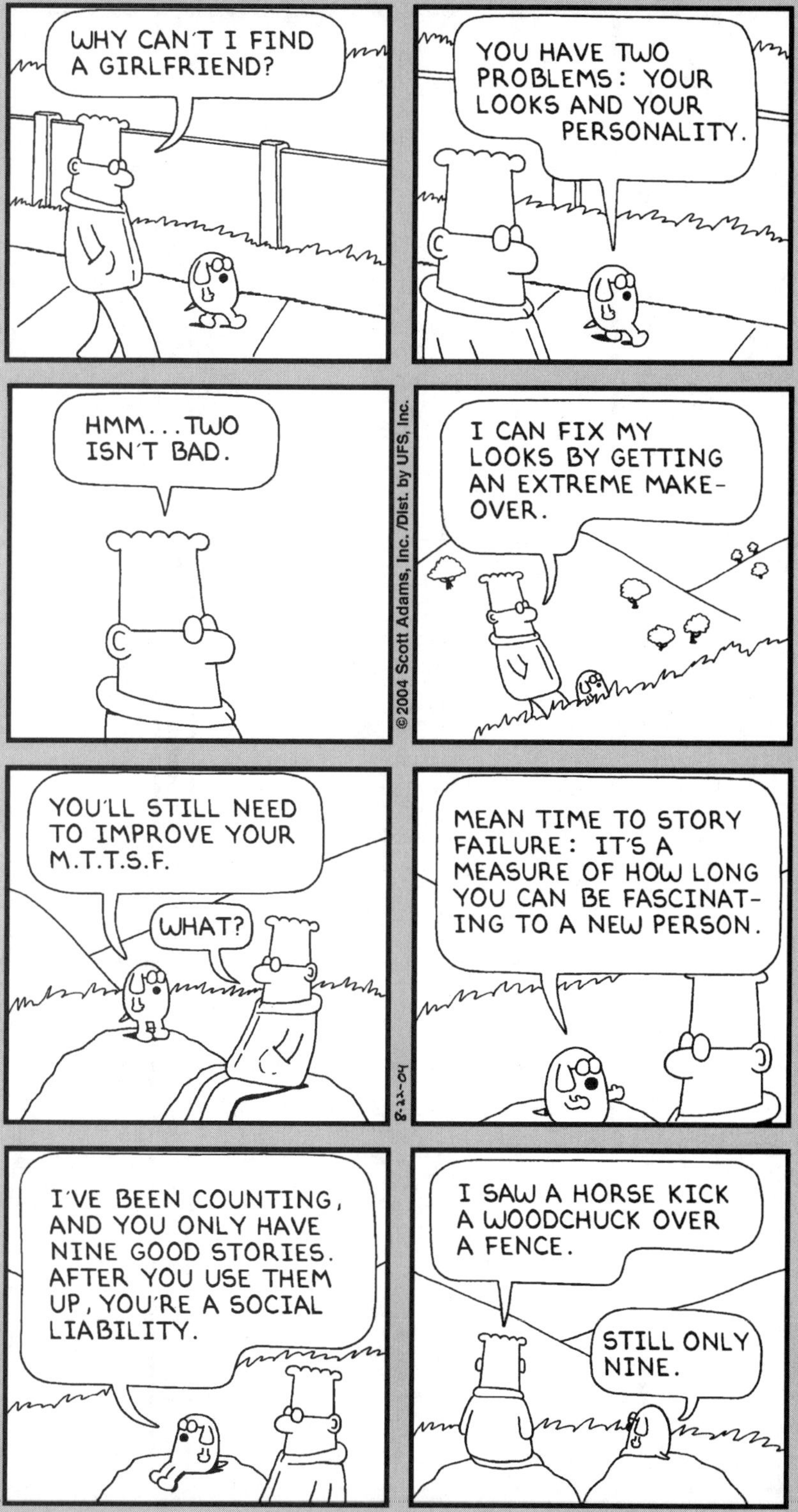
WHY CAN'T I FIND A GIRLFRIEND?
YOU HAVE TWO PROBLEMS: YOUR LOOKS AND YOUR PERSONALITY.
HMM...TWO ISN'T BAD.
I CAN FIX MY LOOKS BY GETTING AN EXTREME MAKE-OVER.
YOU'LL STILL NEED TO IMPROVE YOUR M.T.T.S.F.
WHAT?
MEAN TIME TO STORY FAILURE: IT'S A MEASURE OF HOW LONG YOU CAN BE FASCINATING TO A NEW PERSON.
I'VE BEEN COUNTING, AND YOU ONLY HAVE NINE GOOD STORIES. AFTER YOU USE THEM UP, YOU'RE A SOCIAL LIABILITY.
I SAW A HORSE KICK A WOODCHUCK OVER A FENCE.
STILL ONLY NINE.
©2004 Scott Adams, Inc. /Dist. by UFS, Inc.
8-22-04

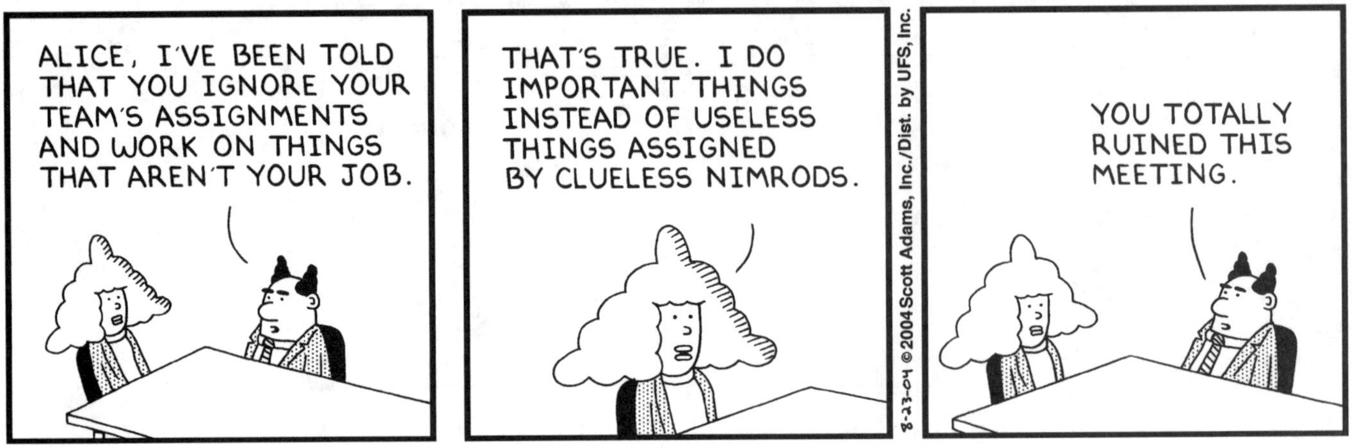
ALICE, I'VE BEEN TOLD THAT YOU IGNORE YOUR TEAM'S ASSIGNMENTS AND WORK ON THINGS THAT AREN'T YOUR JOB.
THAT'S TRUE. I DO IMPORTANT THINGS INSTEAD OF USELESS THINGS ASSIGNED BY CLUELESS NIMRODS.
8-23-04 ©2004 Scott Adams, Inc./Dist. by UFS, Inc.
YOU TOTALLY RUINED THIS MEETING.

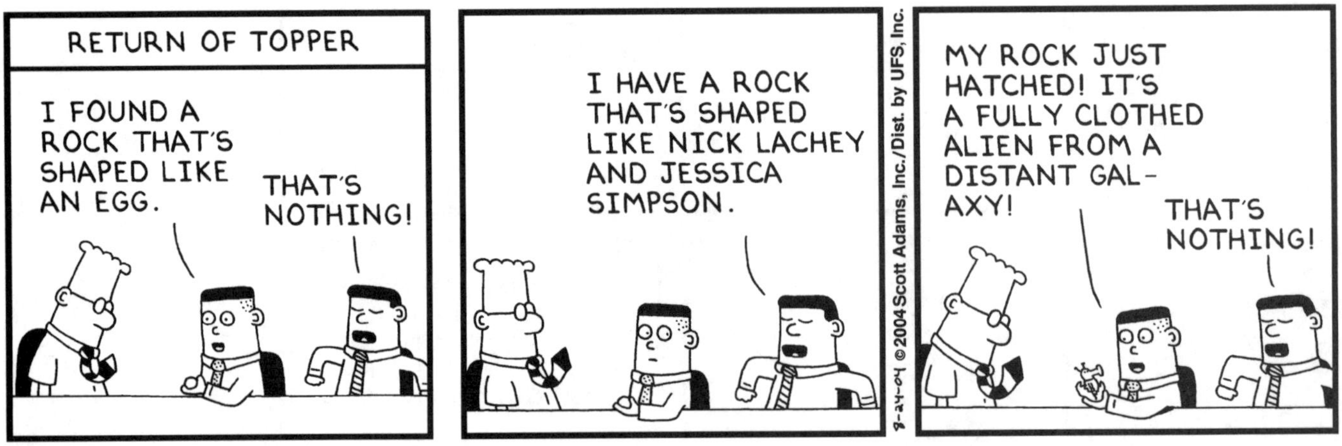
RETURN OF TOPPER
I FOUND A ROCK THAT'S SHAPED LIKE AN EGG.
THAT'S NOTHING!
I HAVE A ROCK THAT'S SHAPED LIKE NICK LACHEY AND JESSICA SIMPSON.
8-24-04 ©2004 Scott Adams, Inc./Dist. by UFS, Inc.
MY ROCK JUST HATCHED! IT'S A FULLY CLOTHED ALIEN FROM A DISTANT GAL-AXY!
THAT'S NOTHING!

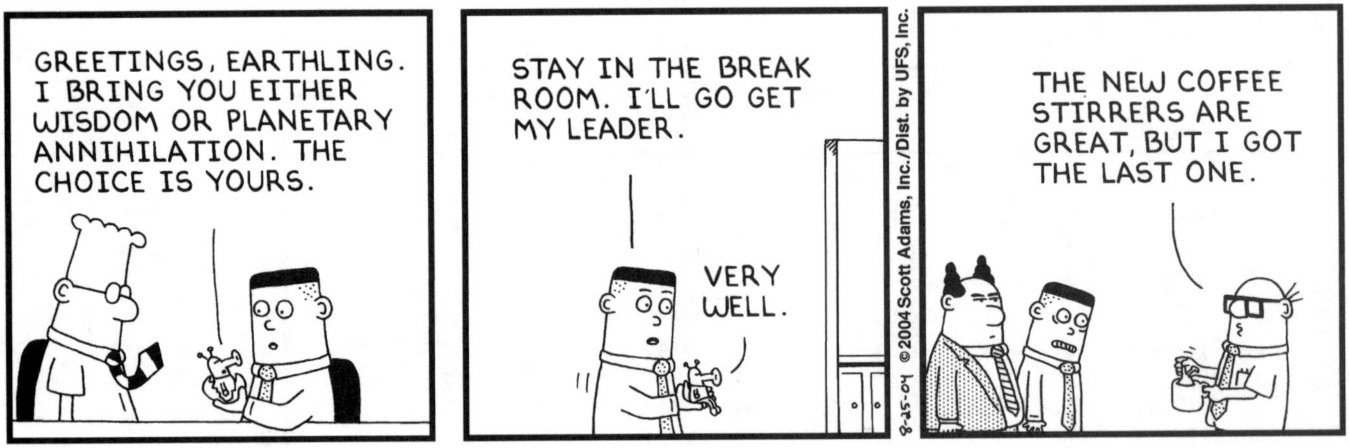
GREETINGS, EARTHLING. I BRING YOU EITHER WISDOM OR PLANETARY ANNIHILATION. THE CHOICE IS YOURS.
STAY IN THE BREAK ROOM. I'LL GO GET MY LEADER.
VERY WELL.
8-25-04 ©2004 Scott Adams, Inc./Dist. by UFS, Inc.
THE NEW COFFEE STIRRERS ARE GREAT, BUT I GOT THE LAST ONE.

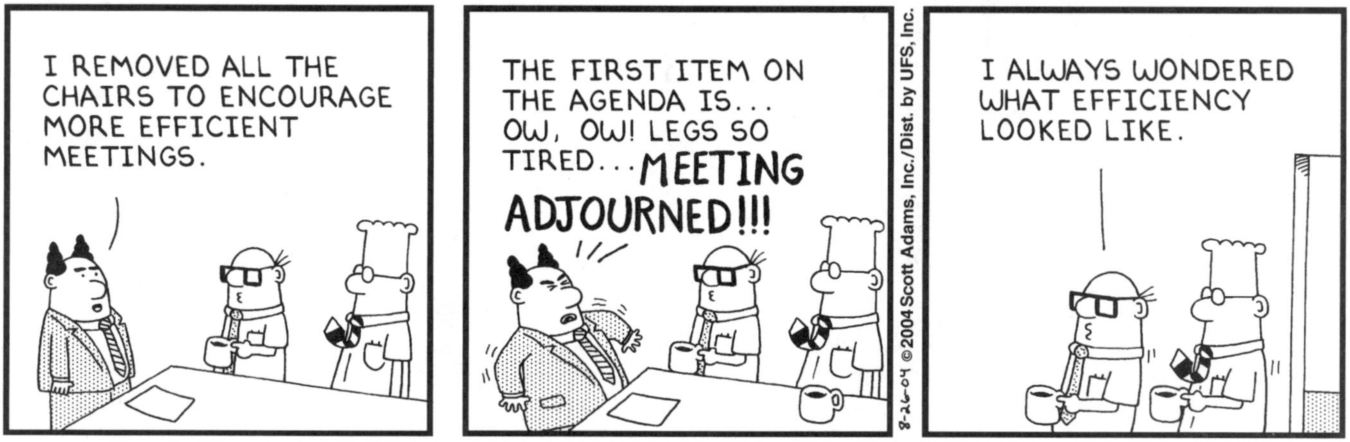
I REMOVED ALL THE CHAIRS TO ENCOURAGE MORE EFFICIENT MEETINGS.
THE FIRST ITEM ON THE AGENDA IS... OW, OW! LEGS SO TIRED... MEETING ADJOURNED!!!
I ALWAYS WONDERED WHAT EFFICIENCY LOOKED LIKE.
8-26-04 ©2004 Scott Adams, Inc./Dist. by UFS, Inc.

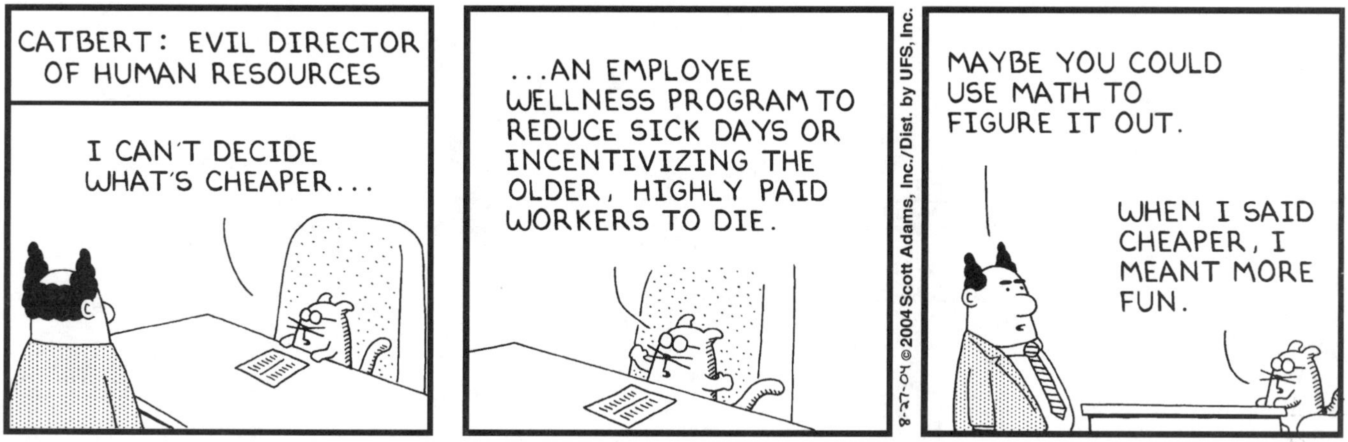
CATBERT: EVIL DIRECTOR OF HUMAN RESOURCES
I CAN'T DECIDE WHAT'S CHEAPER...
...AN EMPLOYEE WELLNESS PROGRAM TO REDUCE SICK DAYS OR INCENTIVIZING THE OLDER, HIGHLY PAID WORKERS TO DIE.
MAYBE YOU COULD USE MATH TO FIGURE IT OUT.
WHEN I SAID CHEAPER, I MEANT MORE FUN.
8-27-04 ©2004 Scott Adams, Inc./Dist. by UFS, Inc.

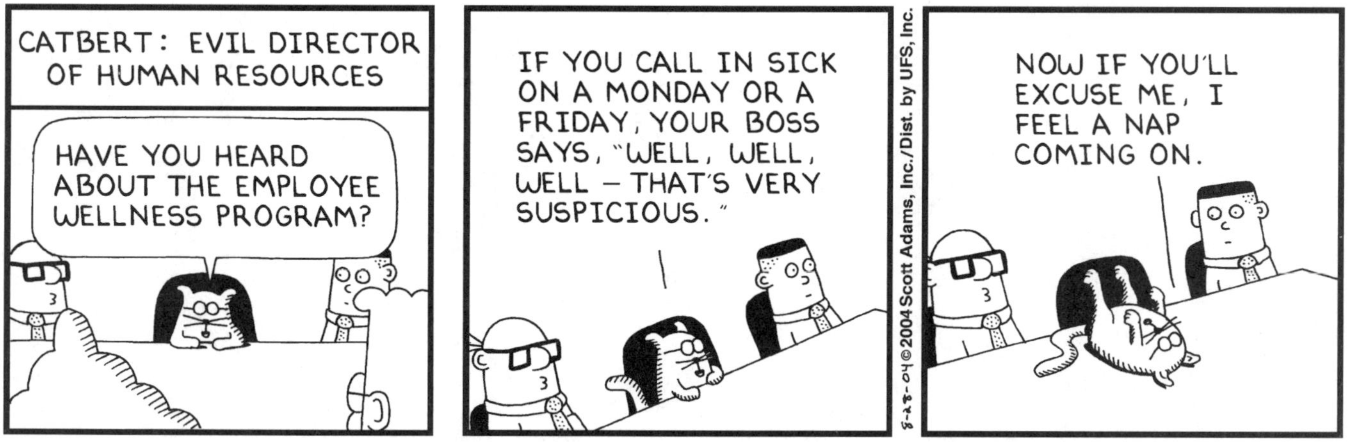
CATBERT: EVIL DIRECTOR OF HUMAN RESOURCES
HAVE YOU HEARD ABOUT THE EMPLOYEE WELLNESS PROGRAM?
IF YOU CALL IN SICK ON A MONDAY OR A FRIDAY, YOUR BOSS SAYS, "WELL, WELL, WELL – THAT'S VERY SUSPICIOUS."
NOW IF YOU'LL EXCUSE ME, I FEEL A NAP COMING ON.
8-28-04 ©2004 Scott Adams, Inc./Dist. by UFS, Inc.

OUR BONUSES WILL DEPEND ON THE RESULTS OF THE EMPLOYEE ATTITUDE SURVEY.
IF WE BOOST OUR MORALE RANK, WE'LL GET BIGGER BONUSES.
GET IT? ALL YOU HAVE TO DO IS SAY YOU'RE HAPPY AND YOU GET MONEY.
WINK WINK WINK
YOU WANT US TO LIE?
NO-O-O-O! HEAVEN FORBID. ABSOLUTELY NO LYING.
BUT IF YOU DID LIE, IMAGINE THE THINGS YOU COULD BUY WITH THAT MONEY.
I'LL HAND OUT THE SURVEYS AND YOU CAN LET YOUR CON-SCIENCE GUIDE YOU.
IS "PARA-DISE" TOO OVER THE TOP?
I'M GOING TO LIE ME UP A NEW COUCH!
8-29-04

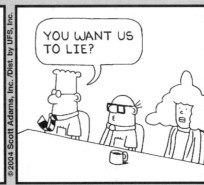

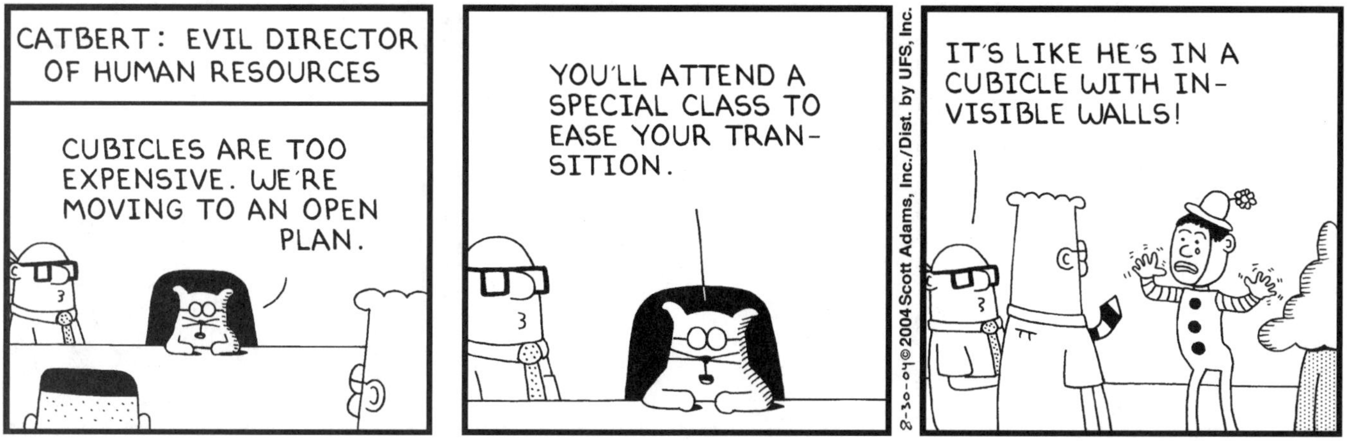
CATBERT: EVIL DIRECTOR OF HUMAN RESOURCES
CUBICLES ARE TOO EXPENSIVE. WE'RE MOVING TO AN OPEN PLAN.
YOU'LL ATTEND A SPECIAL CLASS TO EASE YOUR TRANSITION.
8-30-04 © 2004 Scott Adams, Inc./Dist. by UFS, Inc.
IT'S LIKE HE'S IN A CUBICLE WITH INVISIBLE WALLS!

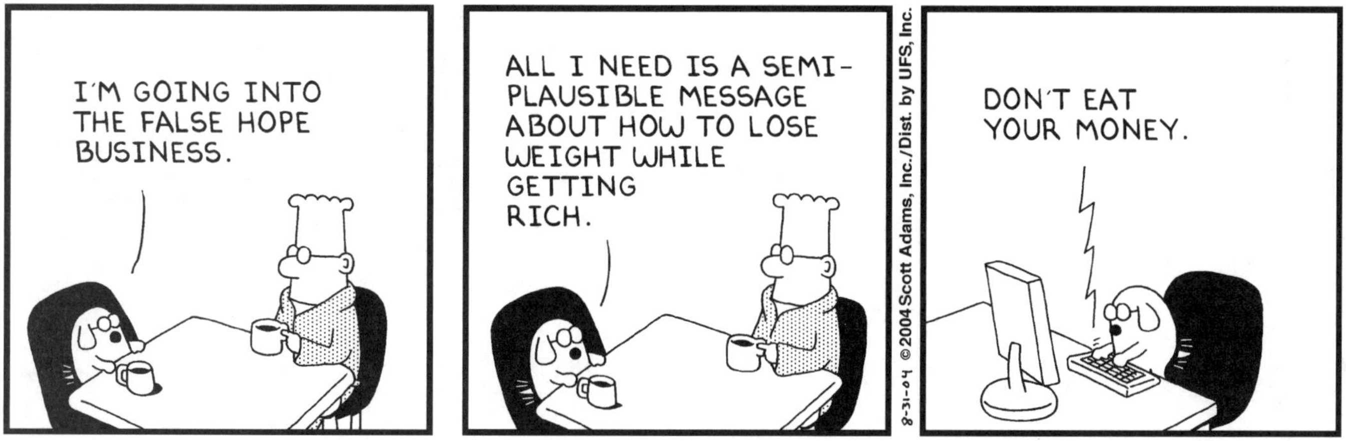
I'M GOING INTO THE FALSE HOPE BUSINESS.
ALL I NEED IS A SEMI-PLAUSIBLE MESSAGE ABOUT HOW TO LOSE WEIGHT WHILE GETTING RICH.
8-31-04 © 2004 Scott Adams, Inc./Dist. by UFS, Inc.
DON'T EAT YOUR MONEY.

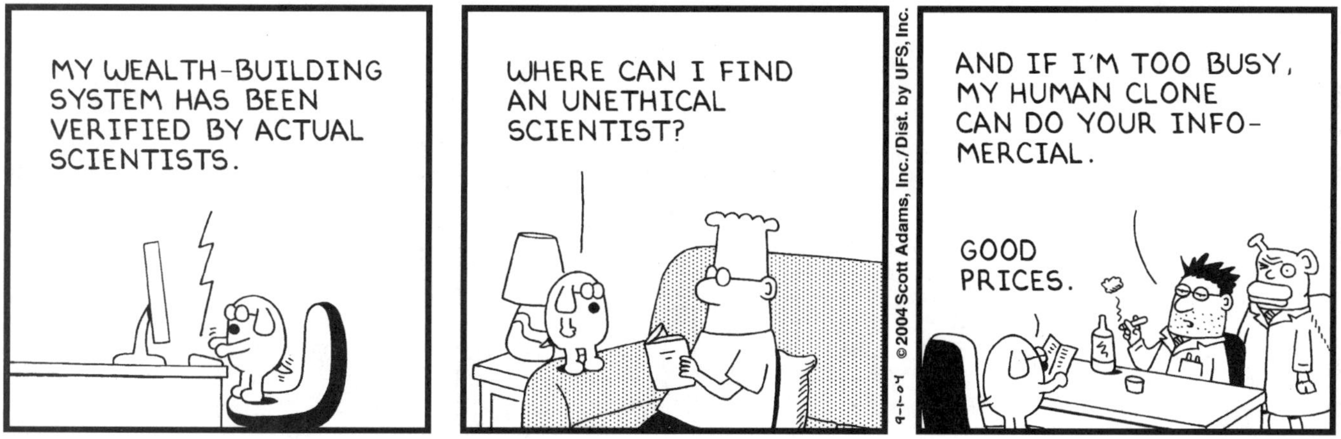
MY WEALTH-BUILDING SYSTEM HAS BEEN VERIFIED BY ACTUAL SCIENTISTS.
WHERE CAN I FIND AN UNETHICAL SCIENTIST?
9-1-04 © 2004 Scott Adams, Inc./Dist. by UFS, Inc.
AND IF I'M TOO BUSY, MY HUMAN CLONE CAN DO YOUR INFOMERCIAL.
GOOD PRICES.

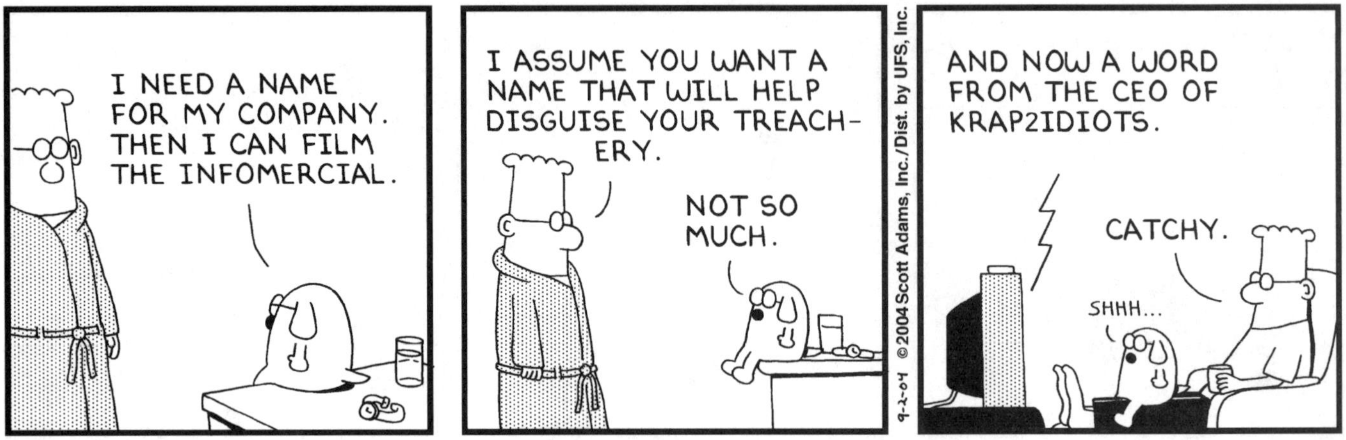
I NEED A NAME FOR MY COMPANY. THEN I CAN FILM THE INFOMERCIAL.
I ASSUME YOU WANT A NAME THAT WILL HELP DISGUISE YOUR TREACHERY.
NOT SO MUCH.
9-2-04 ©2004 Scott Adams, Inc./Dist. by UFS, Inc.
AND NOW A WORD FROM THE CEO OF KRAP2IDIOTS.
CATCHY.
SHHH...

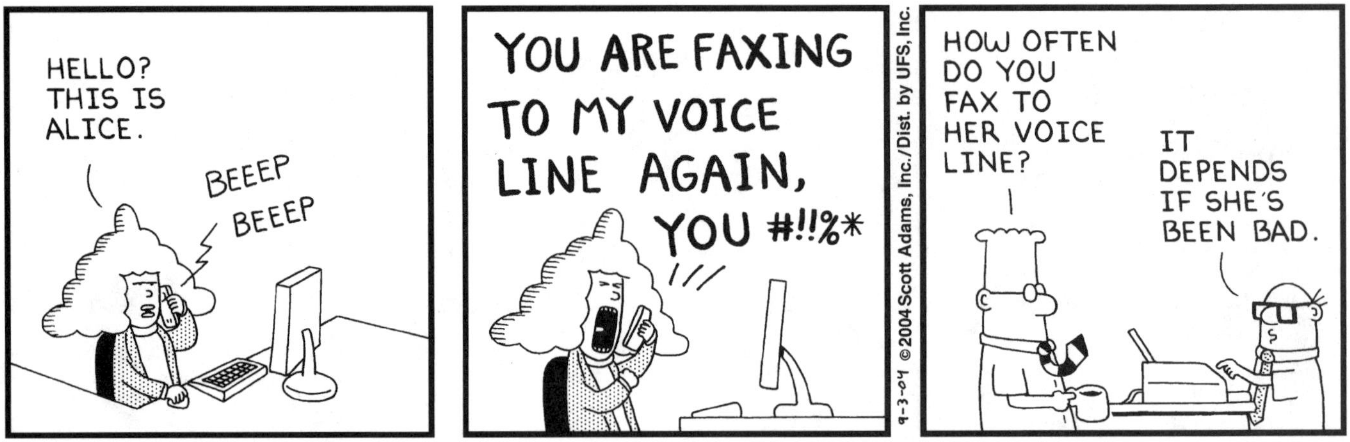
HELLO? THIS IS ALICE.
BEEEP
BEEEP
YOU ARE FAXING TO MY VOICE LINE AGAIN, YOU #!!%*
9-3-04 ©2004 Scott Adams, Inc./Dist. by UFS, Inc.
HOW OFTEN DO YOU FAX TO HER VOICE LINE?
IT DEPENDS IF SHE'S BEEN BAD.

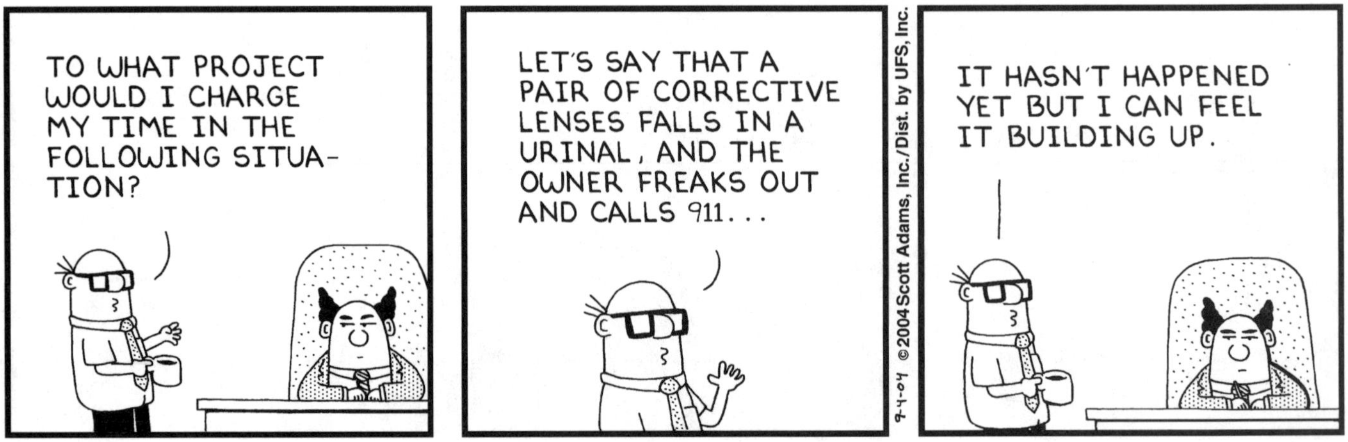
TO WHAT PROJECT WOULD I CHARGE MY TIME IN THE FOLLOWING SITUATION?
LET'S SAY THAT A PAIR OF CORRECTIVE LENSES FALLS IN A URINAL, AND THE OWNER FREAKS OUT AND CALLS 911...
9-4-04 ©2004 Scott Adams, Inc./Dist. by UFS, Inc.
IT HASN'T HAPPENED YET BUT I CAN FEEL IT BUILDING UP.

OUR BUDGET WON'T COVER ALL OF THE PRODUCT DEVELOP-MENT.
WE CAN ONLY DO TWO-THIRDS OF THE FEATURES FOR THAT AMOUNT.
REDUCE THE SCOPE OF THE PROJECT BY ONE-THIRD.
OKAY.
BUT... THEORETICALLY...
©2004 Scott Adams, Inc. /Dist. by UFS, Inc.
NO...DEAR LORD, NO.
9-5-04
IF I LATER GIVE YOU A CHANGE REQUEST TO ADD ONE FEATURE, COULD YOU DO IT FOR THE SAME BUDGET.
ONE? SURE.
DATA GOES IN; MAN-AGEMENT COMES OUT.
ONE? SURE.
CHANGES ARE FREE.
WHERE DO I PUT THE CHANGE REQUESTS?

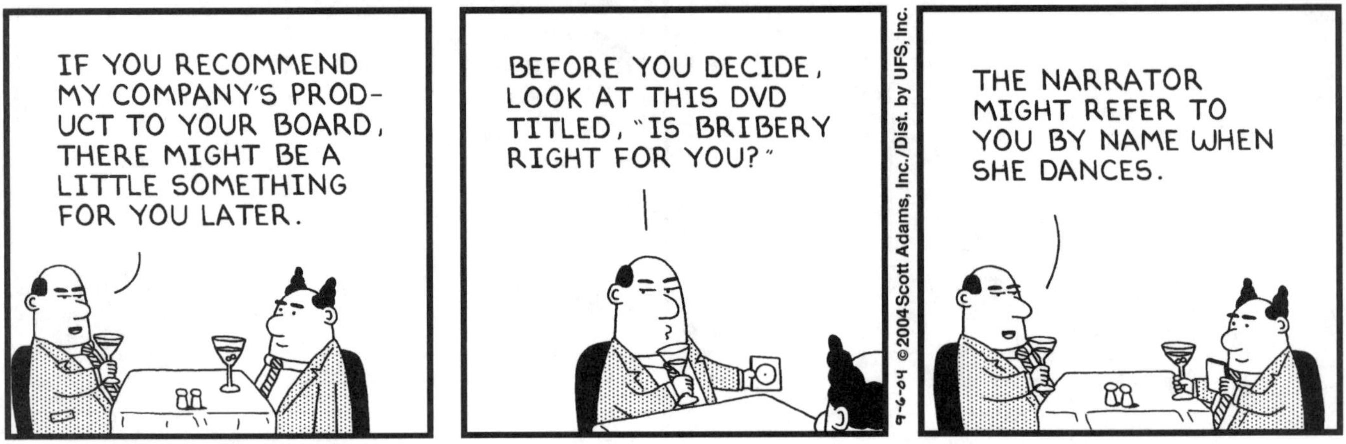
IF YOU RECOMMEND MY COMPANY'S PROD-UCT TO YOUR BOARD, THERE MIGHT BE A LITTLE SOMETHING FOR YOU LATER.
BEFORE YOU DECIDE, LOOK AT THIS DVD TITLED, "IS BRIBERY RIGHT FOR YOU?"
9-6-04 ©2004 Scott Adams, Inc./Dist. by UFS, Inc.
THE NARRATOR MIGHT REFER TO YOU BY NAME WHEN SHE DANCES.

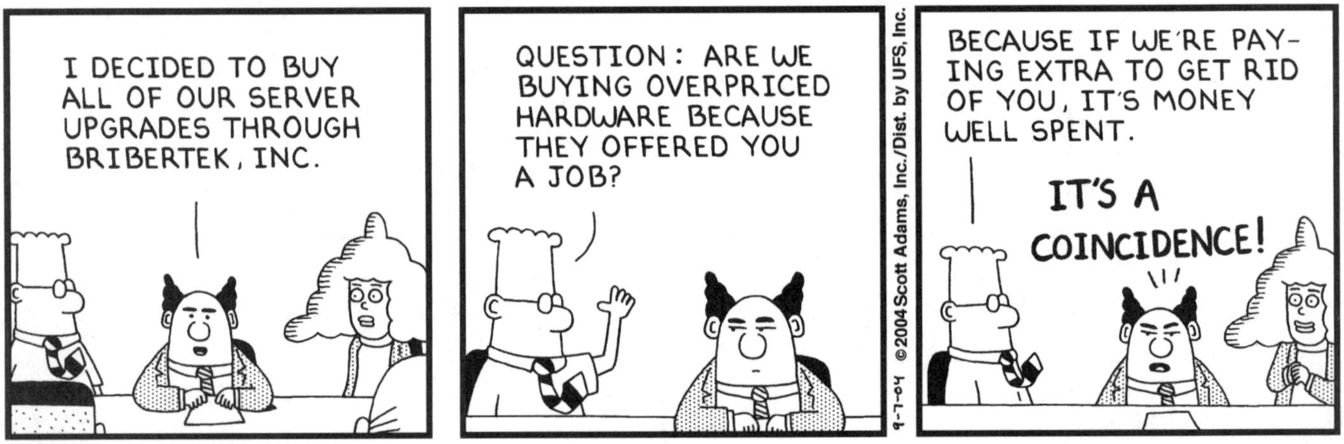
I DECIDED TO BUY ALL OF OUR SERVER UPGRADES THROUGH BRIBERTEK, INC.
QUESTION: ARE WE BUYING OVERPRICED HARDWARE BECAUSE THEY OFFERED YOU A JOB?
9-7-04 ©2004 Scott Adams, Inc./Dist. by UFS, Inc.
BECAUSE IF WE'RE PAY-ING EXTRA TO GET RID OF YOU, IT'S MONEY WELL SPENT.
IT'S A COINCIDENCE!

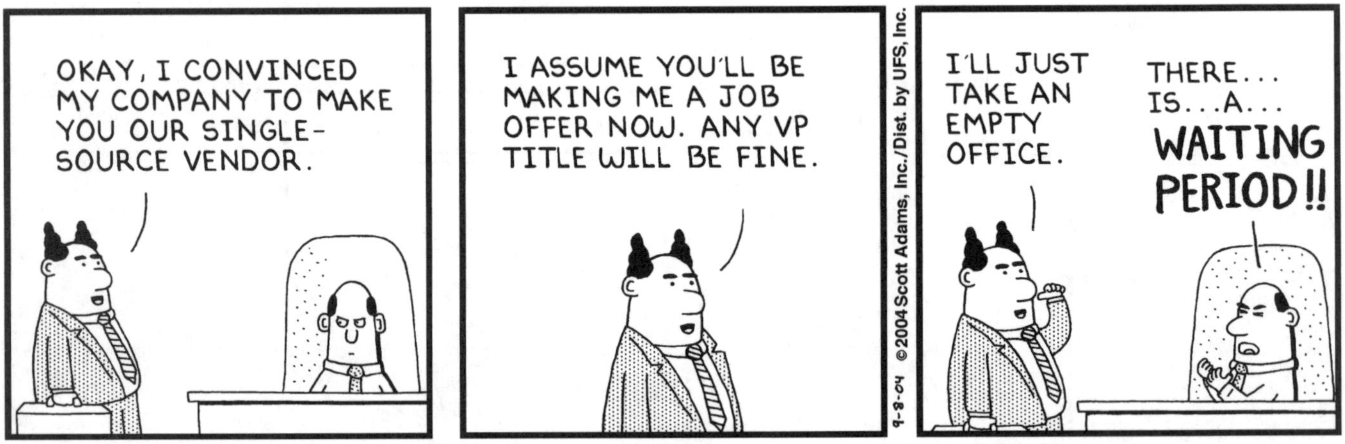
OKAY, I CONVINCED MY COMPANY TO MAKE YOU OUR SINGLE-SOURCE VENDOR.
I ASSUME YOU'LL BE MAKING ME A JOB OFFER NOW. ANY VP TITLE WILL BE FINE.
9-8-04 ©2004 Scott Adams, Inc./Dist. by UFS, Inc.
I'LL JUST TAKE AN EMPTY OFFICE.
THERE... IS...A... WAITING PERIOD!!

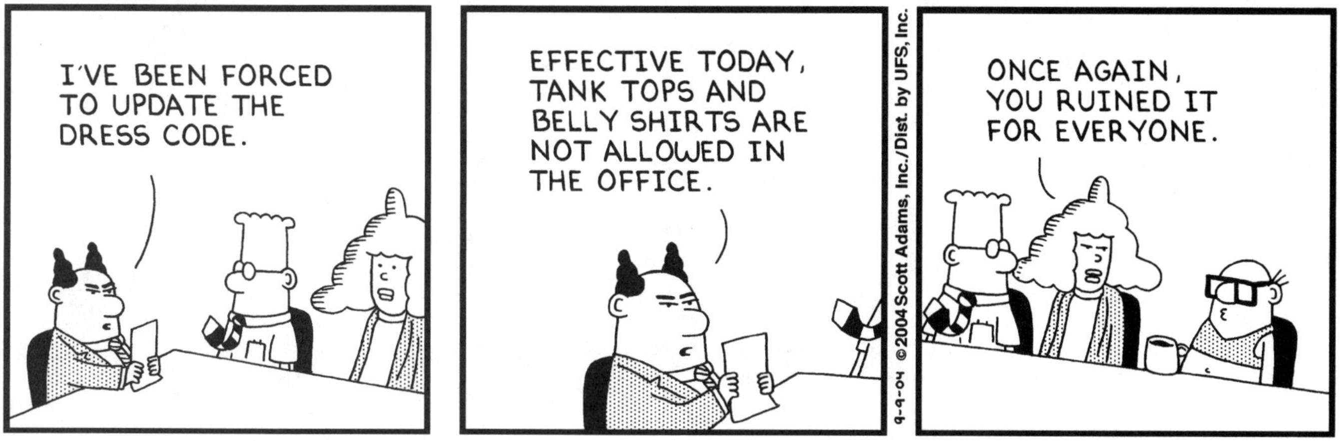
I'VE BEEN FORCED TO UPDATE THE DRESS CODE.
EFFECTIVE TODAY, TANK TOPS AND BELLY SHIRTS ARE NOT ALLOWED IN THE OFFICE.
9-9-04 ©2004 Scott Adams, Inc./Dist. by UFS, Inc.
ONCE AGAIN, YOU RUINED IT FOR EVERYONE.

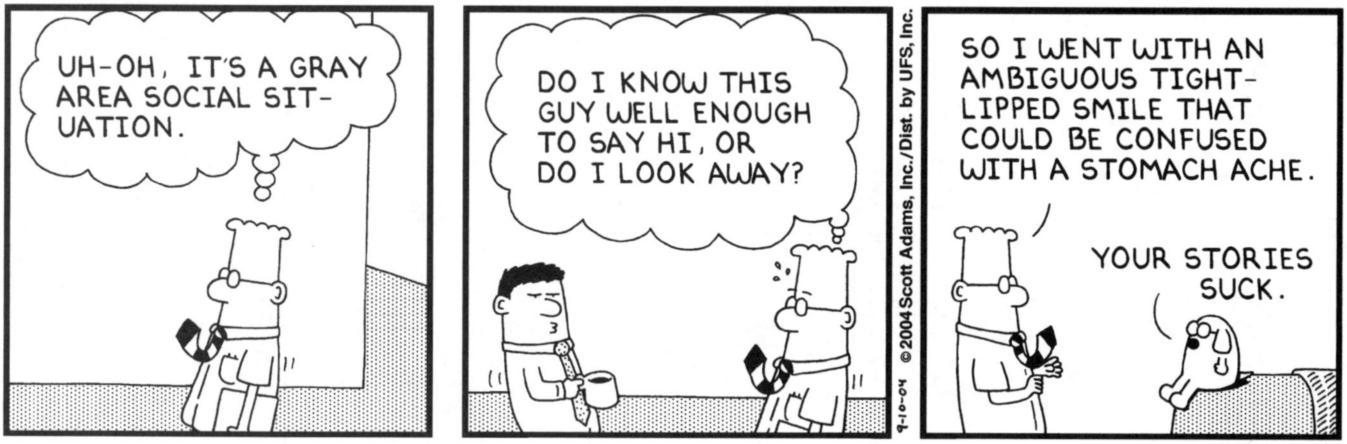
UH-OH, IT'S A GRAY AREA SOCIAL SIT-UATION.
DO I KNOW THIS GUY WELL ENOUGH TO SAY HI, OR DO I LOOK AWAY?
9-10-04 ©2004 Scott Adams, Inc./Dist. by UFS, Inc.
SO I WENT WITH AN AMBIGUOUS TIGHT-LIPPED SMILE THAT COULD BE CONFUSED WITH A STOMACH ACHE.
YOUR STORIES SUCK.

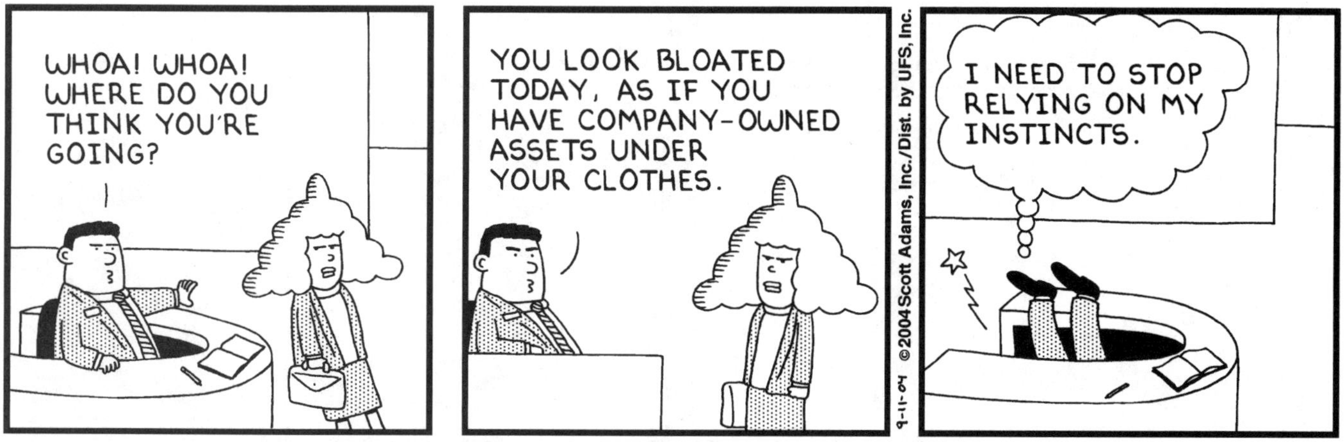
WHOA! WHOA! WHERE DO YOU THINK YOU'RE GOING?
YOU LOOK BLOATED TODAY, AS IF YOU HAVE COMPANY-OWNED ASSETS UNDER YOUR CLOTHES.
9-11-04 ©2004 Scott Adams, Inc./Dist. by UFS, Inc.
I NEED TO STOP RELYING ON MY INSTINCTS.

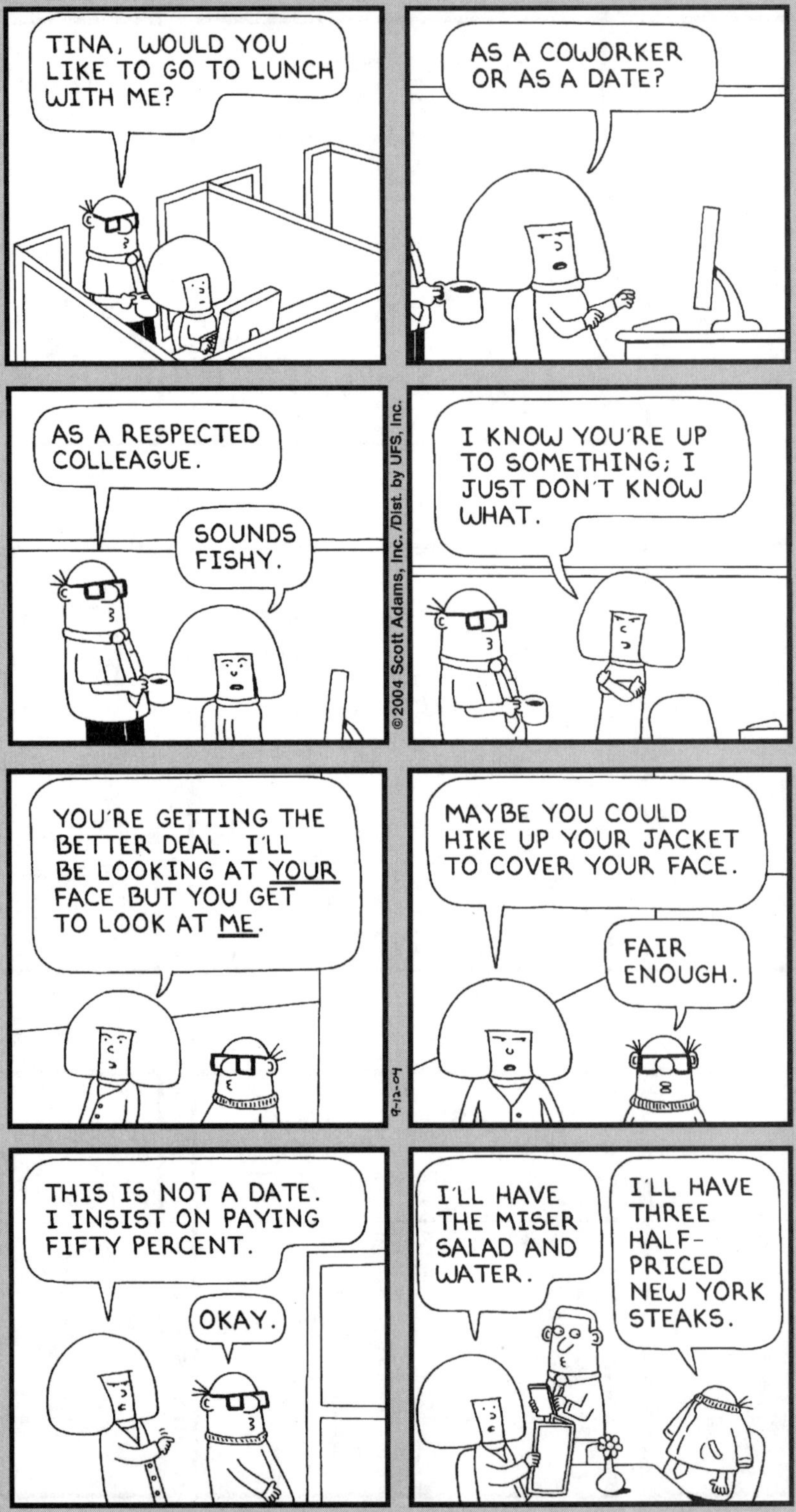
TINA, WOULD YOU LIKE TO GO TO LUNCH WITH ME?
AS A COWORKER OR AS A DATE?
AS A RESPECTED COLLEAGUE.
SOUNDS FISHY.
I KNOW YOU'RE UP TO SOMETHING; I JUST DON'T KNOW WHAT.
YOU'RE GETTING THE BETTER DEAL. I'LL BE LOOKING AT YOUR FACE BUT YOU GET TO LOOK AT ME.
MAYBE YOU COULD HIKE UP YOUR JACKET TO COVER YOUR FACE.
FAIR ENOUGH.
THIS IS NOT A DATE. I INSIST ON PAYING FIFTY PERCENT.
OKAY.
I'LL HAVE THE MISER SALAD AND WATER.
I'LL HAVE THREE HALF-PRICED NEW YORK STEAKS.
©2004 Scott Adams, Inc. /Dist. by UFS, Inc.
9-12-04

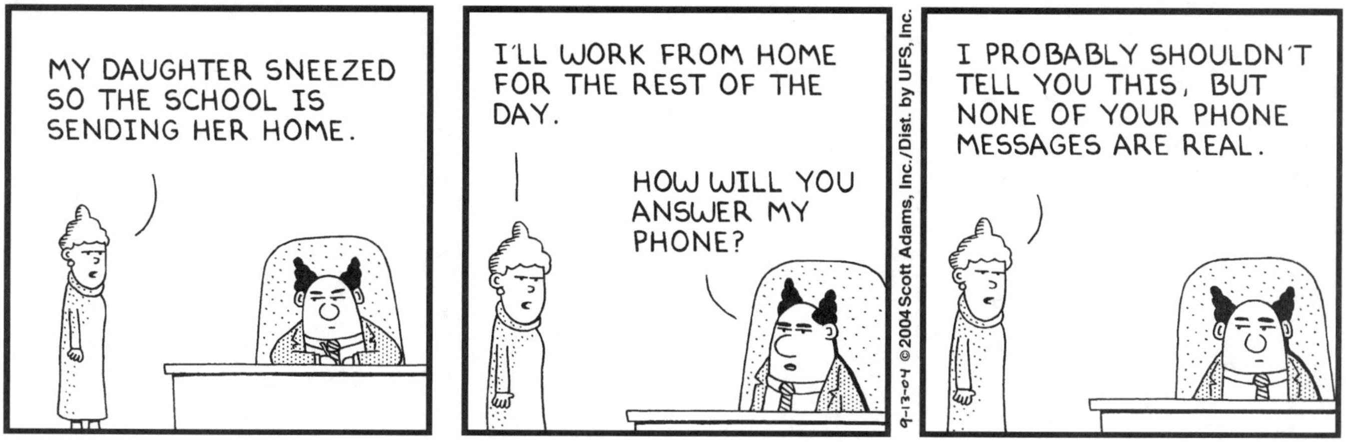
MY DAUGHTER SNEEZED SO THE SCHOOL IS SENDING HER HOME.
I'LL WORK FROM HOME FOR THE REST OF THE DAY.
HOW WILL YOU ANSWER MY PHONE?
I PROBABLY SHOULDN'T TELL YOU THIS, BUT NONE OF YOUR PHONE MESSAGES ARE REAL.
9-13-04 © 2004 Scott Adams, Inc./Dist. by UFS, Inc.

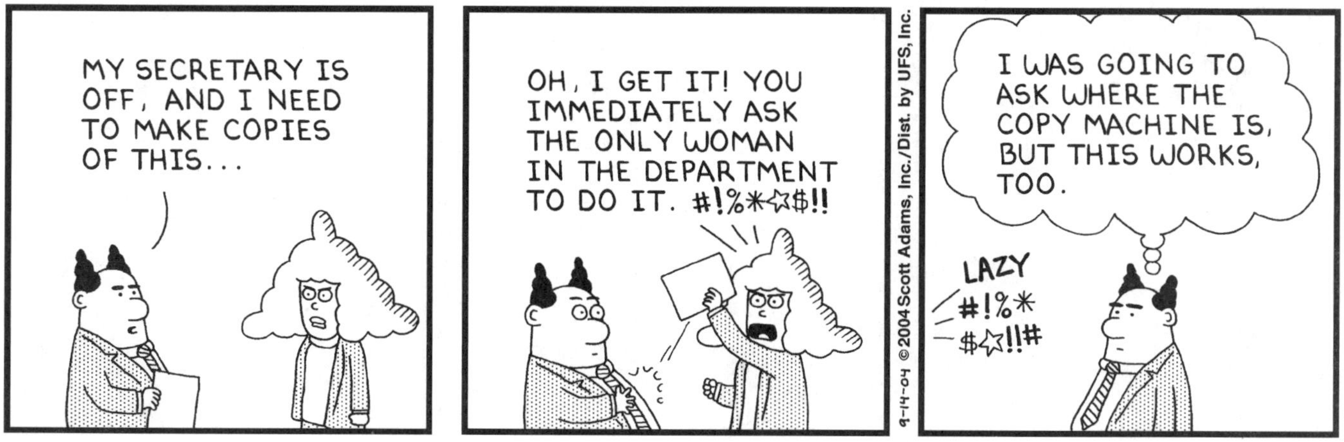
MY SECRETARY IS OFF, AND I NEED TO MAKE COPIES OF THIS...
OH, I GET IT! YOU IMMEDIATELY ASK THE ONLY WOMAN IN THE DEPARTMENT TO DO IT. #!%*☆$!!
I WAS GOING TO ASK WHERE THE COPY MACHINE IS, BUT THIS WORKS, TOO.
LAZY #!%* $☆!!#
9-14-04 © 2004 Scott Adams, Inc./Dist. by UFS, Inc.

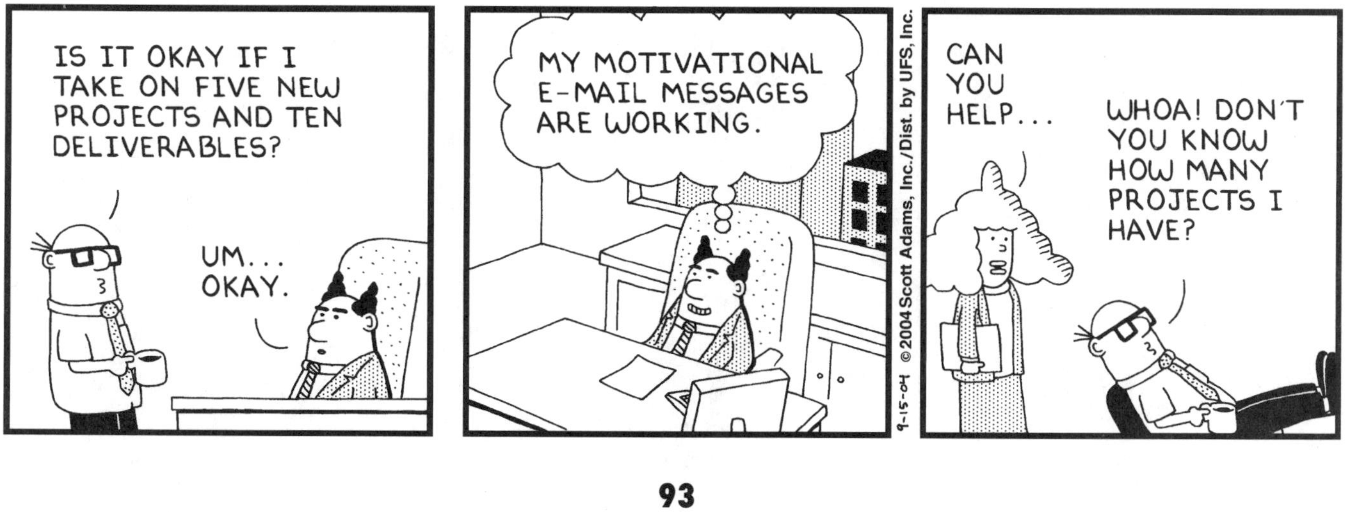
IS IT OKAY IF I TAKE ON FIVE NEW PROJECTS AND TEN DELIVERABLES?
UM... OKAY.
MY MOTIVATIONAL E-MAIL MESSAGES ARE WORKING.
CAN YOU HELP...
WHOA! DON'T YOU KNOW HOW MANY PROJECTS I HAVE?
9-15-04 © 2004 Scott Adams, Inc./Dist. by UFS, Inc.

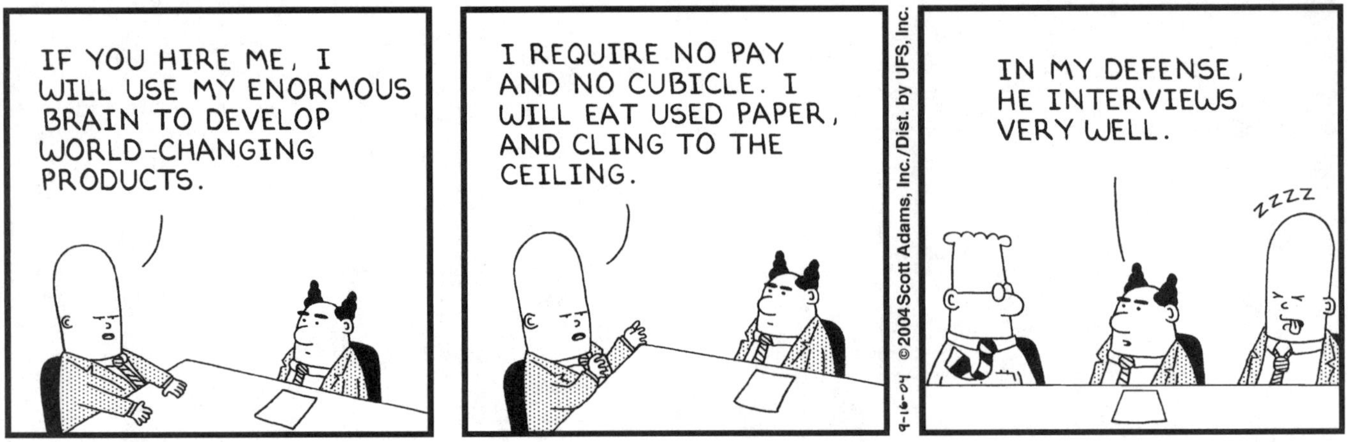
IF YOU HIRE ME, I WILL USE MY ENORMOUS BRAIN TO DEVELOP WORLD-CHANGING PRODUCTS.
I REQUIRE NO PAY AND NO CUBICLE. I WILL EAT USED PAPER, AND CLING TO THE CEILING.
9-16-04 © 2004 Scott Adams, Inc./Dist. by UFS, Inc.
IN MY DEFENSE, HE INTERVIEWS VERY WELL.
ZZZZ

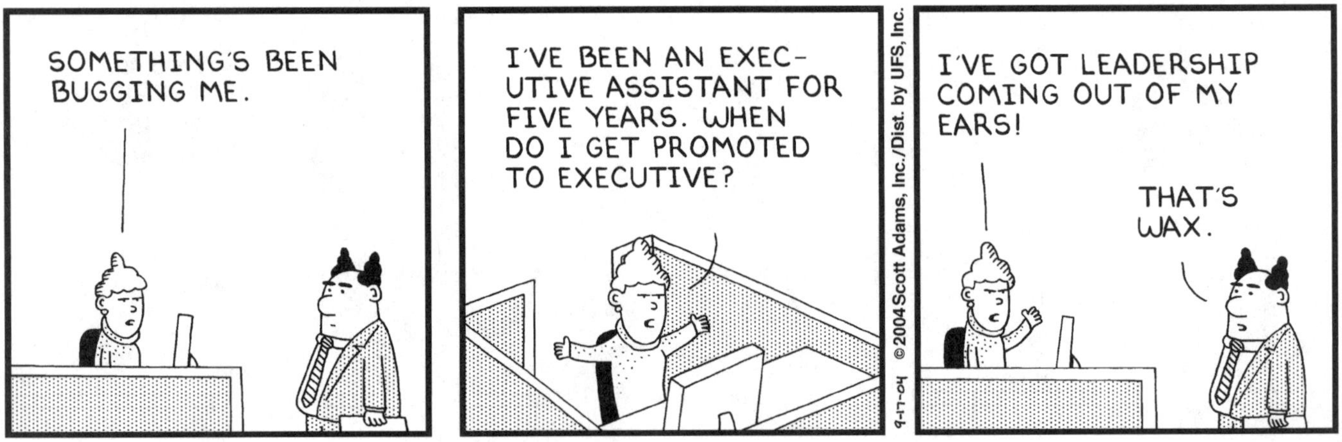
SOMETHING'S BEEN BUGGING ME.
I'VE BEEN AN EXEC-UTIVE ASSISTANT FOR FIVE YEARS. WHEN DO I GET PROMOTED TO EXECUTIVE?
9-17-04 © 2004 Scott Adams, Inc./Dist. by UFS, Inc.
I'VE GOT LEADERSHIP COMING OUT OF MY EARS!
THAT'S WAX.

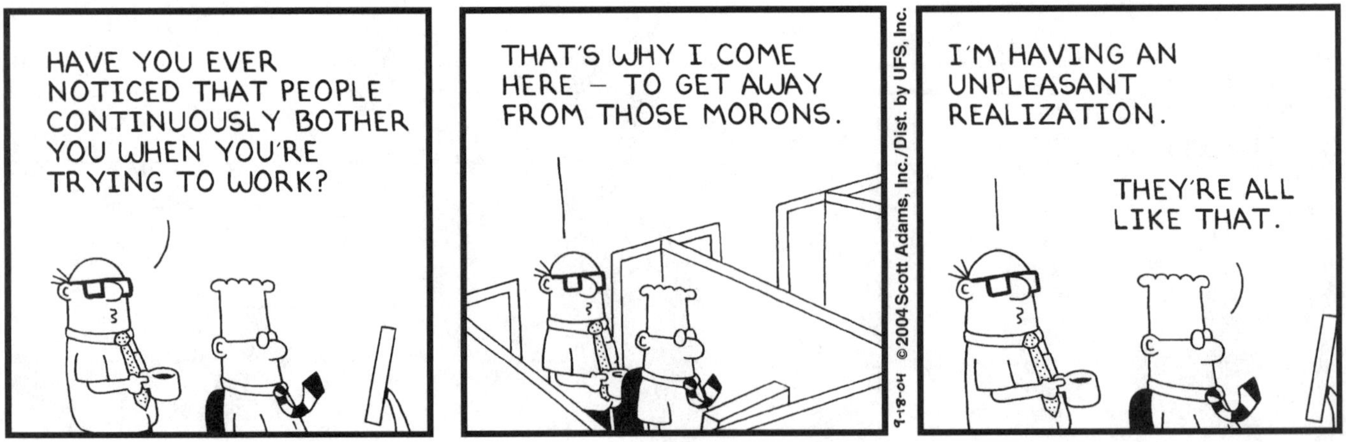
HAVE YOU EVER NOTICED THAT PEOPLE CONTINUOUSLY BOTHER YOU WHEN YOU'RE TRYING TO WORK?
THAT'S WHY I COME HERE – TO GET AWAY FROM THOSE MORONS.
9-18-04 © 2004 Scott Adams, Inc./Dist. by UFS, Inc.
I'M HAVING AN UNPLEASANT REALIZATION.
THEY'RE ALL LIKE THAT.

DO YOU HAVE THE MARKET DEMAND NUMBERS?
I'M IN THE MIDDLE OF SOMETHING. CAN I GET BACK TO YOU LATER?
HOW MUCH LATER?
WHEN DO YOU NEED IT?
AS SOON AS POSSIBLE.
I'LL DO IT AS SOON AS I'M DONE.
WHEN WILL THAT BE?
AS SOON AS POSSIBLE.
WHEN WILL IT BE POSSIBLE?
CUT ME SOME SLACK.
HOW MUCH SLACK DO YOU NEED?
©2004 Scott Adams, Inc./Dist. by UFS, Inc.
9-19-04

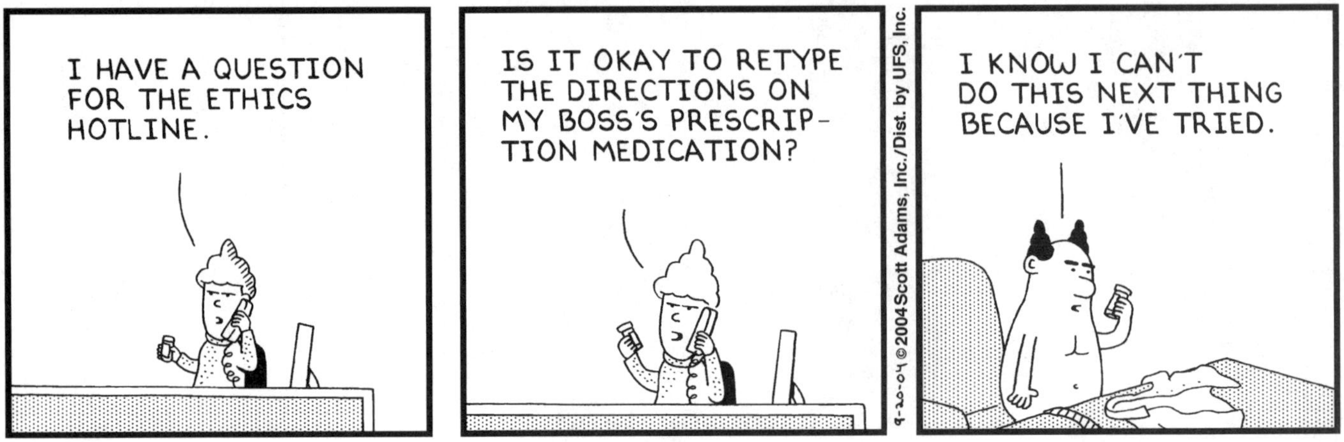
I HAVE A QUESTION FOR THE ETHICS HOTLINE.
IS IT OKAY TO RETYPE THE DIRECTIONS ON MY BOSS'S PRESCRIP-TION MEDICATION?
9-20-04 © 2004 Scott Adams, Inc./Dist. by UFS, Inc.
I KNOW I CAN'T DO THIS NEXT THING BECAUSE I'VE TRIED.

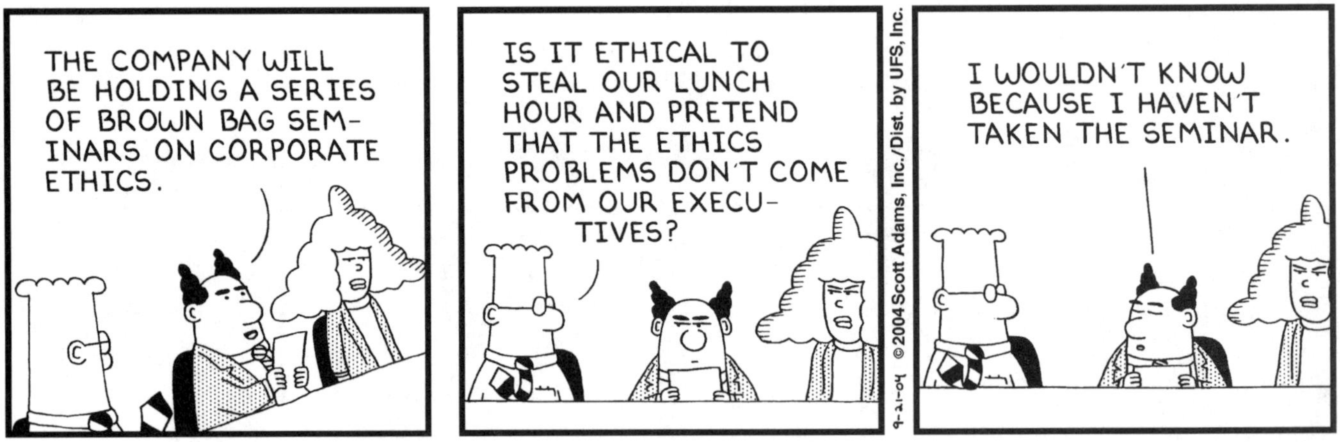
THE COMPANY WILL BE HOLDING A SERIES OF BROWN BAG SEM-INARS ON CORPORATE ETHICS.
IS IT ETHICAL TO STEAL OUR LUNCH HOUR AND PRETEND THAT THE ETHICS PROBLEMS DON'T COME FROM OUR EXECU-TIVES?
9-21-04 © 2004 Scott Adams, Inc./Dist. by UFS, Inc.
I WOULDN'T KNOW BECAUSE I HAVEN'T TAKEN THE SEMINAR.

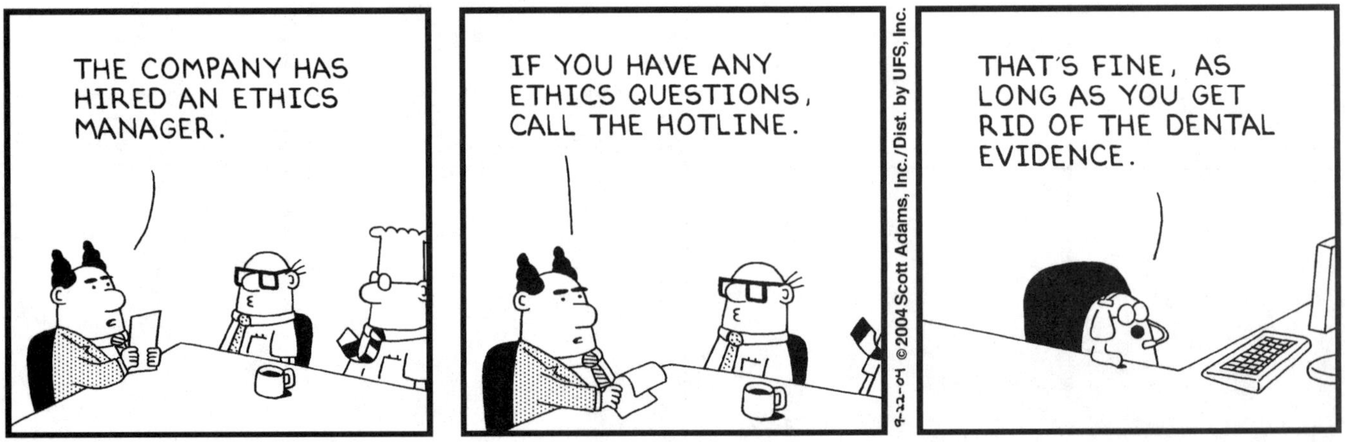
THE COMPANY HAS HIRED AN ETHICS MANAGER.
IF YOU HAVE ANY ETHICS QUESTIONS, CALL THE HOTLINE.
9-22-04 © 2004 Scott Adams, Inc./Dist. by UFS, Inc.
THAT'S FINE, AS LONG AS YOU GET RID OF THE DENTAL EVIDENCE.

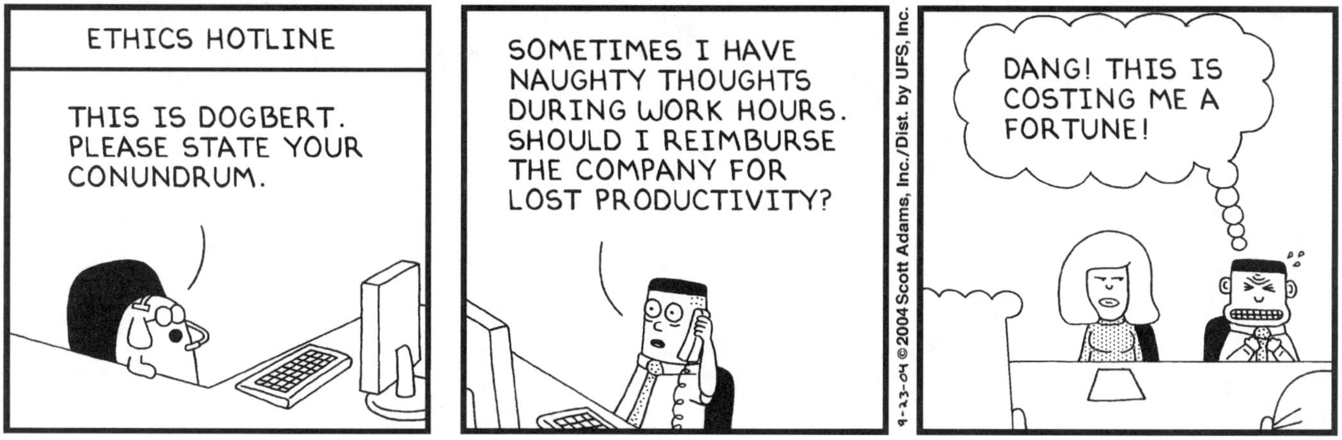
ETHICS HOTLINE
THIS IS DOGBERT. PLEASE STATE YOUR CONUNDRUM.
SOMETIMES I HAVE NAUGHTY THOUGHTS DURING WORK HOURS. SHOULD I REIMBURSE THE COMPANY FOR LOST PRODUCTIVITY?
DANG! THIS IS COSTING ME A FORTUNE!
9-23-04 © 2004 Scott Adams, Inc./Dist. by UFS, Inc.

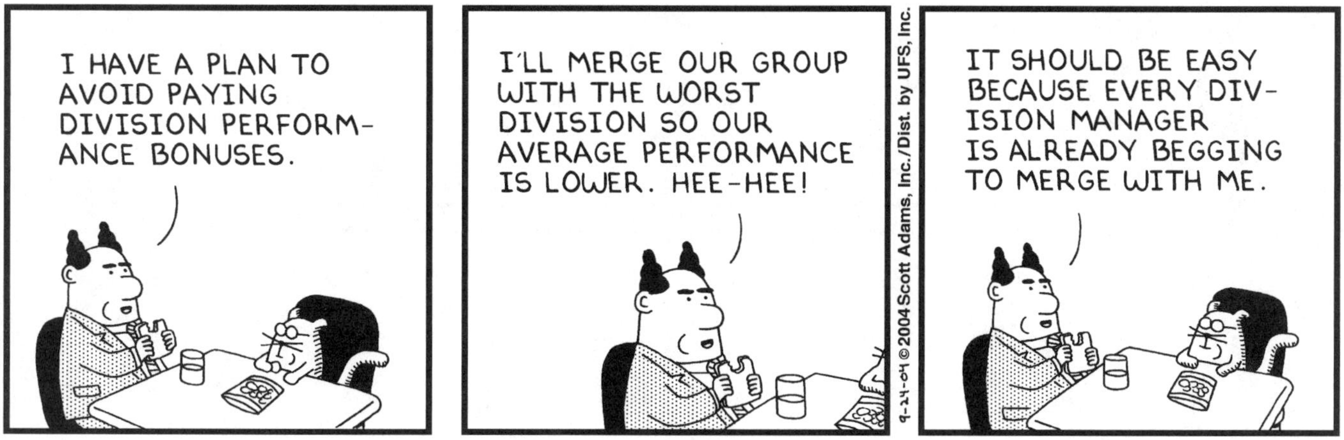
I HAVE A PLAN TO AVOID PAYING DIVISION PERFORM-ANCE BONUSES.
I'LL MERGE OUR GROUP WITH THE WORST DIVISION SO OUR AVERAGE PERFORMANCE IS LOWER. HEE-HEE!
IT SHOULD BE EASY BECAUSE EVERY DIV-ISION MANAGER IS ALREADY BEGGING TO MERGE WITH ME.
9-24-04 © 2004 Scott Adams, Inc./Dist. by UFS, Inc.

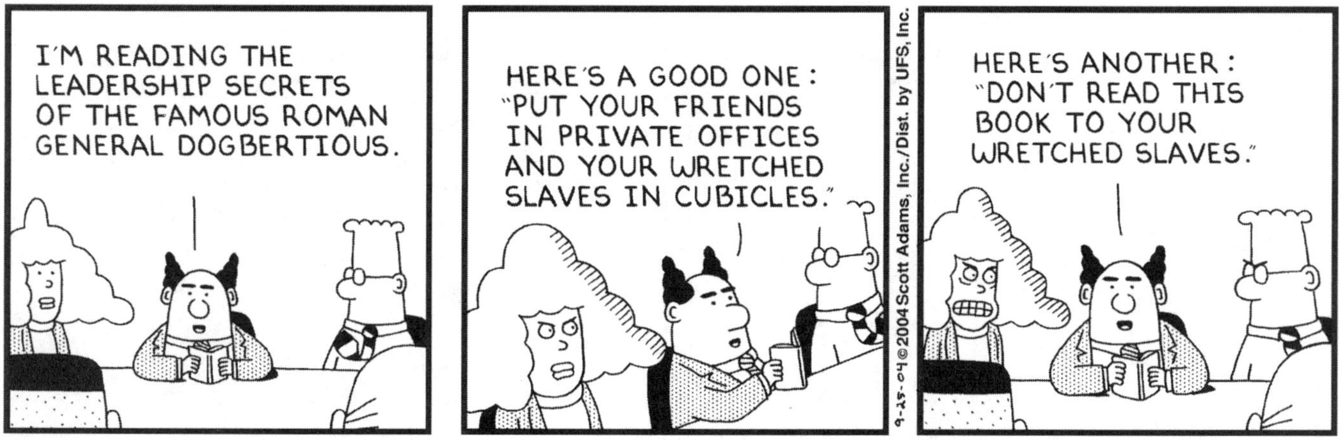
I'M READING THE LEADERSHIP SECRETS OF THE FAMOUS ROMAN GENERAL DOGBERTIOUS.
HERE'S A GOOD ONE: "PUT YOUR FRIENDS IN PRIVATE OFFICES AND YOUR WRETCHED SLAVES IN CUBICLES."
HERE'S ANOTHER: "DON'T READ THIS BOOK TO YOUR WRETCHED SLAVES."
9-25-04 © 2004 Scott Adams, Inc./Dist. by UFS, Inc.

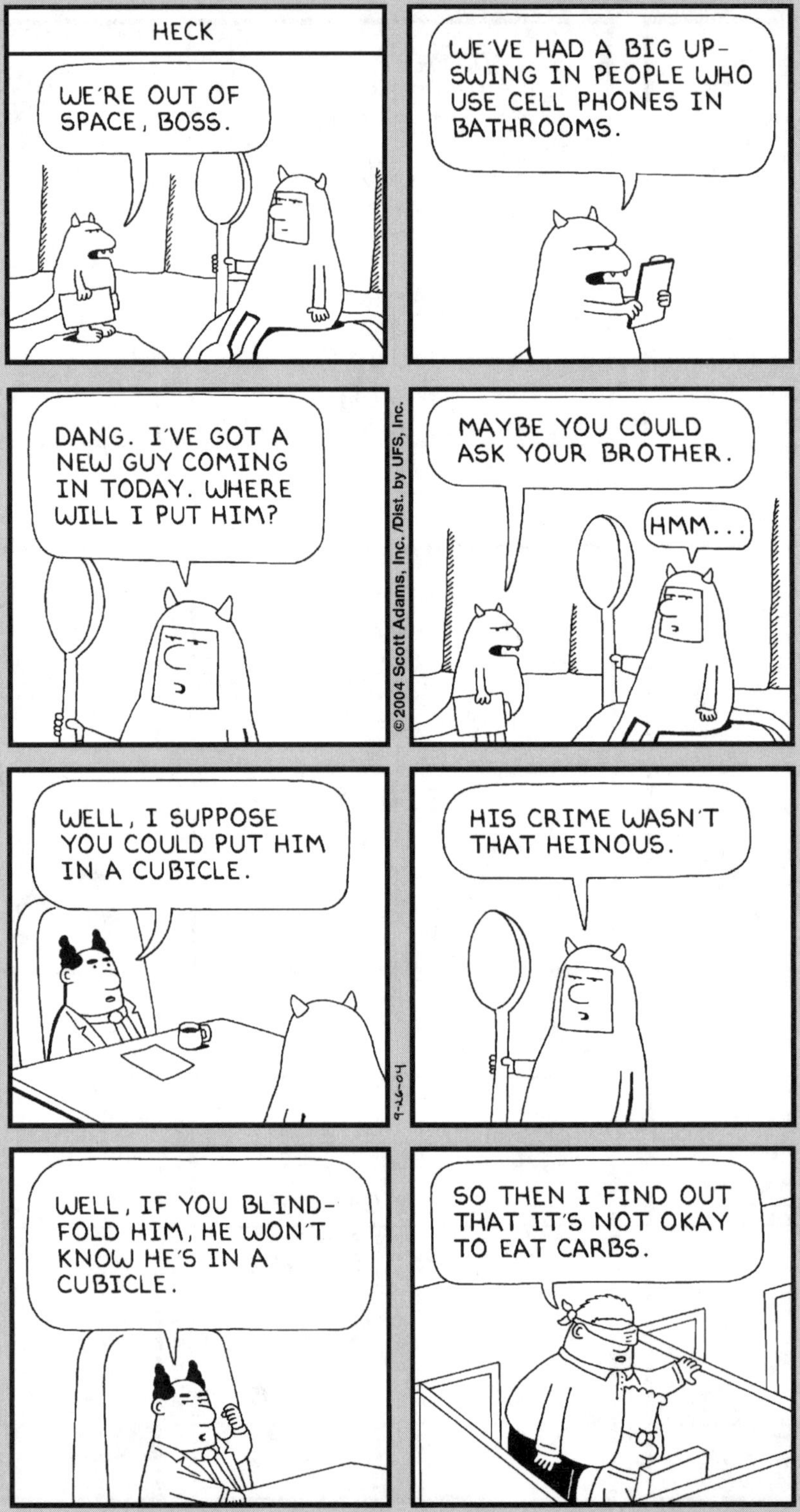
HECK
WE'RE OUT OF SPACE, BOSS.
WE'VE HAD A BIG UP-SWING IN PEOPLE WHO USE CELL PHONES IN BATHROOMS.
DANG. I'VE GOT A NEW GUY COMING IN TODAY. WHERE WILL I PUT HIM?
©2004 Scott Adams, Inc./Dist. by UFS, Inc.
MAYBE YOU COULD ASK YOUR BROTHER.
HMM...
WELL, I SUPPOSE YOU COULD PUT HIM IN A CUBICLE.
9-26-04
HIS CRIME WASN'T THAT HEINOUS.
WELL, IF YOU BLIND-FOLD HIM, HE WON'T KNOW HE'S IN A CUBICLE.
SO THEN I FIND OUT THAT IT'S NOT OKAY TO EAT CARBS.

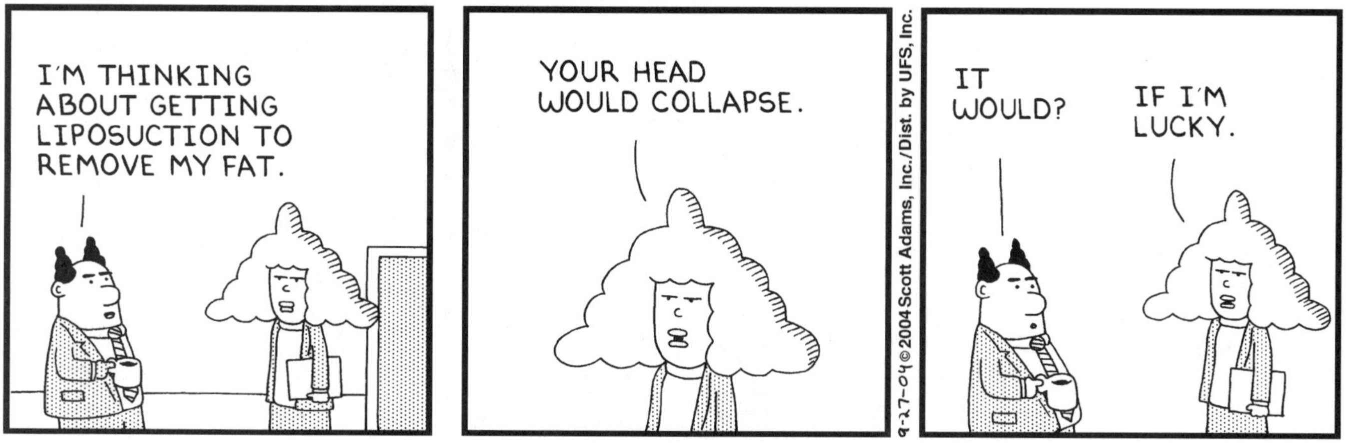
I'M THINKING ABOUT GETTING LIPOSUCTION TO REMOVE MY FAT.
YOUR HEAD WOULD COLLAPSE.
9-27-04 ©2004 Scott Adams, Inc./Dist. by UFS, Inc.
IT WOULD?
IF I'M LUCKY.

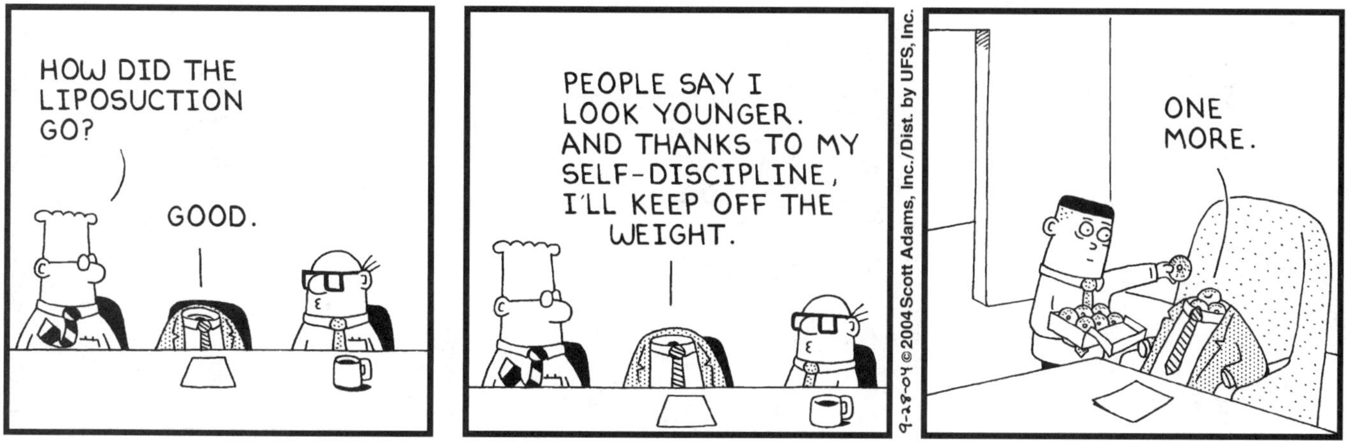
HOW DID THE LIPOSUCTION GO?
GOOD.
PEOPLE SAY I LOOK YOUNGER. AND THANKS TO MY SELF-DISCIPLINE, I'LL KEEP OFF THE WEIGHT.
9-28-04 ©2004 Scott Adams, Inc./Dist. by UFS, Inc.
ONE MORE.

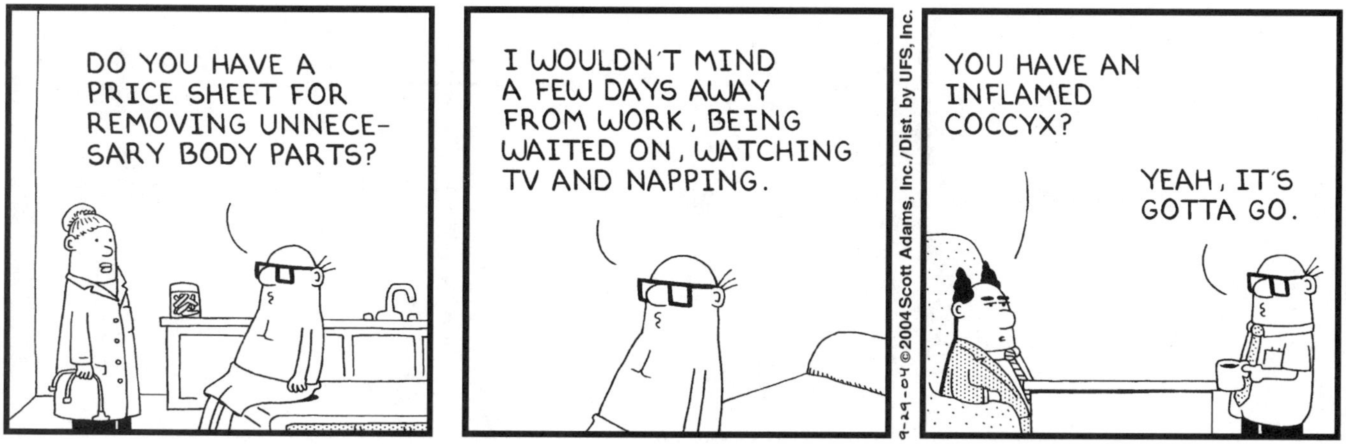
DO YOU HAVE A PRICE SHEET FOR REMOVING UNNECE-SARY BODY PARTS?
I WOULDN'T MIND A FEW DAYS AWAY FROM WORK, BEING WAITED ON, WATCHING TV AND NAPPING.
9-29-04 ©2004 Scott Adams, Inc./Dist. by UFS, Inc.
YOU HAVE AN INFLAMED COCCYX?
YEAH, IT'S GOTTA GO.

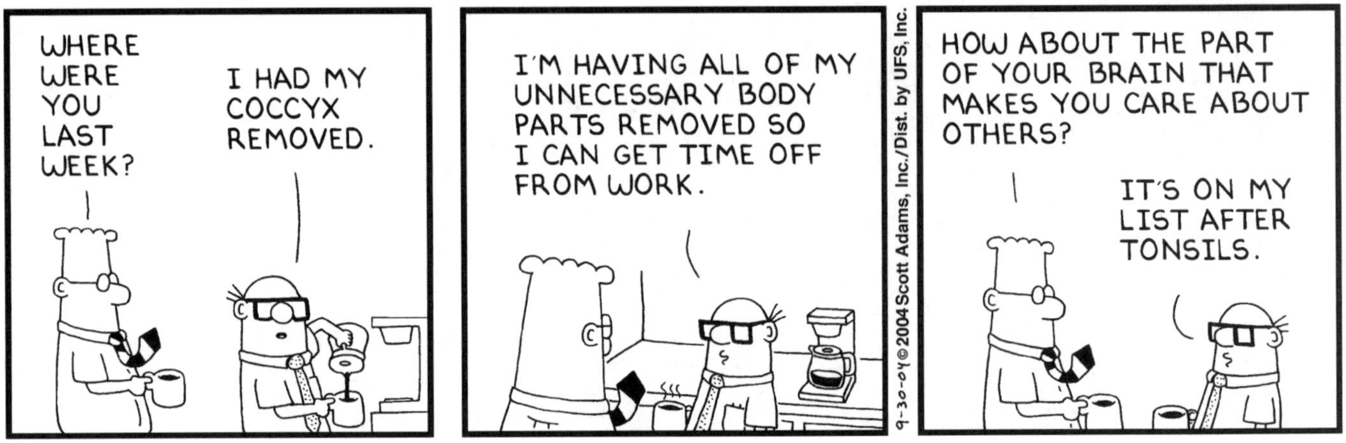
WHERE WERE YOU LAST WEEK?
I HAD MY COCCYX REMOVED.
I'M HAVING ALL OF MY UNNECESSARY BODY PARTS REMOVED SO I CAN GET TIME OFF FROM WORK.
HOW ABOUT THE PART OF YOUR BRAIN THAT MAKES YOU CARE ABOUT OTHERS?
IT'S ON MY LIST AFTER TONSILS.
9-30-04 © 2004 Scott Adams, Inc./Dist. by UFS, Inc.

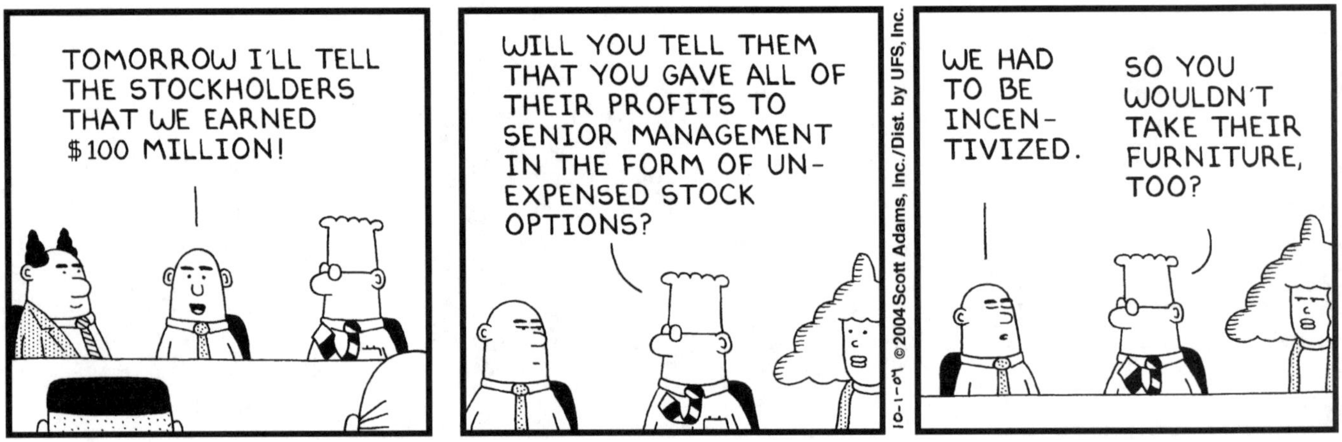
TOMORROW I'LL TELL THE STOCKHOLDERS THAT WE EARNED $100 MILLION!
WILL YOU TELL THEM THAT YOU GAVE ALL OF THEIR PROFITS TO SENIOR MANAGEMENT IN THE FORM OF UN-EXPENSED STOCK OPTIONS?
WE HAD TO BE INCEN-TIVIZED.
SO YOU WOULDN'T TAKE THEIR FURNITURE, TOO?
10-1-04 © 2004 Scott Adams, Inc./Dist. by UFS, Inc.

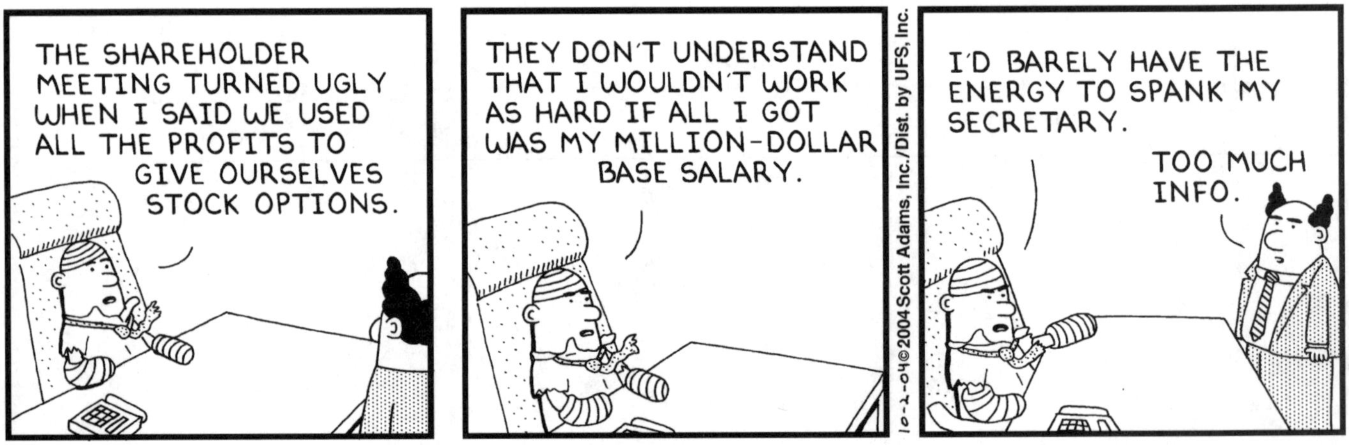
THE SHAREHOLDER MEETING TURNED UGLY WHEN I SAID WE USED ALL THE PROFITS TO GIVE OURSELVES STOCK OPTIONS.
THEY DON'T UNDERSTAND THAT I WOULDN'T WORK AS HARD IF ALL I GOT WAS MY MILLION-DOLLAR BASE SALARY.
I'D BARELY HAVE THE ENERGY TO SPANK MY SECRETARY.
TOO MUCH INFO.
10-2-04 © 2004 Scott Adams, Inc./Dist. by UFS, Inc.

DO YOU WANT TO WATCH WHEN THE NEW EMPLOYEE LOOKS AT HER FIRST PAYCHECK?
OOH-YA!
WHAT DO WE KNOW ABOUT HER?
SHE'S STRAIGHT OUT OF COLLEGE. ALL OF HER PRIOR JOBS PAID HER IN CASH.
PERFECT.
©2004 Scott Adams, Inc./Dist. by UFS, Inc.
EAR GUARDS ON.
MY FIRST PAYCHECK!
DEDUCTIONS??? HMMM...HOW BAD COULD IT BE?
10-3-04
WHAT THE...
NEXT TIME, NO COFFEE.
EH?

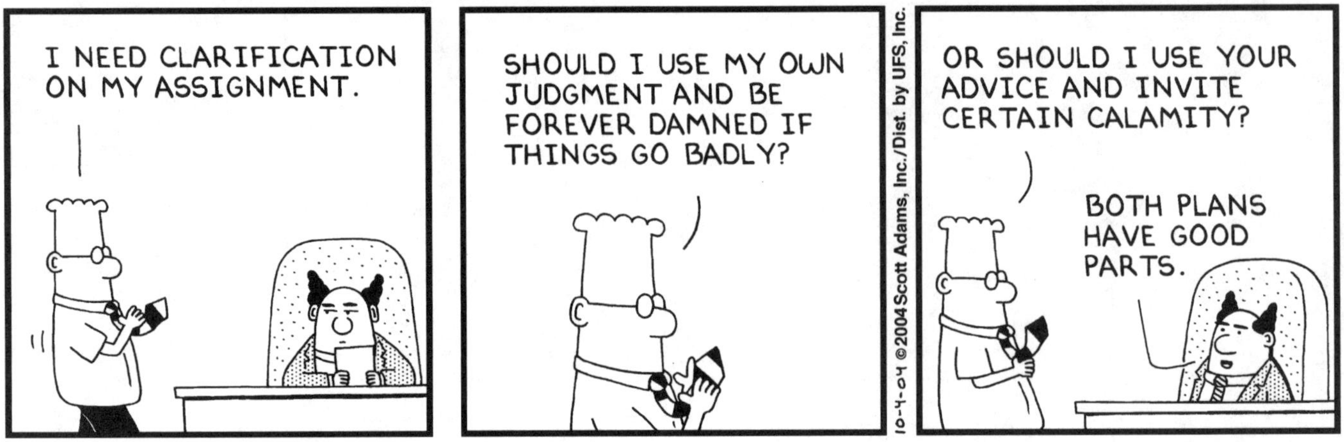
I NEED CLARIFICATION ON MY ASSIGNMENT.
SHOULD I USE MY OWN JUDGMENT AND BE FOREVER DAMNED IF THINGS GO BADLY?
10-4-04 ©2004 Scott Adams, Inc./Dist. by UFS, Inc.
OR SHOULD I USE YOUR ADVICE AND INVITE CERTAIN CALAMITY?
BOTH PLANS HAVE GOOD PARTS.

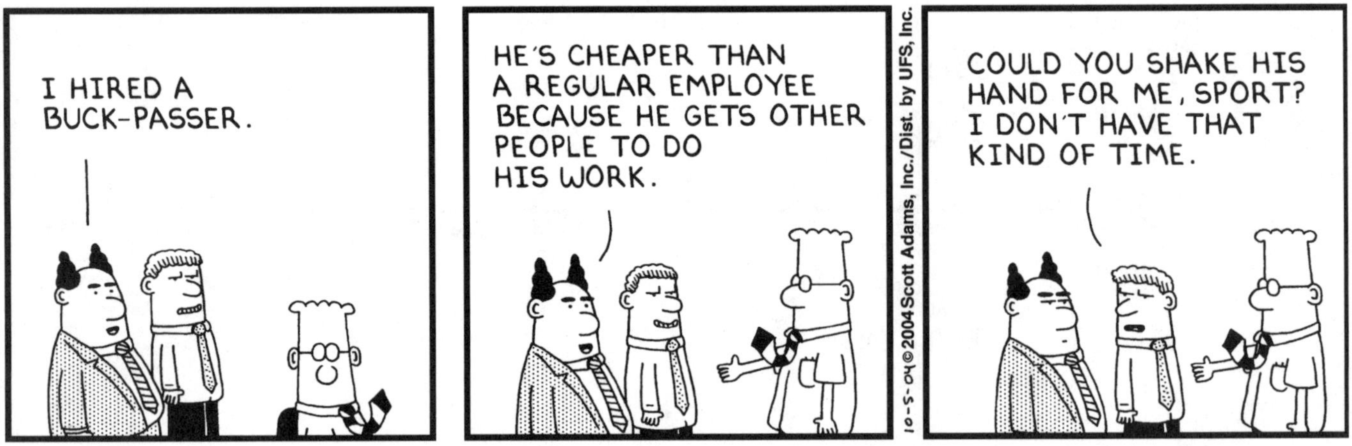
I HIRED A BUCK-PASSER.
HE'S CHEAPER THAN A REGULAR EMPLOYEE BECAUSE HE GETS OTHER PEOPLE TO DO HIS WORK.
10-5-04 ©2004 Scott Adams, Inc./Dist. by UFS, Inc.
COULD YOU SHAKE HIS HAND FOR ME, SPORT? I DON'T HAVE THAT KIND OF TIME.

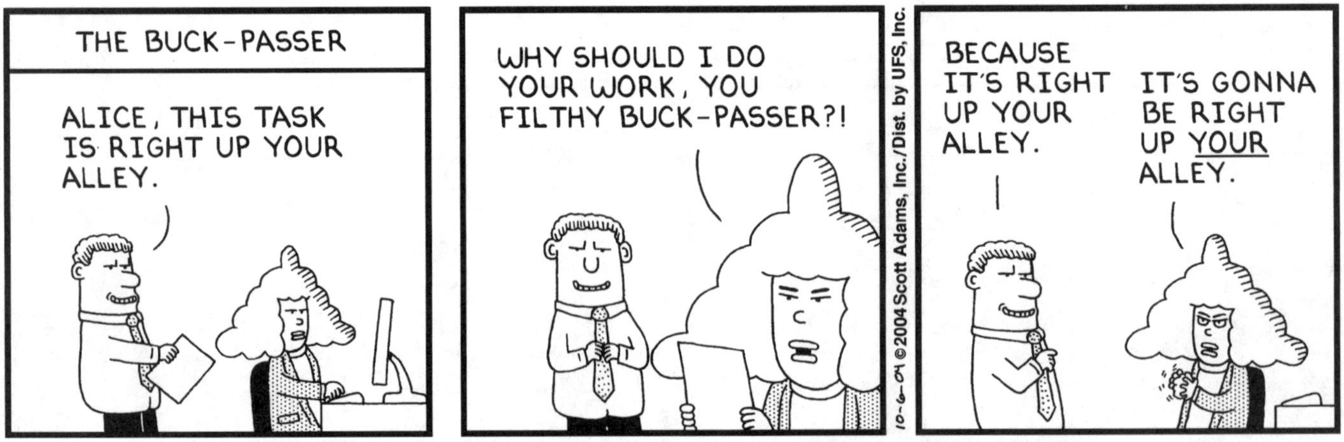
THE BUCK-PASSER
ALICE, THIS TASK IS RIGHT UP YOUR ALLEY.
WHY SHOULD I DO YOUR WORK, YOU FILTHY BUCK-PASSER?!
10-6-04 ©2004 Scott Adams, Inc./Dist. by UFS, Inc.
BECAUSE IT'S RIGHT UP YOUR ALLEY.
IT'S GONNA BE RIGHT UP YOUR ALLEY.

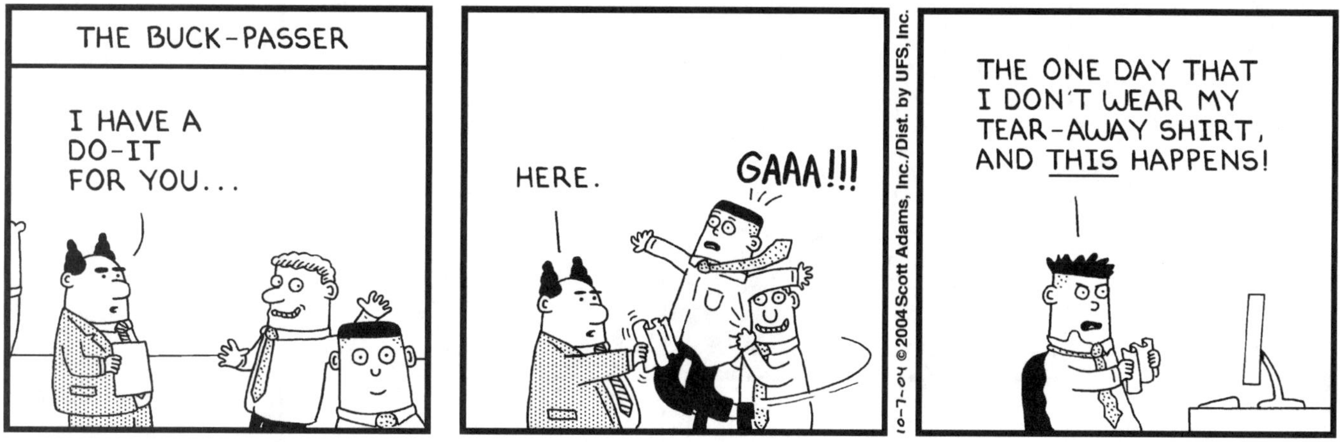
THE BUCK-PASSER
I HAVE A DO-IT FOR YOU...
HERE.
GAAA!!!
10-7-04 © 2004 Scott Adams, Inc./Dist. by UFS, Inc.
THE ONE DAY THAT I DON'T WEAR MY TEAR-AWAY SHIRT, AND THIS HAPPENS!

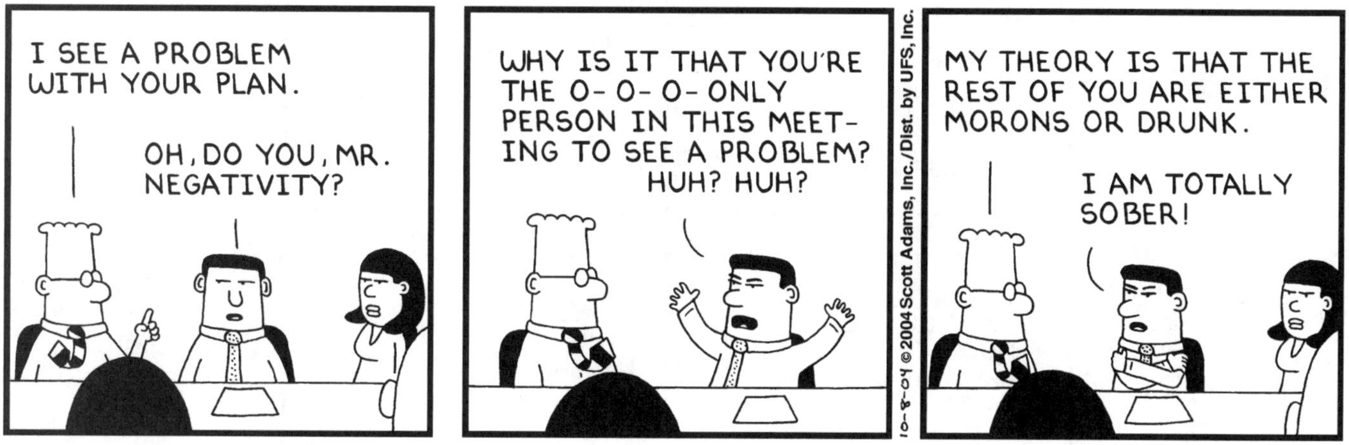
I SEE A PROBLEM WITH YOUR PLAN.
OH, DO YOU, MR. NEGATIVITY?
WHY IS IT THAT YOU'RE THE O- O- O- ONLY PERSON IN THIS MEETING TO SEE A PROBLEM? HUH? HUH?
10-8-04 © 2004 Scott Adams, Inc./Dist. by UFS, Inc.
MY THEORY IS THAT THE REST OF YOU ARE EITHER MORONS OR DRUNK.
I AM TOTALLY SOBER!

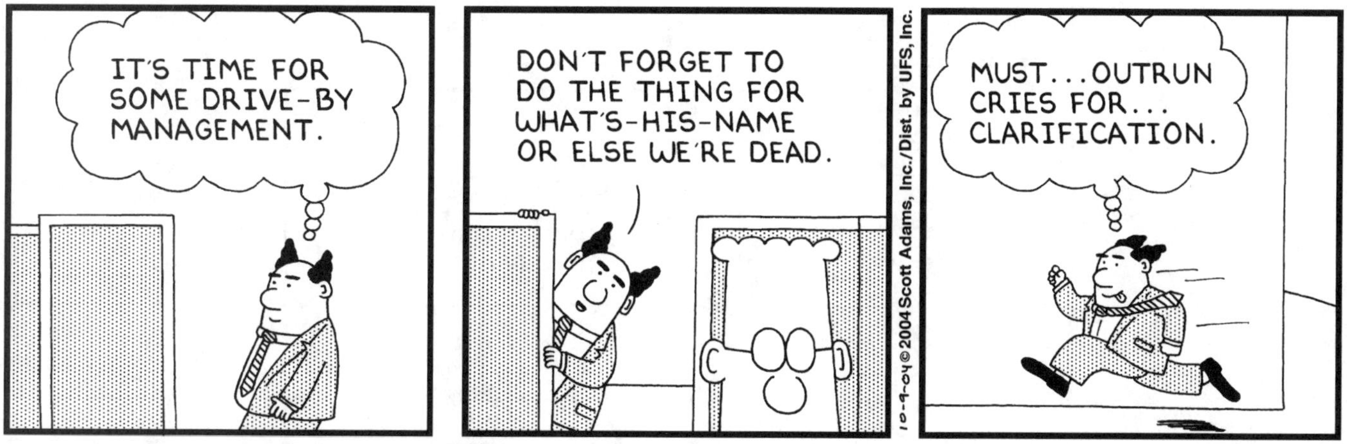
IT'S TIME FOR SOME DRIVE-BY MANAGEMENT.
DON'T FORGET TO DO THE THING FOR WHAT'S-HIS-NAME OR ELSE WE'RE DEAD.
10-9-04 © 2004 Scott Adams, Inc./Dist. by UFS, Inc.
MUST...OUTRUN CRIES FOR... CLARIFICATION.

OUR ENTERPRISE SOFT-WARE COMES IN TWO FLAVORS.
THE PREMIUM PACKAGE BOASTS A FRIENDLY USER-INTERFACE.
THE ECONOMY OPTION DOES THE SAME STUFF BUT THE INTERFACE IS DESIGNED TO RUIN YOUR LIFE.
WE'LL TAKE THE CHEAP ONE.
©2004 Scott Adams, Inc. /Dist. by UFS, Inc.
I CAN TELL BY THE WAY YOU HOLD THE MOUSE THAT YOU'VE NEVER HAD A GIRL-FRIEND.
HEY!
I'LL SEND ROMANTIC INVITATIONS TO ALL THE PEOPLE ON YOUR E-MAIL ADDRESS LIST.
NO!!!
10-10-04
DON'T WORRY – I'LL USE THE TEXT THAT I FOUND ON A GREAT ADULT WEB SITE.
GAAA!
WHEN I SAID THAT YOU NEED TO GIVE A HUNDRED PERCENT, I SHOULD HAVE BEEN MORE SPECIFIC.

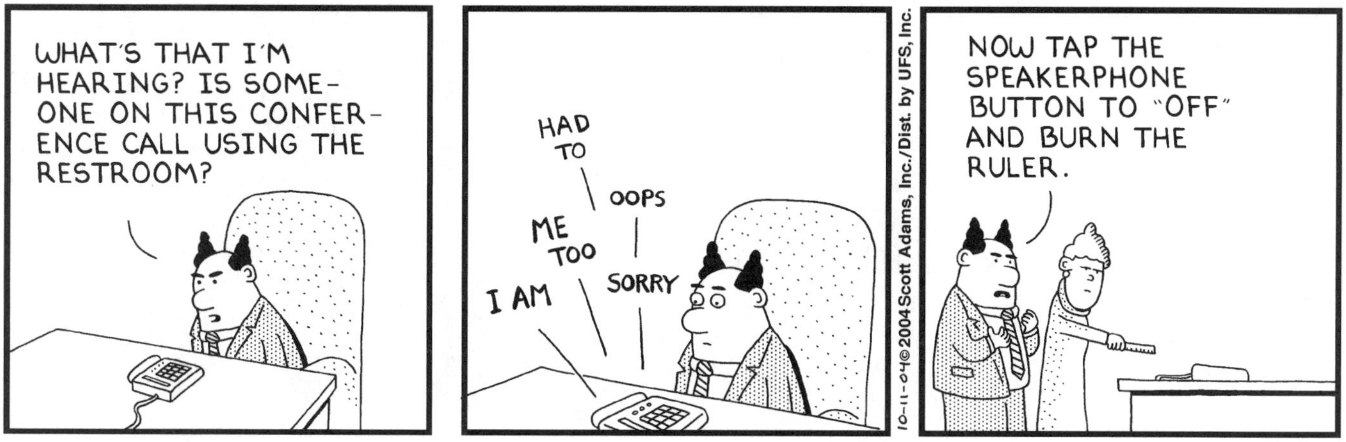
WHAT'S THAT I'M HEARING? IS SOMEONE ON THIS CONFERENCE CALL USING THE RESTROOM?
HAD TO
OOPS
ME TOO
SORRY
I AM
10-11-04 © 2004 Scott Adams, Inc./Dist. by UFS, Inc.
NOW TAP THE SPEAKERPHONE BUTTON TO "OFF" AND BURN THE RULER.

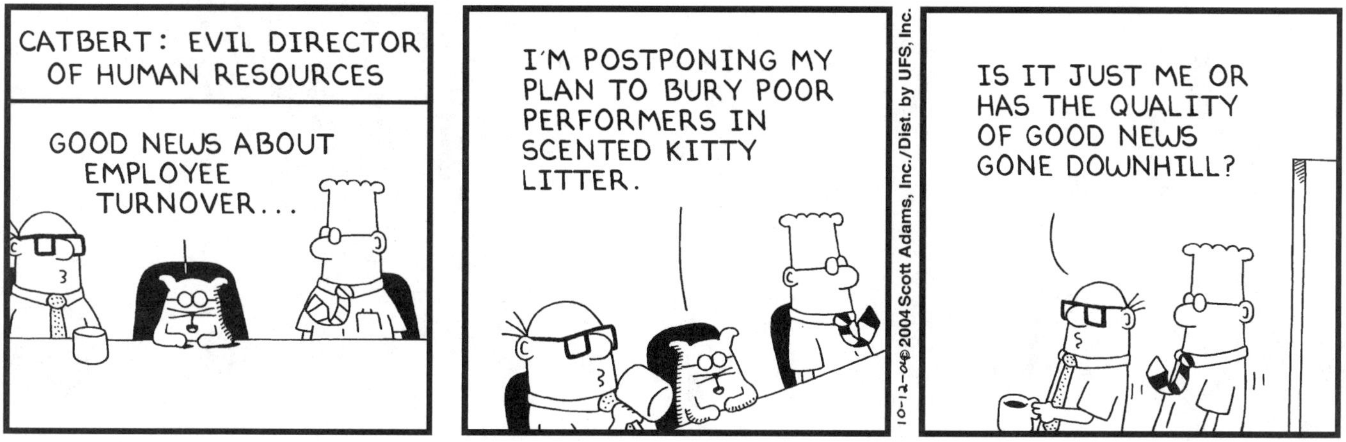
CATBERT: EVIL DIRECTOR OF HUMAN RESOURCES
GOOD NEWS ABOUT EMPLOYEE TURNOVER...
I'M POSTPONING MY PLAN TO BURY POOR PERFORMERS IN SCENTED KITTY LITTER.
10-12-04 © 2004 Scott Adams, Inc./Dist. by UFS, Inc.
IS IT JUST ME OR HAS THE QUALITY OF GOOD NEWS GONE DOWNHILL?

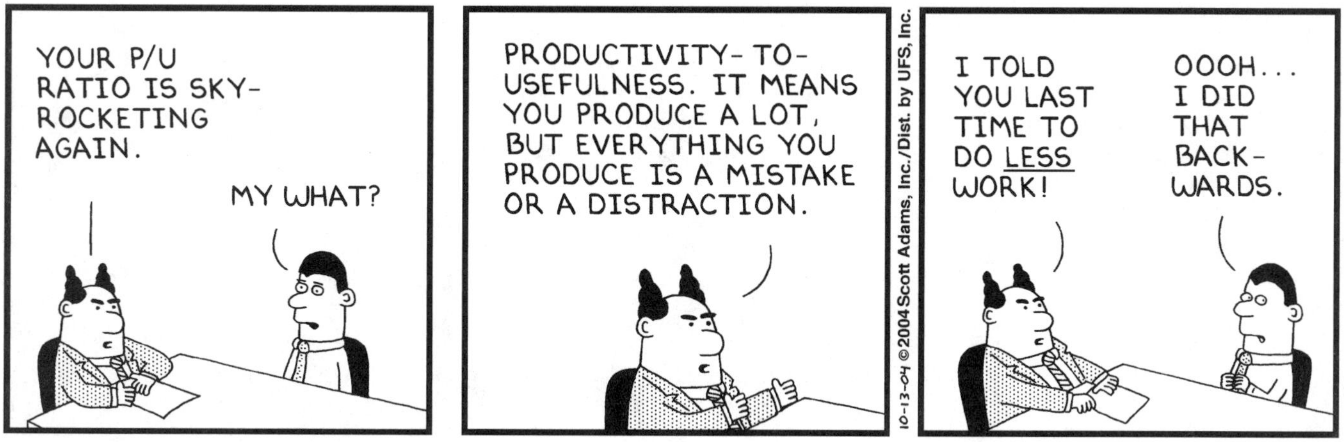
YOUR P/U RATIO IS SKY-ROCKETING AGAIN.
MY WHAT?
PRODUCTIVITY-TO-USEFULNESS. IT MEANS YOU PRODUCE A LOT, BUT EVERYTHING YOU PRODUCE IS A MISTAKE OR A DISTRACTION.
10-13-04 © 2004 Scott Adams, Inc./Dist. by UFS, Inc.
I TOLD YOU LAST TIME TO DO LESS WORK!
OOOH... I DID THAT BACK-WARDS.

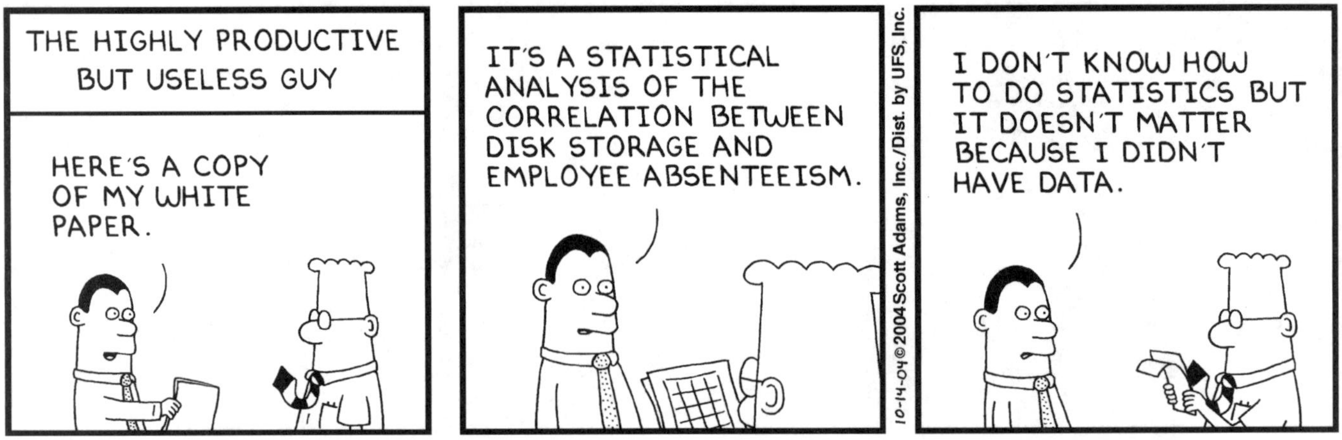
THE HIGHLY PRODUCTIVE BUT USELESS GUY
HERE'S A COPY OF MY WHITE PAPER.
IT'S A STATISTICAL ANALYSIS OF THE CORRELATION BETWEEN DISK STORAGE AND EMPLOYEE ABSENTEEISM.
I DON'T KNOW HOW TO DO STATISTICS BUT IT DOESN'T MATTER BECAUSE I DIDN'T HAVE DATA.
10-14-04 © 2004 Scott Adams, Inc./Dist. by UFS, Inc.

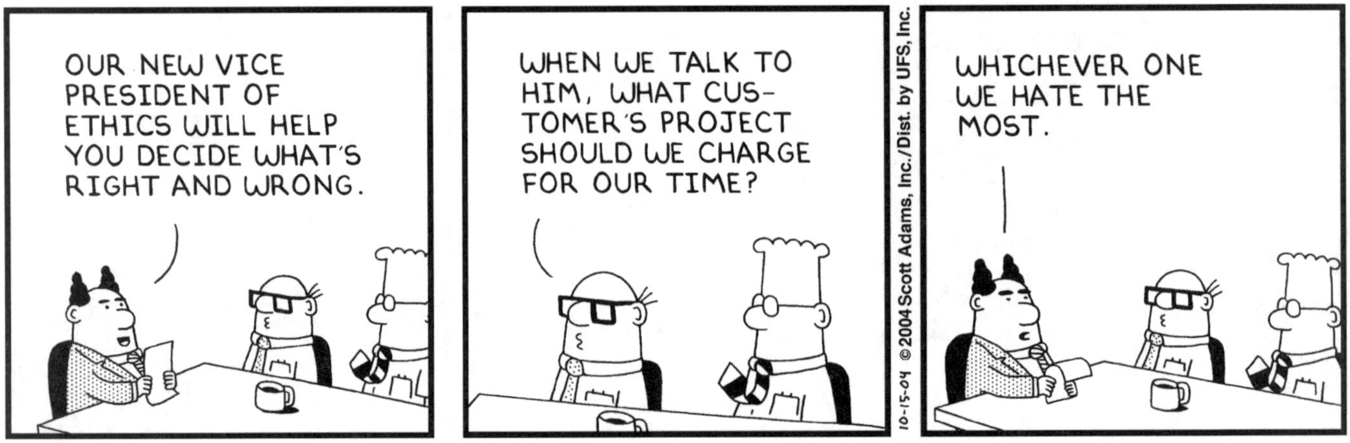
OUR NEW VICE PRESIDENT OF ETHICS WILL HELP YOU DECIDE WHAT'S RIGHT AND WRONG.
WHEN WE TALK TO HIM, WHAT CUS-TOMER'S PROJECT SHOULD WE CHARGE FOR OUR TIME?
WHICHEVER ONE WE HATE THE MOST.
10-15-04 © 2004 Scott Adams, Inc./Dist. by UFS, Inc.

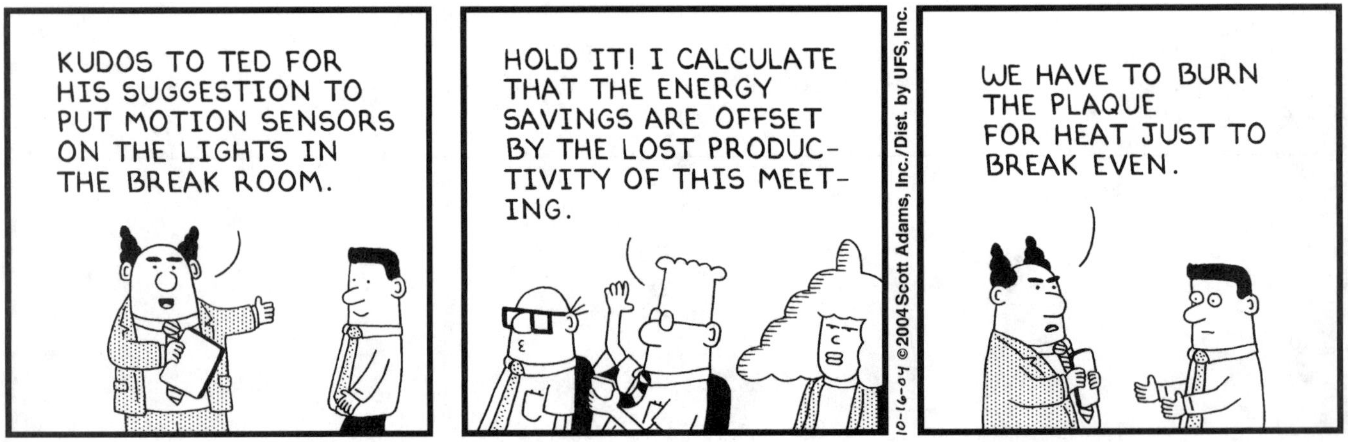
KUDOS TO TED FOR HIS SUGGESTION TO PUT MOTION SENSORS ON THE LIGHTS IN THE BREAK ROOM.
HOLD IT! I CALCULATE THAT THE ENERGY SAVINGS ARE OFFSET BY THE LOST PRODUC-TIVITY OF THIS MEET-ING.
WE HAVE TO BURN THE PLAQUE FOR HEAT JUST TO BREAK EVEN.
10-16-04 © 2004 Scott Adams, Inc./Dist. by UFS, Inc.

WHAT? YOU HAVE NO ACCOMPLISHMENTS THIS MONTH???
WHAT DID YOU DO FOR THE PAST THREE MONTHS?
WELL, I SPENT MUCH OF THAT TIME CORRECTING MISCONCEPTIONS THAT YOU GAVE TO OUR CUSTOMERS.
AND I ATTENDED MEETINGS WITH YOU TO KEEP YOU FROM CREATING ADDITIONAL MISCONCEPTIONS.
I SPENT A MONTH WORKING ON AN OBJECTIVE THAT YOU FORGOT TO TELL ME DIDN'T MATTER.
I FLEW TO THE WRONG CITY FOR A MEETING BECAUSE YOU CONFUSED HOUSTON WITH AUSTIN.
AND I UPGRADED YOUR HOME COMPUTER SO YOU WOULDN'T HAVE TO PAY SOMEONE TO DO IT.
ALLOW ME TO PARAPHRASE: BLAH, BLAH, BLAH, YOU DIDN'T ACCOMPLISH ANYTHING.
© 2004 Scott Adams, Inc./Dist. by UFS, Inc.
10-17-04

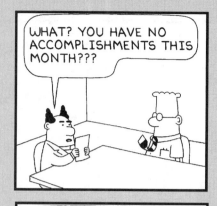

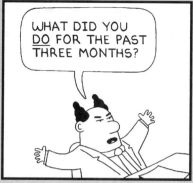

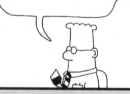

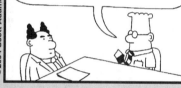

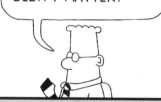

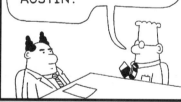

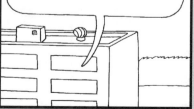

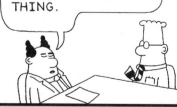

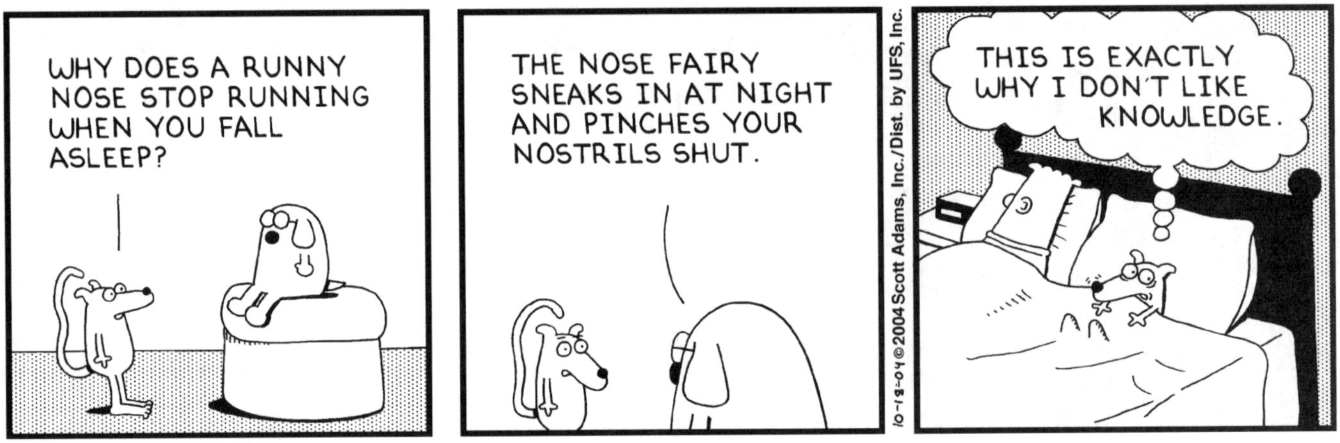
WHY DOES A RUNNY NOSE STOP RUNNING WHEN YOU FALL ASLEEP?
THE NOSE FAIRY SNEAKS IN AT NIGHT AND PINCHES YOUR NOSTRILS SHUT.
10-18-04 ©2004 Scott Adams, Inc./Dist. by UFS, Inc.
THIS IS EXACTLY WHY I DON'T LIKE KNOWLEDGE.

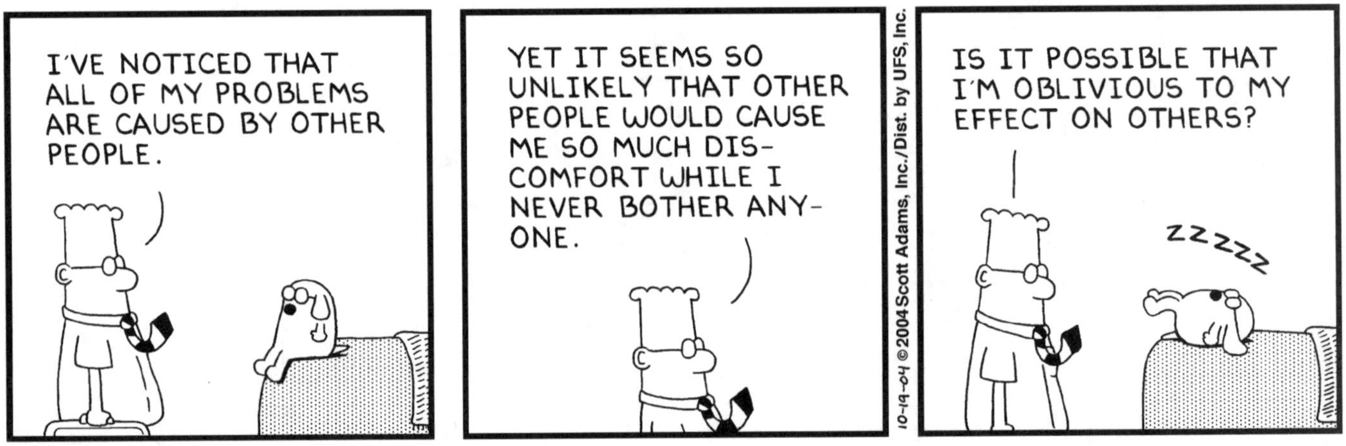
I'VE NOTICED THAT ALL OF MY PROBLEMS ARE CAUSED BY OTHER PEOPLE.
YET IT SEEMS SO UNLIKELY THAT OTHER PEOPLE WOULD CAUSE ME SO MUCH DIS-COMFORT WHILE I NEVER BOTHER ANY-ONE.
10-19-04 ©2004 Scott Adams, Inc./Dist. by UFS, Inc.
IS IT POSSIBLE THAT I'M OBLIVIOUS TO MY EFFECT ON OTHERS?
ZZZZZ

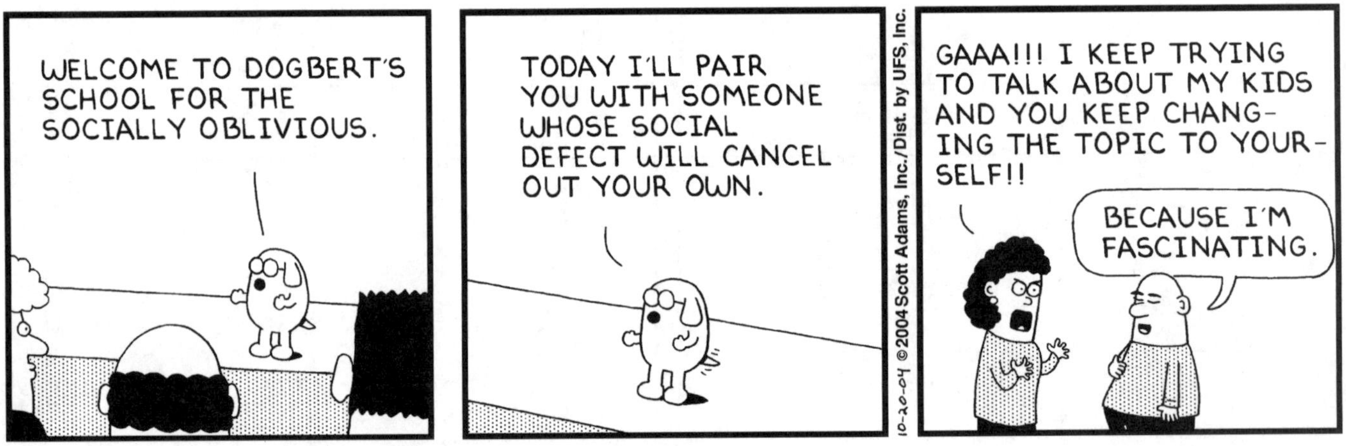
WELCOME TO DOGBERT'S SCHOOL FOR THE SOCIALLY OBLIVIOUS.
TODAY I'LL PAIR YOU WITH SOMEONE WHOSE SOCIAL DEFECT WILL CANCEL OUT YOUR OWN.
10-20-04 ©2004 Scott Adams, Inc./Dist. by UFS, Inc.
GAAA!!! I KEEP TRYING TO TALK ABOUT MY KIDS AND YOU KEEP CHANG-ING THE TOPIC TO YOUR-SELF!!
BECAUSE I'M FASCINATING.

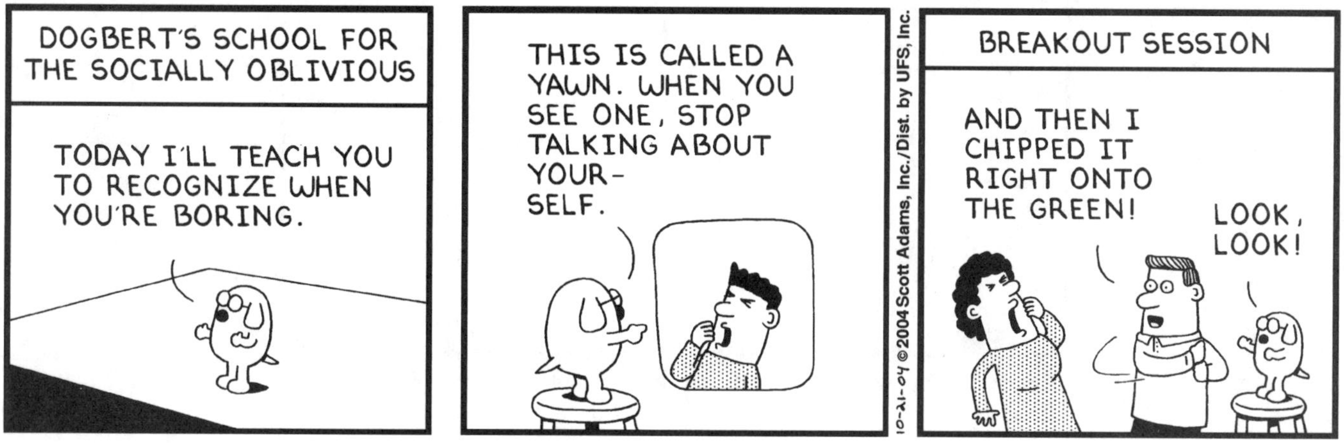
DOGBERT'S SCHOOL FOR THE SOCIALLY OBLIVIOUS
TODAY I'LL TEACH YOU TO RECOGNIZE WHEN YOU'RE BORING.
THIS IS CALLED A YAWN. WHEN YOU SEE ONE, STOP TALKING ABOUT YOUR-SELF.
10-21-04 ©2004 Scott Adams, Inc./Dist. by UFS, Inc.
BREAKOUT SESSION
AND THEN I CHIPPED IT RIGHT ONTO THE GREEN!
LOOK, LOOK!

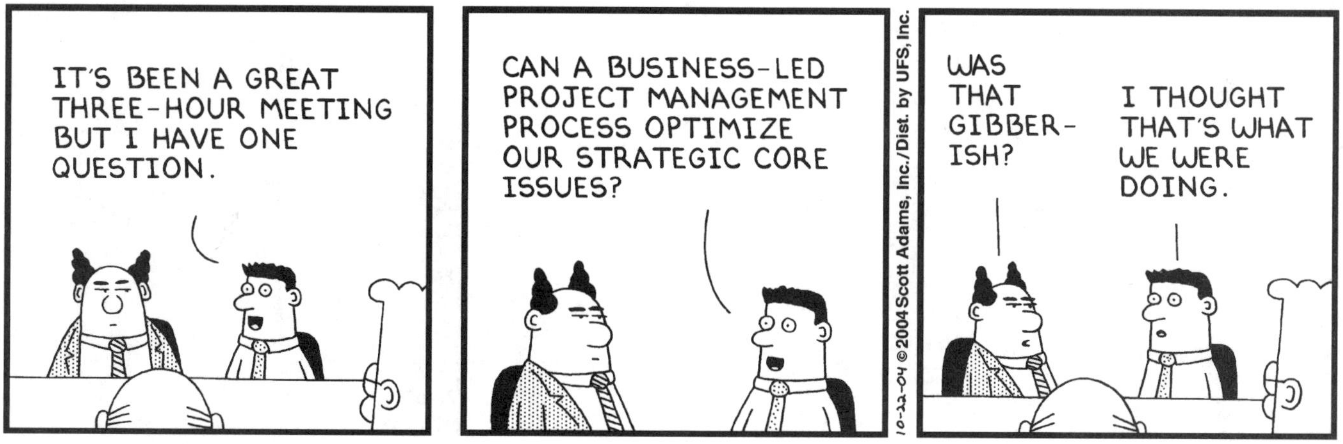
IT'S BEEN A GREAT THREE-HOUR MEETING BUT I HAVE ONE QUESTION.
CAN A BUSINESS-LED PROJECT MANAGEMENT PROCESS OPTIMIZE OUR STRATEGIC CORE ISSUES?
10-22-04 ©2004 Scott Adams, Inc./Dist. by UFS, Inc.
WAS THAT GIBBER-ISH?
I THOUGHT THAT'S WHAT WE WERE DOING.

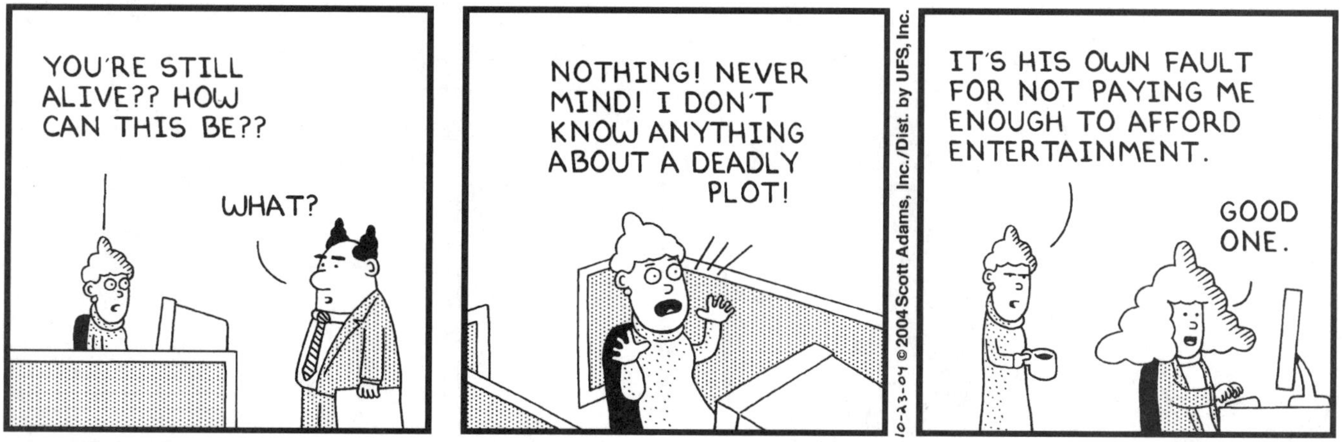
YOU'RE STILL ALIVE?? HOW CAN THIS BE??
WHAT?
NOTHING! NEVER MIND! I DON'T KNOW ANYTHING ABOUT A DEADLY PLOT!
10-23-04 ©2004 Scott Adams, Inc./Dist. by UFS, Inc.
IT'S HIS OWN FAULT FOR NOT PAYING ME ENOUGH TO AFFORD ENTERTAINMENT.
GOOD ONE.

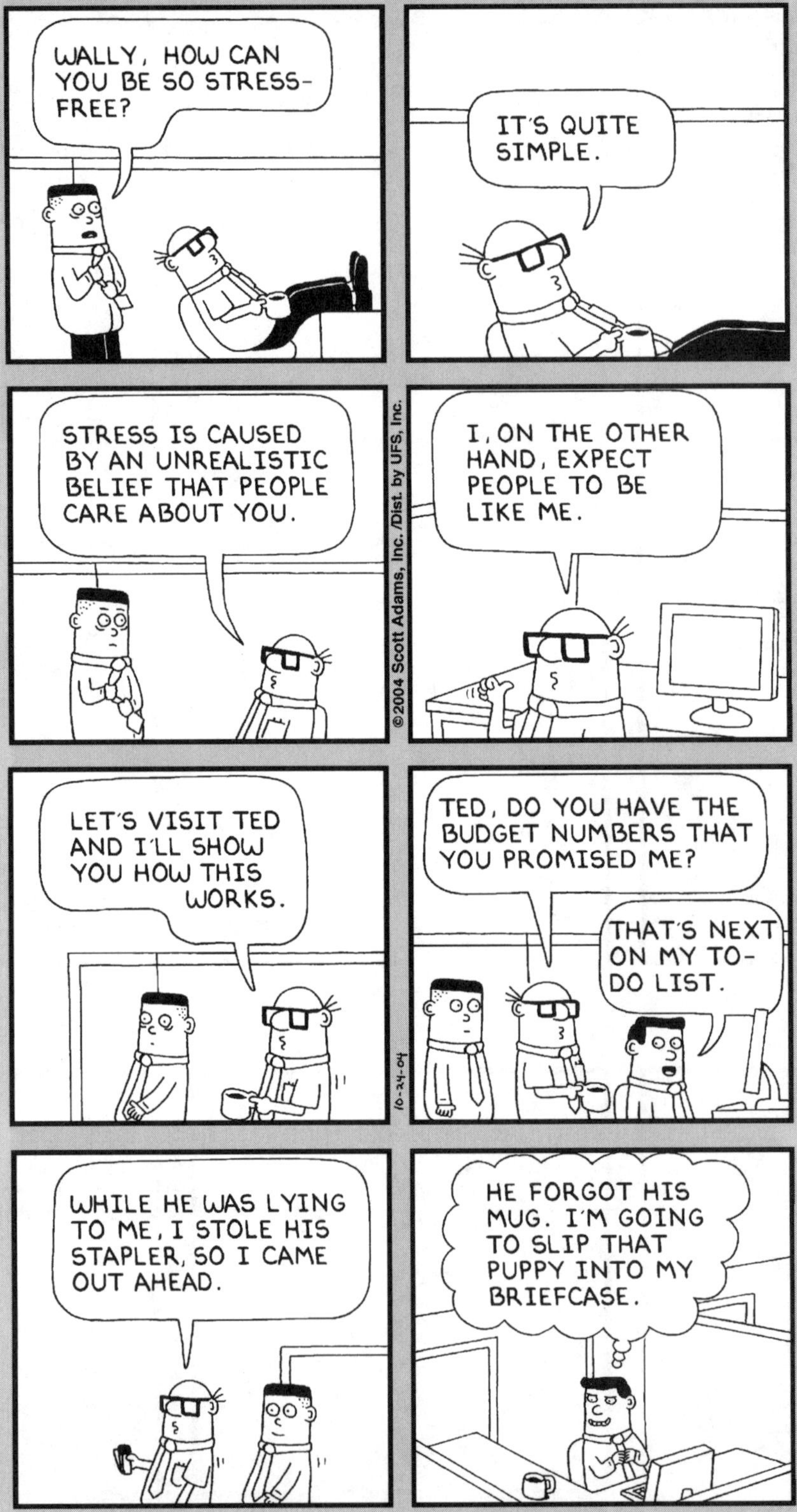
WALLY, HOW CAN YOU BE SO STRESS-FREE?
IT'S QUITE SIMPLE.
STRESS IS CAUSED BY AN UNREALISTIC BELIEF THAT PEOPLE CARE ABOUT YOU.
I, ON THE OTHER HAND, EXPECT PEOPLE TO BE LIKE ME.
LET'S VISIT TED AND I'LL SHOW YOU HOW THIS WORKS.
TED, DO YOU HAVE THE BUDGET NUMBERS THAT YOU PROMISED ME?
THAT'S NEXT ON MY TO-DO LIST.
WHILE HE WAS LYING TO ME, I STOLE HIS STAPLER, SO I CAME OUT AHEAD.
HE FORGOT HIS MUG. I'M GOING TO SLIP THAT PUPPY INTO MY BRIEFCASE.
©2004 Scott Adams, Inc. /Dist. by UFS, Inc.
10-24-04

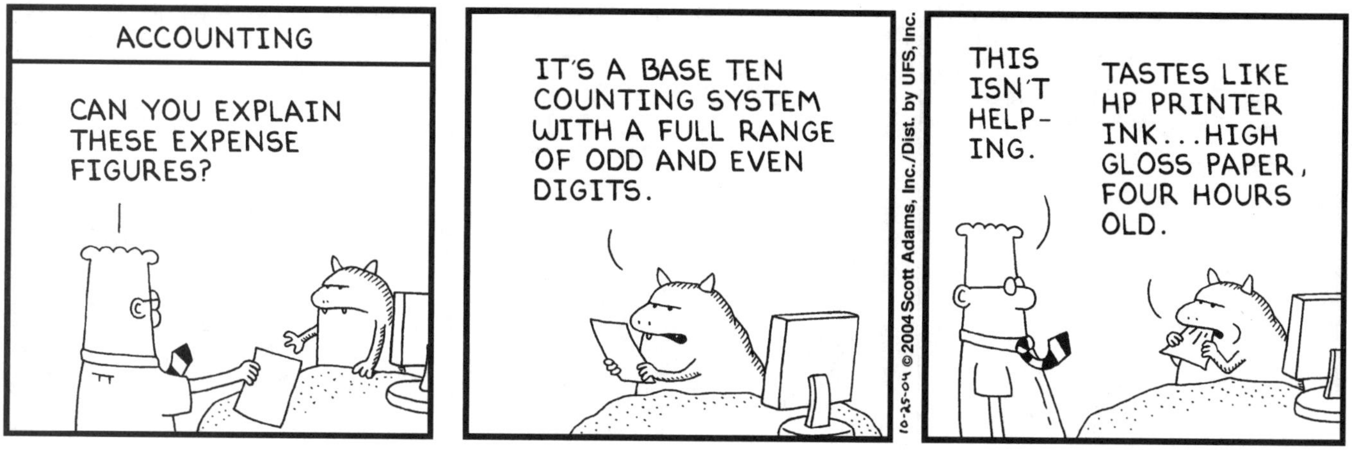
ACCOUNTING
CAN YOU EXPLAIN THESE EXPENSE FIGURES?
IT'S A BASE TEN COUNTING SYSTEM WITH A FULL RANGE OF ODD AND EVEN DIGITS.
10-25-04 © 2004 Scott Adams, Inc./Dist. by UFS, Inc.
THIS ISN'T HELP-ING.
TASTES LIKE HP PRINTER INK...HIGH GLOSS PAPER, FOUR HOURS OLD.

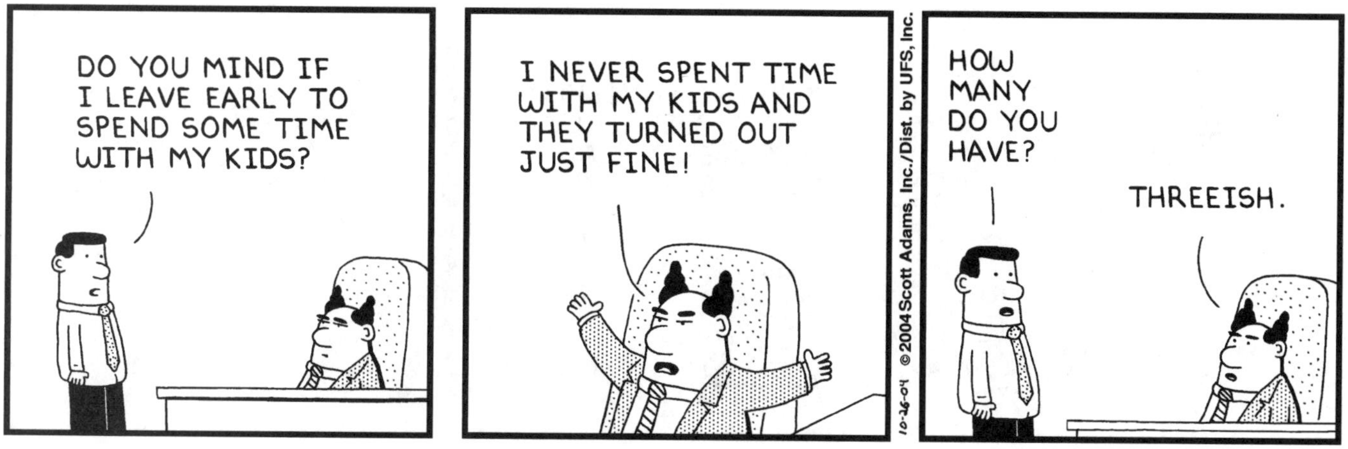
DO YOU MIND IF I LEAVE EARLY TO SPEND SOME TIME WITH MY KIDS?
I NEVER SPENT TIME WITH MY KIDS AND THEY TURNED OUT JUST FINE!
10-26-04 © 2004 Scott Adams, Inc./Dist. by UFS, Inc.
HOW MANY DO YOU HAVE?
THREEISH.

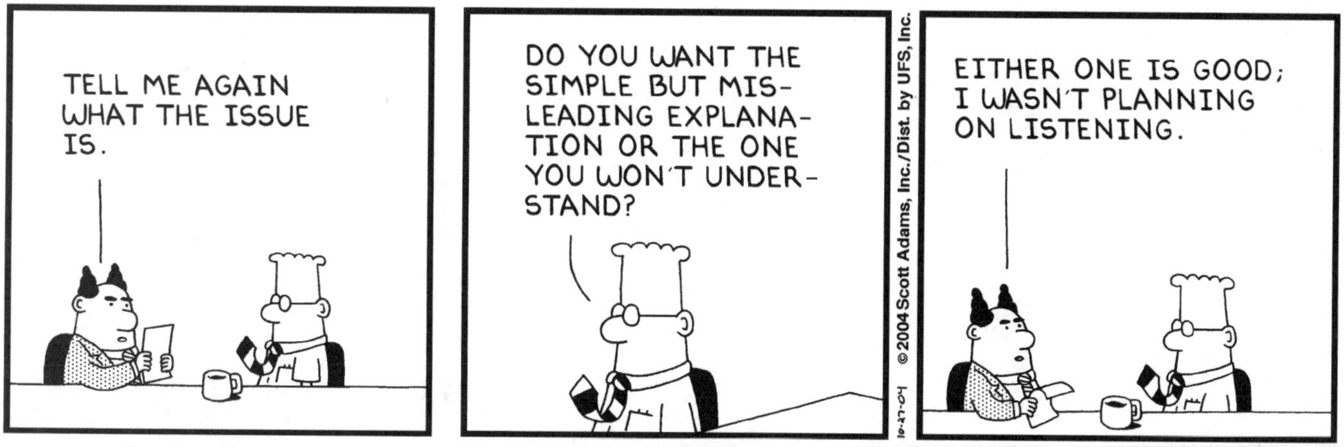
TELL ME AGAIN WHAT THE ISSUE IS.
DO YOU WANT THE SIMPLE BUT MIS-LEADING EXPLANA-TION OR THE ONE YOU WON'T UNDER-STAND?
10-27-04 © 2004 Scott Adams, Inc./Dist. by UFS, Inc.
EITHER ONE IS GOOD; I WASN'T PLANNING ON LISTENING.

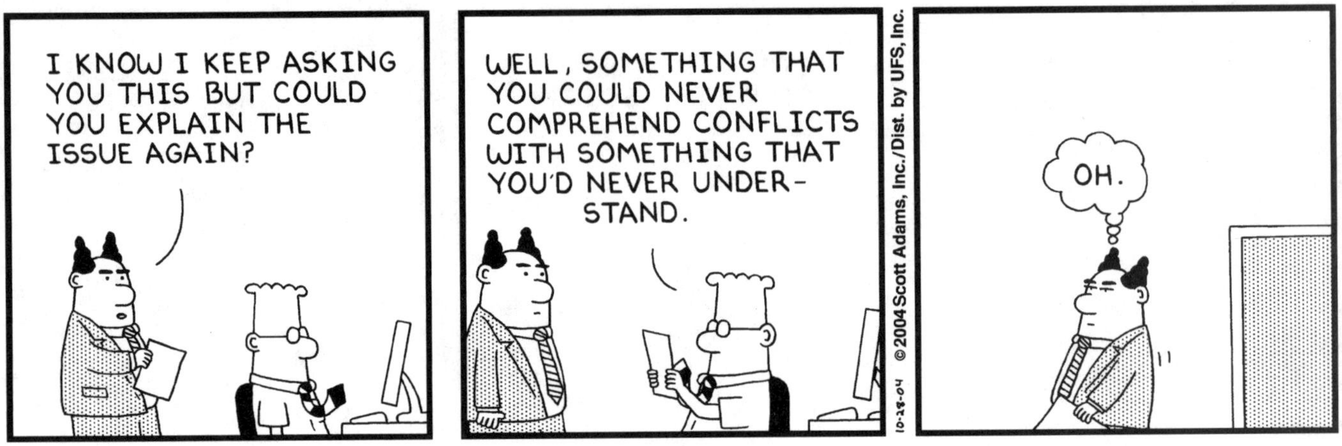
I KNOW I KEEP ASKING YOU THIS BUT COULD YOU EXPLAIN THE ISSUE AGAIN?
WELL, SOMETHING THAT YOU COULD NEVER COMPREHEND CONFLICTS WITH SOMETHING THAT YOU'D NEVER UNDER-STAND.
© 2004 Scott Adams, Inc./Dist. by UFS, Inc.
10-28-04
OH.

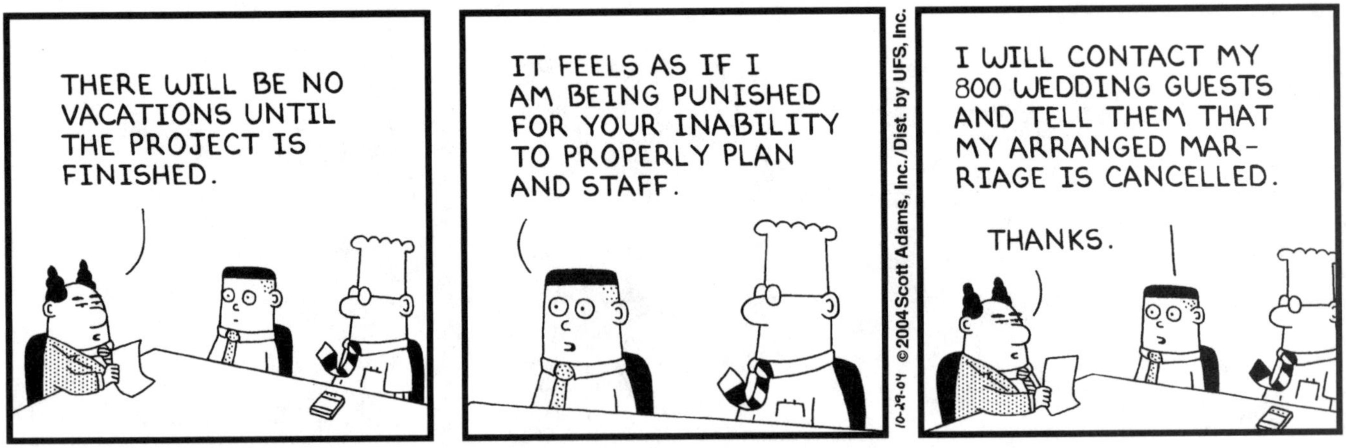
THERE WILL BE NO VACATIONS UNTIL THE PROJECT IS FINISHED.
IT FEELS AS IF I AM BEING PUNISHED FOR YOUR INABILITY TO PROPERLY PLAN AND STAFF.
© 2004 Scott Adams, Inc./Dist. by UFS, Inc.
10-29-04
I WILL CONTACT MY 800 WEDDING GUESTS AND TELL THEM THAT MY ARRANGED MAR-RIAGE IS CANCELLED.
THANKS.

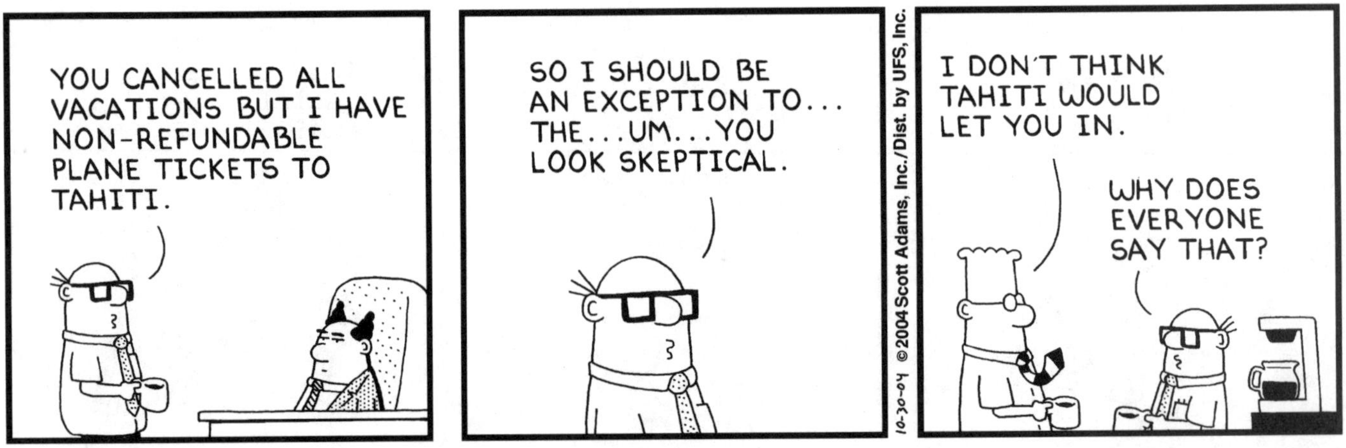
YOU CANCELLED ALL VACATIONS BUT I HAVE NON-REFUNDABLE PLANE TICKETS TO TAHITI.
SO I SHOULD BE AN EXCEPTION TO... THE...UM...YOU LOOK SKEPTICAL.
© 2004 Scott Adams, Inc./Dist. by UFS, Inc.
10-30-04
I DON'T THINK TAHITI WOULD LET YOU IN.
WHY DOES EVERYONE SAY THAT?

THE NEW SENIOR VICE PRESIDENT WILL BE AT MY MEETING.
I HOPE TO IMPRESS HIM WITH MY LEADERSHIP SKILLS.
UH-OH. UNDERLING ALERT.
©2004 Scott Adams, Inc./Dist. by UFS, Inc.
I CAN'T BE SEEN GETTING CHUMMY WITH AN INTERN.
PLEASE DON'T TRY TO MAKE CONVERSATION. DON'T, DON'T, DON'T, DON'T, DON'T.
10-31-04
DID YOU DO ANYTHING FUN THIS WEEKEND?
HERE HE COMES!
GET BACK TO WORK, YOU SLACKING SLACKER!!!
GOOD MOTIVATING! IF HE BLOWS HIS NOSE WITH HIS NECKTIE, YOU'RE MY NEW VICE PRESIDENT.
WAAA!!!

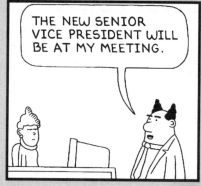

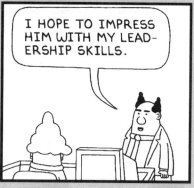

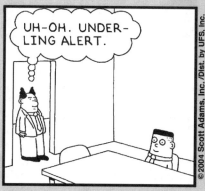

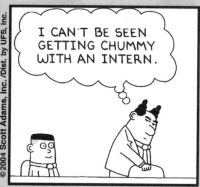

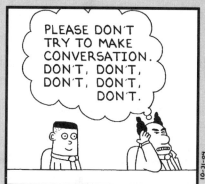

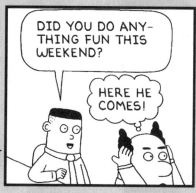

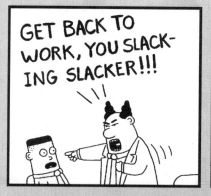

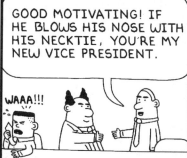

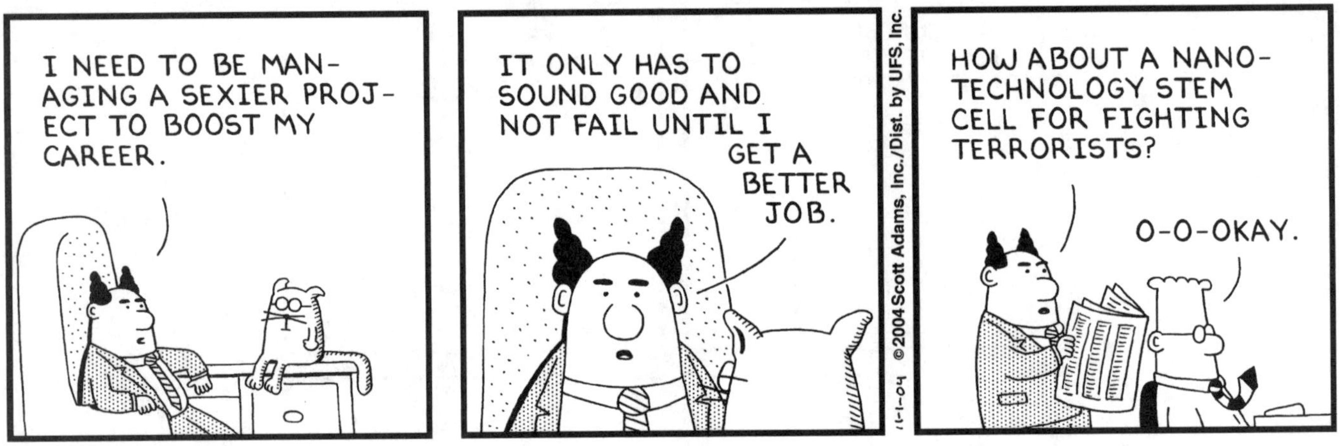
I NEED TO BE MANAGING A SEXIER PROJECT TO BOOST MY CAREER.
IT ONLY HAS TO SOUND GOOD AND NOT FAIL UNTIL I GET A BETTER JOB.
HOW ABOUT A NANOTECHNOLOGY STEM CELL FOR FIGHTING TERRORISTS?
O-O-OKAY.
11-1-04

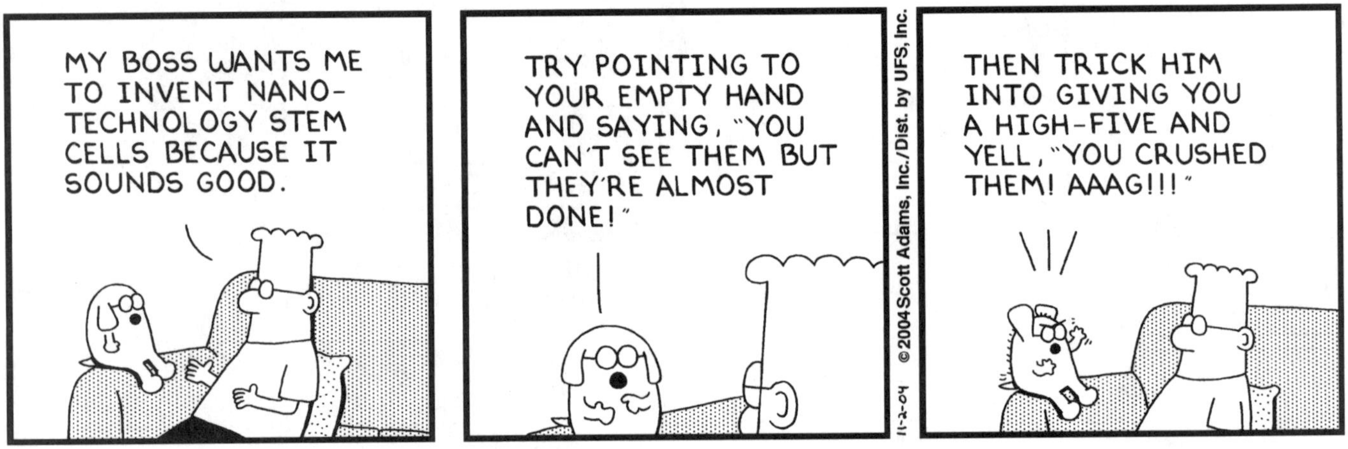
MY BOSS WANTS ME TO INVENT NANOTECHNOLOGY STEM CELLS BECAUSE IT SOUNDS GOOD.
TRY POINTING TO YOUR EMPTY HAND AND SAYING, "YOU CAN'T SEE THEM BUT THEY'RE ALMOST DONE!"
THEN TRICK HIM INTO GIVING YOU A HIGH-FIVE AND YELL, "YOU CRUSHED THEM! AAAG!!!"
11-2-04

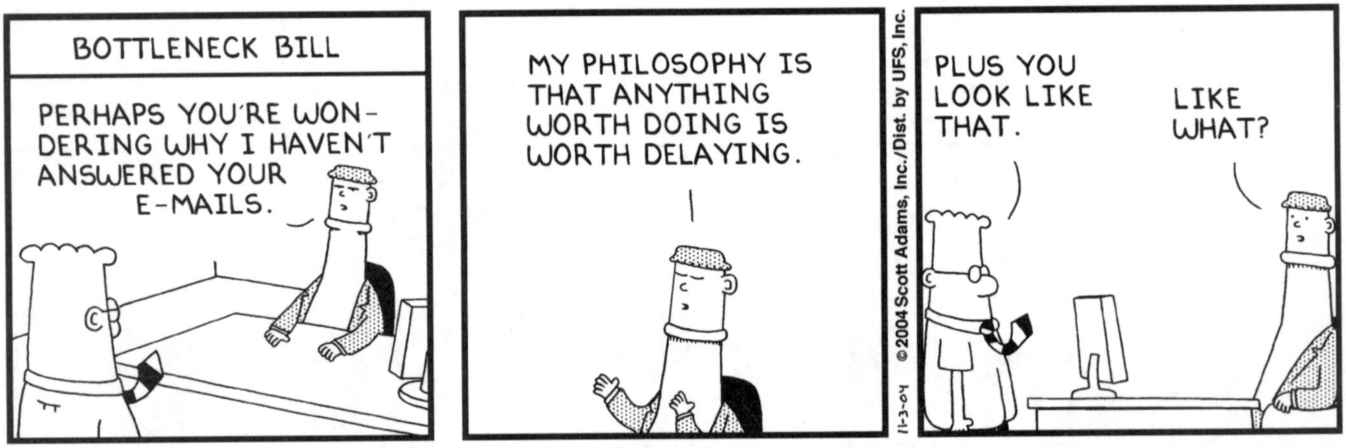
BOTTLENECK BILL
PERHAPS YOU'RE WONDERING WHY I HAVEN'T ANSWERED YOUR E-MAILS.
MY PHILOSOPHY IS THAT ANYTHING WORTH DOING IS WORTH DELAYING.
PLUS YOU LOOK LIKE THAT.
LIKE WHAT?
11-3-04

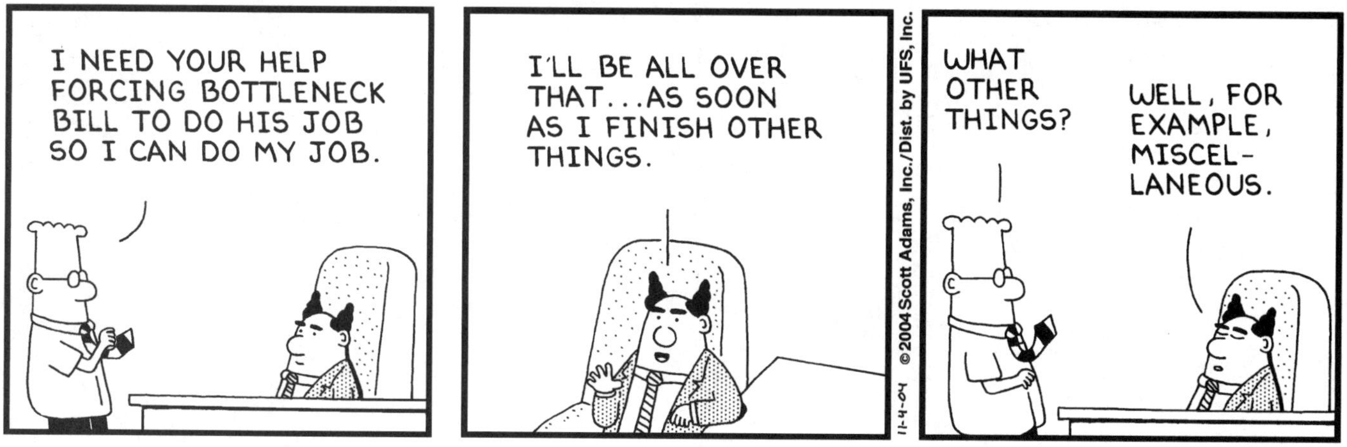
I NEED YOUR HELP FORCING BOTTLENECK BILL TO DO HIS JOB SO I CAN DO MY JOB.
I'LL BE ALL OVER THAT...AS SOON AS I FINISH OTHER THINGS.
WHAT OTHER THINGS?
WELL, FOR EXAMPLE, MISCEL-LANEOUS.
11-4-04 ©2004 Scott Adams, Inc./Dist. by UFS, Inc.

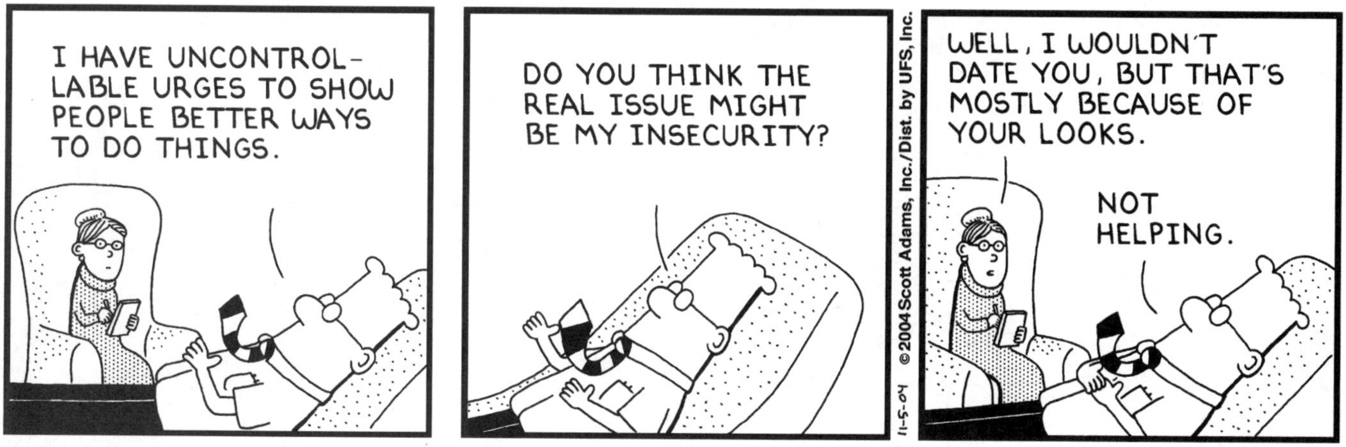
I HAVE UNCONTROL-LABLE URGES TO SHOW PEOPLE BETTER WAYS TO DO THINGS.
DO YOU THINK THE REAL ISSUE MIGHT BE MY INSECURITY?
WELL, I WOULDN'T DATE YOU, BUT THAT'S MOSTLY BECAUSE OF YOUR LOOKS.
NOT HELPING.
11-5-04 ©2004 Scott Adams, Inc./Dist. by UFS, Inc.

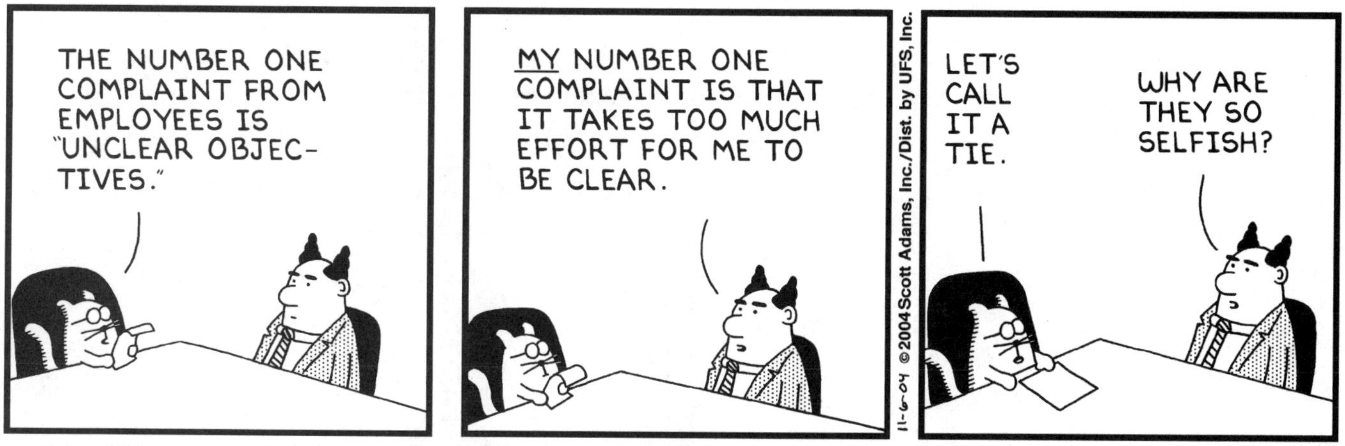
THE NUMBER ONE COMPLAINT FROM EMPLOYEES IS "UNCLEAR OBJEC-TIVES."
MY NUMBER ONE COMPLAINT IS THAT IT TAKES TOO MUCH EFFORT FOR ME TO BE CLEAR.
LET'S CALL IT A TIE.
WHY ARE THEY SO SELFISH?
11-6-04 ©2004 Scott Adams, Inc./Dist. by UFS, Inc.

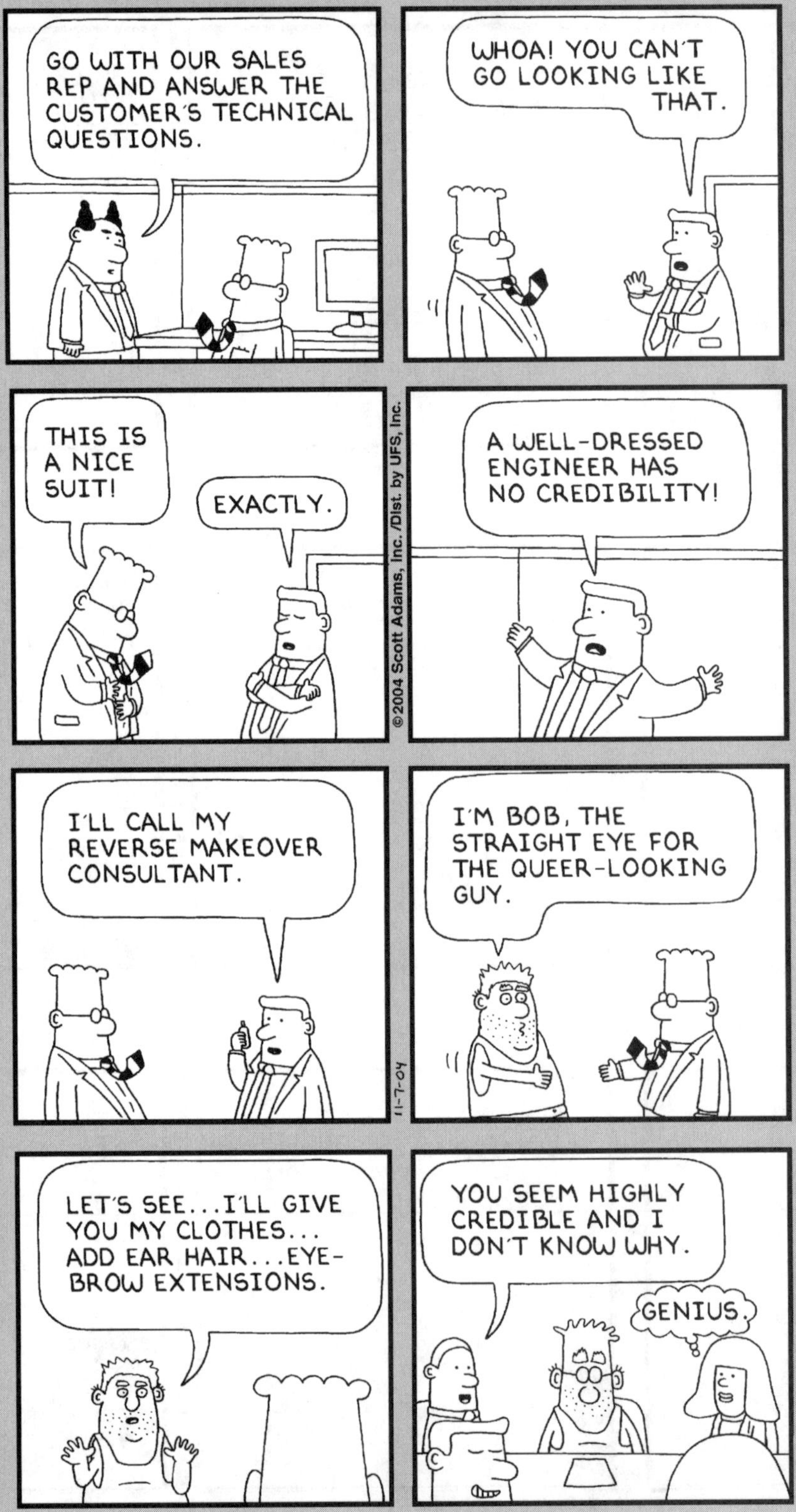
GO WITH OUR SALES REP AND ANSWER THE CUSTOMER'S TECHNICAL QUESTIONS.
WHOA! YOU CAN'T GO LOOKING LIKE THAT.
THIS IS A NICE SUIT!
EXACTLY.
©2004 Scott Adams, Inc./Dist. by UFS, Inc.
A WELL-DRESSED ENGINEER HAS NO CREDIBILITY!
I'LL CALL MY REVERSE MAKEOVER CONSULTANT.
11-7-04
I'M BOB, THE STRAIGHT EYE FOR THE QUEER-LOOKING GUY.
LET'S SEE...I'LL GIVE YOU MY CLOTHES... ADD EAR HAIR...EYE-BROW EXTENSIONS.
YOU SEEM HIGHLY CREDIBLE AND I DON'T KNOW WHY.
GENIUS.

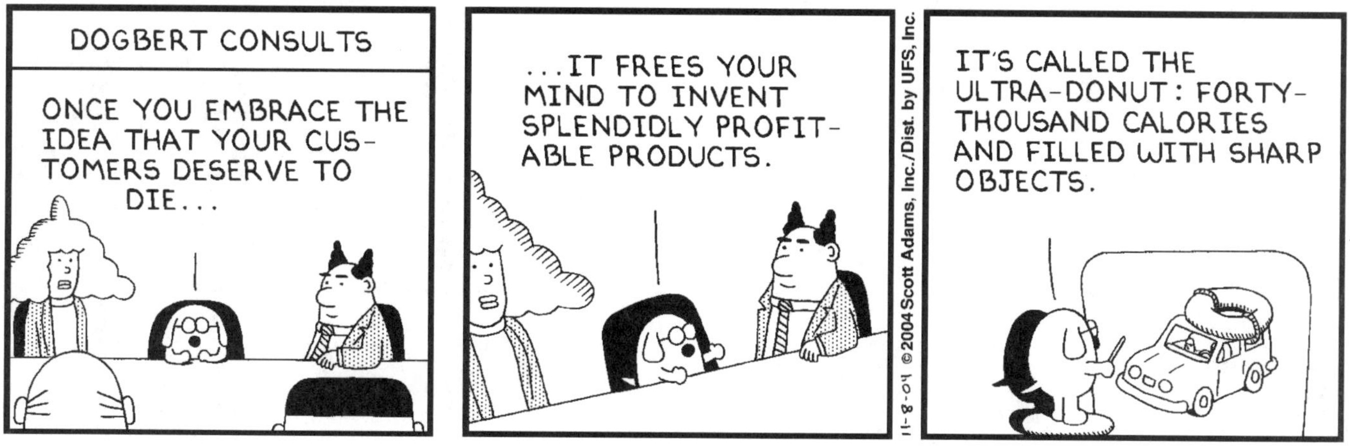
DOGBERT CONSULTS
ONCE YOU EMBRACE THE IDEA THAT YOUR CUS-TOMERS DESERVE TO DIE...
...IT FREES YOUR MIND TO INVENT SPLENDIDLY PROFIT-ABLE PRODUCTS.
11-8-04 ©2004 Scott Adams, Inc./Dist. by UFS, Inc.
IT'S CALLED THE ULTRA-DONUT: FORTY-THOUSAND CALORIES AND FILLED WITH SHARP OBJECTS.

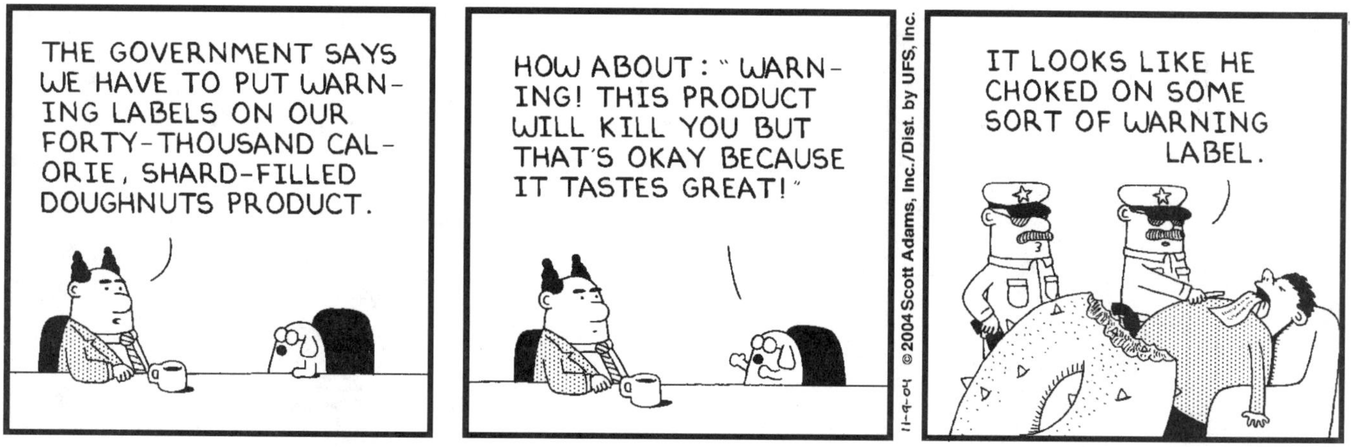
THE GOVERNMENT SAYS WE HAVE TO PUT WARN-ING LABELS ON OUR FORTY-THOUSAND CAL-ORIE, SHARD-FILLED DOUGHNUTS PRODUCT.
HOW ABOUT: "WARN-ING! THIS PRODUCT WILL KILL YOU BUT THAT'S OKAY BECAUSE IT TASTES GREAT!"
11-9-04 ©2004 Scott Adams, Inc./Dist. by UFS, Inc.
IT LOOKS LIKE HE CHOKED ON SOME SORT OF WARNING LABEL.

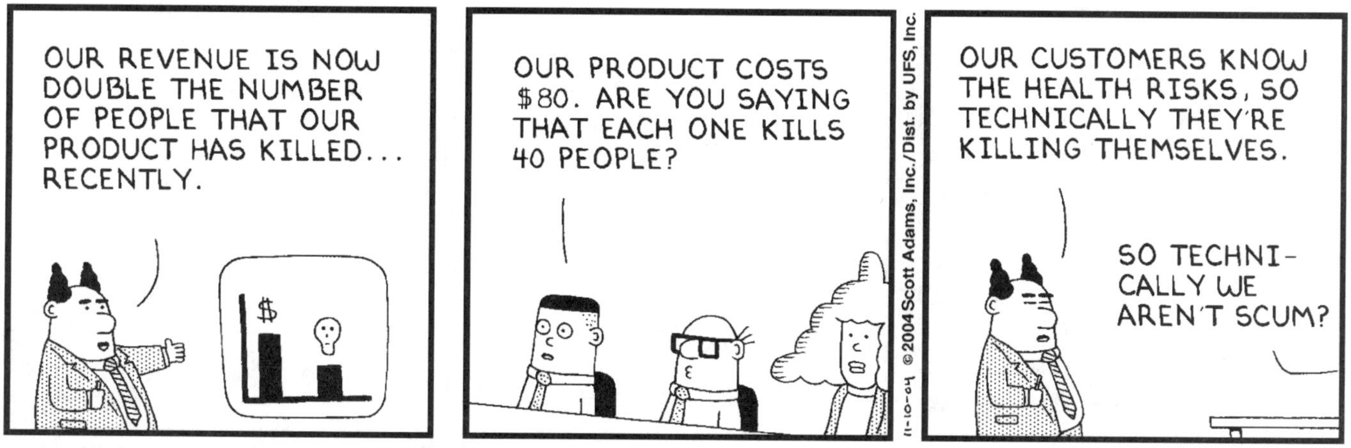
OUR REVENUE IS NOW DOUBLE THE NUMBER OF PEOPLE THAT OUR PRODUCT HAS KILLED... RECENTLY.
$
OUR PRODUCT COSTS $80. ARE YOU SAYING THAT EACH ONE KILLS 40 PEOPLE?
11-10-04 ©2004 Scott Adams, Inc./Dist. by UFS, Inc.
OUR CUSTOMERS KNOW THE HEALTH RISKS, SO TECHNICALLY THEY'RE KILLING THEMSELVES.
SO TECHNI-CALLY WE AREN'T SCUM?

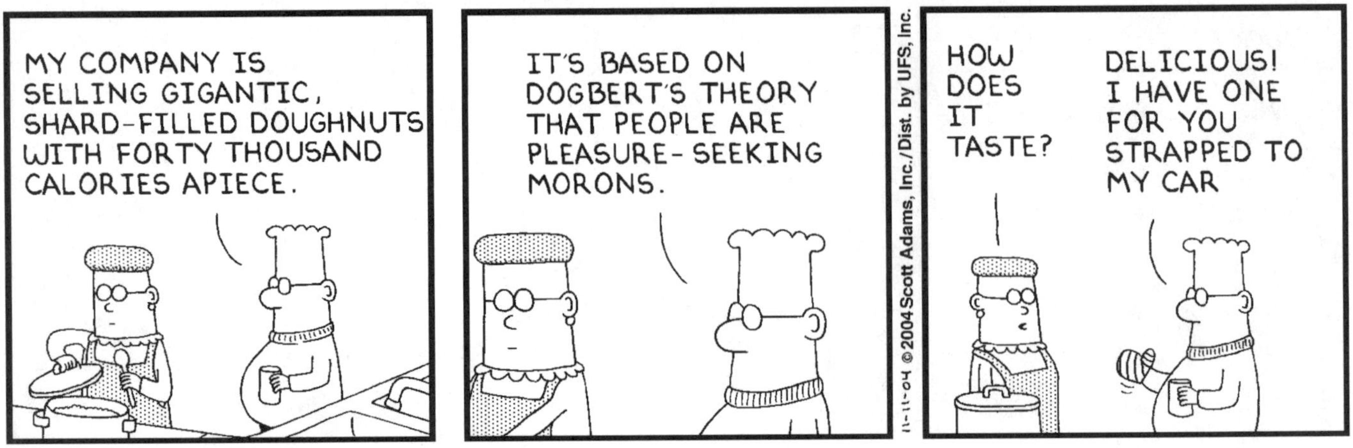
MY COMPANY IS SELLING GIGANTIC, SHARD-FILLED DOUGHNUTS WITH FORTY THOUSAND CALORIES APIECE.
IT'S BASED ON DOGBERT'S THEORY THAT PEOPLE ARE PLEASURE-SEEKING MORONS.
HOW DOES IT TASTE?
DELICIOUS! I HAVE ONE FOR YOU STRAPPED TO MY CAR
11-11-04 ©2004 Scott Adams, Inc./Dist. by UFS, Inc.

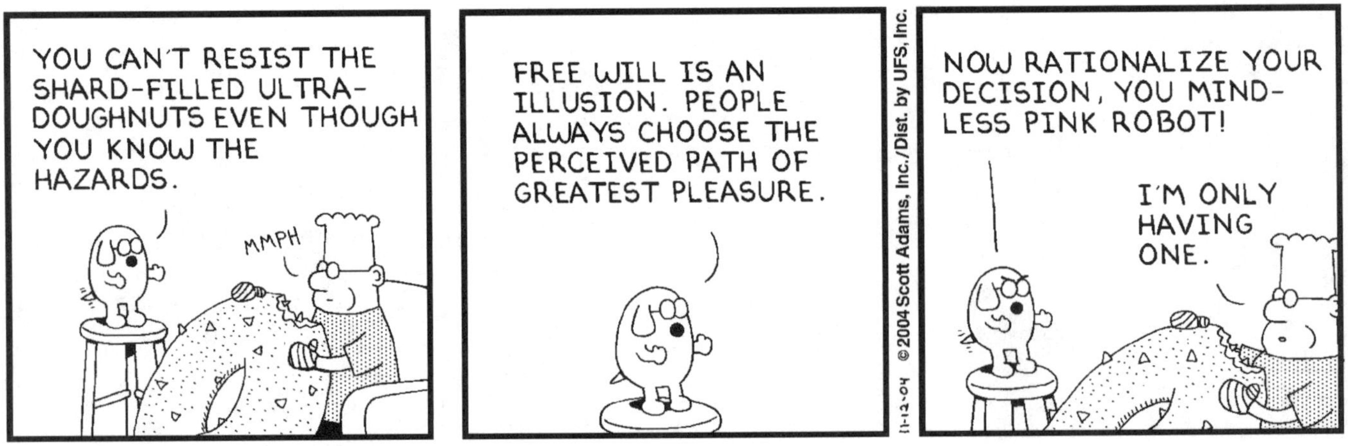
YOU CAN'T RESIST THE SHARD-FILLED ULTRA-DOUGHNUTS EVEN THOUGH YOU KNOW THE HAZARDS.
MMPH
FREE WILL IS AN ILLUSION. PEOPLE ALWAYS CHOOSE THE PERCEIVED PATH OF GREATEST PLEASURE.
NOW RATIONALIZE YOUR DECISION, YOU MIND-LESS PINK ROBOT!
I'M ONLY HAVING ONE.
11-12-04 ©2004 Scott Adams, Inc./Dist. by UFS, Inc.

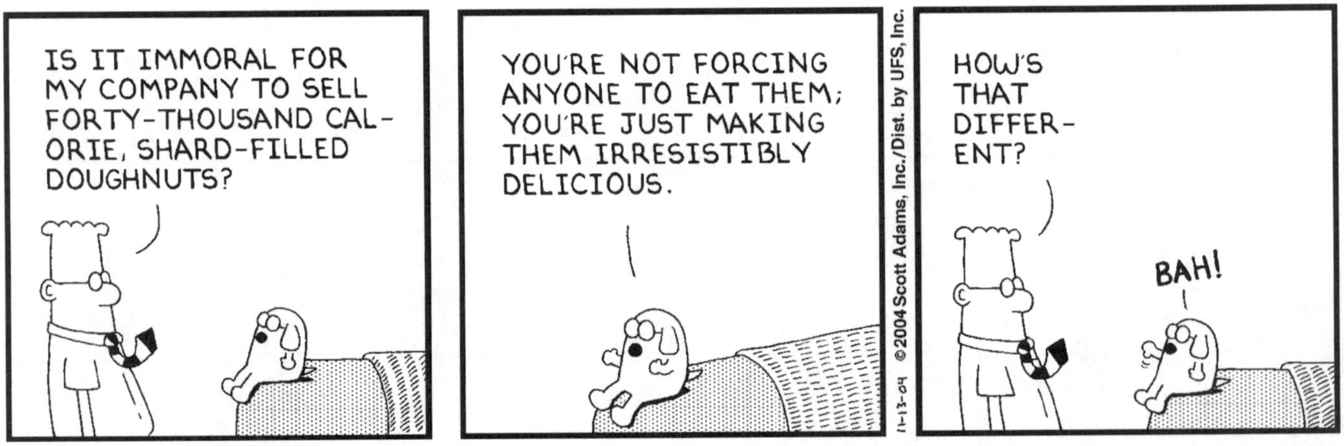
IS IT IMMORAL FOR MY COMPANY TO SELL FORTY-THOUSAND CAL-ORIE, SHARD-FILLED DOUGHNUTS?
YOU'RE NOT FORCING ANYONE TO EAT THEM; YOU'RE JUST MAKING THEM IRRESISTIBLY DELICIOUS.
HOW'S THAT DIFFER-ENT?
BAH!
11-13-04 ©2004 Scott Adams, Inc./Dist. by UFS, Inc.

CATBERT: EVIL DIRECTOR OF HUMAN RESOURCES
EXCELLENT IDEA.
EVIL H.R. DIGEST
CELL PHONES WITH CAMERAS ARE BANNED FROM THE WORKPLACE.
WHY?
WE DON'T WANT YOU TAKING PICTURES OF PROPRIETARY INFORMATION.
©2004 Scott Adams, Inc./Dist. by UFS, Inc.
MOST OF OUR INFORMATION IS IN DIGITAL FORM AND CAN BE E-MAILED ANYWHERE.
THE REST IS ON PAPER THAT CAN BE COPIED, SCANNED OR TUCKED DOWN ONE'S TROUSERS.
11-14-04
MY NEW CELL PHONE WILL BE RENDERED USELESS FOR NO GOOD REASON!
AND YOU AREN'T EVEN BANNING REGULAR CAMERAS!!
THIS ONE GOES IN THE SCRAPBOOK.
SNAP

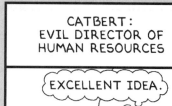

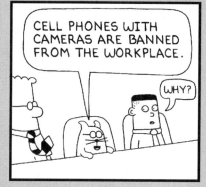

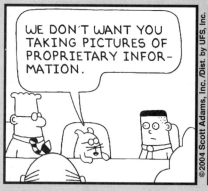

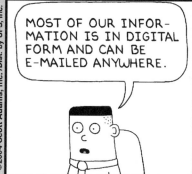

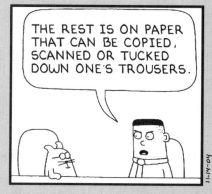

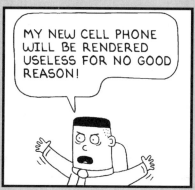

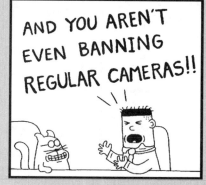

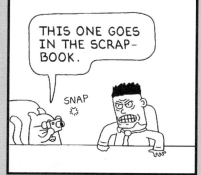

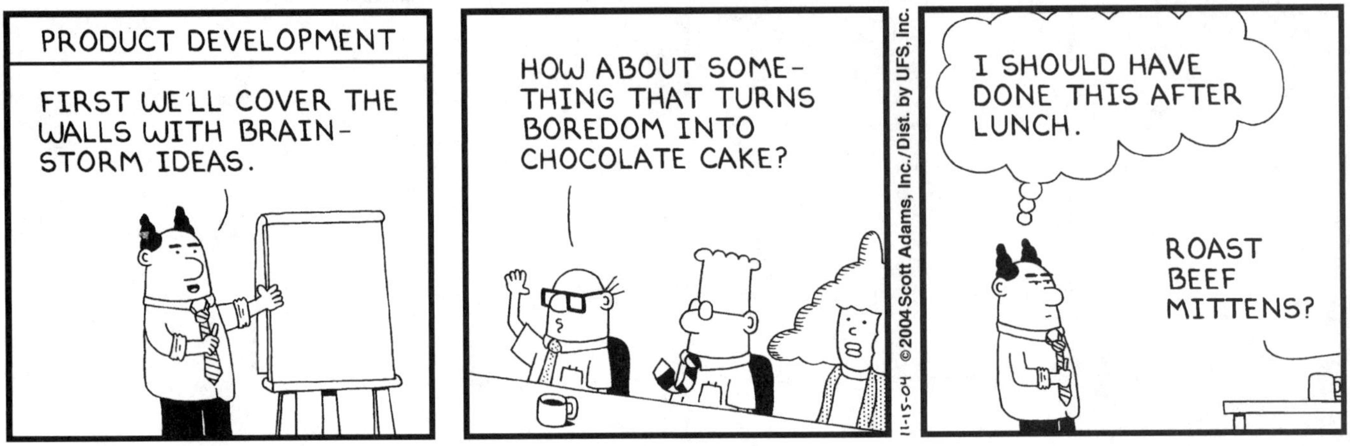
PRODUCT DEVELOPMENT
FIRST WE'LL COVER THE WALLS WITH BRAIN-STORM IDEAS.
HOW ABOUT SOME-THING THAT TURNS BOREDOM INTO CHOCOLATE CAKE?
©2004 Scott Adams, Inc./Dist. by UFS, Inc.
11-15-04
I SHOULD HAVE DONE THIS AFTER LUNCH.
ROAST BEEF MITTENS?

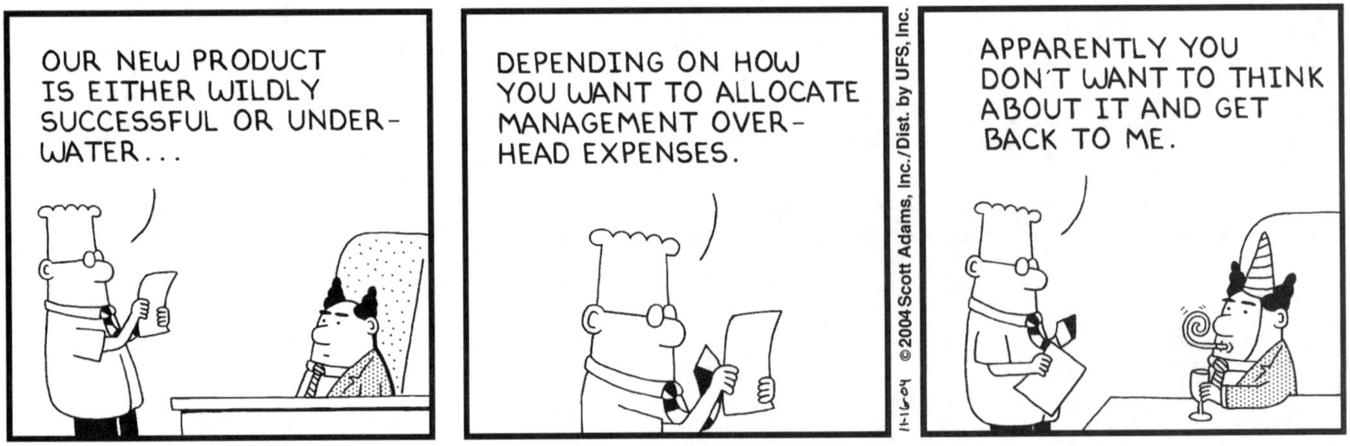
OUR NEW PRODUCT IS EITHER WILDLY SUCCESSFUL OR UNDER-WATER...
DEPENDING ON HOW YOU WANT TO ALLOCATE MANAGEMENT OVER-HEAD EXPENSES.
©2004 Scott Adams, Inc./Dist. by UFS, Inc.
11-16-04
APPARENTLY YOU DON'T WANT TO THINK ABOUT IT AND GET BACK TO ME.

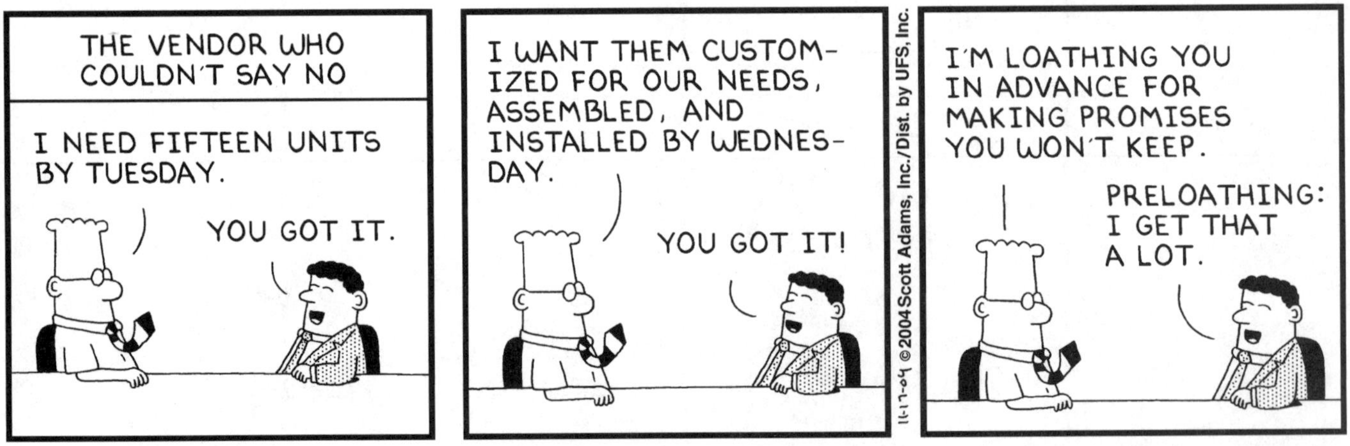
THE VENDOR WHO COULDN'T SAY NO
I NEED FIFTEEN UNITS BY TUESDAY.
YOU GOT IT.
I WANT THEM CUSTOM-IZED FOR OUR NEEDS, ASSEMBLED, AND INSTALLED BY WEDNES-DAY.
YOU GOT IT!
©2004 Scott Adams, Inc./Dist. by UFS, Inc.
11-17-04
I'M LOATHING YOU IN ADVANCE FOR MAKING PROMISES YOU WON'T KEEP.
PRELOATHING: I GET THAT A LOT.

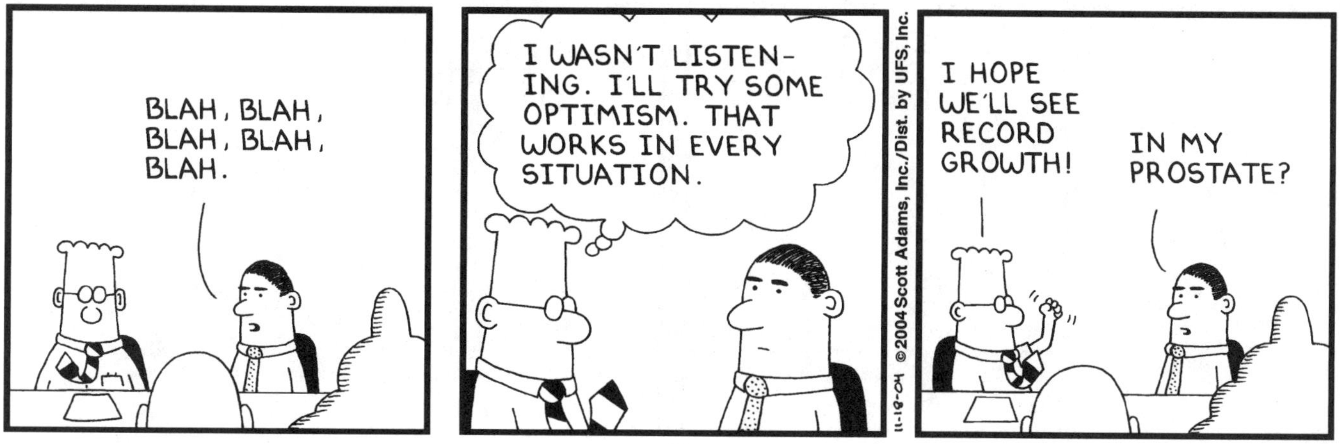
BLAH, BLAH, BLAH, BLAH, BLAH.
I WASN'T LISTEN-ING. I'LL TRY SOME OPTIMISM. THAT WORKS IN EVERY SITUATION.
11-19-04 ©2004 Scott Adams, Inc./Dist. by UFS, Inc.
I HOPE WE'LL SEE RECORD GROWTH!
IN MY PROSTATE?

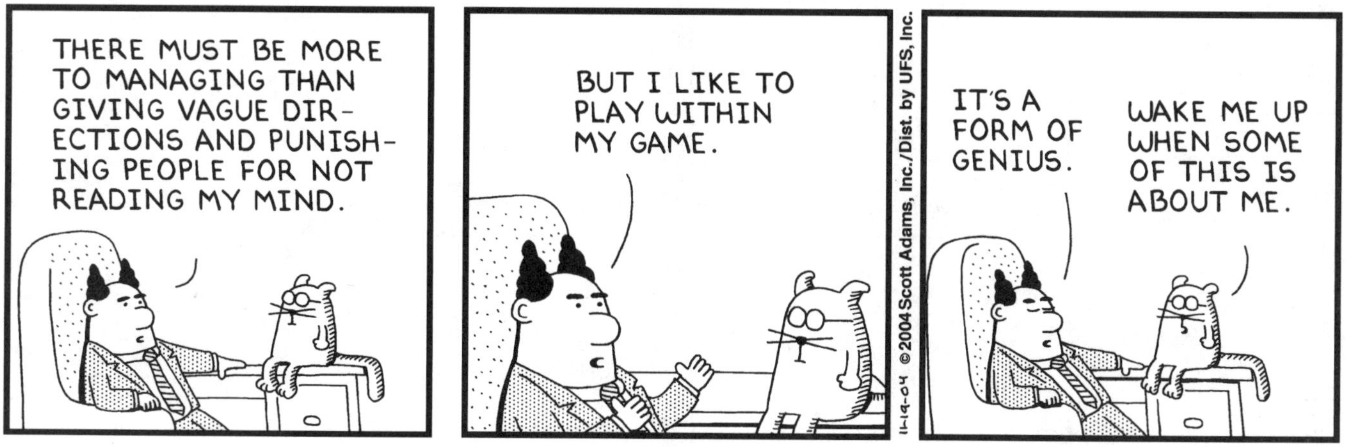
THERE MUST BE MORE TO MANAGING THAN GIVING VAGUE DIR-ECTIONS AND PUNISH-ING PEOPLE FOR NOT READING MY MIND.
BUT I LIKE TO PLAY WITHIN MY GAME.
11-19-04 ©2004 Scott Adams, Inc./Dist. by UFS, Inc.
IT'S A FORM OF GENIUS.
WAKE ME UP WHEN SOME OF THIS IS ABOUT ME.

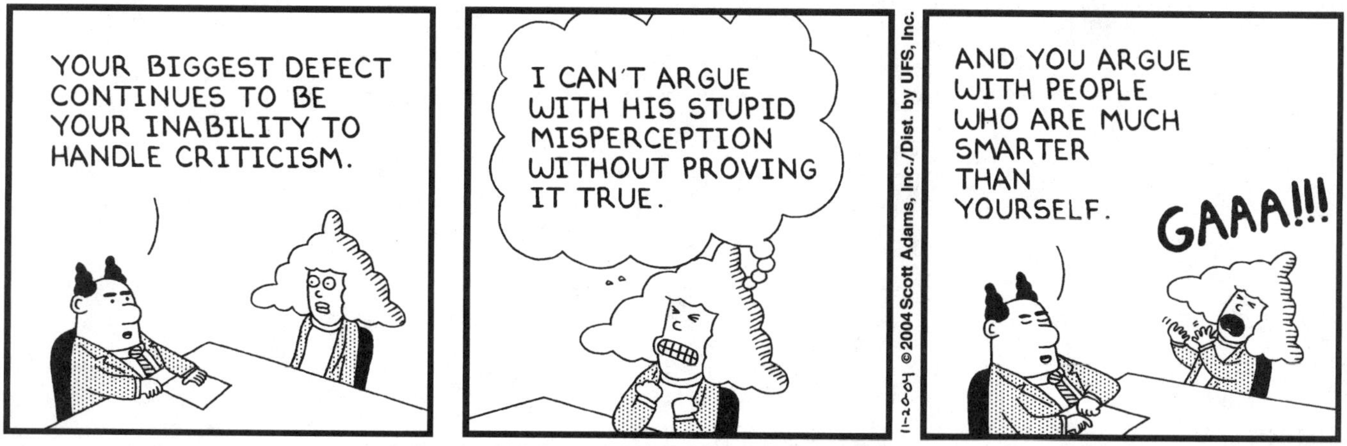
YOUR BIGGEST DEFECT CONTINUES TO BE YOUR INABILITY TO HANDLE CRITICISM.
I CAN'T ARGUE WITH HIS STUPID MISPERCEPTION WITHOUT PROVING IT TRUE.
11-20-04 ©2004 Scott Adams, Inc./Dist. by UFS, Inc.
AND YOU ARGUE WITH PEOPLE WHO ARE MUCH SMARTER THAN YOURSELF.
GAAA!!!

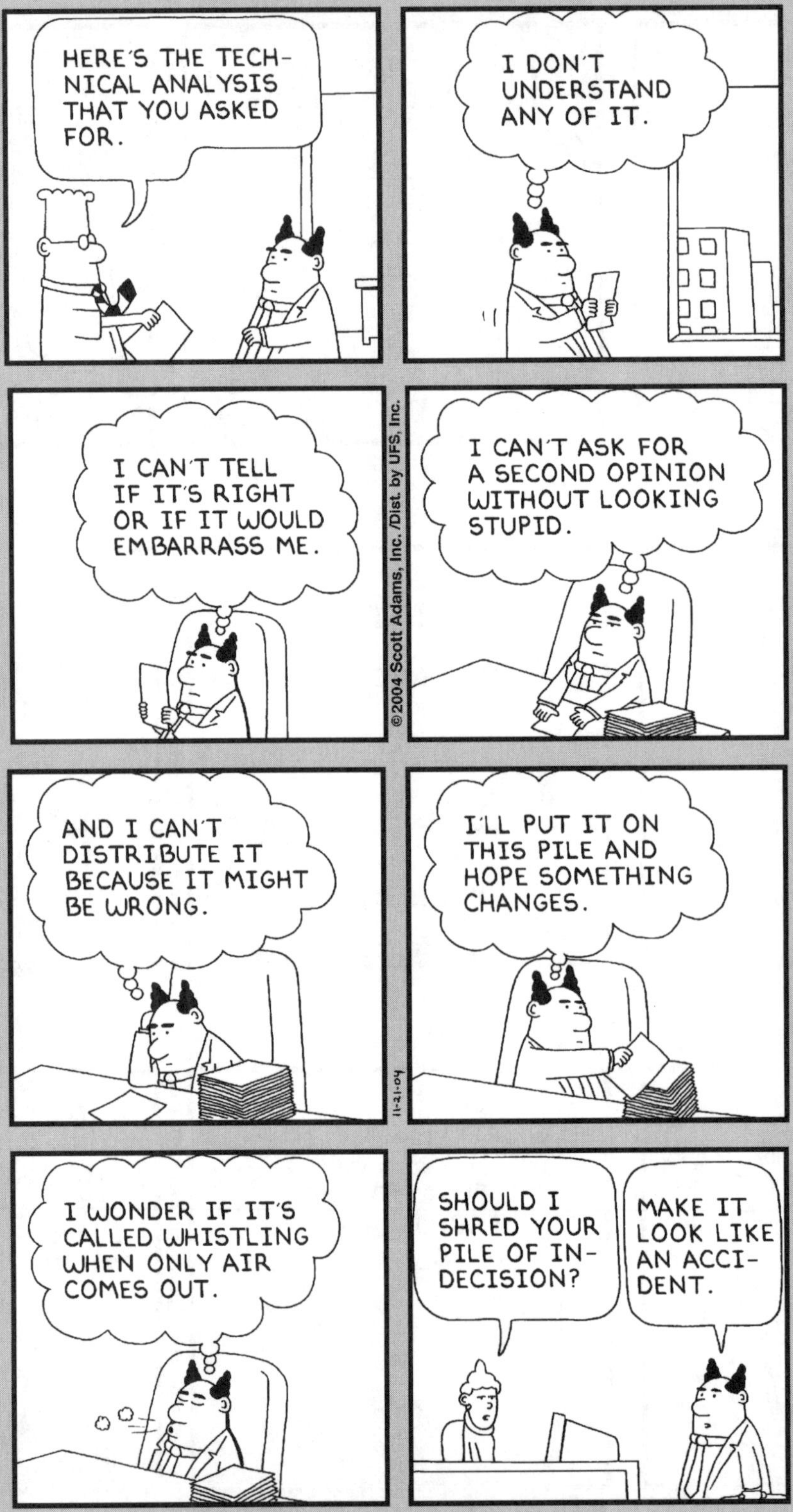
HERE'S THE TECH-NICAL ANALYSIS THAT YOU ASKED FOR.
I DON'T UNDERSTAND ANY OF IT.
I CAN'T TELL IF IT'S RIGHT OR IF IT WOULD EMBARRASS ME.
I CAN'T ASK FOR A SECOND OPINION WITHOUT LOOKING STUPID.
AND I CAN'T DISTRIBUTE IT BECAUSE IT MIGHT BE WRONG.
I'LL PUT IT ON THIS PILE AND HOPE SOMETHING CHANGES.
I WONDER IF IT'S CALLED WHISTLING WHEN ONLY AIR COMES OUT.
SHOULD I SHRED YOUR PILE OF IN-DECISION?
MAKE IT LOOK LIKE AN ACCI-DENT.
©2004 Scott Adams, Inc. /Dist. by UFS, Inc.
11-21-04

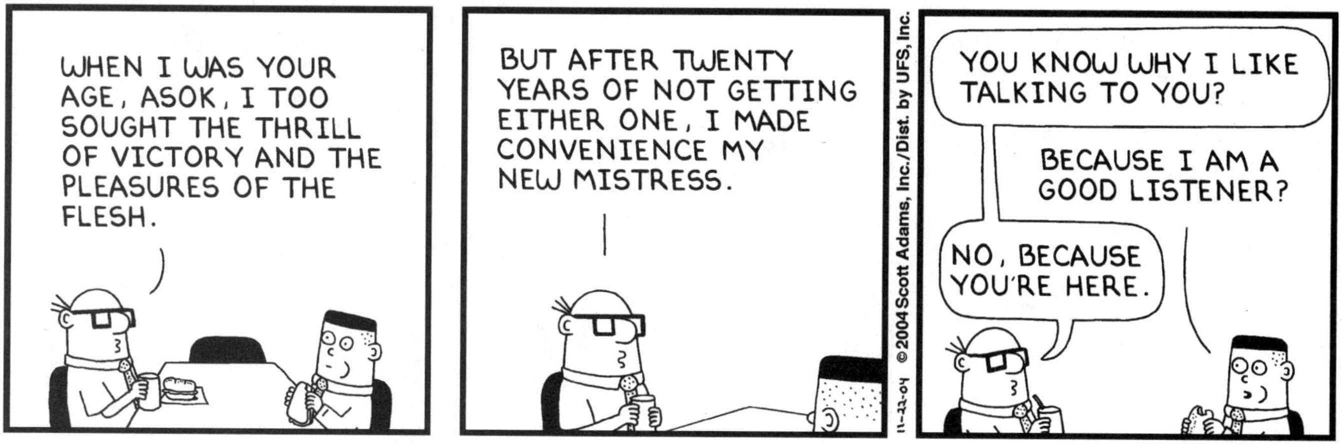
WHEN I WAS YOUR AGE, ASOK, I TOO SOUGHT THE THRILL OF VICTORY AND THE PLEASURES OF THE FLESH.
BUT AFTER TWENTY YEARS OF NOT GETTING EITHER ONE, I MADE CONVENIENCE MY NEW MISTRESS.
11-22-04 © 2004 Scott Adams, Inc./Dist. by UFS, Inc.
YOU KNOW WHY I LIKE TALKING TO YOU?
BECAUSE I AM A GOOD LISTENER?
NO, BECAUSE YOU'RE HERE.

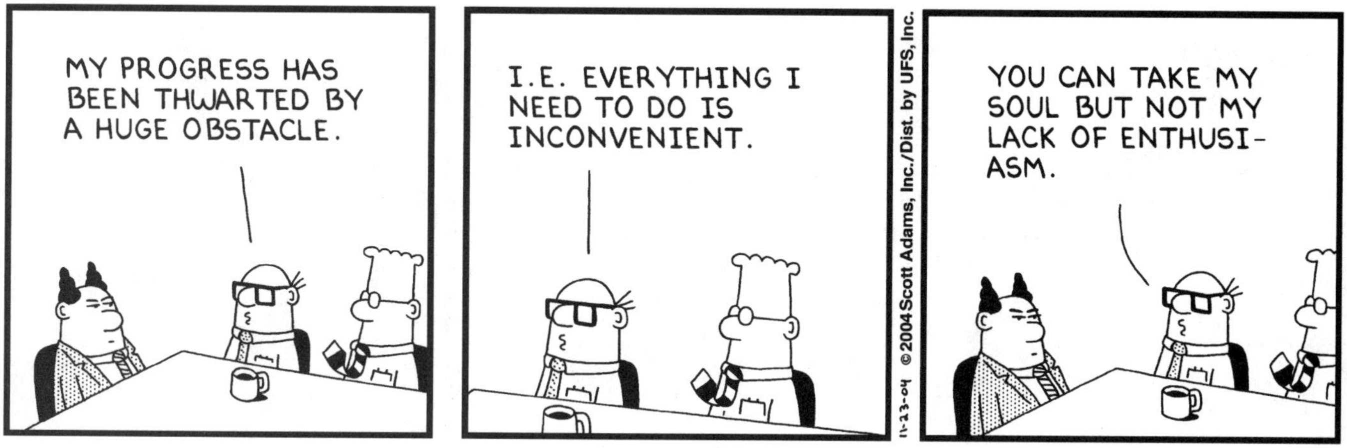
MY PROGRESS HAS BEEN THWARTED BY A HUGE OBSTACLE.
I.E. EVERYTHING I NEED TO DO IS INCONVENIENT.
11-23-04 © 2004 Scott Adams, Inc./Dist. by UFS, Inc.
YOU CAN TAKE MY SOUL BUT NOT MY LACK OF ENTHUSI-ASM.

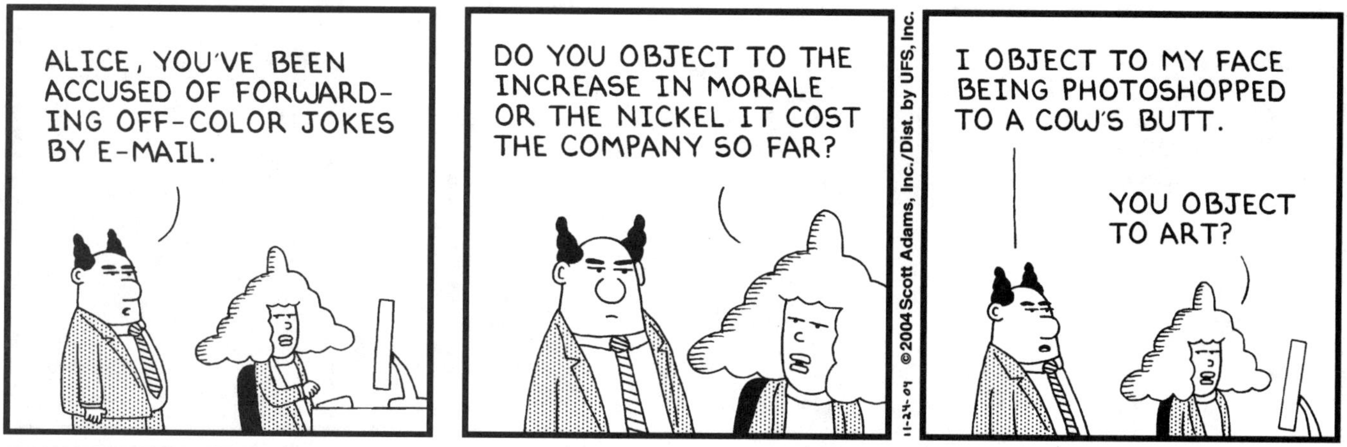
ALICE, YOU'VE BEEN ACCUSED OF FORWARD-ING OFF-COLOR JOKES BY E-MAIL.
DO YOU OBJECT TO THE INCREASE IN MORALE OR THE NICKEL IT COST THE COMPANY SO FAR?
11-24-04 © 2004 Scott Adams, Inc./Dist. by UFS, Inc.
I OBJECT TO MY FACE BEING PHOTOSHOPPED TO A COW'S BUTT.
YOU OBJECT TO ART?

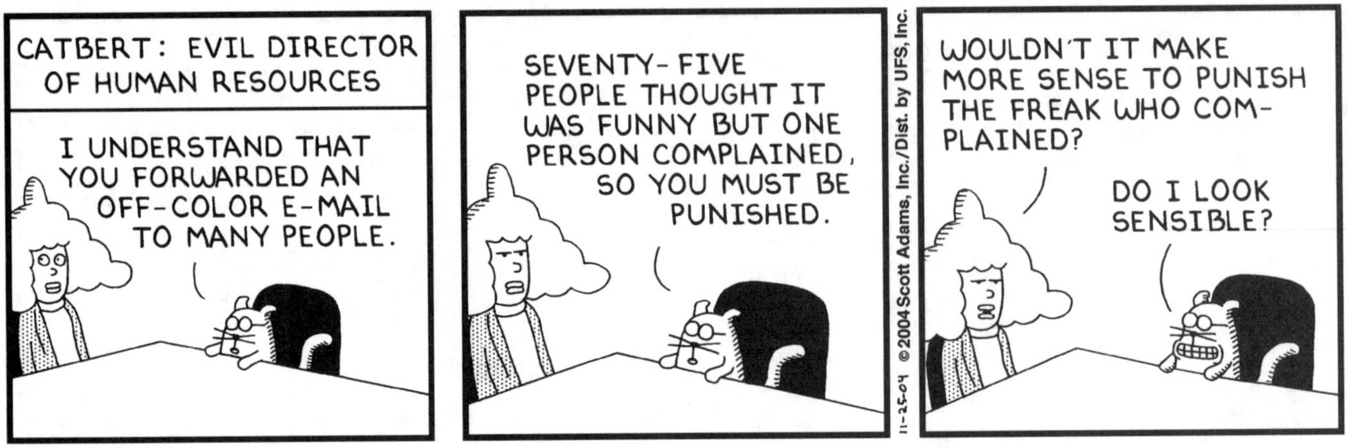
CATBERT: EVIL DIRECTOR OF HUMAN RESOURCES
I UNDERSTAND THAT YOU FORWARDED AN OFF-COLOR E-MAIL TO MANY PEOPLE.
SEVENTY-FIVE PEOPLE THOUGHT IT WAS FUNNY BUT ONE PERSON COMPLAINED, SO YOU MUST BE PUNISHED.
11-25-04 © 2004 Scott Adams, Inc./Dist. by UFS, Inc.
WOULDN'T IT MAKE MORE SENSE TO PUNISH THE FREAK WHO COMPLAINED?
DO I LOOK SENSIBLE?

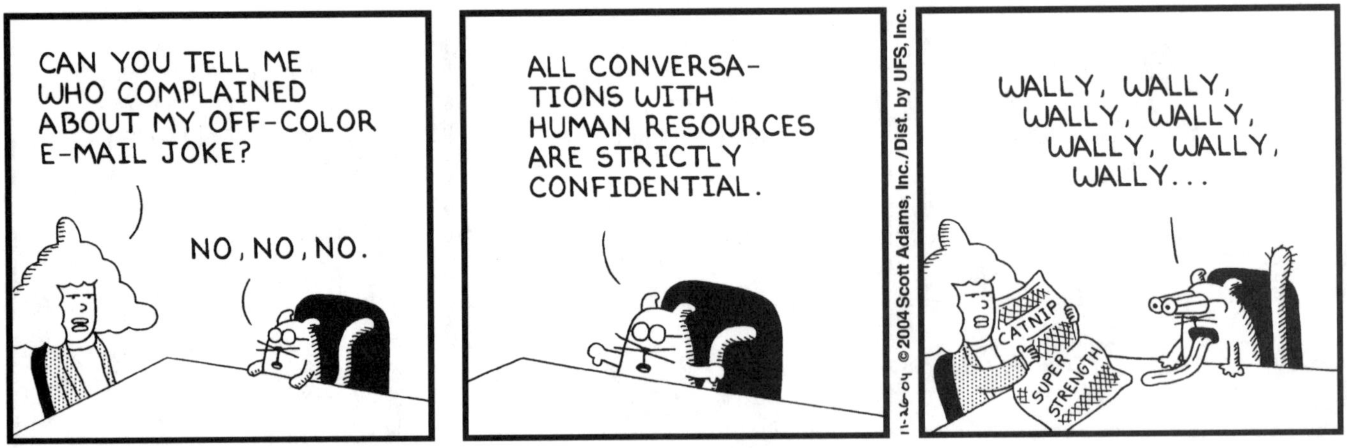
CAN YOU TELL ME WHO COMPLAINED ABOUT MY OFF-COLOR E-MAIL JOKE?
NO, NO, NO.
ALL CONVERSATIONS WITH HUMAN RESOURCES ARE STRICTLY CONFIDENTIAL.
11-26-04 © 2004 Scott Adams, Inc./Dist. by UFS, Inc.
CATNIP
#SUPER STRENGTH
WALLY, WALLY, WALLY, WALLY, WALLY, WALLY, WALLY...

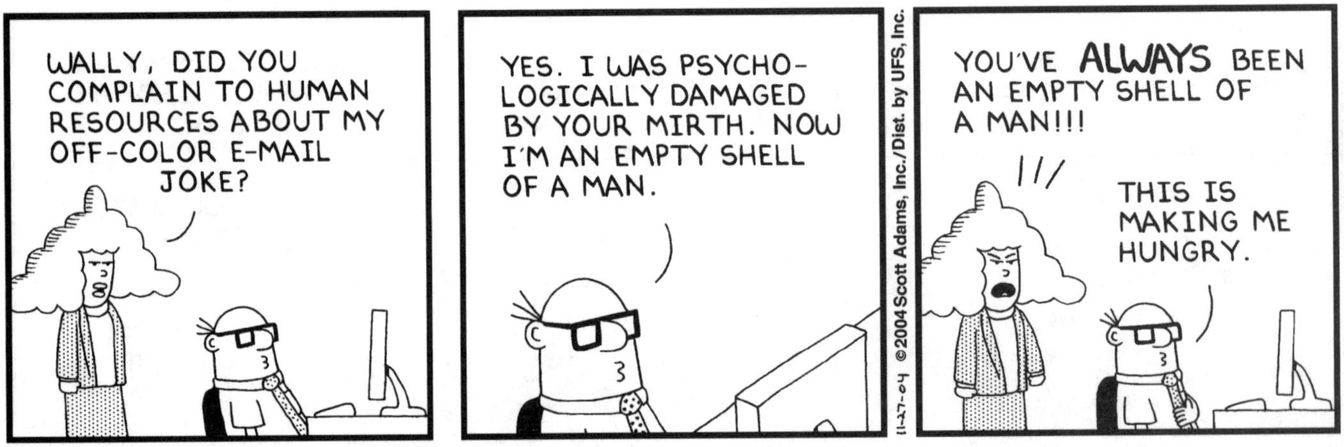
WALLY, DID YOU COMPLAIN TO HUMAN RESOURCES ABOUT MY OFF-COLOR E-MAIL JOKE?
YES. I WAS PSYCHOLOGICALLY DAMAGED BY YOUR MIRTH. NOW I'M AN EMPTY SHELL OF A MAN.
11-27-04 © 2004 Scott Adams, Inc./Dist. by UFS, Inc.
YOU'VE ALWAYS BEEN AN EMPTY SHELL OF A MAN!!!
THIS IS MAKING ME HUNGRY.

WHEN OUR POINTY-HAIRED BOSS ASKS ABOUT YOUR PROJECT, WHAT SHOULD YOU SAY?
I WOULD INFORM HIM ABOUT ANY PROBLEMS.
BIG MISTAKE. IF HE HEARS THAT YOU HAVE A PROBLEM, HE MIGHT TRY TO HELP.
HOW CAN HELP BE BAD?
ASOK, HOW'S YOUR PROJECT?
GOOD, BUT I NEED TO UPGRADE MY DISK DRIVE TO STORE ALL OF THE IMAGE DATA.
FORGET THAT. JUST E-MAIL PIECES OF THE DATABASE TO EMPLOY-EES WHO HAVE EXTRA DISK SPACE.
PLEASE PULL ON THIS UNTIL I LOSE CONSCIOUSNESS.
11-29-04

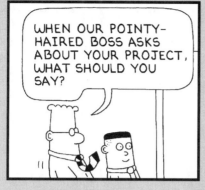

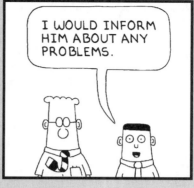

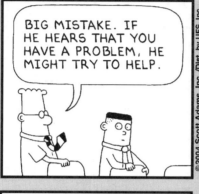

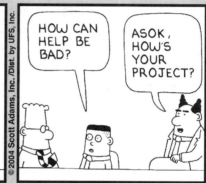

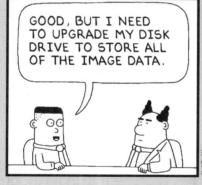

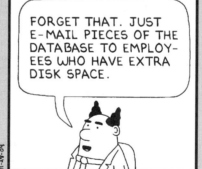

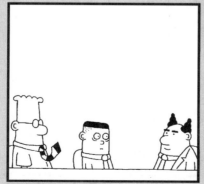

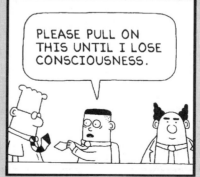

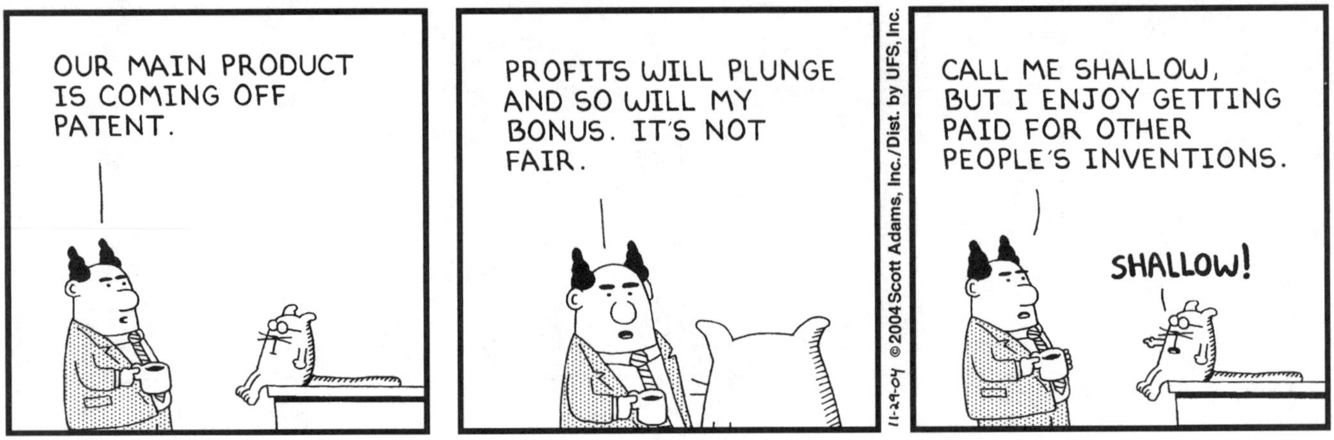
OUR MAIN PRODUCT IS COMING OFF PATENT.
PROFITS WILL PLUNGE AND SO WILL MY BONUS. IT'S NOT FAIR.
CALL ME SHALLOW, BUT I ENJOY GETTING PAID FOR OTHER PEOPLE'S INVENTIONS.
SHALLOW!
11-29-04 © 2004 Scott Adams, Inc./Dist. by UFS, Inc.

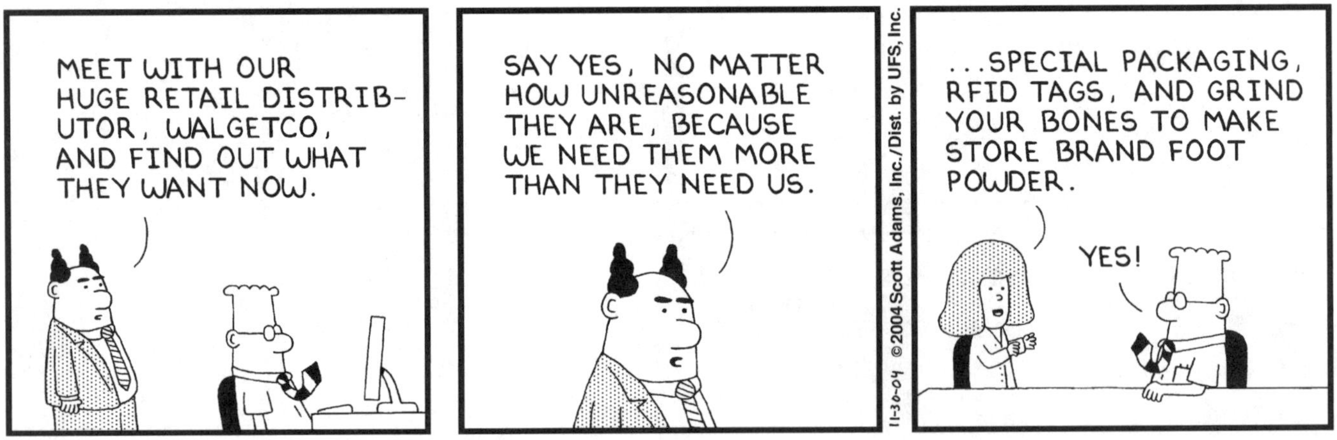
MEET WITH OUR HUGE RETAIL DISTRIB-UTOR, WALGETCO, AND FIND OUT WHAT THEY WANT NOW.
SAY YES, NO MATTER HOW UNREASONABLE THEY ARE, BECAUSE WE NEED THEM MORE THAN THEY NEED US.
...SPECIAL PACKAGING, RFID TAGS, AND GRIND YOUR BONES TO MAKE STORE BRAND FOOT POWDER.
YES!
11-30-04 © 2004 Scott Adams, Inc./Dist. by UFS, Inc.

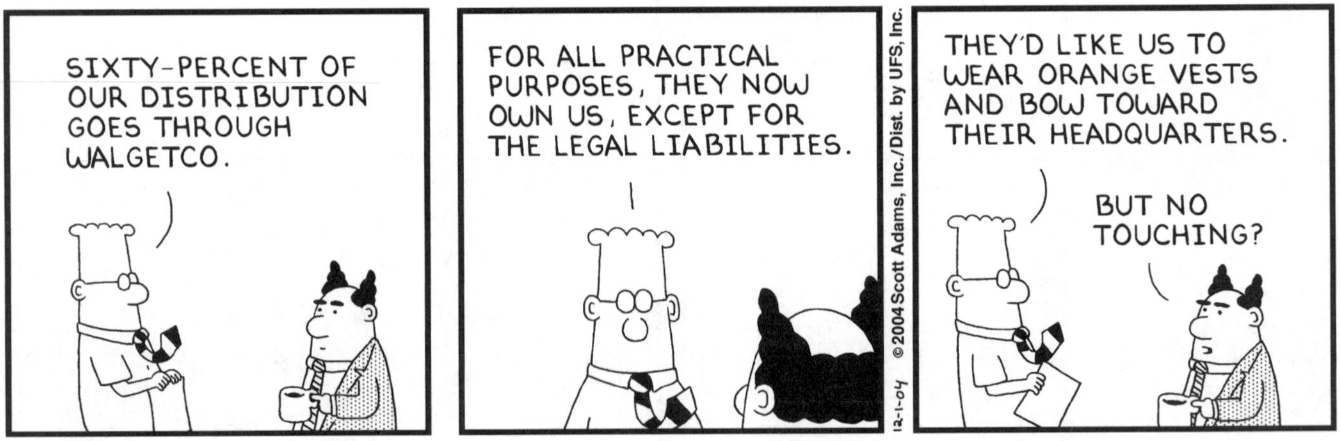
SIXTY-PERCENT OF OUR DISTRIBUTION GOES THROUGH WALGETCO.
FOR ALL PRACTICAL PURPOSES, THEY NOW OWN US, EXCEPT FOR THE LEGAL LIABILITIES.
THEY'D LIKE US TO WEAR ORANGE VESTS AND BOW TOWARD THEIR HEADQUARTERS.
BUT NO TOUCHING?
12-1-04 © 2004 Scott Adams, Inc./Dist. by UFS, Inc.

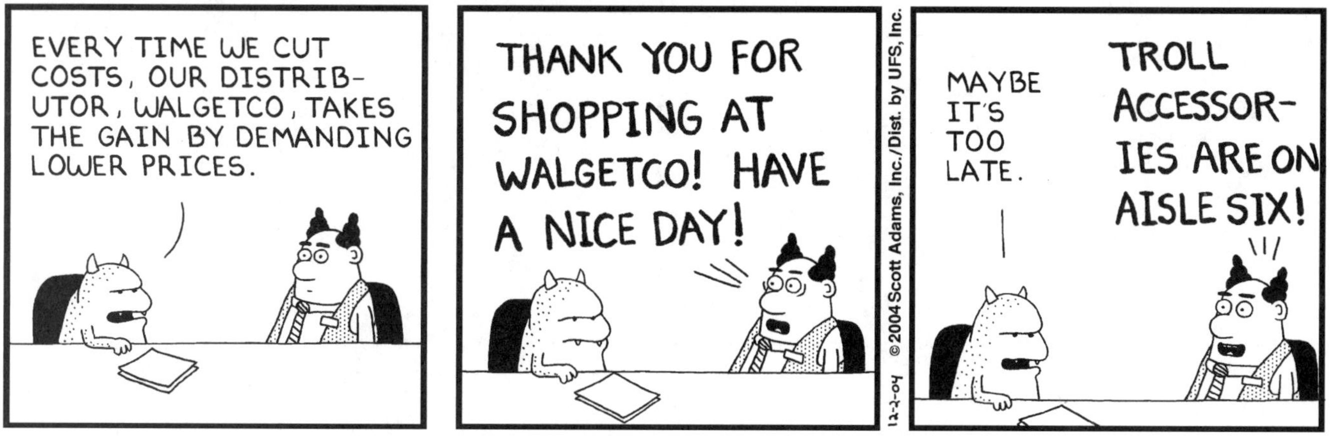
EVERY TIME WE CUT COSTS, OUR DISTRIB-UTOR, WALGETCO, TAKES THE GAIN BY DEMANDING LOWER PRICES.
THANK YOU FOR SHOPPING AT WALGETCO! HAVE A NICE DAY!
12-2-04 © 2004 Scott Adams, Inc./Dist. by UFS, Inc.
MAYBE IT'S TOO LATE.
TROLL ACCESSOR-IES ARE ON AISLE SIX!

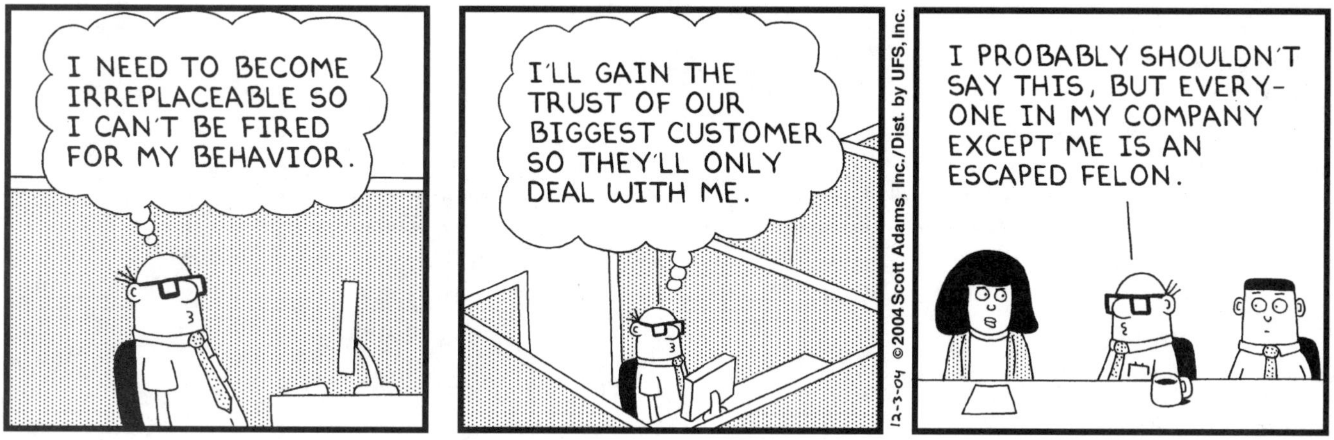
I NEED TO BECOME IRREPLACEABLE SO I CAN'T BE FIRED FOR MY BEHAVIOR.
I'LL GAIN THE TRUST OF OUR BIGGEST CUSTOMER SO THEY'LL ONLY DEAL WITH ME.
12-3-04 © 2004 Scott Adams, Inc./Dist. by UFS, Inc.
I PROBABLY SHOULDN'T SAY THIS, BUT EVERY-ONE IN MY COMPANY EXCEPT ME IS AN ESCAPED FELON.

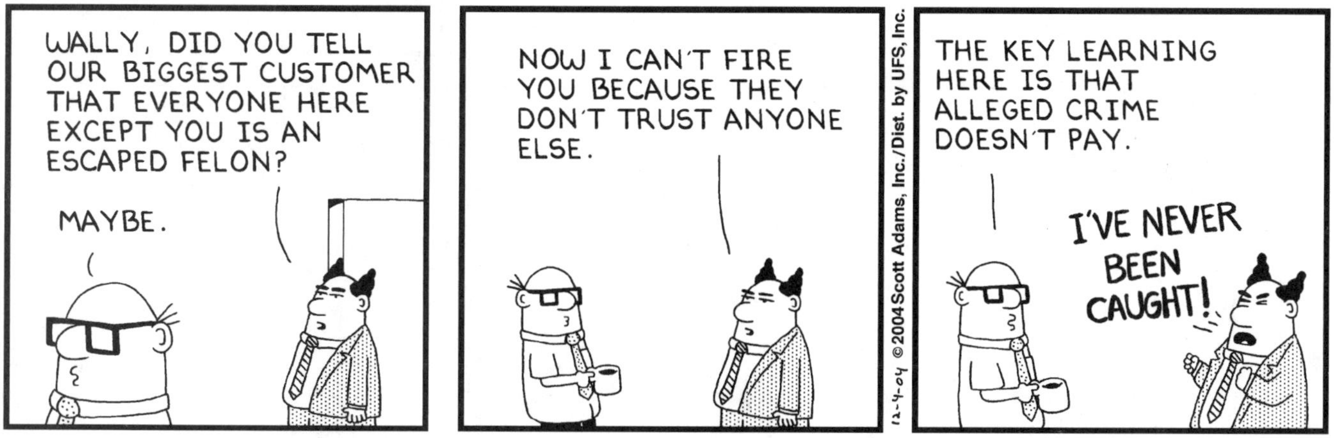
WALLY, DID YOU TELL OUR BIGGEST CUSTOMER THAT EVERYONE HERE EXCEPT YOU IS AN ESCAPED FELON?
MAYBE.
NOW I CAN'T FIRE YOU BECAUSE THEY DON'T TRUST ANYONE ELSE.
12-4-04 © 2004 Scott Adams, Inc./Dist. by UFS, Inc.
THE KEY LEARNING HERE IS THAT ALLEGED CRIME DOESN'T PAY.
I'VE NEVER BEEN CAUGHT!

NOW WHAT?
CREATE A PASSWORD THAT'S AT LEAST SIX CHARACTERS LONG WITH A MIX OF LETTERS AND NUMBERS.
HOW ABOUT 123?
UH, NO.
IT HAS TO INCLUDE LETTERS AND BE AT LEAST SIX CHARAC-TERS LONG.
HOW ABOUT ABC?
LETTERS AND NUMBERS AND AT LEAST SIX CHARAC-TERS LONG!!!
FOURSOME?
GAAA!!!
©2004 Scott Adams, Inc./Dist. by UFS, Inc.
12-5-04

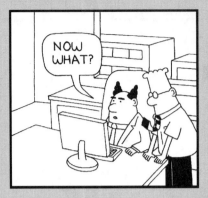

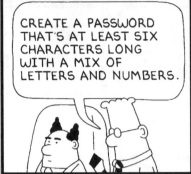

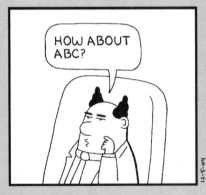

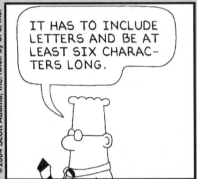

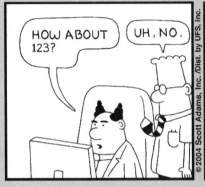

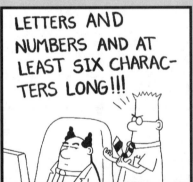

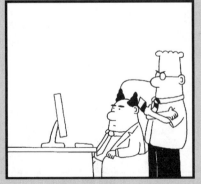

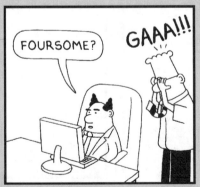